ALLENBY
SOLDIER AND STATESMAN

The general must know how to get his men their rations and every other kind of stores needed in war. He must have imagination to originate plans, practical sense and energy to carry them through. He must be observant, untiring, shrewd, kindly and cruel, simple and crafty, a watchman and a robber, lavish and miserly, generous and stingy, rash and conservative. All these and many other qualities, natural and acquired, he must have. He should also, as a matter of course, know his tactics; for a disorderly mob is no more an army than a heap of building materials is a house.

SOCRATES

FIELD-MARSHAL VISCOUNT ALLENBY OF MEGIDDO AND
FELIXSTOWE, G.C.B., G.C.M.G.

Photo Russell and Sons

ALLENBY

SOLDIER AND STATESMAN

By

FIELD-MARSHAL

VISCOUNT WAVELL

OF CYRENAICA AND WINCHESTER

G.C.B. C.M.G. M.C.

VICEROY OF INDIA

LONDON

GEORGE G. HARRAP & CO. LTD.

SYDNEY TORONTO BOMBAY STOCKHOLM

First published in this edition 1946
by George G. Harrap & Co. Ltd.
182 High Holborn, London, W.C.1

Originally issued in two volumes:
"*Allenby: A Study in Greatness*":
First published September 1940
Reprinted: September 1940;
December 1940; *March* 1941;
December 1941

"*Allenby in Egypt*":
First published January 1944
Reprinted February 1944

BOOK
PRODUCTION
WAR ECONOMY
STANDARD

THIS BOOK IS PRODUCED IN
COMPLETE CONFORMITY WITH THE
AUTHORIZED ECONOMY STANDARDS

Composed in Garamond type and printed by R. & R. Clark, Limited, *Edinburgh*
Made in Great Britain

PREFACE

ALLENBY: SOLDIER AND STATESMAN
were not essential to the story of Allenby's life, and the complete
book would be better balanced without them. Otherwise the
matter of the two volumes . . . . altered
I have already acknowledged in the prefaces to the two previous

I UNDERTOOK the writing of Allenby's biography nearly nine
years ago—shortly after his death. I was then commanding a
division at Aldershot; busy, but not so busy that I could not
hope to complete the work in reasonable time. It took me many
months to collect material, since Allenby had left no record of
his life and no papers. Just as I had got fairly started on the
writing I was sent to command in Palestine, and soon had to deal
with a rebellion there. I returned to England in 1938 to take over
the Southern Command, the largest and busiest in England, and
again could spare little time for writing. When I was ordered
to the Middle East, two months before the outbreak of war,
I had almost finished the account of Allenby's military career,
but had not begun the equally, or more, interesting history of
his work as High Commissioner in Egypt. As I saw little
prospect of writing this while the war lasted I arranged to publish
what had already been done, leaving the Egyptian story till after
the war. The result was *Allenby: A Study in Greatness*, which was
published in 1940. It told of Allenby's life up to the end of the
war against the Turks in 1918.

During the first two years of the war, when my headquarters
were in Egypt, it seemed a pity not to take advantage of
being on the spot and at least to collect material from those
who had known and worked with Allenby, British or Egyptian.
Gradually the volume *Allenby in Egypt*, which completed the
story of his life, was compiled. It was written in spare hours or
half-hours, often separated by days, weeks, or even months,
during two years of intense military work. Some of it was
written during my frequent aeroplane journeys. It was published
at the beginning of 1944. The present volume combines the
contents of the two previous volumes, and thus contains a full
record of Allenby's whole life. It is, in fact, the work as originally
planned.

In this new edition certain portions of the first volume, on
Allenby's military career, have been omitted, since I felt that they

5

were not essential to the story of Allenby's life, and the complete book would be better balanced without them. Otherwise the matter of the two volumes has remained unaltered.

I have already acknowledged in the prefaces to the two previous volumes my thanks to the many friends who have helped me with this biography, and will not repeat them here, though my gratitude to them remains unchanged.

W.

NEW DELHI
November 1945

CONTENTS

7

BOOK II

SWORD AND BATON

BOOK III

PLOUGHSHARE

CONTENTS

Part I

EGYPT: THE PROTECTORATE
(*March* 1919–*February* 1922)

Part II

EGYPT: INDEPENDENCE
(*March* 1922–*June* 1925)

ILLUSTRATIONS

MAPS AND PLANS

INTRODUCTION

ALLENBY THE MAN

Who would true valour see,
Let him come hither;
Here's one will constant be,
Come wind, come weather.

JOHN BUNYAN

Without courage there cannot be truth; and without truth
there can be no other virtue.

SIR WALTER SCOTT

ALLENBY was the last man who would have cared what his
biographer wrote of him, or, indeed, that his biography should
be written at all. He never troubled to explain his successes or
to justify any action he had taken; he bore no grudge against his
critics or detractors; he left behind no account of his life and no
material to compile one; he had, in truth, a certain impatience
with those who recalled past events, saying that it was only the
future that mattered. Yet it is well that an attempt should be
made to tell his story and to paint his portrait. Not only is there
interest in the record of one who was a successful soldier in the
most testing of all wars and a wise, sympathetic administrator in
perplexed countries at difficult times; but also Allenby's character
was of such rare truth and strength that it can serve as a model,
and yet of such humanity—rough, violent humanity at times—
that it can escape the aversion that most people feel towards
anyone held up as a model.

His fame as a soldier rests secure on two brilliant campaigns
in Palestine and Syria. The Great War of 1914–18 was mostly
hard, pitiless, clumsy pounding, and the manœuvres of those five
years that will be remembered and discussed as examples of the
strategist's art are few. Tannenberg, the Marne, the campaigns
on the Russian front in 1914 and 1915, the overrunning of Serbia
and of Rumania, the operations that began at Gaza-Beersheba

and ended with the fall of Jerusalem, the final annihilation of the Turkish armies in Palestine and Syria—these will form the main material for text-book analysis and discussion. In two of them the master-hand was Allenby's; and while it is true that the odds in numbers and equipment were on his side in his victories, the manner of their accomplishment showed a bigness of conception and a firmness of execution that must give him a high place among great captains of war. The opening of the Arras battle in April 1917 showed that even in the close-locked conditions of trench warfare he could plan on original lines: had he remained in France and been given the opportunity he might well have developed a technique in position warfare that would have brought an earlier end to the long conflict; it is notable that two prominent officers of the Tank Corps have recorded that he was the most understanding of the high commanders on the Western Front. Indeed, Allenby had qualities of courage, loyalty, directness of thought and purpose, knowledge of his profession and common sense in the application of his knowledge, that would have made him a great soldier in any age and under any conditions.[1]

He brought these same qualities, together with a patience and a tolerance that were innate in him, though his appearance and manner did not always suggest them, to his task of administrating first the occupied enemy territories that his troops had overrun in Palestine, Syria, and beyond, and later the ancient, baffling land of Egypt at a difficult and dangerous period. His success as diplomat and administrator has been more questioned than his ability as a soldier; and his handling of the Egyptian problem has been bitterly criticized in some quarters. Allenby never replied or defended himself: it was not his way. It will be possible one day to provide a basis on which his actions in Egypt can be better understood and judged, but the later course of events has been the best justification of his foresight and good sense.

The official records and documents of his victories as a soldier and of his success or failure as an administrator will remain available for future strategists and historians to dissect and discuss; but history, and more especially military history, is dry,

---

[1] Had he lived in the Middle Ages he might have inspired a statue in Whitehall like Verrocchio's statue of Colleoni in Venice.

misleading stuff without a clear understanding of the character and motives of the chief actors. It is like tinned food: it lacks the vitamins necessary for health. The aim of this biography is to leave on record, while memory is fresh and many of those who knew him well are still alive, a portrait of Allenby as a man, rather than to describe in detail his achievements in war and peace. He is perhaps too near yet for a final estimate as general and administrator, but he will soon be too far for a contemporary portrait as a man.

Allenby came from the English countryside, of old-rooted English stock. He was the embodiment of those virtues which the Englishman likes to think most typical of his race—tolerance and kindliness, love of peace and order and fair dealing. Allenby had no family tradition of military service, and glory was the last idea that would ever have entered his head. His attitude to soldiering was not that of the professional man-at-arms seeking a bubble reputation, but rather that of the good citizen who bears arms in the defence of peace and trade, but longs always to return from the distasteful necessity of fighting to his beloved country-side or town, to his home and his business. While still a young officer Allenby once confided to a friend that to have a garden and to grow roses was the thing in life that made most appeal to him. But, having once adopted a military career, the deep sense of duty and loyalty which was the guiding motive of his whole life caused him to give of his best unsparingly, and made him sometimes a hard taskmaster to those under him. He had little personal ambition, and never sought advancement; but his character and abilities made it certain that advancement would come to him. Nor did Allenby ever pretend not to enjoy the exercise of power and the privileges and position that it gave him.

His mind had breadth and poise rather than any great depth. He had not a creative and imaginative brain, like Marlborough: his military genius was colder and stiffer, like that of Wellington, the very embodiment of character and common sense. He had the gift of a wonderfully retentive memory, and he stored it wisely, adding a sound knowledge of his profession and much of the learning of a scholar to the lore of the countryside that he had acquired in youth. In all three departments he kept his stock fresh and up to date. Indeed, Allenby's range of information was remarkable, and it was not wise in his presence to lay down the law on any subject, unless very sure of the facts: he was disconcertingly likely to have read more, thought more, and remembered more on the same subject. He made no parade of his knowledge, and never talked for effect; but he would not pass uncorrected any inaccurate or ignorant statement made in his presence. He was studious, and read much; he enjoyed foreign travel, and missed no opportunity to visit fresh countries and see new sights; but most he loved the quiet and peaceful things of life— gardens and birds and old buildings. Fishing was his favourite recreation.

All this does not seem to accord well with his nickname and traditional reputation in the Army as " the Bull." Yet the name was appropriate enough at first sight and knowledge of the man and to some of his moods. His size, bearing, and obvious physical strength were of themselves impressive: the frank, open countenance, with its firm jaw and steady eyes, gave assurance of power and courage; the voice was of a part with the form and face—strong, clear, and confident almost to arrogance. The conscious strength of form, face, and voice could affect very powerfully those who came in contact with him. To those who knew him well, and to those who faced him fairly and without fear, his dominant personality was an inspiration and support; to those who met him for the first time or were at all nervous in his presence he was without doubt alarming and disconcerting, especially in his official capacity. His manner was often gruff and abrupt; his questions were straight and sharp; and he demanded an immediate, direct reply. Any attempt at prevarication, any indefiniteness, even hesitation, might provoke a sudden explosion of anger that could shake the hardiest.

But it needed no long acquaintance with Allenby to realize that his nickname was appropriate to externals only, that the man was big mentally and morally as well as physically, and that, in spite of his volcanic outbursts of temper, his attitude to men was at bottom kindly and tolerant. The outstanding spiritual characteristic of Allenby was a greatness of mind that matched his bigness of body; he was incapable of the least meanness or pettiness of spirit in his dealings with persons or with questions of conduct. However violently his anger might rage, he never cherished a grudge or bore any ill-will. Though intensely self-reliant, he was not obstinate, and would always listen to the views of those who had special knowledge, accepting their advice if he judged it sound. Once his mind was made up he asked no one to share his responsibility. If things went well, he was generous in his acknowledgment of the services of his subordinates; if things went ill, he was sparing of blame and never stooped to shirk his own responsibility or to defend himself.

He was always grave and courteous to women, and all women liked him; to children he was kind and humorous, and children adored him. With men he was reserved, even with those who knew him best, and remained, except on rare occasions, somewhat aloof and Olympian—as little likely to ask for confidences as to give them, so sure of himself as hardly to recognize the existence of doubts in lesser men. His path through life was simple, straight, and direct; neither fear nor favour could ever make him swerve from it, and the end he sought was peace and quiet, the peace of the English countryside from which he sprang.

Such is the outline that the following pages will attempt to develop into a portrait, the portrait of a great soldier and a very gallant and honourable gentleman, whose family motto, *Fide et labore* (" By loyalty and service "), records the faith by which he lived and died.

BOOK I

FORGE

This is the best blade that Weland ever made. Even the user
will never know how good it is.

RUDYARD KIPLING, *Weland's Sword*

CHAPTER I

EARLY LIFE
(1861–82)

I

ORIGINS AND CHILDHOOD
(1861–71)

THE family of Allenby (or Allanby) originally came from Cumberland. The name is apparently derived from Allonby, a village on the coast of Cumberland, or from Ellonby, a hamlet in Inglewood Forest, also in Cumberland. These two place-names are really identical, as Allonby was Allayneby in 1262 and Ellonby was Alanebi in 1228. They are post-Conquest names, meaning the ' by,' or homestead, of Alain, a Breton name, of Celtic origin and uncertain meaning, which came over with the Conqueror. It seems, then, that the founder of the Allenby family was some stout warrior from Brittany, who followed the Conqueror's fortunes to England and received a grant of land on the northern marches, in the debatable land between Norman and Scot, where good skirmishing was always to be had, and only strong hand and good watch could keep the roof on the farm and the cattle from the raider.[1]

The county of Lincoln, to which the most prosperous branch of the family presently moved, and where it is known to have

[1] Professor Ernest Weekley, the well-known authority on surnames and place-names, has provided most of the information in this paragraph.

owned land since the middle of the sixteenth century, lies somewhat off the beaten track of English history and beyond the edge
of the average Englishman's knowledge of his country. He
probably connects it with fens and skating, with a bishop and
cathedral, with country life and with a poacher who has inspired
a cheerful marching tune. If asked for the principal event in its
history he would be most likely to recall King John's lost baggage
in the Wash. In this retired, quiet county the Allenby family
seem to have lived quiet, retired, useful lives, concerning themselves mainly with their houses and their land and their stock,
taking their proper part in local affairs, but making little show
outside, typical of that lesser landed gentry who have been the
backbone of the English race and the principal source of its
greatest names. The type is passing, or has changed. No longer
does the possession of land ensure a comfortable, untroubled
living and the power to support a large family.

Some two hundred and fifty years ago one Thomas Allenby,
by his marriage with Dorothy, daughter of Henry Hinman, of
Swinhope, in the county of Lincoln, brought into the family two
names which have been common in it ever since—Hinman (or
Hynman) and Henry. About a hundred years later another
marriage secured to the family an inheritance of more value than
a name—a strain of the blood of one of England's greatest soldiers
and administrators, Oliver Cromwell,[1] also a man of the Eastern
Counties, and living, like the Allenby family, " neither in any
considerable height, nor yet in obscurity." The marriage which
imported this strain of military and political genius was that of
Hinman Allenby with Anne Raddish, a great-great-granddaughter
of General Ireton and Bridget Cromwell, daughter of the Pro-
tector. Hinman and Anne Allenby established themselves at

[1] It is interesting that a large number of the principal families of England have
inherited the blood of Oliver Cromwell; his descendants, in the female line, have
included a Prime Minister, a Foreign Secretary, two Lords-Lieutenant of Ireland,
and a Viceroy of India. The following contemporary description of Cromwell
indicates that Allenby may well have inherited a part of his qualities: " His body
was well compact and strong . . . his head so shaped as you might see it both a
storehouse and a shop of a vast treasury of natural parts. His temper exceedingly
fiery, as I have known, but the flame of it kept down for the most part, or soon
allayed by those moral endowments he had. . . . A larger soul, I think, hath seldom
dwelt in a house of clay than his was."

Kenwick Hall, near Louth, which remained the principal seat of the elder branch of the Allenby family up to a few years ago. Hinman Raddish Allenby, their son, married in 1819 Elizabeth, daughter of Mr H. Bourne, of Dalby. She and her sister were well-known beauties, and Tennyson, who was in his youth a near neighbour, addressed poems to them.

Of the marriage of Hinman Raddish Allenby and Elizabeth Bourne came two sons, of whom the elder was named Henry Hynman Allenby, and the younger, with the economy proper to a younger son, just Hynman Allenby. This latter was the father of the subject of this biography. He should, in the strict tradition of younger sons, have gone out into the world and adopted a profession, but he seems to have desired nothing more than to lead the life of a country gentleman, as had his ancestors for so many generations. He was educated at home by a private tutor, and then went to Corpus Christi College, Cambridge, which he left, however, without taking a degree. He at one time thought to become a doctor, and even began the study of medicine. But his heart was always in the country and in country occupations and sports—shooting and horses, fishing and boat-sailing. He was of medium height, handsome, kindly, straightforward, and generous, with some artistic and musical talent, but little business acumen. He married in 1859 a woman of remarkable force of character and ability, Miss Catherine Anne Cane, a daughter of the Rev. Thomas Coats Cane.

Mrs Allenby's outstanding characteristic was thoroughness in all she did; in the management of her easy-going husband, her children, the house, the horses, a sailing-boat, a garden, and the villagers of Felixstowe she never left any duty undone, she never wasted time, she was never at a loss. Yet she was not domineering, and her family were all devoted to her. When they were first married she and her husband went to live at Dartmouth, where he kept a small boat, being very fond of sailing. Mrs Allenby suffered daily at first the agonies of the bad sailor; but her strength of will mastered her weakness, and she became in time an excellent sea-woman, and thoroughly competent at handling a boat. She retained her spirit to old age: when she was eighty-one she sat up in her bed, a few hours after an operation for appendicitis, and gave very explicit and forcible instructions through an open window to her gardener, who was doing something in the garden below of which she disapproved.

There were six children of the marriage, three sons and three daughters. The eldest, Catherine Mary (Kitty),[1] was born in 1860 at Kenwick Hall. The first son, the future Field-Marshal, was born the next year, on April 23, St George's Day, at his mother's old home at Brackenhurst, Southwell, Notts. He was given the name of Edmund, together with the two traditional family names of Henry and Hynman. After barely surviving in infancy a serious attack of whooping-cough he grew up straight, strong, and healthy.

When his father died, in 1861, and he found himself better off Mr Allenby and his family left Dartmouth and returned to the Eastern Counties. A second daughter was born, in June 1862.[2] Mr Allenby decided to settle at Felixstowe, and bought Felixstowe House, which remained the home of the family till after the death of Mrs Allenby, in 1922, at the age of ninety-one. Here the three younger children were born, two more sons and a third daughter.[3]

Besides the Felixstowe house, Mr Allenby bought an estate of some two thousand acres in Norfolk, at West Bilney, with some good rough shooting. It was not a successful purchase from the business point of view, for the land in Lincolnshire which he sold to pay for the Norfolk property steadily increased in value, while the Bilney estates steadily declined in the market, and when sold at Mr Allenby's death fetched only half the price originally paid. But it suited his tastes admirably during his lifetime. There was good shooting with which to entertain his friends; the surroundings

[1] She married in 1881 Canon Henry Andrew, vicar of Griston, Norfolk, and died April 7, 1935.

[2] She married Major C. L. Fanshawe, R.E., who died in 1904.

[3] These three children were: (1) Frederick Claude Hynman, born September 21, 1864. He joined the Navy, was present at the bombardment of Alexandria in 1882, and served in the Royal Yacht. He retired as a Captain, and received the C.B.E., for services during the War. He died on August 1, 1934. His elder son, a Major in the 11th Hussars, is the present Viscount Allenby. (2) Helen Henriette (Nellie), born December 15, 1866. She married Thomas Cunningham Porter, for many years senior science master at Eton. He died in 1933. (3) Alfred Hynman, born March 9, 1870.

of wood and field, hedge and lane, stream and pond, were those he had known and loved from childhood; and here he could pass on to his children that deep feeling for the English country-side that he inherited through so many generations. He was one of those rarely fortunate people, rarer now than ever, who know exactly what they like and are in such circumstances that they can do exactly what they like to do. From his forbears he had inherited not only pleasant tastes, but a sufficient competence to indulge these tastes and to live the life that suited him. He was a good whip, and drove a four-in-hand regularly; but he could not afford to pay long prices for his horses, which were not always fully broken; there were often exciting and dangerous moments during his drives. He did not hunt, in deference to the sensibilities of his mother, whose memory he cherished deeply: she had had a passionate tenderness for all animals and weak things, and denounced hunting as a cruel sport. Shooting and fishing did not, however, come under the same ban apparently, and the latter especially was Mr Allenby's favourite pastime. He went often to Scotland to fish, and sometimes to Norway, a far more enterprising and adventurous journey then than now.

He had also a 28-ton schooner-rigged yacht, the *Water Witch*, in which he and his family cruised regularly, and in which he won prizes in the races of the Royal Harwich Yacht Club.[1] Indoors he had some musical and artistic talents, and was an earnest student of the Bible, especially the Old Testament, long passages of which he used to read and expound to his children in the mornings.

The family usually spent the summer at Felixstowe, and moved to the Norfolk property for the autumn and winter. This was an ideal place for children. The house was a smallish Georgian building, with a fine walled garden. It stood in a park, with woods and a rookery close by, through which ran a small trout stream (a tributary of the river Nar), dammed in one place to provide a swimming-pool. The woods were full of birds, and during the seasons of the spring and autumn migrations many

[1] Edward FitzGerald, translator of the *Rubáiyát*, also had a yacht here, called *The Scandal*. He was a friend of the Allenby family, and a striking but untidy figure at Felixstowe.

rare visitors to these islands could be found in them or on the coast near by.

Life in the country really was country life in those days, and the children grew up with little knowledge of towns or factories or crowds or of the stir of business, but with much simple lore of the peaceful countryside and the countryfolk and of the ways of birds and beasts. They rode and drove as a matter of course as soon as they were old enough, or even earlier. Perambulators were almost unknown at that time: panniers on a donkey, or a red pad-saddle with an iron ring round it to prevent falls, served in their place, so the children were on donkey-back or pony-back before they were a year old. Their games and pastimes were of their own devising. In the woods round Bilney they went bird-nesting and fished the stream; as the boys grew up they learned to handle a gun, and there was swimming and boat-sailing in the summer at Felixstowe.

II
SCHOOLDAYS
(1871–78)

Presently the question of the sons' education arose. The means and habits of education in the upper classes were changing. A few generations earlier the squire's son had usually begun (and sometimes finished) his education at the local grammar school, with the sons of the farmers and of the local tradesmen. This wholesome practice ceased as educational opportunities developed and class-consciousness grew, but there was an interval before it became the accepted custom for the sons of the gentry and would-be gentry to go to a public school, and before such schools were available in sufficient numbers to meet the demand. During this interval a private tutor, usually a clergyman, was used in many families. About the middle of the nineteenth century the old public schools (Winchester, Eton, Shrewsbury, Westminster, Rugby, Harrow, and one or two others) were rapidly supplemented. Cheltenham was founded in 1841, Marlborough in 1843, Radley in 1847, Lancing in 1848, Bradfield in 1850, Wellington in 1859, Clifton, Malvern, and Haileybury in 1862. The system of feeding the public schools from recognized private schools took a little longer to develop. Meantime a parson with a bent for teaching and a rectory too large for the needs of his family would often take some of the sons of his neighbours and friends and prepare them for the public schools or university. In this way Edmund Allenby, followed shortly by his brother Claude, went at the age of ten to the Rev. Maurice Cowell, vicar of Ashbocking, about seven miles north of Ipswich and some fifteen miles from Felixstowe. He had previously received his first grounding from a governess, a Miss Simpson.

Edmund Allenby was at this period a quiet, reserved boy, but noticeable even then for his strong, straight figure and frank, fearless bearing. A nephew of Mr Cowell's who afterwards became Bishop Welldon,[1] and was constantly at the vicarage during the time Allenby was there, writes of him:

> Edmund Allenby would not, I think, have been regarded as a boy of outstanding distinction, either in work or in play. But in his lessons, as in his games, he was always painstaking and thorough-going. He was a quiet, strong, manly, conscientious boy, of singular modesty, who never put himself forward. Among his qualities I think I should place first his high ideal of duty: he was one upon whom it was possible to rely in boyhood as in manhood for entirely faithful service.

It was the Welldon family who decided, indirectly, what Allenby's next school should be. His father, hearing that William Welldon, a younger brother of the future bishop and a pupil at Ashbocking, was going to Haileybury, decided to send his son there also. Accordingly in May 1875, when he was just fourteen, Allenby went to Haileybury, which had been founded some thirteen years previously in Hertfordshire, a mile or two south-east of the county town. He thus spent all his schooldays within easy reach of his home. He was placed in the Lower Middle part of the school and in Bartle Frere House (named in honour of Sir Bartle Frere, who after a distinguished career in India was shortly

---

[1] Headmaster of Harrow 1885–98; Bishop of Calcutta 1898–1902; Canon of Westminster 1902–6; Dean of Manchester 1906–18; Dean of Durham 1918–33; died June 1937.

to embark on a stormy term as High Commissioner in South Africa).[1]

There is not much to record of the three years that Allenby spent at Haileybury. He went steadily up the school, and was in the Lower Sixth (the second class) for his last two terms; had he stayed his full time he might have been head of the school, or near it. As prefect he had his first taste of authority and his first proving as a master of men. His selection as school prefect was a tribute to his character, for while members of the Upper Sixth were entitled to that office by virtue of their position, it was given only to those members of the Lower Sixth who were selected as specially suitable by ' The Master ' (as the headmaster of Haileybury has always been termed). Authority came easily to Allenby, who feared no one and loved order and justice. A fellow-prefect writes of him:

> No one in my time justified his selection more completely than Allenby. He was sane, simple, and direct in all he did; he had no difficulties with discipline, which he exercised without harshness and with absolute justice. He was invaluable in a house where the other prefects were not over-strong, and where the housemaster was too gentle in his methods and trusted where trust was abused and believed the impossible best of the wholly unworthy.

Allenby made no mark in the athletic side of school life. He played Rugby football for his house as a forward, but was never in the school fifteen, and there is no record of his appearance on the cricket-field. He cared nothing, now as ever, for the applause or condemnation of his fellows; and the exaggerated renown that athletic prowess brought in the school world made no appeal to him. He was more interested in books and study than in games. The picture that he has left on his contemporaries at school is that of a large, pleasant, good-tempered boy, quiet and rather reserved, somewhat old for his age in thought and manner, with a kindly but slightly ironical sense of humour, who made no special mark in the school, but was respected by all with whom he came in contact. Years later some one remarked to Allenby,

---

[1] One of the houses at Haileybury is now named after Allenby, who left to the school his banner of the Order of the Bath.

" School life was very rough in those days. You had to fight your way up, I suppose." " Nonsense! " replied Allenby. " I never had to fight at all." Even then there must have been something impressive about the large, strong, but peaceable boy that kept him from any necessity to fight; and his good-humour contained no desire to do so.

In the holidays there was the pleasant home life and country pursuits of West Bilney and Felixstowe: in the summer sailing, fishing, swimming, and riding; in the winter shooting, riding, and skating. Country life was not the restless week-end business it has now become in so many places. Golf had not yet come to Felixstowe, nor was tennis much played. But the *Water Witch* was always available for a cruise; there was sea-bathing, and there was fishing. At West Bilney the two elder boys with their father tramped the fields with guns, or sometimes went for long walks through the woods with an axe to cut off dead branches or to blaze trees for cutting. There were horses and ponies, and all the family rode, though hunting lay under the ban of the tender-hearted grandmother. When it froze there were plenty of opportunities to skate. Both his father and mother were keen observers of bird-life, and from them Allenby drew the great interest in and love of birds that was to remain with him all his life. From his mother, a keen botanist with a well-stocked garden, Allenby learned the names and care of flowers and plants.

In February 1878, while Edmund Allenby was still at Haileybury, his father died. The West Bilney property was sold soon afterwards, and the family henceforward lived entirely at Felixstowe.

III
ROYAL MILITARY COLLEGE, SANDHURST
(1878–82)

At the end of the summer term of 1878 Allenby left Haileybury. It had been decided that he should go up for the entrance examination to the Indian Civil Service, which was then considered to offer the best career for young men of ambition and brains. The examination was so stiff and the competition for admission so keen that for all except the most brilliant boys cramming was considered a necessity. Accordingly Allenby went to Wren's cramming establishment in Powis Square, Bayswater, which specialized in coaching for the Indian Civil Service. He went up twice for the examination, in 1879 and 1880, but was unsuccessful on each occasion, though failing only narrowly (according to family tradition, for the marks are not now available) at the second attempt. This was undoubtedly a great disappointment; but the severity of the competition may be judged by the fact that in the 1879 examination 174 candidates sat for 24 vacancies, while in 1880 the figures were 182 and 26, and few but boys with brains and ability much above the average faced the examination. The subjects offered by Allenby in 1879 were English composition, Greek,[1] Latin, French, mathematics (pure and mixed), chemistry, and mechanical philosophy (which included mechanics, heat, and astronomy)—a sufficiently formidable syllabus for a boy of eighteen, though of what value much of it would have been for the better government of the inhabitants of India is not easy to determine. If character could have been assessed in marks Allenby would have been lost to the Army.

At this time, when it was necessary to make new choice of a profession, young Allenby, who had lost the guidance of his father, must have looked to his mother for advice. It was quite natural that some of those who failed for the Indian Civil Service should turn to the Army for a career;[2] in fact, other openings were limited, for commercial business was not in those days considered a suitable occupation for a gentleman. Allenby, though he had no family tradition of Army service and no influence to help him in a military career, decided to go up for the Royal Military College at Sandhurst. In December 1880 he did so and passed fifth.

Allenby began his military career as a cadet of the Royal Military College on February 10, 1881. Military life came easily to the young Allenby. With his smart, well-set-up figure and

[1] " A good Greek scholar was lost in Allenby," his tutor said.

[2] There are curious similarities between the careers of Allenby and Colonel Sir Henry McMahon, G.C.M.G., G.C.V.O., K.C.I.E. They were at Haileybury together; both went to Wren's to cram for the I.C.S.; both failed and entered the Army through Sandhurst; both were High Commissioners for Egypt.

alertness, he can have been little trouble to the drill-sergeant; and his gospel of unfailing loyalty to those set over him made him ready to accept without outward questioning the restrictions of the military code and the conservatism of regulations. With the same gospel a weaker character or less acute mind would soon have become rigid and routine-ridden; but Allenby had too open and well stored an intelligence ever to be a mere automaton. He was to become that rare thing in a professional army, the perfect subordinate who yet retains the capacity for independent action; he could always be trusted to carry out the orders and intentions of his superiors with complete loyalty, but he never lost the power to think and act independently.

Among fellow-cadets were two, L. E. Kiggell [1] and the Hon. H. A. Lawrence,[2] who during the Great War occupied in succession the responsible post of Chief of the General Staff to Sir Douglas Haig; one who held many high administrative posts in the Army, G. F. Ellison;[3] a celebrated writer and explorer, F. E. Younghusband;[4] and two well-known novelists, H. A. Vachell and Egerton Castle.

The year's course was divided into two terms; at the end of each term one batch of cadets at the College passed out and received their commissions, while the next batch, who had completed one term, became ' seniors ' instead of ' juniors,' and were eligible for promotion to the posts of under-officers, of whom there was one for each of the ten divisions. These appointments were much-coveted distinctions. Again Allenby's character and qualities received recognition. He was transferred from his own division (of which H. A. Lawrence, a great friend of Allenby, became under-officer) to be under-officer of another division, No. 4. The path of one promoted from outside is not always smooth, but Allenby knew how to inspire loyalty as well as to give it, and established his authority naturally and without friction.

During the years he was at the crammers' and at Sandhurst Allenby spent some time abroad. In the summer of 1879 the

[1] Lieutenant-General Sir Launcelot Kiggell, K.C.B., K.C.M.G.
[2] General the Hon. Sir Herbert Lawrence, K.C.B.
[3] Lieutenant-General Sir Gerald Ellison, K.C.B., K.C.M.G.
[4] Sir Francis Younghusband, K.C.S.I., K.C.I.E.

whole family, together with Mr Andrew,[1] the curate of Walton, near Felixstowe, spent some eight weeks in Belgium, Germany, and Switzerland; and Allenby then acquired a taste for foreign travel that never left him. In the winter of 1880–81, before going to Sandhurst, he spent two months at Saumur (where the French Cavalry School is), in the family of a French Protestant clergyman, M. Davaine, improving his French. Allenby retained a warm feeling for French people all his life. In 1881, during one of the Sandhurst vacations, he went with Lawrence and another fellow-cadet to Rome. Here he became ill with diphtheria, spending some little time afterwards convalescing at Felixstowe. During this convalescence he occupied himself in making pen-and-ink drawings, for which he had some talent. He had the eye and hand of an artist, could he have found time to cultivate it; but, like Wellington with his fiddle, he put aside his artistic leanings on becoming a soldier.

In December 1881 Allenby passed out of Sandhurst " with honours," being bracketed twelfth on the list with Kiggell, also destined for a distinguished career. On May 10, 1882, just after his twenty-first birthday, he was gazetted to a commission in the 6th Inniskilling Dragoons, then stationed in South Africa.

IV
THE YOUNG ALLENBY

It is time to sum up the influence of origin, upbringing, and home life on Allenby's character and career. He was of hard, sound North Country stock on both sides. His forbears had lived on the land for some centuries, free, independent, and fearless, usually in easy enough circumstances, but never so rich as to lose energy and vitality. He inherited the best traditions of the English spirit—freedom, good-humour, courage, love of fair play—which had been bred and preserved in his ancestors for many generations.

From his father he had a perfect and straightforward honesty,

[1] He married Allenby's eldest sister, and became Canon Andrew (see p. 19 n. 1).

kindliness, and generosity, love of sport, some talent for music and drawing—gifts of good-fellowship that would smooth his way through life, and would bring him the respect and appreciation of those who travelled with him. From his mother he had a gift more momentous than all these for his future success, but more uncomfortable for himself and for others—absolute and unsparing thoroughness in all he did. He was to say with truth at the height of his success, " I owe everything to my mother." The text she gave him, which stayed always in his actions, was, " Whatsoever thy hand findeth to do, do it with thy might." It would not always be appreciated by those under him. We shall find, perhaps, that the influence of the easy-going father was uppermost in the first part of his life, and that of the determined, active mother in the latter part, after he had begun to rise to high rank. Not that Allenby was not thorough from the start: while still awaiting appointment to a regiment he went through a full and practical course of horse-shoeing with the Felixstowe blacksmith.

He thus started his life as a commissioned officer with qualities and advantages that would mean success and high position, if luck was with him and if high position was his aim. He had absolute courage, moral and physical; he was loyal and honest by tradition and upbringing; he had brains above the average; he had strength and health and good looks; and he had money sufficient for his needs, yet not so much as to induce idleness or extravagance. And there had been much in his upbringing that would help him as a soldier. His wanderings with gun or rod or axe had given him field-craft and woodcraft, and had trained his eye for observation; [1] the sailing of a boat had developed skill with his hands and resource in an emergency; he was a strong swimmer, and could sit a horse; as a prefect at Haileybury and under-officer at Sandhurst he had learned something of the handling of men. Many young men who joined the Army in those days of unhurried country life had similar qualities. But few had learned to study books also, as Allenby had, and few had his experience of foreign travel, and could actually speak to those

[1] His mother had required him in early years to give her an account of all he had seen in his morning rambles, and sometimes to draw a map of his route.

28

queer foreigners in their own language.[1] It was a well-equipped
young man, more mature than most subalterns, more reserved
and thoughtful, who received his first step towards a Field-
Marshal's baton in the spring of 1882.

[1] The British officer is, though, a much better linguist than is supposed; probably
no other army has a higher proportion of officers who have a good working knowledge of some language, European or native. Allenby spoke French with determination rather than great accuracy, but could always understand it and make himself
understood.

CHAPTER II

THE REGIMENT

(1882–96)

I

EARLY SERVICE IN SOUTH AFRICA

(1882–83)

ALLENBY began his military service at a period when the old red-coated, long-service, close-ranked, horse-power, shock-action Army had just begun to develop into the modern khaki-clad, short-service, open-order, mechanized, fire-plan force. After the Napoleonic wars the British people unbelted the sword that Wellington had wielded with such effect, hung it on the wall with a sigh of relief, and went back to the business of making money, with the fixed hope of not having to use a military force again for many years, if ever, save only for ceremony at home and police work abroad. But the Crimean War betrayed what rust had gathered on the old-fashioned weapon, which even Wellington himself had neglected to keep serviceable during the years of peace; and the Indian Mutiny immediately after showed that a different system was required if we were to continue to seize and hold an Empire abroad.

While our rulers were considering the problem—of which no one has yet produced an entirely satisfactory solution—of how to organize the army of a people with a taste for empire in distant lands and a great distaste for military service, Prussia startled the world with her victories over Austria and France, and introduced into Europe the new system of ' a nation in arms,' with rapid mobilization and great masses of short-service troops, trained and led by a body of long-service professional (really professional) officers and N.C.O.'s.

There followed from about 1873 onward a period of some twenty years during which all the European nations refashioned their armies on the Prussian model. At this hour of much-needed

MR AND MRS HYNMAN ALLENBY

AND THEIR FAMILY

The old lady is Mrs Allenby (Lord Allenby's grandmother), the girl in front is Lord Allenby's eldest sister (afterwards Mrs Andrew), and the one behind Edmund Allenby is a younger sister (afterwards Mrs Fanshawe).

EDMUND ALLENBY ABOUT 1870

VISCOUNTESS ALLENBY
Photo Hay Wrightson, F.R.S.A., London

reform Great Britain was fortunate enough to find the first of her two great War Ministers, Mr (afterwards Lord) Cardwell. The reforms he introduced during his period at the War Office, from 1868 to 1874, were far-reaching, and they stood the test of time—almost too well. These reforms laid the foundations of the British Regular Army that was tested in the South African War of 1899–1902, found wanting in many respects, and then brought to a high level of efficiency by another great War Minister, Mr Haldane, in time for the vortex of 1914. So that Allenby came into the Army on a rising market, at a time when its fortunes and efficiency were on the upgrade and the neglect of half a century was being gradually repaired. At the actual moment, however, the reputation of the Army in the field lay under the shadow of a series of disasters—Isandhlwana in 1879, Maiwand in 1880, Majuba in 1881.

Chance rather than design had guided Allenby thus far. He had been sent to Haileybury because the son of a friend of his father's had gone there; Haileybury's associations with India had probably been the cause of his attempting to enter the Indian Civil Service; his friendship at the crammers' with many boys who were working for the Army had led him to turn to a military career after his failure in the Indian Civil examination. Of the influences that guided his appointment to the Inniskilling Dragoons we have now no record,[1] but the choice was a fortunate one. The regiment had fine traditions of service; it had among its officers a number of men who were to rise to high distinction and responsibility; and it was stationed in an eventful country at an eventful time.

The regiment had been raised in Northern Ireland just on two hundred years earlier, to fight for the Protestant cause against King James. It had a fine fighting record and traditions, and had always borne a high reputation for efficiency. It was one of the less expensive cavalry regiments, which may have been a reason why Allenby joined it, for his income was not a large one.

[1] Curiously enough, when he had gone up for the Sandhurst examination a year or two before he had been accosted near the door by an impoverished ex-soldier, who had wished him success, and on receiving a satisfactory coin had added, " May you be a captain in the Inniskillinger Dragooners ! "

The Inniskillings had arrived in South Africa and landed at
Durban, in Natal, in February 1881, just before the disaster of
Majuba on February 27. Before they could reach the front
Gladstone's Government had ordered an armistice; peace was
concluded without further fighting, and later in the year the
independence of the Transvaal was recognized. By April 1882
the regiment had settled down under canvas at Pinetown, seventeen miles from Durban. Here Allenby joined it, together with
J. W. Yardley,[1] who had been at Sandhurst with him, and who
became his closest friend in the regiment.

Few countries and few periods could have offered greater
interest for the active mind or scope for the active body than the
South Africa of the 1880's. It was from the European point of
view an almost empty land, the wealth and potentialities of which
were just being realized. There were, it is true, large numbers of
natives, of an inconveniently warlike type, who claimed to
possess the lands in the interior, but they were just a part of the
' white man's burden,' and which particular breed of white man
should bear the burden—and pocket the profits, if any—was the
real question to be decided.

The long struggle between Boer and Briton for control of that
vast, obscure interior was nearing a crisis. In the first part of the
century British sea-power had wrested Cape Colony and Natal
from the original Dutch settlers, a part of whom had withdrawn
north to found new republics in the Transvaal and Orange Free
State. Round their ill-defined borders lay lands as yet un-
appropriated by whites—Zululand to the east, Bechuanaland to
the west, the country of the Matabele to the north. The next ten
years were to decide whether Boer or Briton should ' protect ' or
annex these territories. Ten years or more previously Britain
had absorbed Basutoland, between Cape Colony and Natal, and,
following the discovery of the Kimberley diamond field, Griqua-
land West. In 1877 she had boldly annexed the Transvaal itself,
disordered within by bankruptcy and threatened without by the
warrior state of Zululand, and had broken the power of the Zulus
and their chief Cetewayo in the war of 1879–80. But she had
failed to reconcile the Boers to British rule, and in 1881, after the

[1] He was afterwards a well-known amateur steeplechase rider. He died in 1920.

Majuba defeat, had again recognized the independence of the Transvaal, retaining only some shadowy ' suzerainty.'

So that in 1882 the Boer was for the moment insolently in the ascendant. He saw only the small Regular garrison (one cavalry regiment, two and a half battalions), the inept leading and low training of the despised ' rooinek,' as shown at Majuba, and the poor quality of many of the British immigrants. He knew nothing of the mighty power behind this unimpressive outpost, or of the real temper and quality of the British people when roused to fight; and he thought and acted in accordance with his contempt.

The protagonists of their respective nations in this struggle were two remarkable men, Cecil Rhodes and Paul Kruger. Rhodes, the princely money-grubber, the unscrupulous dreamer, the tolerant Imperialist, the backwoods apostle of education, had just entered the Cape Assembly, of which he remained a member for the rest of his life; Kruger, the shrewd, narrow, fanatical pioneer, who had spent his whole life as hunter, farmer, and warrior, struggling with wild nature and savage man, was at the height of his power and prestige as President of the Transvaal and as one of those who had wrested its independence from a mighty Empire.

Such was the South Africa to which Allenby came: a land with a wonderful climate, but with sudden death at close hand in many forms; a land of boundless opportunity and constant strife; a land where courage and enterprise were at their highest, and rascality abounded; a land to which came the hardy pioneers and needy adventurers of many races; a restless, untamed, immature land; a great Dominion in the rough. Here Allenby was to serve his first apprenticeship in the field, and twenty years later to make his name as a commander. Curiously enough, also, at the very time of his first landing in South Africa events were taking place in the extreme north of the same continent that were to provide the scene and opportunity for his last service, forty years later. In July 1882 British naval forces, in which Allenby's brother Claude was serving, bombarded Alexandria, and two months later a British force was in occupation of Cairo, an event which roused in the Imperialistic mind of Rhodes the dream of an all-red route from Cape to Cairo under British control. Allenby was to see this dream fulfilled, as well as Rhodes' other dream of Dutch and British working together in a united South Africa.

It might be thought that a cavalry subaltern would have little opportunity or desire to meditate on such problems, and would receive little encouragement to do so. But the Inniskillings had among their officers at this time a remarkable group of men, who were to play a considerable part in the development and administration of Africa. R. E. R. Martin, then a Major, was afterwards Commissioner in Swaziland and in Rhodesia, and became Sir Richard Martin, K.C.B., K.C.M.G.; A. C. M'Kean and E. G. Pennefather, captains, served with distinction in Colonial forces, as did also Raleigh Grey and Patrick Forbes, subalterns, who joined a year earlier than Allenby. Grey led the Bechuanaland Police Force in the notorious Jameson Raid of 1895, and was one of those tried and sentenced for participation in it; he was later reinstated, and did much valuable work in the development of Rhodesia, receiving the K.C.M.G. for his services. There were also in the regiment " Mike " Rimington, who became a celebrated column commander in the Boer War, and commanded the Indian Cavalry Corps in France in the Great War; J. Stevenson-Hamilton, for many years Warden of the Kruger Game Reserve; and Richard Crawshay, who was well known later as administrator, hunter, and naturalist in Nyasaland. Rhodes himself was a friend of the Inniskillings, and knew many of the officers personally. There must have been much discussion in the mess of African politics and problems, besides the usual talk of sport and amusement. Allenby had also opportunities to meet and talk with such men as Sir Theophilus Shepstone, who had annexed the Transvaal in 1877 and had administered it during the greater part of the period it remained under British rule, Colonel Dartnell, who commanded the Natal police, and other well-known administrators and pioneers. With his alert and well-stored mind he was able to take full advantage of such opportunities.

II
ZULULAND AND BECHUANALAND
(1883–85)

Allenby soon found his feet in the regiment. He was quick to learn the course of exercises prescribed for young officers, and was soon passed as efficient by the adjutant; the regimental sergeant-major of those days, Mr Bramley, reports him as having been noticeably good with the sword. He had ridden from boyhood, and was always a strong, intrepid horseman, though never a very polished one. His weight and physical make-up were against his mastering the more delicate arts of horsemanship, but he rode boldly and well to hounds or at polo, and on parade or in the field fully satisfied the standard of military horsemanship of those days, which was somewhat rougher and less exacting than now. He was liked and respected both by his brother-officers and by his men, and was at all points a proved and trusted subaltern when he received, a little more than a year after joining, his first experience of service in the field.

Of the three great territories (Zululand, Bechuanaland, Matabeleland) still remaining at this time under native control (though both Briton and Boer were pressing in on them), Zululand was the first to require military intervention. In the settlement after the Zulu War of 1879–80 the fierce Cetewayo had been deposed and exiled, and his country had been divided between thirteen tribal chiefs. Disputes and disturbances soon became so frequent that, in spite of his previous record of tyrannies and cruelties, it was decided to carry out a partial restoration of Cetewayo, who had been to England, where he had posed as a leopard with an entirely new set of spots and had professed himself a loyal friend of England. His protestations deceived those at home who knew not Zululand nor the Zulus.

The country was divided into three portions. Cetewayo was to be king over the major part, comprising two-thirds of his old dominions; one part remained under a chief named Usibebu; and the third part, called the Reserve, was placed under British protection. Cetewayo landed at Port Durnford in January 1883, and was escorted to his capital, Ulundi, by two troops of the Inniskillings. Allenby was not with this force, but went up to Eshowe, in the Reserve, with a small British column in September of the same year.

The restoration of Cetewayo had not been a success; disregarding all his undertakings, he had attempted again to place the whole country under his subjection. But his star had set, and after several defeats at the hands of Usibebu he surrendered to the British at Eshowe on October 15, 1883. His sudden death on February 8, 1884, solved the problem of how to dispose of this unwanted chieftain, but did not resolve the troubles of Zululand, where Boer encroachments in the north had produced a fresh complication. On May 21, 1884, the Boers proclaimed Dinizulu, son of Cetewayo, King of Zululand, and then aided him to dispose of Usibebu, who was overpowered and fled to Eshowe. Allenby with his troop took part in an extensive reconnaissance over the Reserve lasting some weeks, and later acted as escort to a Boer delegate who had come to discuss the affairs of Zululand with the British authorities.

Matters on this eastern flank of the Transvaal had to be left in this unsatisfactory condition for a time, since a more serious Boer encroachment on the west threatened to place all Bechuanaland in their power, and thus to shut off the British from the third great territory open to exploitation—Matabeleland, in the north. Accordingly, the Inniskillings returned to Pinetown at the end of November 1884, embarked at Durban for the Cape, and encamped at Wynberg, to form part of a column under Major-General Sir Charles Warren for service in Bechuanaland. Here they were equipped with corduroy jackets and Bedford cord breeches in place of the red uniform which had been up to then the campaigning as well as the parade dress of the British soldier.

The purpose of the expedition was to eject from Bechuanaland certain Boer freebooters who had, in defiance of treaties, set up two small independent republics—that of Stellaland, round Vryburg, and that of Goshenland, farther north. The importance of ousting the Boer from these territories lay in the fact that the one road to the north between the Transvaal and the Kalahari Desert lay through them; Rhodes called it the Suez Canal of Cape Colony, the key of its road to the interior. In all probability no Imperial force would, however, have been sent had not the Germans in 1884 proclaimed a protectorate over Damaraland and Namaqualand (afterwards German South-west Africa), and thus threatened to join hands with the Transvaal and hem in Cape Colony on the north.

Sir Charles Warren's force of some 4000 men was trained to the Orange river, then the terminus of the railway, and marched thence to Barkly, on the Vaal river, which was reached in January 1885. President Kruger met General Warren on January 22, and tried to induce him to proceed no farther.[1] But he continued the march, reaching Vryburg in February and Mafeking, nearly nine hundred miles from the Cape, on March 11. The republics of Stellaland and Goshen broke up without a shot being fired, and the Boer adventurers withdrew. The advanced part of the column remained for some time at Mafeking, pushing reconnaissances to the north through the Kalahari Desert, where Allenby found some good sport and made some interesting visits to native chieftains. The return march to the Orange river was made in July and August, and by October the regiment was back in Natal, at Pinetown. Bechuanaland was formally taken under British protection on September 30, 1885.

It has been thought worth while to give some little space to these two small expeditions because they form a very definite stage in Allenby's military education as well as in the expansion of British rule in Africa. Though there was no fighting in either Zululand or Bechuanaland, the experience of these two years from the autumn of 1883 to the autumn of 1885, during which he had been almost continuously on active service, must have been invaluable to Allenby. He learned the conduct of the minor operations of war, such as patrols, outposts, reconnaissances, the protection of camps and convoys, in circumstances when a mistake or carelessness might have meant loss of life, and not merely a reprimand at a powwow; he learned the care of man and

---

[1] Rhodes was with Warren on this occasion, and he and Kruger crossed swords for the first time. Kruger is said to have at once recognized him as his rival in the struggle for power in South Africa, and to have remarked, " The racehorse is swifter than the ox, but the ox can draw the greater load."

horse on the march and in bivouac under rough conditions of climate and country; and he learned under skilled and practised guidance. Sir Charles Warren had had previous experience of colonial warfare, and was a prudent and capable soldier, so that his expedition was thoroughly well organized and run.[1] And the Inniskillings had deservedly acquired a great reputation for their efficiency and discipline in the field.

Also Allenby made the acquaintance in these two years of many interesting types, British, Boer, and native—administrators, adventurers, hunters, chieftains. Rhodes himself accompanied the Bechuanaland expedition for part of the time, and Allenby used to relate in after-years how it had once fallen to him on a very cold night in bivouac to share a blanket with Rhodes, who was a guest of the regiment. Allenby presently awoke, shivering, to find that Rhodes in his sleep had pushed him from under the blanket and had wrapped it round himself. Rhodes apologized profusely when aroused, and the two again composed themselves to slumber. But in a very short time the same thing happened again; and eventually, after his third ejection from the blanket, Allenby went off to find some one less restless—satisfied, however, that British interests in South Africa were safe in the hands of one who was so acquisitive and tenacious even in his sleep. Allenby met also such characters as John Dunn, the white chief of a Zulu tribe, Montsioa, the Bechuana chief, who had struggled for a life-time against the Boers, and Van Niekerk, ex-President of Stella-land and the 'bad boy' of the Bechuanaland imbroglio. With these and many others his broad, receptive mind found points of contact and interest. Altogether, few young subalterns have ever had a better two years' training than had Allenby from 1883 to 1885.

III

SOUTH AFRICA

(1886–90)

In May 1886 the Inniskillings moved from their camp at Pinetown to Pietermaritzburg, the capital of Natal, about seventy-

[1] His reputation as a commander was lost in the Spion Kop disaster, fifteen years later, in the Boer War.

five miles by rail from Durban. Shortly afterwards Allenby went home for a two years' tour of duty at the cavalry depot at Canterbury. There is little record of these two years. Allenby's commanding officer at the depot remembers him as a loyal and conscientious officer who always did his work well and as a keen and dashing fox-hunter. He was promoted captain in January 1888, and in the summer of that year returned to South Africa, bringing with him a draft of the regiment and a few couples of fox-hounds. With these latter, until they succumbed to the various hazards that beset dog-life in South Africa, he hunted jackal and small buck in the hills outside Pietermaritzburg.

The greater part of the regiment was at this time in Zululand, which had again become the scene of serious trouble. Dinizulu had proved almost as truculent and turbulent as his father, and showed the same obstinate prejudice against seeing his lands occupied by white settlers, whether British or Dutch. It ended as such differences of opinion between white men and black men always have ended in the long run or the short run. Great Britain in May 1887 annexed Zululand, except the New Republic, where the occupation by Dutch settlers had already been recognized. Next year Dinizulu made a last effort to throw off white dominion, and there was some fighting between May and August 1888. Allenby did not arrive back from England in time to accompany the regiment to Zululand, and was employed for some time after his arrival in collecting remounts and performing other base duties in Natal; by the time he reached Zululand most of the fighting was over.[1] In September his leg was injured by his horse falling with him, and he was sent down-country to Natal in an ox-wagon.

In October regimental headquarters and the greater part of the regiment returned to Pietermaritzburg, though part of the regiment remained in Zululand for another six months. In Pietermaritzburg the younger officers of the Inniskillings settled

---

[1] Dinizulu at least ended his chieftainship with dignity. He slipped through the columns which were hunting him, got to Maritzburg, and walked into Government House, saying to the Governor, " I am a king, and surrender only to the representative of the Great White Queen." He was exiled to St Helena, allowed to return to Zululand in 1898, was tried for treason in 1908, and died on a farm in the Transvaal in 1913.

down to the relaxations and amusements proper to light-hearted cavalry officers—polo, racing, shooting, dances, and other entertainments provided by the hospitable people of Natal.

Allenby rode boldly, had strength and good looks (of which last he was quite unconscious), danced well, and could talk on many subjects, so was popular in all classes of society. He never had the passion for sport which was characteristic of most young cavalry officers of the time: it was with him a relaxation, not the main object of life. He played polo, and played well, but racing had no attraction for him. Anything in which there was the slightest suspicion even of finesse was anathema to him; and he was, of course, far too heavy to ride races himself. He had, however, a grey mare which even with his weight on her back was so remarkably fast at polo that he was persuaded to enter her for the principal race at the next gymkhana meeting. "What name is the pony to run under?" inquired the race secretary. "Oh, anything you like," replied the rather bored and busy owner. So Captain Allenby's Anything You Like duly appeared on the card and won her race with ease, as she did several others.[1] Allenby acted as Mess President during much of the time in South Africa. With characteristic thoroughness he studied with a butcher the choosing of meat, and visited the baker to see how bread was made; he rode many miles to find plants for the mess garden or flowers for the mess table. He was known to his friends as "Apple-pie" (sometimes shortened to "Pie"), a play on his name and probably also a tribute to his love of order.

A brother-officer [2] writes of him at this time:

At this period of his career, whatever may have been his own secret thoughts and ambitions, Allenby was not regarded by his brother-officers in general as what used to be known in peacetime as a 'keen soldier.' He carried out all his military duties with complete efficiency, played polo, liked a little rough shooting, but all with rather an air of *insouciance*, so that many thought of him

---

[1] Allenby brought his pony back with him, and she became his wife's mount after his marriage.

[2] Lieutenant-Colonel James Stevenson-Hamilton, who joined the Inniskilling Dragoons a few years after Allenby, and was Warden of the Transvaal Government Game Reserves from 1902 to 1926.

as one constitutionally easy-going who took nothing seriously. He was popular with all ranks; he had a strong sense of humour, with just a touch of irony in his good-natured comments. A great reader on all manner of subjects unconnected with his profession, he could hold his own in conversation with older men who had made a special study of the subject under discussion. He held original ideas on many matters, military and civil, and did not hesitate to give expression to them, however contrary they may have been to accepted standards. He was always a little detached in manner, and did not court familiarity. But he would go out of his way to be kind to newly joined officers and to put them at their ease if necessary. He was an acute judge of character, and when he conceived a dislike it was invariably found to be justified, sooner or later. He hated and despised to an exceptional degree anything in the least savouring of sharp practice, of immorality, or of cowardice, moral or physical. In nearly everything else he was, even as a young man, exceedingly tolerant. He had a strong scientific bent, which expressed itself in various ways, but found its chief outlet in love of natural history.

Early in 1889 Allenby was appointed Adjutant of the regiment. From this moment his general outlook seemed to change and his air of good-natured *insouciance* was replaced by a determined thoroughness which was sobering to the more thoughtless of the young subalterns. It was as though with the acceptance of responsibility he put aside the easy-going outlook on life that he had inherited from his father, and took on the gospel of thoroughness laid on him by his mother. He soon made the most careless of subalterns understand that duty came before their pleasure and parade before their leisure, and that there was a serious side to soldiering. As an officer who knew him well in his official capacity puts it, " There was no wheeling before the C.O.; a few words, short, sharp, and decisive, from the Adjutant were sufficient." The same officer [1] gives a good picture of him in his unofficial moments:

He had never the herd instinct, and was at his best with a few friends. He had no desire to hold the floor on all possible occasions.

[1] Major-General Sir Thomas O'Donnell, K.C.I.E., C.B., D.S.O. He was Medical Officer to the Inniskilling Dragoons in South Africa from 1887 till 1890.

If there was a heated argument in the mess on such a vital issue as, say, the date of the next gymkhana, he would listen with an amused smile and make no attempt to rush into the fray. Never a great talker, he got to the root of the matter straight away in his short, crisp, rather staccato style. He was a first-rate judge of men, and had a wonderful knack of hitting off anyone's character in a short sentence or with a caricature. He was toying with a pencil and paper one day as we talked of a mutual friend. Presently he tossed me the scrap of paper; it was a caricature of our friend with all his little foibles and characteristics staring me in the face. He had a great sense of humour, and saw the comic side of a situation in a moment.

Once we rode together on leave from Etchowe to Maritzburg, a three-day trek. I picture him now in the glorious sunshine of a spring morning on the veldt, his handsome face lit up with the joy of living, taking the keenest interest in the animals and birds—he loved birds—on our way, and as pleased as a schoolboy that his little red-roan pony, named The Pink 'Un, could live up all day with my much bigger pony carrying three stone less. It was difficult to imagine that this was the same man who with a look and a few words could reduce the most insubordinate subaltern almost to a state of tears.

Allenby's consideration for his men at a period when such consideration was by no means a matter of course is illustrated by an incident remembered by one who was a corporal in the regiment at this time. On a day when drill was being done over rough ground at a fast pace the corporal's horse put his foot into a hole hidden by the long grass and crashed with him. It was the traditional custom in those rougher days for the farrier-sergeant-major to be sent to the scene of the casualty to inquire anxiously about injury to the horse, careless of any injury to the rider. On this occasion the Adjutant rode up and asked the corporal whether he was hurt, and, seeing that he was shaken by the fall, ordered him to ride his horse quietly back to barracks.

While Adjutant Allenby was called by his commanding officer, Colonel Martin, and by others of his friends, " the Mouthpiece." The nickname arose from a remark made by Allenby himself, _à propos_ of some orderly-room mandate: " I am but a sounding brass and a tinkling cymbal, the mouthpiece of a greater than I."

In November 1889 Allenby's career was nearly ended by a

serious accident at polo. He was crossed by another player who was unable to control his pony, and came down very heavily on the hard ground on head and shoulder. He lay unconscious for some time, and every one believed him to be fatally injured. Presently he recovered a little, and was found to be suffering from severe concussion of the brain and a dislocated shoulder: he had had an extremely narrow escape from breaking his neck. It was some months before he was fit enough to resume duty.

In 1890 the Inniskillings were suddenly ordered home, at a time when Allenby and a brother-officer were planning an expedition to Nyasaland, then known as British Central Africa, and still in the stage of primitive administration and of an unofficial war with the Arab slave-traders whose interests were threatened by British occupation. The regiment embarked at Durban on October 10 on H.M.S. *Himalaya*, one of the last of the old troopships manned by the Royal Navy. She proceeded alternately by steam and sail, taking nearly five weeks over the voyage home. The Inniskillings landed at Portsmouth on November 13, after nearly ten years' service in South Africa.

In these years Allenby had passed from youth to manhood, from apprentice to craftsman. He had learned the soldier's motley trade, and had gained knowledge of himself and his fellows in a good school. The cavalry arm gives the best military training possible for the young officer who means to learn and has the character and capacity to do so. He has responsibility out of sight and call of his immediate superior earlier and more entirely than his *confrères* of the artillery and infantry. He ranges wider, has to look farther ahead, to decide more quickly; in his care for man and horse, often at a distance from his unit, he has to solve small administrative problems not taught in books or barrack-room routine; in his sports of hunting and polo he has to think at speed, if he thinks at all, and to make decisions at once, if he is capable of deciding.

Allenby was fortunate, too, in spending his early service abroad rather than at home, where in those far-off, unregenerate days precise and stereotyped parade movements under the adjutant and drill-sergeant formed the chief military occupation, where the ambitious subaltern sought distinction in the hunting-field, on the polo-ground, on the racecourse, and even in the ballroom rather than in any manœuvre area, and where there was always the temptation to waste time and money in London. Instead, Allenby had passed his early service mainly in camp or bivouac, on the open veldt, in a manœuvre area nearly a thousand miles square from Cape Town to Mafeking, from St Lucia Bay to the Kalahari Desert. If he had seen little actual fighting in the Zululand and Bechuanaland expeditions, he had learned to handle a patrol or picket under the unseen but hostile and critical eyes of watching natives, who had read no text-books, but had studied warcraft from boyhood, and who seldom left a mistake unpunished. He had known the attraction and repulsion of South Africa, a land of sunshine and sudden storm, of bleak bareness and hidden wealth, of simple homeliness and stark savagery. But for the offer of the Adjutancy he might well have joined the pioneers of Rhodesia, as did so many of his friends. His knowledge of South Africa and its peoples was to serve him well when he returned less than ten years later with the expedition that was to bring the Dutch republics under British control. The discovery in 1885 of gold on the Witwatersrand, where the bare veldt then was and Johannesburg is now, had really, though few yet knew it, destroyed the last chance that those sturdy, uncompromising farmers in the Orange Free State and Transvaal would be left to their primitive hunting and farming and praying, and to their treasured independence from outside interference. And no further trek was possible, since the British under Rhodes and his lieutenant, Jameson, had occupied the country of the Matabele (now Rhodesia). The Boers were, as their leader, Paul Kruger, expressed it, " shut up in a kraal," or, as the modern German would claim, " subjected to a policy of encirclement."

IV

GARRISON LIFE AT HOME

(1890–96)

The Inniskillings were quartered at Brighton for the first three years after their return from South Africa. The conditions of service, the requirements of training, and the standard of polish were, of course, very different from those to which they had become accustomed during their campaigning life in South Africa. On Allenby as Adjutant fell much hard work to maintain the efficiency and smartness of the regiment in the new atmosphere. He found time, however, to play polo, to hunt and to shoot in due season. He made the acquaintance at this time of a Mr Kenneth Angelo, who owned a deer forest in Inverness-shire, and he used to spend a week or two with him each autumn in the stalking season. This friendship was to have momentous consequences for him.

Allenby's period as Adjutant came to an end in 1893. The Adjutant, the Colonel's staff officer and representative, had in those days much greater power and responsibility than now, and regiments run entirely by the Adjutant were not uncommon. During a considerable part of Allenby's tenure of office the commanding officer was away, which fact increased the influence of the Adjutant. Allenby, however, with his usual complete loyalty, never made any attempt to usurp power or to put himself forward.

The experience of responsible work as Adjutant inspired him to make an attempt to enter the Staff College, a somewhat unusual proceeding in those days—almost eccentric, indeed, in a cavalry officer. The Staff College had not then assumed the exaggerated importance it now holds in the eyes of the average officer, nor become the Mecca to which every devout subaltern feels compelled to make pilgrimage. Only some sixty to seventy officers competed annually for thirty-two vacancies, of which eight were by nomination of the Commander-in-Chief. Perhaps the syllabus deterred many; it demanded a high standard of mathematics, a detailed knowledge of fortification and topography, and considerable proficiency in foreign languages. Allenby began to read hard for the examination as soon as he had completed his Adjutancy, and spent some weeks with a crammer in London. He went up first for the examination in 1894 (the examination then took place in August), and though his percentage of marks was high (over 70 per cent.), he failed by a few marks to reach the qualifying minimum in military topography. Next year he passed

45

in successfully, being the only cavalry officer to do so, or even to qualify.[1]

Meanwhile the Inniskillings had gone from Brighton to Shorncliffe, and thence, after a winter at Manchester, with good hunting in Cheshire, to Edinburgh. From here Allenby left them to join the Staff College in January 1896, the first officer of his regiment to enter that seat of military learning.

[1] The examination comprised three papers in mathematics, two in fortification, two in tactics, two in military history, one each in topography, military law, administration, and geography, and one obligatory and two optional in foreign languages (of which four only were admissible—French, German, Hindustani, Russian). Allenby was 21st out of sixty-eight candidates, and obtained the highest marks (90 per cent.) in French. First on the list was J. E. Edmonds (now Sir James Edmonds, C.B., C.M.G., the official military historian), and the second was Captain G. M. W. Macdonogh (later Lieutenant-General Sir George Macdonogh, G.B.E., K.C.B., K.C.M.G.), both officers of the Royal Engineers.

CHAPTER III

THE STAFF
(1896–99)

I
THE STAFF COLLEGE
(1896–97)

THE names of those who have successfully passed the course of the Staff College since its foundation in 1859 are inscribed on wooden panels in the central hall and principal passages of the building. On the panel which records those students who joined the college in January 1896 and passed out in December 1897 the names of Major E. H. H. Allenby, of the 6th Dragoons, and Captain D. Haig, of the 7th Hussars, stand next to each other.[1]

The careers and characters of these two men, who were the most famous commanders of British forces in the Great War, have many resemblances and some striking differences. They were practically of an age, Haig less than two months younger than Allenby; they were of similar stock and fortune, since each came of an old-established country family of good repute and comfortable circumstances, but of no particular eminence. Both lost their fathers early and owed much to their mothers for their upbringing. Neither was intended originally for a military career. Both had the essential qualities of greatness—absolute courage, moral and physical, strength of purpose and constancy, a high sense of duty, and a fine generosity of spirit. Both were

---

[1] Haig, who had sat for the examination in 1893, but had failed in mathematics, received a nomination in 1895 and joined in 1896. Others in the same term who greatly distinguished themselves later were Sir Richard Haking (a corps commander in France), Sir Thompson Capper (who died of wounds received at Loos in command of a division), Sir George Macdonogh (head of the Intelligence branch in France and at the War Office during the War, and afterwards Adjutant-General), Sir William Furse (a divisional commander of the War and Master-General of Ordnance later), Sir George Forestier-Walker (a divisional commander of the War), and Sir James Edmonds (Deputy-Engineer-in-Chief in France and now official military historian of the War).

hardy and enduring of body and handsome of face and form. Both, though self-reliant, were reserved and aloof, both in their different ways somewhat alarming to approach. Both were liked and admired by women for their strength, and welcomed by children for their gentleness. Neither took any notice of women's admiration, but both adored children.

Thus in spirit and in body they were fellows—strong, enduring, and upright; but in mind there was a wide difference between them. Allenby had the finer perception and the greater knowledge; his intelligence had, as already shown, a wide range and many interests outside soldiering; he took every opportunity to visit new places and to acquire fresh learning. He was earnest and thorough in his profession, but it was by no means his only, probably not even his first, interest. Haig, on the other hand, had a single-track mind, intensely and narrowly concentrated, like a telescope, on the one object; except his profession of soldiering, and later his family, he had no real interests of any kind, and little knowledge; nor had he any desire for knowledge, unless it bore on his own special subject. Very quick of temper in his youth, he had so disciplined his mind and body to serve his fixed purpose that he seldom showed anger or impatience. Allenby, by nature of a more tolerant humour, indulged as the years went on in frequent outbursts of violent temper. Haig, secure in his own self-confidence, seldom listened to the opinion of others; Allenby, equally strong-willed, would always pay heed to those who had knowledge. Haig recorded all events in a carefully kept diary; Allenby made no note whatever of his acts or thoughts, and destroyed practically every letter or paper he received. Haig had a deeply religious strain, and was a regular churchgoer; Allenby, though a constant student of the Bible, made little observance of the outward forms of religion.

To sum up, Allenby was the more broad-minded and the more human; Haig, by virtue of concentration, the more technically efficient. Their differences in character can be attributed partly to their respective nationalities. Haig was Scottish to the bone, Allenby was English to the core. The two men never understood each other well, nor were easy in each other's company. Allenby himself once told one of his staff of a meeting during the War between himself and Haig alone. They had important matters to discuss, but from sheer shyness of each other neither uttered a word. They parted with a mutual, but still unspoken, resolve never to meet again without others present.

At the Staff College, where their paths first met, Haig was an outstanding personality in his batch, for whom the highest honours were predicted both by his instructors and by his fellow-students; Allenby made no special mark, and his work, though of good quality, was undistinguished. He was always inclined to listen and to absorb knowledge, rather than to talk and exhibit it. He was remembered by his fellow-students chiefly for his remarkable appetite, his good humour, and his Mastership of the Staff College Draghounds, a post carrying considerable distinction and responsibility.[1] The Master of the Drag is elected each year by the students of the term concerned. For the season 1896–97 Haig, who was a better horseman than Allenby, was the obvious choice, and his election was confidently expected. But Haig was not popular with his fellow-students, and Allenby was. At the meeting held to elect the Master Allenby was chosen. He duly succeeded an old Sandhurst friend of his, Herbert Lawrence, and made a most successful Master, though his falls were frequent. He won the heavy-weight point-to-point race on his chestnut gelding Chisel. A point-to-point did not consist of prepared fences in those days. There were three flags only, and riders could take any course outside them. Allenby rode his own line a little wide of the majority, and came up at the finish to beat by a head Captain Mackenzie,[2] of the Seaforths. Allenby also made a remarkably good speech at the hunt dinner to the farmers.

Allenby had married at the end of his first year at the Staff College. At the house in Scotland of his friends, the Angelos, he had met in 1895 Miss Mabel Chapman, the third daughter of a Wiltshire landowner.[3] He had seen her for a few days only, but

[1] One fellow-student remembers Allenby as notorious for his unpunctuality. If so, he cured himself of the fault, for he was an extremely punctual man in later life.

[2] Major-General Sir Colin Mackenzie, K.C.B.

[3] There were three other daughters, of whom the eldest married Canon Tupper-Carey, Chaplain at Monte Carlo; the second, Sir Arthur Downes, a distinguished public servant; and the youngest, Admiral Charles Napier.

had been strongly attracted by her; and when he again found her there in August next year he made up his mind with his usual swiftness and directness, and by the end of a week they were engaged. Miss Chapman's father at first disapproved strongly of his daughter throwing herself away on a young cavalry officer with poor prospects. But his objections were soon overcome, and the marriage took place at the bride's home, Donhead St Andrew, in the south-west of Wiltshire, on December 30, 1896, during the winter vacation of the Staff College. After a short honeymoon in London the Allenbys began married life in a house on a hill just above Camberley, within a mile or so of the Staff College.

The union of these two was, from the beginning to the end, a true and ideal one. Mrs Allenby looked on life with the same clear courage and directness as her husband, and had in her gentle way as great a strength of will as he. Like him, she had been brought up to a country life, and loved birds and gardens; like him, she rode well and boldly to hounds. She could share his adventures in travel, his liking for fresh sights, and his appreciation of the old and quiet and lovely things of life.

Allenby was promoted Major in May 1897. He completed the course at the Staff College at the end of that year. He received a good report as a thoroughly practical soldier, and was recommended for the appointment of Brigade-Major to a cavalry brigade. He had found time while at the Staff College to qualify as Army interpreter in French. He also knew some German, and visited Germany during one vacation.

II

THE CURRAGH

(1898–99)

Allenby received the appointment for which he had been recommended almost immediately on leaving the Staff College. In March 1898 he took up the post of Brigade-Major (or Adjutant, as it was termed at that time) to the 3rd Cavalry Brigade in Ireland, at the Curragh. Lord Downe, late of the 10th Hussars, a charming personality and a good soldier, was the brigade commander. The brigade included the 8th and 14th Hussars, Allenby's own regiment, the Inniskillings, and two batteries of Horse Artillery. This was the only staff appointment ever held by Allenby: the remainder of his career was spent as a commander. His natural genius was for command, but he had also the qualities required for a staff officer, for he was hard-working, accurate, and methodical, he wrote good, clear English, and he could get orders carried out without friction. Of his loyalty there could never be any question. Though he was always a stickler for the Regulations, he interpreted them with common sense and forbearance, and he was liked as well as respected by the officers of the brigade.

Ireland was in those days a highly popular station for the sporting soldier. Hunting was good and cheap, and there was plenty of fishing and rough shooting to be had. The Allenbys hunted, fished, and cultivated their garden, which they made one of the best at the Curragh. In his letters home from South Africa Allenby remembers continually the garden at Simla, their house, and laments its fate of neglect on their departure. Their only child, Michael, was born in January 1898 at Donhead St Andrew, Mrs Allenby's Wiltshire home. He was to grow to the promise of a brilliant and useful life, and to lay down that life prematurely in the Great War.

Allenby's appointment was ended by the outbreak of the South African War. He rejoined his regiment, which was one of the first ordered to the theatre of war, in October 1899 as a squadron commander, and embarked on s.s. *Persia* at Queenstown at the end of that month.

CHAPTER IV

THE SOUTH AFRICAN WAR

(1899–1902)

I

THE COMING OF WAR

THE Boer War marks a turning-point in our history. It was the climax of British Imperialism, of the time—the last time—when we were aggressively sure of ourselves and of our destiny. Though it is not, perhaps, an episode of our history in which we have reason to feel great pride, politically or militarily, yet it is certainly not one of which we need be ashamed. That two stiff-necked peoples, with a background of past quarrels and injustices, might come to a proper respect for each other, and thus to union, a war was practically inevitable; and it had in the end healthful consequences both for South Africa and for the British Army. No more of its origin and course will be related here than is necessary for the understanding of Allenby's part in the operations.

Since Allenby had left South Africa, nine years earlier, friction between Briton and Boer had developed a heat at which fire was bound to occur before long. The discovery in 1885 of gold on the Witwatersrand—the low range of hills that forms the watershed of the great South African plateau between the Orange and Limpopo rivers—had brought an influx into the Transvaal of so great a body of gold-seekers and their satellites that they soon came to outnumber the other whites in the Transvaal. These 'Uitlanders,' as they were termed, the great majority of whom were British subjects, formed a serious problem for the narrow, suspicious Dutch farmers and their stubborn, Biblical old President, Paul Kruger. The Boers grumbled that their country was being overrun by undesired and undesirable foreigners. The Uitlanders, on the other hand, complained that, though the taxes they contributed provided by far the greater part of the republic's revenue, they were denied a fair franchise or equitable treatment. The criminal folly of the Jameson Raid at the end of 1895 confirmed the Dutch in their hatred of the British and in their refusal of any rights or privileges to the Uitlanders. The dispute dragged on for another three years. In June 1899 a conference at Bloemfontein between Kruger and Milner, the British High Commissioner in South Africa, showed that the gulf between their respective points of view was unbridgeable.

Thereafter both parties prepared for war, the British slowly and reluctantly, the Boers convinced that their day had come. The British garrison, which in January 1899 consisted of two cavalry regiments and half a dozen battalions, was reinforced in August and September by some 10,000 men from India and the Mediterranean. The two Dutch republics—for the Orange Free State had resolved to support the Transvaal—determined to strike before more troops could be sent. They mustered their commandos at the end of September; and, on the British Government responding by ordering the mobilization of an Army Corps, sent, on October 9, 1899, an ultimatum that had been prepared some time earlier. It was unacceptable, as it was meant to be, and was, in fact, a declaration of war on the British Empire.

It seemed on the face of it an impudent, if gallant, challenge. A handful of farmers, with little military organization, faced the might of a great empire. Yet it was not from the Boer calculations so desperate an enterprise as it seemed to the outside world. They had a considerable initial superiority for at least several weeks, since the total British garrison amounted, at the beginning of October, only to some 27,000, of whom one-third were Colonial troops, while the two republics could muster 60,000 fighting burghers—to whom any success would add large numbers of the Dutch inhabitants of Cape Colony, only too ready to throw off their British allegiance if it could safely be done. And, in the experience of President Kruger and his advisers, both British troops and British Governments could be made to yield without great difficulty. Finally, they had encouragement to hope for the intervention in their favour of one or more of the Great Powers of Europe. They entered the war, then, with a vision of quick and easy successes in the field like Majuba and Doornkop, a great rising of fellow-Dutchmen in Cape Colony, a driving of

the hated British into the sea from which they came, the intervention of Europe to safeguard their victory, and a wholly Dutch
South Africa at last. They could not know the indomitable
determination and staying-power of the British nation when
roused, nor that the British Navy had then such unchallenged
supremacy as to overawe, during three years, a Europe united for
once in shrill condemnation of the Islanders and in sympathy for
the Boers. That no intervention was attempted was one of the
greatest demonstrations in history of the value of sea-power,
though never a shot was fired by those silent, unseen fleets.[1]

II

THE VOYAGE TO SOUTH AFRICA
(*November–December* 1899)

The Inniskillings embarked at Queenstown by squadrons in
three separate ships during the last week of October 1899. The
first two ships, with headquarters and A and B Squadrons, had
uneventful passages; but the third ship, on which was Allenby
with C Squadron, had a difficult and dangerous voyage. The
Persia, an Anchor Line boat of about 3500 tons, sailed four or five
days later than the other two, and at once ran into a heavy gale
which caused much discomfort and the loss of a number of horses.
Later, when about twenty miles from St Vincent, in the Cape
Verde Islands, and about six miles from the rocky island of San
Antonio, the screw shaft broke, and the ship lay helpless in a heavy
swell, with the wind driving her on to the cliffs of San Antonio.
A boat manned by Inniskilling volunteers under the ship's second
officer set out to sail to St Vincent for aid; it was dismasted by a
squall, rescued by a shore boat, and taken into St Vincent, where
by great luck lay the cruiser *Diadem* and a tug which had arrived
the day previously from Liverpool. The story of events on board
the *Persia* meanwhile is told in a letter from Allenby to his wife:

---

[1] It is odd to remember in these days of long-range naval warfare that in 1900 two
thousand to three thousand yards was regarded as the normal range of engagement
for battleships, and that in all ships cutlasses for boarders or to repel boarders were
still carried. The range of torpedoes at that time was some eight hundred yards only.

CHAPTER IV: THE SOUTH AFRICAN WAR

At 6 A.M. yesterday our screw shaft broke. Heavy swell and stiff breeze dead on shore, 20 miles from St Vincent and 6 miles from the island of S. Antonio, straight on our lee. We made all the distressful signals that are known, but though we saw some villages and a lighthouse on shore, no notice was taken. So we sent 6 volunteers from my men and an officer of the ship in a small boat to sail to St Vincent for help. They got it in the end, or we shouldn't be here, and we didn't know, till we were retrieved, that their mast was carried away, that they were picked up by a Portuguese shore boat, and towed here, to St Vincent, where they found a tug. Well, we really had quite a dramatic and satisfactory day. The ship was being steadily carried in towards the most beautiful bit of mountain scenery I have ever seen. A steep rocky island, with mountains up to 3000 or 4000 feet. Lovely green valleys and little villages with cliffs that reminded one of Doré's illustrations of Dante's *Inferno*. But we couldn't see much chance of landing, and the probability was that there would be no anchorage, as the charts showed 70 fathoms right up to the mountain-sides, where the rollers were spouting up 2 or 300 feet high. A lot of sharks came round in the morning, and we had great practice at them with revolvers, but did not do them much harm. After a time we got all our boats out. The arrangement was that if we took to the boats they should all try to get to the lee of the island and land. The captain and I and 6 men would remain, with one boat, on the off-chance of the anchor catching, and would leave when there was no chance for the ship or the horses. At last, at about 3 P.M., a tug hove in sight, and at that moment, to our considerable relief, our anchor, which was hanging with 60 fathoms of chain, caught and held, and we swung to it, $\frac{1}{2}$ a mile from shore.[1] Then the tug got us, and we were right, but we couldn't get the men out of the boats, which, 11 in number, were swinging astern in a very heavy swell, and with all the tow-ropes twisted up, and the boats bumping and jumping all over the place. Then up came the *Diadem*, a cruiser, and signalled that she would pick up the boats. . . . She sent a boat and picked off our men from our boats. We could not get them up again and

---

[1] Actually it was Allenby who persuaded the captain to let the anchor hang. The captain said that the charts showed deep water, and there was no possibility of the anchor finding hold, but Allenby insisted that the off-chance should be taken.

in a very short time they were all swamped and broken away, except one. We were then towed in here to St Vincent, the cruiser following up as a convoy. It was lucky our anchor caught hold when it did, as otherwise I think we should have lost a lot of men and the whole ship and horses. Still it was a most cheerful shipwreck. The men behaved like bricks, and those in the boats looked on it as a sort of picnic. They spent the night in the man-of-war, and are very pleased with themselves. The trouble now is that we have no boats and can't go on without them, and it will probably take a week or more to repair our shaft. . . . We've had a really unlucky voyage so far; 21 horses have died.

The coolness and common sense displayed by Allenby on this occasion gave all on board great confidence in his leadership. The squadron had to wait over a fortnight at St Vincent while another ship, the *Goth*, of the Union-Castle Line, came out from England to replace the disabled *Persia*.

Allenby and his squadron finally landed at Cape Town on December 11, during that " Black Week " in which the British nation was shaken out of its complacency and stirred to action by the successive disasters of Stormberg, Magersfontein, and Colenso. The remainder of the Inniskillings was with French's force in front of Colesberg, near the Orange Free State border, and Allenby received orders to join it at once as second-in-command, to replace Rimington, who had been detailed to raise a local irregular force.[1] Allenby went by train to Naauwpoort Junction, leaving his squadron to follow later.

III

THE FIRST PHASES OF THE WAR

(*December* 1899–*February* 1900)

The opening events of the war, had brought shocks and disappointments to both sides; each had under-estimated the other, and each had been disillusioned. The Boer plan was to make their main initial effort against Natal, the northern part of which lay in a salient between the Transvaal and Orange Free State, and

---

[1] It became famous during the war as " Rimington's Tigers."

was thus open to invasion from two sides. Other commandos were to deal with the small British force on the Bechuanaland border, near Mafeking, and others to occupy the diamond fields of Kimberley. They reckoned easily to overrun Natal and reach its port of Durban, and that this success, together with the occupation of Kimberley and Mafeking, would rouse all the Dutch of Cape Colony, some 40,000 fighting men, to rise in rebellion and join them against the British. Thus reinforced, they could drive the British to the coast, and make their task of reconquering the interior impossible.

For the British the danger was a very real one, to which they had tardily awakened after the failure of the Bloemfontein conference. The troops hastily sent from India and the Mediterranean in August and September were intended to secure Natal from the threatened invasion. For the defence of Bechuanaland and Kimberley only local forces were available, but selected Regular officers were sent to take command—Baden-Powell,[1] then a young Brevet-Colonel of cavalry, to Mafeking, and Kekewich, an infantryman, to Kimberley; Plumer,[2] another infantry soldier, led a few hundred irregulars in Rhodesia. The small forces in Cape Colony could do no more than hold, with inadequate detachments, the principal railway bridges and junctions at Orange River Station, De Aar, Naauwpoort, and Stormberg, and hope to keep the enemy in check by bluff. Thus only in Natal had the defence any strength, and even there it was dangerously weak. But it was not believed that irregulars like the Boers, with little military training, would have much offensive power against Regular troops; and it was hoped that the defence in Natal and elsewhere would hold until the Army Corps and Cavalry Division from the United Kingdom could land. Once this imposing force was concentrated there could be no question, it was felt, of its ability to end by a direct advance on Bloemfontein and Pretoria any pretence of the Dutch republics to oppose the might of Great Britain. Sir Redvers Buller had been selected for command—a

---

[1] Lieutenant-General Lord Baden-Powell, G.C.M.G., G.C.V.O., K.C.B., founder of the Boy Scouts organization.
[2] The late Field-Marshal Lord Plumer, commander of the Second Army in France during the Great War.

brave, stolid, burly man, who looked just as the public expected a British general to look, and was popular accordingly; he had made his name largely by his personal courage in small wars, but had little real knowledge of the arts of generalship. He always had the liking of his troops, even after his repeated failures.

The Boer invasion of Natal ended in a stalemate—the siege of Ladysmith. There was a moment when the invaders, had they been content merely to blockade the British forces in Ladysmith, might have overrun the rest of Natal and have reached its capital, Pietermaritzburg, and its port, Durban. But their leader, Joubert, was old and cautious; [1] the British attacks at Talana and Elandslaagte had somewhat shaken Boer confidence; their organization was ill-fitted for a prolonged invasion, and the opportunity was allowed to pass. But the British plan had been completely dislocated by the events in Natal. The Army Corps that was to advance triumphantly on Bloemfontein was broken up before it was landed. The greater part, under Buller himself, was hurried east to save Natal and relieve Ladysmith, while a portion only, under Lord Methuen, advanced to the relief of Kimberley. The bulk of the Cavalry Division was placed in the centre opposite Colesberg, with the mission of checking any further enemy advance from the Free State into Cape Colony. It was under General French,[2] with Haig as his principal staff officer; after taking part in the early fighting in Natal they had escaped together by the last train to leave Ladysmith.

Allenby landed, as we have seen, at a gloomy moment: within one week three severe reverses had befallen the British forces. Gatacre, on French's right, attempted to improve his position at Stormberg by a night operation, mismanaged it, and met disaster; Methuen's advance on Kimberley was checked by the repulse of his night attack at Magersfontein; and, worst shock of all, Buller failed with heavy loss to cross the Tugela at Colenso and to relieve hard-pressed Ladysmith. A pause of two months followed, while the British gathered fresh strength. The opening moves of the campaign had effectively shaken their complacency and removed

[1] See *Commando*, by Deneys Reitz, Chapter II.
[2] Afterwards Field-Marshal the Earl of Ypres, leader of the British Army in France 1914-15.

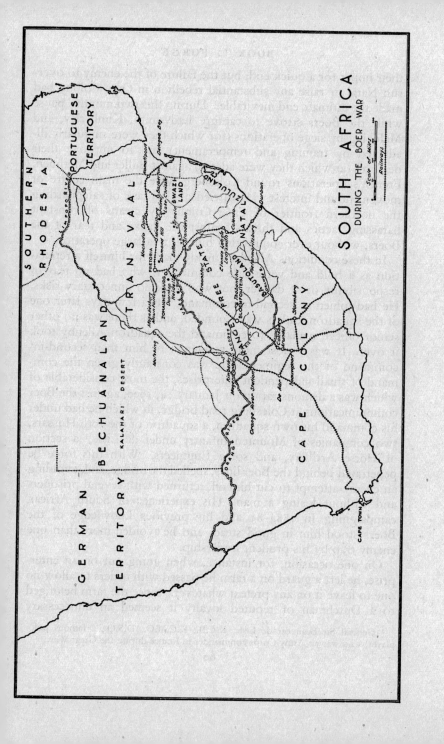

SOUTH AFRICA
DURING THE BOER WAR

Scale of Miles

Railways

their hopes for a quick end, but the failure of the enemy to over-run Natal or raise any substantial rebellion in Cape Colony had made the ultimate end inevitable. During this two months' pause while the Boers strove to capture Ladysmith, Kimberley, and Mafeking by siege operations (for which they were singularly ill-adapted by training and temperament) and to improve their defences (at which they were adepts) against Buller and Methuen, French's operations round Colesberg were the main centre of movement and interest. He carried out his task of safeguarding the northern frontier of Cape Colony by means of constant harassing tactics and threats against the flanks and rear of the Boers, without ever committing himself to a large operation.

In these conditions Allenby quickly made for himself a reputation as a bold and yet a safe commander, who had no fear of responsibility or of danger, but who took no unnecessary risks. He had joined as second-in-command, but a few days later one of the squadron leaders was wounded, and as there was no other senior officer available to command the squadron Allenby took it over. It was a post more congenial to him than second-in-command of the regiment. He was constantly given the command of small independent enterprises, the most considerable of which was a demonstration on January 14, 1900, against the Boer communications at Colesberg road bridge, in which he had under his command his own squadron, a squadron of the 10th Hussars, two companies of Mounted Infantry under de Lisle,[1] a section of Horse Artillery, and some Engineers. With this force he penetrated behind the Boer lines, shelled the bridge, and, avoiding an enemy attempt to cut him off, returned with several prisoners and without losing a man. His experience of South African campaigning in 1884–85 and his previous knowledge of the Boers stood him in good stead, and he avoided more than one enemy trap by his prudent leadership.

On one occasion, for instance, when going out on an enterprise, he left a guard on a farm he passed with orders to allow no one to leave it on any pretext whatever. Since the farm belonged to a Dutchman of reputed loyalty it seemed an unnecessary

---

[1] General Sir Beauvoir de Lisle, K.C.B., K.C.M.G., D.S.O., a famous polo-player, who was an Army Corps commander in France during the Great War.

precaution, but a month or two later the corporal of this guard recognized in a batch of Boer prisoners a youth from this very farm who had on this occasion attempted to pass the guard on some pretext. He then realized the prudent wisdom of his squadron commander. At another time Allenby, believing his squadron had been seen by the enemy going into bivouac, moved after dark, leaving his fires burning; at dawn the old bivouac suddenly came under heavy fire. Such precautions may seem elementary, but it was exceptional for them to be taken by the British Army of 1899–1900.

Once his knowledge of, and interest in, the ways of birds and beasts saved Allenby from a dangerous ambush. With another officer he had ridden ahead of his squadron to reconnoitre a farm-house, apparently deserted and surrounded by a low wall. After scanning it for a while with his field-glasses he remarked to his companion, " Did you ever see ducks perching on a wall before? " And, riding back to the squadron, he gave the order to retire. As soon as the movement began heavy rifle-fire broke out from behind the wall. The Boers had placed the ducks, with a well-founded contempt for the average English patrol's knowledge of natural history, on the wall behind which they were hiding, to entice their enemy into thinking the farm safe and get them to ride up to it to buy poultry and eggs.

No officer, in fact, carried out General French's policy of harrying and alarming the enemy without becoming heavily engaged or unnecessarily losing lives more efficiently than Allenby. His courage was so natural to him that he did not have to take unwise risks to himself and to his men to prove it. He had no use for displays of bravery where bravery had no utility.

The Earl of Dunmore (Lord Fincastle of those days) writes of Allenby:

In the operations around Colesberg under French he seemed to me one of the few men who had the courage to exercise his own judgment. He wasn't out to earn a reputation by some unnecessary and futile charge. But no man had greater courage or was more ready to take great risks if the circumstances justified his doing so.

So that when, at the beginning of February, a cavalry force was collected under French on the Modder river, to attempt the relief of Kimberley and to support Lord Roberts' flank march on Bloemfontein, Allenby's squadron was taken to form part of it, though the remainder of his regiment was left opposite Colesberg.

Allenby's letters to his wife during the Boer War give a complete record of his movements and of the events in which he took part. They are typical of the man, straight, concise, and clear. He was always a very conscientious letter-writer, and to the end of his life answered practically every letter he received in his rather unformed, sprawling, but perfectly legible handwriting. His letters had no pretence to literary grace, were always short and to the point, and never went beyond it. Not even his wife had a gossiping letter from Allenby. His letters during this early period show well his attitude towards war. He writes without any depression at the uncomfortable conditions or the news of British reverses, nor with any elation at the opportunity of distinguishing himself or desire to do so. He looks on fighting as part of the day's work, to be done as efficiently and to be ended as expeditiously as possible, but does not conceal his opinion of the stupidity of war. He says much in praise of others and little or nothing of his own successes; for the enemy he has no bitterness and much admiration and kindness. Flowers interest him as much as, or more than, fighting. He is full of longing for home and for his small son Michael. Two typical extracts follow:

November 6, 1899

I have too happy a life at home to make a really good soldier. I catch myself often half hoping that the war may be over by the time we arrive.

January 5, 1900

They tell me these Boers are fighting splendidly and most pluckily, although they occasionally fire on an ambulance. I think myself that they mistrust us and that they fancy we are bringing up ammunition by stealth if our ambulance goes out during a fight, as they are very civil to our people when they are collecting wounded after a fight. Fincastle went out to pick up the wounded yesterday, and met several Boers who said what a pity the war was, what a mistake it was for two Christian nations to be shooting each other like wild beasts. We got about 20 prisoners yesterday, such rough, unkempt fellows, but quite pleasant and polite. I must say I rather like Brother Boer.[1] It's satisfactory in a way to be up here as 2nd in command, but I'm not ferocious and I don't want any particular distinctions.

IV
KIMBERLEY AND BLOEMFONTEIN
(*February–April* 1900)

When the shocks of the Black Week roused the British nation and Government to a realization of the task before them they sent to South Africa their two most proved Generals—the veteran Lord Roberts, who had served over forty years in India, and, as his Chief of Staff, Lord Kitchener, the recent conqueror of the Sudan. They reached Cape Town on January 10, 1900. Reinforcements from England were arriving daily, and many local corps were being formed.

Of the three possible lines of advance into the Dutch republics —through Natal, directly on Bloemfontein by Colesberg, or to Kimberley along the western railway line, where Methuen's force, after its defeat at Magersfontein, lay on the Modder river opposite Cronje's commandos—Roberts chose the last. The topography of the northern frontier of Natal was too favourable to the defence, while the direct advance on Bloemfontein would be slow —especially as the Boers still held the bridge at Norval's Point over the Orange river—and liable to attack from both flanks. Further, the relief of Kimberley was becoming urgent; in fact, one influential and autocratic person besieged in that town, Cecil Rhodes, made no secret of his belief that it was the most pressing task of the military forces. Accordingly Roberts made up his mind to concentrate under cover of Methuen's force, to outflank Cronje on the east, relieve Kimberley, and thence move on Bloemfontein. In Natal the puzzled, groping Buller was left to work out his own and Ladysmith's salvation by a somewhat costly process of trial and error.

In its essentials Roberts' plan was, like most successful plans in

---

[1] Later in the war he wrote in a letter, " The Boer if treated the right way is a very decent fellow. I know that very few of my countrymen agree with me, but I have always liked and admired the Boer, and always shall."

war, simple almost to the point of crudity—a feint at Cronje's right and then a quick side-step round his left. The rest depended on the marching powers of man and horse. But elaborate arrangements had to be made to deceive the enemy and to make the outflanking force mobile; in the careful execution of these details lay the difficulties and success of the plan. Many years later, in Palestine, Allenby was to make and to execute successfully a very similar plan.

The activity of French and his cavalry in front of Colesberg was continued, so as to direct the attention of the enemy to that line of advance, till the moment came for the bulk of the mounted men to slip away for the projected ride to Kimberley.

Allenby's squadron marched from Rensburg to Arundel on February 2, and went on next day to Naauwpoort, where it entrained for Modder River Camp, arriving there on February 4 after a trying nineteen hours in the train. The cavalry was being assembled in a hot, dusty camp south of the Modder river, where Allenby had bathed just fifteen years before on his way to Bechuanaland with Warren's expedition.

The movement began on February 11, south-east from Modder Camp to Ramdam Farm, where the striking force assembled. Thence the Cavalry Division, followed by two infantry divisions, was to cross the Riet river and strike north-east to the Modder again, arriving, if all went well, outside the flank of Cronje's position, and moving round it on Kimberley. Speed was the essence of the plan, but speed was not easy without great sacrifice and exertion. February is the hottest month of the year on the South African plateau; water was scarce, and there was little or no grazing for the cavalry horses and transport animals on the bare, scorched, dusty plains. A large proportion of the army's transport was by slow-moving ox-wagon. The distances were considerable—over twenty miles to Ramdam, twelve miles to the Riet river, and twenty-five miles thence to the Modder. On February 12 the drifts over the Riet were secured in face of some opposition, and on the 13th the cavalry crossed the long, waterless stretch between the rivers. Allenby's squadron, which had had some fighting as advanced guard to his brigade on the 12th, was again heavily engaged as right-flank guard. By a masterly

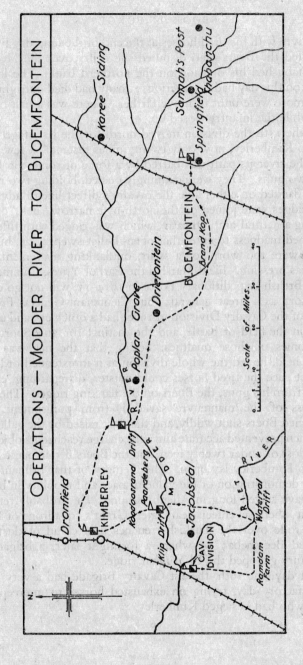

OPERATIONS—MODDER RIVER TO BLOEMFONTEIN

Karee Siding

Sannah's Post

Springfield

Thabanchu

Bloemfontein

Brand Kop

Driefontein

Poplar Grove

MODDER RIVER

Koodoosrand Drift

Paardeberg

Kilp Drift

Jacobsdal

CAV. DIVISION

Waterval Drift

RIET RIVER

Ramdam Farm

KIMBERLEY

Dronfield

Scale of Miles.
0   5   10   20   30   40

N.

manœuvre with his tired horses at the end of the long day French outwitted the Boers who disputed the drifts over the Modder, and established his division on the northern bank. The loss in horses on this day had been serious; many had died outright, and many more were unfit to move farther. There was a halt on the 14th while the infantry closed up.

On the 15th the division moved north for the last stage of its dash to Kimberley, now only twenty miles distant. A few miles from the river its path was barred by a force of some 900 Boers with two guns. They were cunningly posted, holding two ridges which flanked on either side the cavalry's direct line of advance; these ridges were joined on the north by a narrow ' nek,' or col, forming a natural amphitheatre, which was ringed with rifle-fire. It seemed madness to enter that open, bullet-swept zone, but the horses were too worn for a swift, outflanking movement, and time was pressing. Field-Marshal the Earl of Ypres, Commander of the British Expeditionary Force in 1914–15, will not go down to history as a great general; but Lieutenant-General French, leader of the Cavalry Division in 1900, had a quick eye and a bold heart on the field of battle, and the instinct for an opportunity that comes of those qualities. Seeing that the nek was only lightly held, he led the whole division at it in extended order, at the best pace the tired horses could muster, disregarding, except by fire from his guns, the Boers on the flanking ridges. The very boldness of the manœuvre saved it from punishment. The astonished Boers shot wildly, and the dust raised by the galloping horsemen prevented accurate aim; the charge reached its objective with a loss of under twenty men, and the Boers fled in panic. The road to Kimberley lay open. The memory of that brilliant feat, and its demonstration of the value of pace and mobility in battle, must have stayed long in Allenby's mind. He probably remembered it when, seventeen years later, Grant's squadrons of Light Horse rode over the Turkish trenches in a cloud of dust and captured Beersheba; or when, a fortnight later, a brigade of Yeomanry galloped the El Mughar ridge.

Next day, the 16th, the 1st Cavalry Brigade had a very hard, unsatisfactory day, trying on exhausted horses to intercept the Boers who had besieged Kimberley.

So ended " the longest week I ever spent," as Allenby wrote to his wife; " my property now consists of the dirty clothes I live and sleep in day and night, a cloak, a saddle blanket, a tooth-brush, a box of cigarettes, and a tube of lanoline." His squadron was reduced to forty-two horses. The squadron of New South Wales Lancers was now attached to it and put under his command. They remained under him till their return to Australia in the following October. The exhausted brigade now had a few days' rest.

Allenby resumed his acquaintance with Rhodes, who entertained him to dinner, and, remembering his old friendship with the Inniskillings, sent firewood, soup, and other comforts to his squadron. The supply-wagons of the Cavalry had been left behind on the Riet, and did not rejoin for many days. They were lucky to rejoin at all, for that great leader of guerrillas, Christian De Wet, had pounced on the convoys at Waterval Drift, on the Riet, and had captured a large portion of the army's supplies.

Meanwhile important events were taking place on the Modder. Cronje, who had obstinately refused to believe that the clumsy, headlong English could ever march or manœuvre, suddenly found himself with the cavalry between him and Kimberley and the infantry almost between him and Bloemfontein. He tried hurriedly to escape east along the Modder, but French, taking the only brigade fit to move (it had not been launched in pursuit of the besiegers of Kimberley), headed him off at Koodoosrand Drift after a march of thirty-five miles, and with a much inferior force stood boldly in his path—another example of the power of well-handled horsemen, which did not leave Allenby's memory. Cronje went to ground in the bed of the river, and was soon surrounded by the infantry. Lord Kitchener's impetuosity caused unnecessarily heavy losses in an attack on the Boer laager, and the sudden intervention of De Wet from the south made a temporary gap in the lines of investment. But the odds against stubborn old Cronje were too heavy, and on February 27, the anniversary of Majuba, he surrendered with his force of 4000. Meanwhile Allenby's squadron, with the rest of the 1st Cavalry Brigade, leaving Kimberley on the 21st, had rejoined French at Koodoosrand. It was engaged in the line of investing troops up to the time of the surrender.

A few days after the capture of Cronje's force Buller had at last relieved Ladysmith, and the whole basis on which the Dutch republics had built their war plan had crumbled. They were now invaded, instead of invaders, and a large proportion of the burghers were demoralized and ready to submit. All the efforts of the fiery De Wet, of the gallant De la Rey, of the implacable Steyn, and even of old President Kruger himself could not hearten the burghers into a resolute defence of the road to Bloemfontein. If Lord Roberts' army could have acted energetically now the war might have been ended in a few months. Unfortunately it was in no state to do so. Men, horses, and transport animals were all on short rations (caused largely by De Wet's raid on the communications during the march to Kimberley), and were worn by their exertions.

The army halted for a week on the Modder and then moved on Bloemfontein. There were two actions on the way, at Poplar Grove (March 7) and Driefontein (March 10). At the first of these the Boer resistance was half-hearted, but the horses of the cavalry were too exhausted to make either the turning movement round the flank or the pursuit effective. At Driefontein some of the Boers fought desperately, and our infantry had severe losses. Again the condition of the cavalry horses hampered their usefulness and prevented pursuit. On March 12 Allenby's squadron led the final advance on Bloemfontein and seized some kopjes to the south; under cover of this the remainder of the brigade turned the defences of the town, which surrendered next day. A staff officer [1] from the 6th Division sent forward to keep touch with the cavalry at this time has given an interesting picture of his first impressions of Allenby:

> I joined up with Allenby's squadron, and was with it when it occupied Brand Kop, the big hill overlooking Bloemfontein. My first impression of him was that he was the typical heavy dragoon, obviously a good squadron leader. That night I changed my mind. We bivouacked together on the top of Brand Kop, and as we were smoking round a bivouac fire he started talking about the future of the British Army. I remember him saying that our existing organiza-

[1] Captain F. B. Maurice, now Major-General Sir Frederick Maurice, K.C.M.G., C.B.

tion was utterly out of date, and he put the reforms that we must go for in the following order: (*a*) a properly trained General Staff; (*b*) the peace organization of the Army to be the same as the war organization, units and formations to be commanded and trained in peace by the men who would lead them in war; (*c*) promotion above the rank of captain to be by selection; (*d*) the organization of the military forces to be uniform throughout the Empire. All this sounded revolutionary in March 1900, and I was deeply impressed, and thereafter watched Allenby's career with great interest.

At Bloemfontein the exhausted army sank down for a long rest. A relaxation of effort was inevitable, for the force had no stable line of communication till the railway from Colesberg to Bloemfontein was repaired and reopened. But the prolongation of this rest, due in part to an easy optimism that the war was already won, gave the wavering burghers a breathing-space and fresh heart, and probably lengthened the war by nearly two years. Another lesson that Allenby remembered to good purpose in later years—never to allow a beaten enemy time to recover, whatever the hardships and sacrifices required of the troops. At the time he welcomed the halt as much as anyone, for his men had been worked up to their limit and his horses beyond it. The Brigade-Major of the 1st Cavalry Brigade has recorded that he kept a special list of officers who could be trusted with important tasks and independent missions; Allenby's name stood at the head of the list, an honour which brought more than a normal share of danger and exertion.

His squadron was bivouacked with the remainder of the 1st Cavalry Brigade at Springfield, a few miles east of Bloemfontein. The baggage of the brigade had not been with it since Modder Camp, and no tents were available. The men slept on the bare ground, often in mud, for rainstorms were frequent. The officers of the army round Bloemfontein at this time made a ragged appearance. Few possessed a spare coat or breeches, and many had grown beards during the last month's continuous marching and fighting. Allenby had not, but had " shaved about every third day," and had repaired his own clothes with what he regarded as considerable success. There was a good deal of sickness, caused by exertion, exposure, and bad water; soon there was a disastrous epidemic of enteric, a disease which throughout the South African campaign claimed more casualties then the bullet.

Allenby and his men and horses had only ten days' rest before they entered on a fresh spell of nearly a fortnight's continuous hard duty. It began on March 22, when Allenby, with a hundred men, was sent to escort a convoy to Thabanchu, some forty miles east of Bloemfontein, to which a part of the cavalry had been sent. Almost complete peace was believed to exist for many miles round Bloemfontein, and careless optimism was the fashion with many. But Allenby was not the man to neglect military precautions at any time; he knew the Boers better than most, and that so long as De Wet and his like were at large a small convoy moving without support was in no little danger. He handled it, especially on the return journey with surrendered arms and ammunition, with all possible speed and concealment, and brought it safely back past Sannah's Post, where only a few days later the cavalry force to which he had taken his convoy was to suffer ambush and disaster. To the men of his own squadron Allenby's vigilance was normal, but one of another regiment who rode with him on this march has recorded his deep and lasting impression of the skill and care with which this minor operation of war was conducted.

In all Allenby's letters to his wife during this period there is hardly one word of criticism of commanders or of operations except this, written after a disaster caused by careless protective arrangements: " I can't excuse any man who is caught napping. One is always liable to be smashed by superior force, but one should never be caught unprepared to do one's best." He adds, characteristically, " However, I hate criticizing, and I hate war."

The day after his return Allenby was on the move again. All the cavalry round Bloemfontein for whom mounts could be found, some 650 only, went north under French to join the 7th Division at the Glen, fourteen miles distant. A bridge over the Modder had been destroyed by the Boers, and the enemy entrenched a few miles north of the river had to be driven off, so that the Engineers could repair it. This was accomplished by the action of Karee Siding on March 29. The cavalry were under shell-fire, but not heavily engaged. They returned to Springfield on the 30th. Next day came the news of Broadwood's disaster at Sannah's Post; the remainder of the cavalry hurried to the rescue, but were too late. In the evening Allenby was sent on a mission to Colville, the commander of the 9th Division. He rode through the night, and returned at dawn next day, having covered forty-five miles on his charger Pirate. The 1st Cavalry Brigade rescued some of Broadwood's wounded, but could do no more. A few days later the brigade moved out again, to operate against some Boers located to the south-east. But by this time it had only 120 horses fit to move, and it was obvious that the cavalry could do no more till it was rested and remounted.

<h2 style="text-align:center">V</h2>

THE TRANSVAAL: COMMAND OF THE INNISKILLINGS
(*April* 1900–*January* 1901)

On April 7 the remainder of the Inniskillings, who had been left opposite Colesberg, arrived at Bloemfontein, and the regiment was reunited after two months' separation. Shortly afterwards the commanding officer was placed in charge of a cavalry depot, from which he was presently invalided home. Allenby took over temporary command of the Inniskillings, which he held till January 1901, when he was given charge of an independent column.

During April, while the advance into the Transvaal was being prepared, the regiment rested near Bloemfontein, except for occasional spells of outpost or escort duty. It did not, however, receive remounts till a day or two before the advance began, and the horses then issued were soft and quite unfit for hard marching. The result naturally was that heavy wastage began again at once.

The advance of Lord Roberts' main army from Bloemfontein to Pretoria, some three hundred miles, occupied just over one month, from May 3 to June 5. There were many engagements, but no battle. Lord Roberts' tactics were to advance, with his greatly superior numbers, on as broad a front as possible, so as to overlap each successive Boer position. The Boers used their superior mobility, their knowledge of the ground, and their skill in defence to such effect that they never were actually outflanked, though always compelled by superior numbers to retire after engaging and delaying the British advanced forces with more or less success.

The Cavalry Division operated beyond the western wing of the army, but their effectiveness as an outflanking force was, as in the advance to Bloemfontein, crippled by the state of the horses. The division had remained at Bloemfontein for several days after the infantry march began, in order to complete the issue of remounts. It then hurried after the main army by forced marches. This was, naturally, disastrous to the newly arrived remounts; and when Kroonstad, 140 miles distant, was reached six days later nearly half of the horses of the cavalry had succumbed or were unfit to move farther. The horses were over-loaded, even if they had been hard in condition; three days' rations were invariably carried, though the supply-wagons were reaching the divisions daily. This wasteful method of over-marching and overloading remounts before they were conditioned continued practically throughout the war, and was largely responsible for its length. Rightly did Kipling's Sikh trooper (in his tale *A Sahibs' War*) remark, " The army . . . used horses as a courtesan uses oil: with both hands."

It did not take the Inniskillings long to realize that they had in Allenby a commanding officer who was equal to every occasion in the field, and in whom they could place complete trust; nor did it take the Higher Command any longer to understand that in the Inniskillings under Allenby's command they had a unit that was always handled with dash, discretion, and common sense, and could be sent with confidence on any mission. But the first engagement after leaving Bloemfontein was a 'regrettable incident,' almost a disaster. On May 10 a squadron of the Inniskillings, sent on under higher orders without support—a mistake Allenby never committed—was cut up by a superior force, and the whole brigade was for a while in danger of heavy casualties. Allenby's imperturbability soon restored order and confidence.

After a halt of a week at Kroonstad the advance was resumed. The Vaal was crossed practically without opposition on May 24,[1] and British troops were once again in the Transvaal, nearly twenty years after the Majuba surrender. On the march from the Vaal to Johannesburg, which was occupied on May 31, the cavalry had constant skirmishing under artillery- and rifle-fire; and the Inniskillings were able to appreciate the skill with which their commander led them and saved them from unnecessary casualties. Just before the fall of Johannesburg the regiment bivouacked at Doornkop, where Jameson's raiders had been brought to bay and captured, an incident which had contributed largely to causing the war.

About this time the Inniskillings received an official notification that a Carmelite monk, Father Knapp, was to be attached to the regiment as chaplain. There was some consternation at the announcement, and anxious canvassing as to which of the squadron messes was to receive this unknown quantity, who sounded so little likely to adapt himself to the life of a cavalry regiment in the field. He fell, by lot or otherwise, to the head-quarters mess of Allenby and the regimental Staff, and proved to be not only " quite the best specimen of Army Chaplain I've ever met," as Allenby wrote home, but a charming companion. He remained with the regiment during almost the whole of Allenby's command, and in 1901 spent six months with Allenby's column.[2]

The advance from Johannesburg to Pretoria was made with little fighting, for the Boers had become demoralized by their inability to stem the flood of the British invasion. But the Cavalry Division had one exciting evening and night when General French, in pursuit of an enemy rearguard, pressed on late in the afternoon of June 3 into the narrow Kalkheuvel Pass, flanked by rocky heights on either side. The advanced guard was ambushed and checked, General French and his staff coming under close and heavy fire; at the same time a small party of Boers opened fire

---

[1] The morale of the Boers was falling very low at this time (see Chapter XII of *Commando*, by Deneys Reitz, a fascinating account of the war from the enemy's side).

[2] Father Knapp was killed with the Irish Guards at the Battle of Cambrai in 1917, after winning the Military Cross.

from the heights on the flank. There was some confusion, and Allenby's coolness and resource were again much in evidence; he promptly engaged the enemy on the flanks, kept down their fire, and soon had the situation in hand. But the cavalry spent most of the night jammed in the narrow pass in an uncomfortable and dangerous situation, till the front could be cleared and a bivouac established in the plain beyond the defile.

Pretoria, in spite of its fortifications, fell without a struggle, and the 1st Cavalry Brigade was sent on to Waterval, north of the town, to release the British prisoners there. No opposition was expected, but a force of Boers under De la Rey suddenly appeared, attacked the covering troops, and shelled impartially the rescued prisoners, their late gaolers, the train waiting to remove them, and the cavalry escort. There was considerable confusion, and Allenby's competence in such circumstances was recognized by his being left to cover the withdrawal, which he did, in face of superior numbers, with his usual calmness and skill. When the released British prisoners had steamed away to Pretoria and the Boer attackers had been driven off, the Inniskillings found themselves in the dark, with a crowd of Boer prisoners (the late gaolers of Waterval), and with no very clear idea of the way to Wonder Boom Farm, some eight miles distant, where they had been ordered to spend the night. Inquiry among the prisoners for a guide revealed that the owner of the farm was present, and, further, that he was an old friend of Allenby and the Inniskillings, having met the regiment at the time of Warren's Bechuanaland expedition. Allenby was delighted to renew his acquaintance, and the regiment proceeded to his farm under his guidance. It was a bitterly cold night, and the subaltern on duty found in the early morning that Boer prisoners and the Inniskilling troopers of their guard were sleeping together in comradeship under the same blankets. Somewhat scandalized at this fraternization with the enemy, he hurried to Allenby and woke him. " Let them be," said Allenby; " that will do more to ending this stupid war than anything else."

The surrender of Pretoria was held at the time to mean the virtual end of the war, and Lord Roberts opened negotiations for a general surrender with Botha, who had with difficulty halted some seven thousand dispirited burghers fifteen miles east of the capital. But at the critical moment came news of De Wet's successes in the south against the long, vulnerable line of British communications ("I am beginning to dislike this De Wet," wrote Allenby to his wife; "he is keeping the war alive"), and Botha announced that the Transvaalers would fight to the last. Accordingly Roberts advanced east against the Boer position, an extremely strong one along a range of hills. There followed the curious battle of Diamond Hill, fought on June 11 and 12, in which the Boer force of 7000 to 8000 men with twenty guns became extended over twenty-five miles of front in its determination not to be outflanked, in which after two days' fighting at close range the casualties on either side were under two hundred, and in which the defending force, with its enemy in a thoroughly uncomfortable and even dangerous position, suddenly lost heart and gave up the battle. Roberts' force had not the mobility for pursuit, and returned to Pretoria.

There followed a month's pause spent in rest and refitting and in hopes of an early peace. That Allenby's knowledge and ability were recognized as much as his fighting qualities was shown by his appointment to a Committee of Cavalry Reorganization. The records and results of that committee have passed into oblivion, but the advice given by Allenby may perhaps be judged by a sentence in a letter he wrote home about this time: "It is not so much reorganization that the cavalry want as a little common sense."

The small organized remnant of the Transvaal Boers was now on the railway-line from Pretoria to Delagoa Bay covering the seat of their Government—a railway carriage near Komatipoort. In mid-July (midwinter in South Africa) Lord Roberts moved eastward again, but after advancing as far as Middelburg decided to break off operations because of the weather, and to await junction with Sir Redvers Buller's Natal army, which was now moving slowly northward through the Eastern Transvaal. The cavalry were left on a thinly stretched line in front of Middelburg. Allenby showed his skill in defence by holding for three weeks with a small force an outpost line of seven or eight miles in face of an active enemy, without any untoward incident. In the middle of August Sir Redvers Buller's force came up on the right of the line held by Allenby; and the advance on Komatipoort was resumed soon after, the cavalry being transferred to the left flank, where it worked through difficult hill country. On August 27 at Bergendal Farm, about a hundred miles west of Komatipoort, was fought the last regular engagement of the war. When the Boers were driven from this position and Komatipoort lay open their last object of defence and their last line of communication was gone. The aged President Kruger left by Delagoa Bay for Europe in the fruitless hope of persuading one or more of the great Continental Powers to more active measures of sympathy with the Boer cause than mere abuse of England; most of the remaining artillery was destroyed; and the stubborn burghers still remaining in the field broke up into the small bands that were to keep the war alive so gallantly for almost two years more.

While the main British force went slowly on to Komatipoort the cavalry turned south to Carolina, and thence over almost trackless hills to Barberton, an important gold-mining centre. The capture of Barberton was one of the most brilliant feats of the war,[1] and the advance to it from Carolina was led by Allenby and the Inniskillings on every day, except the last. It was typical of Allenby's practical view of things that when offered, in recognition of his fine work during the advance, the honour of leading the entry into Barberton with his regiment on the final day he declined on finding that it would mean extra work for his tired horses and men, and asked to be allowed to move quietly by a better road with the guns. Shortly after the occupation of Barberton Allenby was sent to seize and guard the Sheba group of mines, some fourteen miles away in the mountains above the town. Here the regiment remained for over a fortnight, in high and difficult hills where wheeled transport could not be taken, and the scattered squadrons were fed by aerial tram or pack-donkeys.

[1] Kipling's returned South African warrior (in his poem *Chant-pagan*) remembers it with pride:

> " Me that saw Barberton took
> When we dropped through the clouds on their 'ead,
> And they 'ove the guns over and fled."

Early in October the Cavalry Division was ordered back to Machadodorp, on the railway east of Middelburg, whence it was to proceed south to Carolina and then by Ermelo and Bethel through the Eastern Transvaal (the area known as the High Veldt), slowly and methodically clearing up these districts in preparation for the expected peace. Little opposition was anticipated; and the division trailed with it a large and cumbrous convoy containing fourteen days' supplies. The hopes of a peaceful march were soon rudely dispelled. The leading brigade was heavily attacked the day after leaving Machadodorp, and scarcely avoided disaster; and for nearly a fortnight the division was continually engaged. Hampered by its unwieldy convoy, it was unable to take the offensive against the confident and elusive commandos who swarmed round its flanks and rear. The loss of their capital and the freedom from any obligation to defend a line of communication or fixed point had given the Boers full scope for the guerrilla tactics in which their military genius lay, and had produced a complete change in their morale. The dispirited men who had failed to hold strong natural positions a month or two before now attacked in the open with boldness and skill.

On October 16, the day the force left Carolina, the Inniskillings had a brief but dangerous fight. The regiment was acting as advanced guard to the left column, and its foremost troops surprised a Boer laager near Lake Chrissie. If the remainder of the brigade had been available to support the advanced guard a notable success was in its hands. Unfortunately the brigade had changed its plans and direction, had halted some miles back, and was now going into bivouac. The brigade staff had omitted to inform the advanced guard of this change of plan, with the result that not only was a great opportunity missed, but the advanced squadron was in danger of being overwhelmed and the whole brigade of being caught at a disadvantage. The Boer commando, realizing that the British advanced guard was isolated, rallied and made a determined attack. Allenby galloped up to the firing-line and took in the situation. He found his best friend, Yardley, on a low hill, endeavouring with a small body of men to check the Boer rush, but very closely pressed. " Curate," said Allenby to him, "you're in a tight place. I'll bring you support as soon as I can, but you must hold this kopje till you're killed, to cover the brigade behind." Yardley was badly wounded, one of the officers with him was killed and two others were wounded, and there were some twenty casualties among his men. But their gallant resistance gave time for Allenby to bring up the rest of the regiment and two guns; and after a sharp action at close range the Boer attack was driven off, and the brigade behind saved from disaster. Characteristically enough, Allenby in a letter to his wife gives no more space to this stirring little fight than to a description of some wild-flowers which had interested him.

For another ten days, till Heidelberg (just south-east of Johannesburg) was reached, the force had to fight a continual series of flank and rearguard actions. Then it returned to Pretoria, and the Inniskillings went into camp for the first time after eight months of bivouac in the open. The Cavalry Division was now broken up. The 1st Cavalry Brigade remained in being, though seldom operating as a brigade, for another two months, when it also was broken up, its units being allotted to small independent columns, of which Allenby received the command of one.

Meanwhile the commanding officer of the Inniskillings, who had been invalided home, was placed on half-pay, and Rimington was promoted to command the regiment. This was undoubtedly something of a disappointment to Allenby (though his letters to his wife voice no word of complaint), for Rimington, although senior to him, had been away from the regiment for over a year, in command of his own corps of Rimington's Guides. Allenby, who had been with the Inniskillings ever since they left England a year before (he was the only one of the original officers who had not been killed, wounded, captured, or sent home sick), might reasonably have hoped that Rimington would receive promotion outside the regiment, and that he would be confirmed in the command of the unit he had led so ably for the last nine months. One who commanded a squadron under him for those nine months [1] writes of him:

[1] Lieutenant-Colonel J. Stevenson-Hamilton.

78

I had the privilege of commanding a squadron under him during the whole of this period, and I am sure that every one in the regiment agreed that it was a pure delight to serve under him. We were in the field without a rest during the whole time of his command. There were constant anxious periods against the formidable, cunning, and elusive foe, but Allenby was more than equal to each emergency as it arose. He was always quiet and cool, and knew just what to do, and how to do it. Daring and cautious as the varying occasion required, he ensured that every task the regiment was ordered to perform was achieved with success and credit. As a result the Inniskillings used to be detailed for more than their fair share of advanced and rear guards when trouble was expected. Where Allenby differed from so many other commanders at that time was that, while having himself a better general appreciation of each situation than anyone else present, he was always ready to listen without prejudice to any reasonable objection which might be made to an order given under a misapprehension of the situation, and he never rejected any information merely because it did not happen to fit in with his preconceived ideas. He never committed the mistake, responsible for so many unfortunate incidents in the South African War, of failing adequately to support detached units. Thus, if a squadron was sent to seize a hill, which might or might not be occupied by the enemy, Allenby never failed to be ready to cover it with fire from the main body should resistance be encountered. Also to any officer sent on detached duty he was always careful to give the widest latitude—" These are merely general orders; don't be tied to any definite line; carry out the work in the way that seems best." In cases of failure he always gave careful consideration to the explanation, and if satisfied, not only said so plainly, but took entire responsibility, and ' saw the officer through ' with Higher Authority, if the latter was inclined to be critical. A subordinate leader, therefore, always carried with him the right sense of responsibility in every detached duty he undertook, and had no fear, so long as he acted reasonably, of being afterwards found fault with for not having carried out the letter of his orders. Apart from his own skilled leadership, I believe Allenby's habit of trusting his subordinates formed one of the reasons for the reputation which the regiment acquired during the campaign with the cavalry division. During the advance on Pretoria three squadrons of the 1st Brigade, acting under the direct orders of the brigadier, were placed in an impossible position, and were cut to pieces. The enemy came on, and for a time the situation of the brigade itself seemed a perilous one, and there was even some temporary confusion. It was Allenby's complete *sang-froid* and his unhesitating grasp of the right thing to do that re-established confidence and enabled the advance to be continued after only a slight delay.

During the temporary lulls of an action he used to display his well-known power of detachment, and would talk with animation on any and every subject, quite divorced from the business in hand, from the Descent of Man to the habits of insectivorous birds; ready, however, at any moment to ' change gear,' and snap out the right emergency order. It was this power of temporary detachment of mind, coupled with the ability to pick up the dropped thread in a moment, which, with his never-failing sense of dry humour, kept him always cheerful and free from the outward appearance of worry which in the South African War showed itself in so many commanders of less ability.

He showed his innate love of wild-life preservation even during the stress of the campaign, and I recollect being amused at the consternation of the subalterns when he rebuked them for shooting buck out of season. During the many hours we used to spend during an advance sitting by our horses awaiting the order to move on he liked nothing better than to study the habits of the termites whose small mounds covered the ground everywhere, and I have seen him so engrossed in a fight between rival parties of these creatures, or in a raid on them by black ants, that one would imagine he had nothing else in the world to think about.[1]

An officer in another regiment who was attached to the Inniskillings for some time gives the following impressions of Allenby and the regiment:

Allenby going into action (he was a magnificent figure on a horse) seemed to radiate courage from his whole face. We were all a little afraid of him, but he really was terribly kind. There is no doubt in my mind that the Inniskillings was then the finest fighting cavalry regiment in the Army. But their methods were those of the bush-

---

[1] A friend who met him shortly after the South African War and questioned him on his experiences found that the subjects on which he was willing to discourse were not his engagements or any aspect of the war, but the habits of a peculiar form of caterpillar which he had encountered and studied there.

rangers; every officer had his own Cape cart, which he had to maintain himself as best he could on the country.

VI

THE COLUMN COMMANDER
(*January* 1901–*May* 1902)

The ' column ' period of the war, which now began, lasted for nearly eighteen months. The area of operations, which included the Transvaal, the Orange Free State, and Cape Colony, was approximately equal to the combined areas of France, Germany, Belgium, and Holland. There were few towns or railways and no made roads, the most part was open, rolling plain with few obstacles, admirably suited for the tactics of mobile riflemen, and there was bush country for shelter and hill country for refuge when the commandos were too closely hunted. The Boers made full use of their advantages. No people in its hour of need has surely produced a company of leaders in the field superior in skill and constancy to Botha, De Wet, De la Rey, Smuts, Beyers, Kemp, and others. And the men they led were the refined essence of their people, the core from which the dross had fallen away. There may have been 50,000 burghers still under arms at the beginning of 1901; at the final surrender in May 1902 there were little more than 20,000. To effect this reduction Great Britain had to spend something like a million and a half pounds a week and to maintain over a quarter of a million troops in the field. No other people than the South African Dutch could have withstood privation, danger, and ruin so long; no other nation than the British would have spent blood and treasure so stubbornly for so little apparent result.

This period of the war, during which Lord Kitchener was in chief command, passed through several phases. At first it was hoped that the numerous small, mobile columns would so hustle and harry the commandos remaining in the field that they would recognize the futility of further resistance and sue for peace. The failure of this hope led to the policy of clearing the country of all means of subsistence, of destroying the farms, of concentrating the women and children in camps, of driving off or slaughtering all cattle and sheep, and of burning the crops and grass. This policy of destruction was much condemned, and was, naturally, distasteful to the men who carried it out; but it was a stern necessity. If it hardened the enemy's resistance at the time, it broke it in the end. (" It's beastly work, but ought to be done thoroughly if done at all," wrote Allenby.) Finally, in the latter part of 1901 and beginning of 1902, the country was fenced into areas by the great blockhouse lines; and the system was introduced of ' driving ' an area by a line of columns, till the Boers in it were penned against some natural obstacle or some part of the fortified line of blockhouses. This ended the long war at last.

The Boer leaders meanwhile, some of whom, though not all, were wise in strategy as well as in tactics, had seen that the last hope of tiring out British endurance or closing British purse-strings was by carrying the war into British territory. Accordingly the main efforts of their best men and best leaders centred on the invasion of Natal and Cape Colony.

Natal, with its rampart of hills, was comparatively easy to defend, and the enemy never penetrated beyond the borders; but the great open spaces of Cape Colony were never cleared of small parties of Boers, who rode to within sight of the sea, and once almost to within raiding distance of Cape Town. The problems and difficulties of dealing with the elusive enemy may, perhaps, be compared with the difficulties of combating the submarine campaign in the Great War. The commandos moved over the trackless veldt to raid a convoy or attack an isolated column with the secrecy of U-boats on a trade route, and after their attack disappeared as silently and swiftly from the columns that gathered to net them. They were sometimes destroyed or crippled, as the U-boats were; but, like them, they took a heavy toll of their slower, less wary opponents.

Allenby was one of the few original column commanders whose military reputation and physical endurance survived to the end of that wearing test.[1] Almost alone of them, he never

---

[1] " The war about to be waged required commanders possessing attributes but rarely associated with advancing years: the power of remaining long hours in the saddle, of enduring extremes of temperature and of climate, of bivouacking on

suffered a reverse or lost a convoy, yet few were as active or daring in search of the enemy. He maintained the same coolness and vigour in action, the same trust in and support of his subordinates, the same vigilance in protective measures, that had gained him so high a reputation as regimental commander. His lack of personal ambition and absolute loyalty both to the orders of his Chief and to his fellow-commanders were qualities by no means universal among the column leaders of the time, of whom a number were striving jealously for distinction and reward under a strict and exacting Chief, who excused no failures and did not discourage competition among his subordinate commanders. There were few who could write with perfect truth, as Allenby wrote to his wife when a somewhat over-coloured account of his captures appeared in the Press, " I always try to state in my reports exactly what happened without any ornamentation, so I am not responsible for the exaggerated form of the official version "; or who had the loyalty and sense to recognize, on receiving an order which completely upset his plans, that " My column is only one pawn in the game, and the man with the chessboard in front of him has a bigger view than I, who can only see one square on the board, or at most two." Towards the end of the war he wrote, perhaps with some justification, " I am beginning to think that I am one of the few commanders out here who do not play to the gallery, and tell lies to push themselves. But this is blasphemous ! "

The strength and composition of his column varied a little from time to time; its essential elements were two regiments of cavalry, a battery of Horse Artillery, a long-range gun, one or two pom-poms, and half a battalion of infantry. The Scots Greys were with Allenby till the end of 1901, when they were transferred to another column,[1] being replaced by the 13th Hussars; the Carabiniers (6th Dragoon Guards) were with him throughout. The

sodden ground with no covering but a blanket, of thriving on hard biscuits and bully beef, and of yet remaining fresh and alert, ready to risk their reputations and their lives in the keen pursuit of a skilful foe." (" *The Times* " *History of the War in South Africa*, vol. v.)

[1] The Scots Greys after leaving Allenby were twice involved in small affairs in which they were somewhat heavily punished by the enemy. Was different luck or different leadership responsible?

infantry was changed more frequently; Royal Inniskilling Fusiliers, Lancashire Fusiliers, and Durham Light Infantry were with the force at various times. The *rôle* of infantry with a mobile column was monotonous and wearying—hard marching by day, outpost work at night, and little prospect of even seeing the enemy unless he attacked the supply-wagons or the camp. An officer of the Royal Inniskilling Fusiliers, who was in after-years closely connected with Allenby, describes thus his first sight of him:

As a second lieutenant of eighteen I was ordered to South Africa to join my regiment, which formed part of a mobile column commanded by Major (temporary Lieutenant-Colonel) Allenby, operating in the Transvaal. News of its whereabouts was difficult to obtain, but I eventually joined it one evening after dark. Next morning, the battalion paraded at daybreak; while we were waiting to move off three or four officers galloped to the front of the column, led by a big man on a black horse. As they passed groans and uncomplimentary exclamations arose from the ranks, and I naturally inquired from my colour-sergeant the reason of the extraordinary reception accorded to my future commander. The explanation came: " Well, you see, sir, when Mr Allenby is going to march us twenty miles he always rides the big black horse, and when we are not going far he rides the wee pony. Glory be to God, he has ridden that big horse for the past three days! " Two days afterwards the " wee pony " was ridden, and he and his rider were greeted with loud cheers.[1]

Any detail of the column's trekking would be as wearisome to read as it often was to perform. A brief summary will suffice. In the early part of 1901 the column was one of a number which operated under Sir John French in the Eastern Transvaal against Louis Botha. March was spent on the Swaziland border, where heavy rains had swollen the rivers and made movement difficult, men and horses being reduced to half-rations. In April the column moved north and operated for a time near Middelburg (on the Pretoria–Delagoa Bay line). In May it returned to Pretoria, and from then till the middle of September operated in the

---

[1] Allenby's sobriquet with some of the troops in his column was " Old Knobkerrie," from the stick he carried.

Western Transvaal about the Magaliesburg range of hills. Allenby and his column had been promised a rest after a hard spell of work, but were immediately railed south to Natal to assist in repelling Botha's threatened invasion. Most of October was spent on the borders of Zululand, in a country Allenby had known well in 1888.

At the end of that month he went with his Brigade-Major to Pretoria to ask from Lord Kitchener a rest for his tired horses and an opportunity to get them fit. This was a constant and justified complaint of the commanders of mobile forces at this period—that they were kept so continually on the move and transferred so often from the direction of one General to that of another, all in a hurry to make a bag of Boers and their own reputation, that their horses were always overworked and weary, and no district was ever thoroughly and systematically cleared. ("They are in such a hurry they can't finish a job, but rush off on another chase, like a half-broken pointer," complained Allenby.) Lord Kitchener promised a fortnight's rest; but on return to his column Allenby found it hurriedly on the move for a forced march to Bakenlaagte, near Ermelo, where Benson's column had suffered disaster. For the remainder of 1901 the column was in the Eastern Transvaal, usually working as one of a group of columns under General Bruce Hamilton.

Towards the end of the year even Allenby's iron constitution and imperturbable spirit showed signs of the strain of over two years' continuous warfare in the field, during which he had had no holiday and had never had a roof over his head for more than a very occasional night or two. He went down with influenza, and after a week in hospital at Pretoria spent ten days' leave in Durban. About the same time Mrs Allenby, sensing from his letters his weariness of spirit and need of her, determined to embark for South Africa. She arrived at Durban early in 1902. Allenby, whose column was engaged in the final great 'drives' in the Transvaal and north of the Orange River Colony, did not find opportunity to meet her till the middle of May, when the negotiations which ended the war were in progress and operations were in suspension. Peace was declared on May 31, a peace which paved the way to eventual reconciliation of the two peoples who had fought so stubbornly, and to a united South Africa.

No one welcomed the end of the campaign with greater delight and relief than Allenby. He had spent two and a half years continuously in the field with hardly a rest and without sight of his wife and small son, who were so constantly in his thoughts. There is hardly a letter that he wrote home during that period that does not express his distaste for war and his longing for peace and the gardens of England. His accounts in those letters of his fights and marches are brief and perfunctory, but a new wild-flower receives affectionate and understanding description, as in this extract from a letter written in October 1901 from the Zululand border:

I found the most gorgeous wildflower to-day that I have ever seen. Imagine a brilliant golden-yellow marguerite, rather cup-shaped, measuring $4\frac{1}{2}$ inches across—I measured it with a tape. The outer petals are in two layers, springing from a neat corolla of green spines. The centre is a deeper gold colour, and is rather like the orange centre of a white water-lily. The plant is low and bushy, its leaves growing in spikes like a young spruce fir. Each spine of the leaves is edged with sharp prickles that one can't handle comfortably. The leaves when squashed smell like a mixture of juniper and myrtle. A lot of it is growing on a little hill near here, but I only saw one flower. Unfortunately it is spring;[1] and if I dug up a root it would die; and we shan't be here in the autumn (at least I hope not!). I have never seen the plant at home. I may have made a discovery. If so, I should name it *Mabella Aurea*.[2] I enclose some of the spines off the flower stem. There is a very fine gladiolus about these parts, pretty plentiful: primrose yellow, with deep orange-red spots and stripings. That too I have never seen at home; but it is probably known, as it is well distributed in these parts. The scenery here is good, but Boers are too numerous. I am off, at an early hour, to try for some of them.

Again, in the same letter:

Only a few Boer scouts seen to-day. The country here is covered with spring flowers; mostly of the marigold or marguerite type, of

[1] October is in the South African spring.
[2] Mabel was Mrs Allenby's name.

all colours, white, scarlet, mauve, purple and bright yellow. All the bush is green, too, and the grass sprouting; so that the country is quite good to look at. If there were no Dutchmen about, and one had not to be always on the look-out and on the move, I should like to bring you here to look at this part of the world. I always think it is the most picturesque corner of South Africa. I know it pretty well too, and could guide you as well as any native. I should like you to see the ' Kaffir-Boom ' in flower. The flower comes on before the leaves; and the tree is like a big fig-tree, clothed in brilliant, scarlet, sweet-pea flowers. It glares in the bush like a red lamp. In about six weeks the whole of the valley will be golden with the thorn-bush (mimosa) blossom. There are about a dozen different kinds of this mimosa bush, native to the land, all thorny and all with the yellow mimosa bloom, but the blossoms are of different shapes.

And, after a few lines about the operations and a grumble at the way his horses are overworked by ambitious infantry Generals, he goes on:

To change the subject. This would be a lovely site for a house, if there were no Dutchmen about. Beautiful scenery; and a quick-running river, full of fish. Climate good, as long as you are in a house. Everything will grow here. Pineapples, bananas, roses, trees of all sorts, beautiful grass and endless numbers of wildflowers. If this war ever ends, you and I must come here and live cheap, while Mick's doing his schooling. I saw yesterday the most beautiful bell heather. The bells were coral-pink in colour; growing in clusters, each bell about two inches long. The veldt here is now carpeted with flowers. I have seen a lot of the yellow flower I told you of at the beginning of this letter. It is very free-flowering. Yesterday I saw one clump about 2 feet across, with 30 full-blown blossoms. I expect to get to Vryheid to-morrow evening or next morning.

These extracts have been given at some length since they show so clearly Allenby's love of flowers and interest in nature. War was to him a tedious, distasteful business, which interfered with enjoyment of the quiet and beautiful fruits of the earth. Yet, since soldiering was his profession and thoroughness was the very root of his character, he ended the war acknowledged as one of the best younger leaders it had produced. He received as rewards for his services a Companionship of the Bath, brevet promotion to Colonel, and appointment to command the 5th Lancers.[1] He had celebrated his forty-first birthday just before the conclusion of hostilities by having a ' salute ' of forty-one pom-pom shells fired at a small party of Boers seen at long range in the open.

The other future Army commanders of the Great War besides Allenby had been among the column commanders of South Africa. Haig led a group of columns in Cape Colony; Smith-Dorrien, the future commander of the Second Army, already a Major-General, was at the beginning of 1901 in the North-eastern Transvaal;[2] Plumer, who was to succeed Smith-Dorrien in the Second Army in 1915 and to lead it to the end of the War, was usually to be found working quietly and efficiently in the Eastern Transvaal with a column or group of columns; Rawlinson (Fourth Army) had a roving commission in the Orange River Colony or Transvaal; Byng, who took over the Third Army from Allenby when he went to Palestine in 1917, normally ranged over the Orange River Colony; and Gough, the future commander of the Fifth Army, had a small force of Mounted Infantry, which his impetuosity led to defeat and capture in a trap carefully prepared by the Boers during Botha's attempted invasion of Natal.[3]

[1] His service in the Great War, of course, brought further honours to Allenby. In 1915 he was created a Knight Commander of the Bath (he became Knight Grand Cross in 1918), and in 1917 a Knight Grand Cross of the Order of St Michael and St George. In 1919, after the close of the War, he received the thanks of Parliament, a grant of £50,000, promotion to Field-Marshal, and a Viscounty. He chose as his title Viscount Allenby of Megiddo and Felixstowe.

[2] He left South Africa in May 1901 to take up an important appointment in India.

[3] Gough himself was captured, but escaped and was picked up by Allenby's column, which had gone to the rescue.

CHAPTER V

PREPARATION FOR ARMAGEDDON
(1902–14)

I

COMMAND OF THE 5TH LANCERS
(*August* 1902–*October* 1905)

ALLENBY was quartered in England during the whole twelve years between the South African War and the Great War. He never soldiered in India. These were quiet, peaceful years, but years of hard work and thought for soldiers who had the efficiency of the Army at heart. The South African conflict had revealed our complete lack of organization for any war larger than an expedition against a savage tribe, and had shown how far behind the times was much of our equipment and training. Allenby, as regimental and brigade commander, and later as Inspector-General, had a large part in the reorganization and training of the cavalry arm, a greater share in which, however (as in all our preparations up to 1914), must be credited to his single-minded fellow-student at the Staff College, Douglas Haig.[1]

Allenby took over command of the 5th Lancers at Colchester, to which station they had proceeded on their return from South Africa. He quickly proved that he could train a regiment in barracks and on the manœuvre ground as ably as he could lead one in the field: the two faculties by no means always go together. The root of Allenby's method in peace as in war was trust in his subordinates; he gave his squadron commanders a clear picture of what he expected, and then left them a free hand. He once said that he would like to see inscribed in the room of every

[1] Haig after the South African War took over the command of his regiment, the 17th Lancers, but in 1903 Kitchener, now Commander-in-Chief in India, asked for him as Inspector-General of Cavalry. He accordingly went to India, and was promoted Major-General in 1904, five years before Allenby, though both had received Brevet-Colonelcies in the same *Gazette* at the end of the South African War. In 1906 he returned to the War Office, as Director of Staff Duties, to assist Haldane in his reorganization of the Army.

commander this precept of Confucius: " My people become good of themselves." Though strict, he was no martinet, and maintained discipline rather by the force of his personality than by the severity of his awards in the orderly room. Some officers used, in fact, to think him too easy with the men, by the standard of those days. He had always hated punishment; as a squadron commander he had been heard to say to a malefactor, " Go away! I am far too angry with you to trust myself to punish you." And, indeed, the fear of Allenby's wrath was a greater deterrent to many than the cells. A dressing down from him was not an experience that the hardiest cared to repeat.

A characteristic that some found singular in Allenby, with his broad and independent mind, was his strict insistence on conformity with Regulations. He would say that as long as an official regulation was in force it must be obeyed; if it was a bad regulation one should try to have it altered. There is a type of mind which sticks narrowly and pedantically to written regulations, rather than exercising personal judgment; this, naturally, was not the cause of Allenby's attitude, which was simply an expression of the scrupulous loyalty to superior authority which was one of his guiding principles throughout life.

An account of Allenby from one of the officers of the 5th Lancers shows how he impressed those who served under him:

Under a brusque manner there was unbounded human sympathy. He expected all one could give, but was always ready to help in sickness or in trouble. He had a keen sense of humour and was very quick at repartee.[1] He was intolerant of any prevarication and insisted on an answer yes or no. But he was sympathetic with ignorance, and was a most willing and capable teacher. " Think to a finish," was a very favourite remark of his. He would shoulder full responsibility for any fault found by higher authority, and had consequently the unfailing loyalty of all ranks.

He had a great grasp of the smallest details of regimental life, and

---

[1] This gift of formidable repartee lasted him to the end of his military career. A Medical Officer in Egypt, who sought to excuse the presence of flies in a cookhouse for which he was responsible by saying that the battalion using it had only been there a few days, was met by the instant retort: " I didn't ask how long the battalion has been here. I asked how long these damn' flies have been here, and why! "

during an inspection nothing escaped him. His questions were sometimes most disconcerting, but behind them lurked often a great sense of humour, which though not apparent at the time would be revealed later by a hint.

On manœuvres his ability to use ground as cover was quite uncanny. Once on Salisbury Plain he surrounded with the regiment the headquarters and transport of an opposing division; the blank surprise on the face of the divisional commander when called upon to surrender was interesting. He commanded the Cavalry Brigade during the manœuvres when troops of the Aldershot Command landed at Clacton. The brigade was always early afield, and the standing joke amongst the men was: "Well, what did Allenby capture for breakfast this morning?"

He was an intensely keen fisherman and good with the dry fly. When the regiment was at West Down Camp on Salisbury Plain for manœuvres, there was many a gallop to Netheravon after the day's work, rod in hand, fishing till the last streak of daylight, then a gallop home in the dark, in which rabbit-holes seemed to have no terrors for him.

After two years at Colchester the 5th Lancers joined the 1st Cavalry Brigade at Aldershot, of which Kenna, Allenby's staff officer in South Africa, was Brigade-Major. A year later, in October 1905, Allenby returned to Colchester as Brigadier-General in Command of the 4th Cavalry Brigade.

In August 1905, just before he gave up command of the 5th Lancers, Allenby was awarded by the Royal Humane Society a testimonial for saving life. He was staying on a yacht which his father-in-law had chartered for Cowes Week, and went out for a sail in the yacht's dinghy with a Miss Papillon, the mate of the yacht, and the cabin-boy. It was a rough day, and a sudden squall capsized the boat, which sank. Neither Miss Papillon nor the mate could swim, and Allenby supported them both for twenty minutes, at the same time encouraging the cabin-boy, who was becoming exhausted. But for his strength and coolness some at least of the party would have been drowned. They were rescued by boats from another yacht just when Allenby was contemplating the desperate venture of trying to swim ashore with his burden.

II

THE 4TH CAVALRY BRIGADE
(*October* 1905–*October* 1909)

On the military side there is little to write of the four years during which Allenby commanded a cavalry brigade. The brigade was a scattered one, with regiments at Colchester, Norwich, and Hounslow. One of these, the 19th Hussars at Norwich, was commanded from the beginning of 1908 by one of the most brilliant of the rising generation of soldiers, Sir Philip Chetwode,[1] who was to be Allenby's principal lieutenant in Palestine. Each was quick to recognize the worth of the other, and from now until the end of the Great War their careers were closely associated. Allenby trained the brigade with his usual ability and common sense, and commanded it with decision and vigour.

Here is, perhaps, the place to say something of the roughness of manner, the violence of temper, and the vehemence of speech which became commonly associated with his name in the Army, and gave him his title and reputation as " the Bull." There is a certain irony in the qualities of this gallant but low-brow animal being attached in the general mind to one who was the most highly informed and scholarly of soldiers and at heart the most kindly and tolerant of men. Nor was Allenby's courage the blind, unreasoning impetuosity of the charging bull: he was cool and observant in danger. Yet the name fitted him in some ways. He looked as solid, as unchangeable, and often as dangerous as his namesake; and at certain well-known ' red rags ' would charge as unhesitatingly. Also it cannot be denied that in Allenby increasing authority brought increasing asperity. He who had been a noticeably easy-going young officer and a good-humoured squadron-commander, was a strict Colonel, an irascible Brigadier, and an explosive General.

' Explosion ' best describes the typical manifestation of Allenby's wrath; it was sudden, violent, and disastrous—soon

---

[1] Field-Marshal Sir Philip Chetwode, Bart., G.C.B., O.M., G.C.S.I., K.C.M.G., D.S.O.

over, but it usually left the victim or victims visibly shaken and unnerved. What was the explanation of this flaw in Allenby's fine and generous nature? For it must be judged a flaw that he failed to curb his anger. Curious as it may sound to many, Allenby's lack of control was, originally at least, due partly to shyness. He had never been a ' good mixer '; he admitted few to friendship and almost none to intimacy; he would have preferred in many ways the life of a recluse and a scholar. It was an effort and an embarrassment to him that as he rose in rank he had continually to deal with an increasing number of fresh, sometimes uncongenial, personalities. His great contemporary Haig, also a shy and lonely man, met the same problem by withdrawing coldly into an impenetrable armour of restraint and reserve; Allenby, with less self-discipline, exploded outwardly.

Two causes chiefly provoked his outbursts—a lack of zeal for the King's service and a want of frankness in conduct or of directness in speech. He, who always gave unsparingly of his best, was deeply angered by any slackness or carelessness in the performance of duty or by neglect of orders; the most straightforward of men, he was exasperated by any subterfuge or evasion. Failure, if genuine effort had been made, he pardoned easily; nor did he treat ignorance harshly. At his most blustering he seldom used an oath, but his anger was none the less formidable. In his later years, when he was aware of his reputation, he sometimes consciously lived up to it; but to the end he never realized quite how alarming he could be. One officer, of considerable service and experience, collapsed altogether while being reproved by him, and had to be led hastily away. Allenby was genuinely surprised: " What affected him like that? I wasn't even really angry with him." His gusts of temper cleared Allenby's mind of all rancour; he never bore a grudge, and would often go out of his way to do a kindness to one who had been the object of his unsparing condemnation shortly before.

In his home life these years between the two long wars were very happy ones for Allenby. He watched his deeply loved son Michael grow up into a boy after his own heart, fearless, unspoilt, intelligent, and healthy. Michael was indirectly the means of sowing the first seed of the Boy Scouts organization. His governess, Miss Loveday, had been trained to use for children's outdoor occupations a little red book, *Aids to Scouting*, written by General Baden-Powell for soldiers. One day she and Michael had climbed a big cedar-tree in the drive from which to make observations of birds and animals and to note the sounds of the countryside. Allenby happened to return home on horseback and rode under the tree. He did not look up, and as he passed below Michael cried out, "Father, you're shot! A soldier should look above as well as around him!" General Baden-Powell, on a visit to the Allenbys, was told of this incident and of the use to which his book was being put. He decided to rewrite the book as *Scouting for Boys*, and from this grew the Boy Scouts movement.[1]

The Allenbys' home at Colchester, Roman Hill House, had a pleasant garden, open fields, a small wood full of wildflowers, and a stretch of water (which they stocked with rainbow trout [2]), so that they were enabled to live the country life that both loved. Colchester was within easy distance of Felixstowe, where Allenby had spent so much of his boyhood, and where his mother still lived. For recreation he hunted, fished, or shot in due season; but he gave up polo, as his weight made him too expensive to mount. In all his pursuits his wife was his constant companion. Together they taught their son the love that both had inherited of country life and of books and learning. On a New Forest pony, a present from his grandfather, Michael was instructed in horsemanship by a sergeant-major in the riding-school and by his father in the hunting-field.[3] Presently he went to his first school, at Westgate-on-Sea.

Allenby and his wife spent much of his leave in foreign travel. In February and March 1908 they made a trip to East Africa, visiting Mombasa, Nairobi, and the Victoria Nyanza, in those days a much more unusual journey than now. This interest in

[1] Lord Baden-Powell has related this story in his book *Lessons from the 'Varsity of Life*.
[2] According to the gardener, Allenby caught them all before he left.
[3] On leaving Woolwich in 1915 Michael showed the profit of his instruction by being second in the riding competition.

travel and in seeing fresh parts of the world, not those usually visited by tourists, remained with Allenby to the end of his life. His robust frame and health enabled him to stand the fatigues of travelling better than many much younger men, and his keen interest in new sights, and especially in new bird-life or animal-life or strange plants and flowers, never flagged. He had given up smoking soon after the South African War, for fear of its effect on his eyesight, which was remarkably keen. One of his outdoor accomplishments was the throwing of a boomerang, which he could manage expertly.

III
INSPECTOR-GENERAL OF CAVALRY
(1910–14)

He was wont to speak plain and to the purpose, like an honest man and a soldier. SHAKESPEARE, *Much Ado about Nothing*

Allenby was promoted Major-General in September 1909, at the age of forty-eight. Of the cavalrymen who were more or less his contemporaries and were destined to hold high posts in the Great War, Haig reached General's rank at forty-three, Byng at forty-seven, and Robertson (who spent ten years in the ranks) at fifty-one. After a period of half-pay, part of which he spent travelling in South America, Allenby was appointed Inspector-General of Cavalry in the spring of 1910. His work took him to all the cavalry stations in Great Britain and Ireland; his head-quarters were in London, at the Horse Guards. He had to give up the country life he loved so much and take a house in London, in Onslow Square. He never again had an English garden of his own. Pressure of work and reasons of economy (Allenby's private income was small, and much of it was spent on his son's education) led him at the same time to give up hunting.

Allenby's training of the cavalry was on sound and practical lines. He held a middle course between the hotheads who would have it that the 'cavalry spirit' demanded the solution of all problems by shock action and those who would have discarded the lance and sword altogether and treated the cavalry merely as mobile riflemen.[1] He supported the introduction of machine-guns and stressed the value of fire-power,[2] but taught that many opportunities for intervention by mounted action and the sword would still occur on the modern battlefield. He may not have been gifted with that foresight which enabled some critics, writing years after the War, to predict so accurately its tactical course; but he did help to produce a mounted arm that was in 1914 more realistic in its outlook and more effective in the field than any of the other cavalries of Europe.

A staff ride which he ordered and directed in 1911 in the Eastern Counties gives proof of considerable prevision. It was based on a Blue Force (Germany) invading Redland (France) by passing through a neutral state (Belgium), while the army of an overseas Power, the Hibernians, with a strength and organization corresponding to the British Expeditionary Force, landed at Newhaven (Boulogne) to support Redland. The exercise studied the action of the Hibernian Cavalry Division throughout the phases of disembarkation, an approach march to the north, reconnaissance of the advancing Blue Force, and then withdrawal in face of superior numbers to avoid envelopment—a very intelligent anticipation of 1914.

Cavalry in retreat was a subject which Allenby frequently discussed before the War, and in which he constantly exercised his brigades. The last staff ride of the Cavalry Division was held in May 1914. The final day of this exercise dealt with retreat; and the last words of the official address given by Allenby to the officers of the Cavalry Division before the War recommended them to study the ' manœuvre in retreat.' He once turned to a civilian friend while riding with him on Salisbury Plain and said suddenly, " How would you set about firing a forest to cover a retreating army? "

[1] Erskine Childers, the author of that best of all spy stories, *The Riddle of the Sands*, had raised a heated controversy on the *rôle* of the cavalry by a cleverly argued book, *War and the Arme Blanche*, based on the events of the Boer War and the war in Manchuria, and introduced by a foreword from Lord Roberts.

[2] In his remarks at a lecture on cavalry given at the Royal United Service Institution in November 1910 Allenby said, " We do not make sufficient use of machine-guns. The weapon is not properly understood. . . . Personally I believe that it is going to have an enormous future before it as a cavalry weapon."

But if the British cavalry was better trained than any of its contemporaries, and at least as well equipped, there were serious faults in its organization. A division of four brigades, each of three regiments, besides artillery and other auxiliary arms, was a most unwieldy formation for a divisional staff to handle. The German cavalry division had six regiments only, in three brigades of two regiments each; this was considered by the nation which had studied war most deeply the largest number of mounted men that could be handled by a divisional staff. And the overgrown British division, twice the size of the German, was not even allowed a permanent staff in peace-time, and was seldom assembled for training. In the four years preceding the War it was trained as a division twice only—in 1910 on Salisbury Plain and in 1912, when Army manœuvres took place in the Eastern Counties. In 1911 a drought caused its concentration to be cancelled, and in 1913 considerations of economy. The Inspector-General of Cavalry, who became commander of the division in war, had no staff officer in peace and took over a war staff formed by officers taken from various appointments and brought together for the first time on mobilization.

It was a serious blot on our otherwise admirable preparations for war that the formation likely to take first contact with the enemy should be so unhandily organized and so freshly staffed.[1] Of soldiers, Haig, who did more than anyone to shape our 1914 expeditionary force and was himself a cavalryman, must bear the primary responsibility; and Allenby must share it for his acquiescence. But the real fault lay in the false financial economy which insists on the limitation of staffs in peace to the bare minimum required for peace-time routine. The limitation of the peace strength of units is a grave disadvantage in training for war, but the limitation of staffs is an even more dangerous economy. The starved body can more quickly and easily be recuperated than the starved brain.

While the soundness of Allenby's teaching and the effectiveness of his methods were recognized and appreciated by all thinking cavalrymen, it cannot be said that he was a popular Inspector.

---

[1] The danger had been emphasized in a report by the then Inspector in 1907, and was doubtless expressed also by other Inspectors.

To begin with, though a strong horseman, he was not a polished one, and hardly the cavalry's idea of how a dashing leader of British chivalry should ride. And to the great majority of cavalry officers, who had no opportunity of knowing him closely, his manners seemed as rough as his horsemanship. The average cavalry officer, though just as keen and efficient as his infantry comrade, and usually quicker-witted, did not take so kindly to strict discipline. To him Allenby's insistence on the exact observance of detail seemed irksome and needless. There was the chin-strap rule, for instance. No previous Inspector had ever deemed it necessary that the cavalry should always wear the chin-strap of the service cap actually on the chin. To Allenby it seemed obvious; why was the chin-strap there except for use? And when the cavalry were operating at speed, as cavalry ought to operate, caps frequently fell off unless properly secured. Either the man lost his cap—and had to pay for it—or time was wasted and the cohesion of the formation was spoilt by men or officers falling out to recover their caps.[1] Logic and common sense were on Allenby's side when he decreed that the chin-strap should be worn under the chin at all times, but to many the rule seemed tiresome, and it was at first evaded. Allenby, of course, had his way, and woe betide the officer or man who appeared before him without his chin-strap down! But it did not enhance his popularity.[2] Another order of which Allenby demanded strict observance was that the rifle should be thrust right down in the rifle-bucket. The soldier was fond of placing an old sock or rag at the bottom of the bucket, but Allenby had an unerring eye for rifle-butts which were even a sock's width above the normal level. It was useless for the soldier to protest that the rifle was driven home to the bottom; Allenby insisted on investigation, and in ninety-nine cases out of a hundred some foreign body was found at the end of the bucket.

[1] " I have seen regiments charge, waving their swords in the air, some of the men holding their helmets or their caps on with their sabre hand." (From remarks by Allenby at a lecture on cavalry.)

[2] This resistance to the wearing of chin-straps marks an odd change in military fashion. Up to the beginning of the twentieth century at least, the line of the chin-strap on a sunburnt face was a recognized trade-mark of the soldier. And " lean on your chin-strap " was an ironical adjunction of the old soldier to the tired recruit.

Allenby's inspections were famed, and often dreaded, for their thoroughness, for the searching nature of the questions to which he expected an immediate and direct answer, and for the explosions which might follow a vague or unsatisfactory reply. But, as the 5th Lancers had found,[1] behind the most awkward questions there often lurked a sense of humour. On one occasion, when inspecting a regiment, he stopped suddenly and said to the squadron commander, " Do all your men wear socks? " " Why, of course, sir," said the scandalized commander. " I wonder," replied Allenby. " Dismount that trooper " (pointing to a man in the ranks), " and let him take off his boots." The man was found barefooted. " There you are, you see," said Allenby. " Not at all what I would have expected in a well-conducted squadron! " Later, when the inspection was over, the crestfallen squadron commander summoned courage and asked Allenby, " General, how did you know that man had no socks? " " Well," said Allenby, " he was my batman once. I could never make the fellow wear them; I wondered whether you had been more successful."

On another occasion at the conclusion of an inspection he demanded to see the regiment's pioneer stores. After some delay the key was found and the store opened, to reveal a floor covered with cabbage-stalks, on which a number of black and white rabbits were contentedly browsing, their hutches being formed by the canvas collapsible boats which were one of the principal items of the pioneer stores. The Colonel looked at Allenby in consternation, to find with relief that he was rocking with laughter.

Allenby was no respector of persons, and senior officers, even his Brigadiers, sometimes suffered reproof in public and felt his barbed force of repartee. On one occasion, for example, when training the Cavalry Division, he set an exercise for a Saturday morning. It was timed to conclude by noon, and many officers had made arrangements for week-end leave. But the operation went wrong, and Allenby ordered it to be repeated. The afternoon was well advanced when he assembled the officers for his criticism of the exercise. As he began his opening remarks, the

[1] See p. 90.

Brigadier chiefly concerned stepped forward and interrupted him with, "I am ready to admit at once, sir, that what occurred was entirely my fault.". If he hoped by thus taking the blame to cut short the conference, he was mistaken. Allenby merely turned to him with the remark, "But I have yet to hear a suggestion, General ——, that it was anyone else's," and proceeded with his detailed criticisms. To another Brigadier he once remarked, more crudely, "There are fools, dam' fools, and you, General ——."

On the tactics, discipline, and general readiness for war of the cavalry Allenby's four years as Inspector left a wholesome and invigorating impression. On the human side, while the force and straightforwardness of his personality were recognized and respected, he did not succeed in gaining the full confidence of the cavalry. The last thing he ever sought was popularity, and he was right; but he was too careless of the effect his brusque manner and occasional roughness had upon his subordinates. "Roughness . . . ," wrote that wise man Francis Bacon in his essay on *Great Place*, "is a needless cause of discontent." And Allenby's opportunities in peace of commanding the division as a whole were too few to enable him to prove himself as its leader. On the manœuvres of 1912, indeed, his handling of the cavalry was somewhat severely criticized; he was held, in spite of an advantage in numbers, to have been outmanœuvred in the enclosed fields of East Anglia by the commander of the mounted forces on the other side.

Allenby himself had little doubt for some years before 1914 that Germany intended war when an opportunity came. He paid several visits to France, watched the French troops on manœuvres, and made himself acquainted with the probable theatre of operations on France's northern frontier. In 1912 he had been nominated as commander of the Cavalry Division if war came. In August 1914 he was fifty-three years of age, in full mental and bodily vigour, as well fitted to meet the physical fatigues and mental shocks of active service as any commander in any of the great armies that faced each other. The longest day's work could not tire him, the most unexpected and unwelcome news could not shake his iron nerve. Neither his courage nor his common sense was likely to desert him in the gravest peril or in the most sudden emergency. He had proved himself in the field during the long years of the South African War, and that experience was still fresh in his memory. He always slept well and ate well. He had read much and thought much of war, especially of the war that was now to begin. He was well prepared for the leadership of a force in the field, and those who knew him best could foresee his rise to greatness if chance favoured him. The most loyal of subordinates, he had nevertheless the strength of mind and character for independent command. In one respect only was his readiness for war lacking: he had failed to win the confidence and liking of those under him. Only the few who knew him well recognized his mental powers. To the Army at large, and to the majority of the cavalry he was to lead, he was " the Bull," a rough, violent, headstrong soldier, a ' bonny fechter,' perhaps, and a man not likely to lose his head in a tight place, but hardly a great general. Such was the penalty in reputation that his brusqueness in manner, the result largely of a natural shyness, had brought him.

BOOK II

SWORD AND BATON

The badge of rank for general officers is a crossed sword and baton, the point of the sword to the front and the edge of the blade outwards. The badge of rank for a Field-Marshal is crossed batons on a wreath of laurel.

Dress Regulations for the Army

CHAPTER VI

THE CAVALRY IN FRANCE
(*August* 1914–*May* 1915)

I

MOBILIZATION AND ENGAGEMENT
(*August* 4–24, 1914)

THE Great War saw the virtual passing from the battlefield of the cavalry arm, though not, it is hoped, of the cavalry spirit, which will still find expression in controlling and exploiting the mobility of armoured vehicles. The fighting power of men on horses, who have dominated war or taken an important share in it since the days of Alexander of Macedon, has—fortunately for the horse—practically vanished in face of modern weapons. Alexander was the first great commander to show how battles and campaigns could be won by the speed and endurance of horses and the boldness given to their riders by that speed. The exploits of Allenby's mounted men in Palestine, twenty-two and a half centuries later, are likely to be recorded as the last decisive successes of cavalry dependent on horses, and Allenby himself as the last great cavalry general. *From Alexander to Allenby* may be the title of some future history of the horsed cavalry arm. Yet it is alleged that Allenby failed as a leader of cavalry in 1914, that his Cavalry Division did not cover the British retreat as it should have done, that he lost control of it at the most critical moment, and that it missed its opportunity in pursuit when the Germans in their turn retreated from the Marne. To refute or uphold these accusations it is necessary to examine closely the conditions in which the cavalry had to work, the orders Allenby received, and the human and personal circumstances of the opening stages of the conflict. Man adapts himself rapidly even to the shocks of a world war; but the atmosphere of the first collisions is strange and tense, and brings many surprises. The events must be judged accordingly. The British cavalry in 1914 at least accomplished more than the horsemen of any other of the armies at war.

The Cavalry Division landed at Havre, and there entrained for Maubeuge, in the vicinity of which it was concentrated by August 20. It consisted of the 1st, 2nd, 3rd, and 4th Cavalry Brigades, commanded by Brigadier-Generals Briggs,[1] de Lisle,[2] Gough,[3] and Bingham[4] respectively; two brigades of Horse Artillery (four batteries of four guns each, armed with 13-pounders); a field squadron of Royal Engineers; and a signal squadron. A 5th Cavalry Brigade, under Sir Philip Chetwode, had also been mobilized, but was independent of the Cavalry Division.

The brigades were living organizations, the division was not. The brigades had usually been quartered as a whole, had trained as a whole, and were commanded and staffed in war as they had been in peace. But since the brigades lay far apart—at Aldershot, Salisbury Plain, in Ireland, and in the east of England—and the Treasury was economical, the division had rarely been collected or exercised as a whole, and its staff was improvised. The one permanent element, its commander, had impressed his personality on the training of the cavalry, but had failed to win their liking or their confidence. As a result, the division was a collection

---

[1] The late Lieutenant-General Sir Charles Briggs, K.C.B., K.C.M.G., who later in the War commanded an Army Corps.

[2] General Sir Beauvoir de Lisle, K.C.B., K.C.M.G., D.S.O., commander of an Army Corps in the War and of the Western Command after the War.

[3] General Sir Hubert Gough, G.C.B., G.C.M.G., K.C.V.O., commander of the Fifth Army from 1916 to the early part of 1918.

[4] The late Major-General the Hon. Sir Cecil Bingham, G.C.V.O., K.C.M.G., C.B.

of four brigades, well trained, well equipped, well mounted, and confident, but owing a somewhat critical and suspicious allegiance to divisional headquarters, which had thus an almost impossible task to handle this unwieldy formation in circumstances of the utmost difficulty and danger, into which they were plunged at once without any opportunity to settle down.

The British Expeditionary Force that landed in France in August 1914 was tied to the French war plan. The British Command had had no hand in framing this plan nor knowledge of its strategy. It is remarkable that a great military nation like the French should have produced, after much study of the possibilities of a conflict so long foreseen, so vicious a project as this Plan XVII, based on faulty Intelligence and a faulty conception of war. More remarkable still were the skill and fortitude that enabled them to recover from it. If plans made in peace could ensure success in war France was doomed. If ever a plan deserved victory it was the Schlieffen Plan; if ever one deserved defeat it was Plan XVII.

In the original deployment the Cavalry Division was placed behind the British right. This disposition has been strongly criticized; it has been said that Sir John French should have placed it from the outset on the exposed left flank.[1] This is to ignore the Intelligence available and the plan to be executed. There was at this time no suspicion that the right of the German wheel through Belgium extended so far west as to overlap the British left. On the contrary, the information furnished by Joffre's headquarters indicated that the British Expeditionary Force was outside the right of the German First Army; and the plan was that it should pivot on its right and attack the German flank. The position of the cavalry is therefore intelligible: it was to pass across the front of the B.E.F., and thus reach its left flank, after the intended wheel, by the shortest route (see map opposite). On August 21, in execution of the first stage of this plan, the

[1] There was a complete misunderstanding between Sir John French and Lanrezac, commander of the Fifth French Army, as to the use to be made of the British cavalry. The latter got it into his head that the cavalry was to be employed as mounted infantry and kept as a reserve. (See Brigadier-General Spears' book *Liaison*, Chapter VI and Appendix XII.)

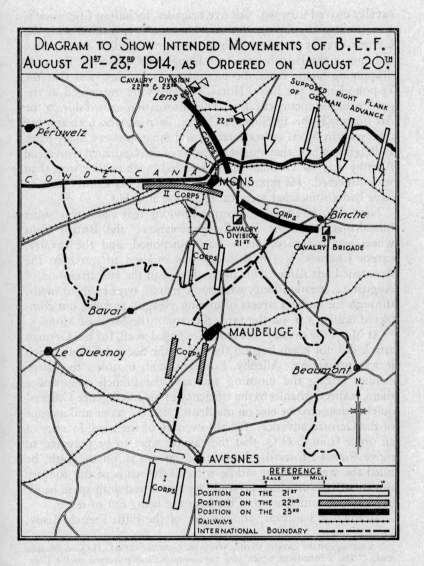

DIAGRAM TO SHOW INTENDED MOVEMENTS OF B.E.F.
AUGUST 21ˢᵀ–23ᴿᴰ 1914, AS ORDERED ON AUGUST 20ᵀᴴ

CAVALRY DIVISION 22ᴺᴰ & 23ᴿᴰ
Lens
22ᴺᴰ

SUPPOSED RIGHT FLANK OF GERMAN ADVANCE

Péruwelz

CONDE CANAL

MONS

II CORPS

I CORPS

Binche

CAVALRY DIVISION 21ˢᵀ

5ᵀᴴ CAVALRY BRIGADE

II CORPS

Bavai

MAUBEUGE

Le Quesnoy

I CORPS

Beaumont

N.

I CORPS

AVESNES

REFERENCE
SCALE OF MILES

POSITION ON THE 21ˢᵀ
POSITION ON THE 22ᴺᴰ
POSITION ON THE 23ᴿᴰ
RAILWAYS
INTERNATIONAL BOUNDARY

cavalry moved forward. All five brigades, including Chetwode's, were under Allenby on this day. Contact was gained with the German cavalry patrols, which were roughly handled, the superior training of the British horsemen being early obvious. The only disquieting factor from the tactical point of view was that the 13-pounders of the Royal Horse Artillery were outranged by the guns with the enemy cavalry. The information gained during the day (mainly by his Intelligence Officer, Barrow, who with another officer sat in Mons railway-station and rang up every likely place in Belgium where they might get news of the Germans) convinced Allenby that the German right extended much farther west than was suspected. He reported accordingly, but his reports seem to have had a somewhat sceptical reception at G.H.Q.[2]

Next day, however, it became obvious that there was some miscalculation in the French appreciation; the British right wheel was cancelled, or at least postponed, and the cavalry, except Chetwode's 5th Brigade, was ordered to move to the threatened left flank. This move, begun in the late afternoon of August 22, meant a long, wearisome march, over cobbled roads, through the endless streets of mining villages, and was not completed until 3 A.M. on the 23rd, the day of the battle of Mons.

At Mons the cavalry was hardly engaged at all, for the German attack did not reach beyond the left of the Second Corps, which it was protecting. Allenby, however, who motored to Valenciennes during the morning and saw the French commander there, realized (thanks to the efficiency of his Intelligence Officers) quicker than anyone else on the British side the scope and menace of the German advance. On the evening of the 23rd, in spite of an order from G.H.Q. that the cavalry were to be prepared to move forward towards Valenciennes at 5 A.M. on the 24th, he filled the wallets of his saddle with all the maps of the country towards Paris on which he could lay hands and with spare handkerchiefs, in anticipation of the baggage being out of reach.

Meanwhile Lanrezac, commander of the Fifth French Army,

---

[1] A message to the Cavalry Division from the General Staff at G.H.Q. on this date read: " The information which you have acquired and conveyed to the Commander-in-Chief appears to be somewhat exaggerated. It is probable that only mounted troops supported by Jägers are in your immediate neighbourhood."

on the right of the British, attacked in front by the German Second Army and on the right flank by the Third, had ordered a retreat. Not only did he omit to inform his ally, but he actually sent a request to Sir John French to advance to the attack, an action which would have exposed the B.E.F. to certain disaster. Fortunately, however, Sir John French became aware, late on the 23rd, of Lanrezac's retreat. Staff officers were summoned to G.H.Q. at Le Cateau, and orders for retreat were issued at 1 A.M. on the 24th. Lanrezac's conduct on this occasion made the British Commander-in-Chief deeply suspicious of his allies and influenced his attitude towards them for some time to come.

II
THE RETREAT
(*August 24–September 5, 1914*)

In all the trade of war, no feat
Is nobler than a brave retreat.
SAMUEL BUTLER, *Hudibras*

To cover a retreat is a traditional *rôle* of cavalry, but in actual history there are few instances of its having done so if the retreat has been prolonged or closely pressed. In theory mounted men should have more endurance than infantry, and be better fitted for the strain of constant rearguard actions; in practice they become used up sooner. The infantryman who gets a respite has only to care for himself and his rifle; the cavalryman has also to forage for his horse. Thus, while cavalry may sacrifice themselves to give the remainder of the army a clean break away, as at Königgrätz in 1866, in any prolonged retreat the brunt of the rearguard work has usually fallen on the infantry. Ney covered the last tragic stages of the retreat from Moscow, and Craufurd the retreat to Corunna, each with a handful of riflemen; and cavalry played no great part in Wellington's retreat from Burgos. It would, in fact, be difficult to find any instance where cavalry have shown greater skill and endurance in retreat than the British cavalry did in the withdrawal from Mons to the Marne.

The retirement could hardly have started in more unfavourable conditions for cavalry, who require room for manœuvre if they are to exploit their principal weapon of mobility. This manœuvre room they never had till the Second Corps turned and shook itself free of its pursuers at Le Cateau. On August 24, when the retreat began, the Second Corps, which the Cavalry Division had to cover, was in close contact with the enemy, and the German mounted troops were already beyond its left flank and threatening its line of retreat. To add to his responsibilities and to the cares of his already overloaded staff, the 19th Infantry Brigade was now put under Allenby's orders. The brigade had been formed from battalions intended to protect the lines of communication, was but newly arrived in France, and was not fully equipped.

Since there was no room for cavalry on the closely engaged front of the Second Corps, Allenby's chief preoccupation on the morning of the 24th was with the threat to the left flank and rear. At about 7 A.M., when all seemed to be going well with the retirement of the Corps, he withdrew the cavalry some miles, to take up a position well to the flank and guard the further retreat of the infantry against any threat from the west. This withdrawal, as it turned out, was premature. The 5th Division became hard-pressed, and its commander, Sir Charles Fergusson,[1] asked Allenby for assistance. Allenby's response was immediate. He at once went back with the 2nd and 3rd Cavalry Brigades, who took prompt action to relieve the pressure at the cost of somewhat heavy losses. This was the rearguard action of Élouges, which caused more casualties to the British Expeditionary Force than had the Battle of Mons on the previous day.

August 25 was a most difficult day for the Cavalry Division. The obstacle of the Forest of Mormal, with no good roads from north to south, lay diagonally across the line of retreat and separated the two Corps of the B.E.F. The Second Corps and the Cavalry Division were forced into a narrow corridor between the forest and the enemy columns, and the cavalry had again little room for manœuvre. The direction of retirement imposed by the roads was not straight to the rear, but diagonally towards the dangerous west flank, threatened by the progress of the great

[1] General Sir Charles Fergusson, Bart., G.C.B., G.C.M.G., D.S.O., later commander of the Seventeenth Corps.

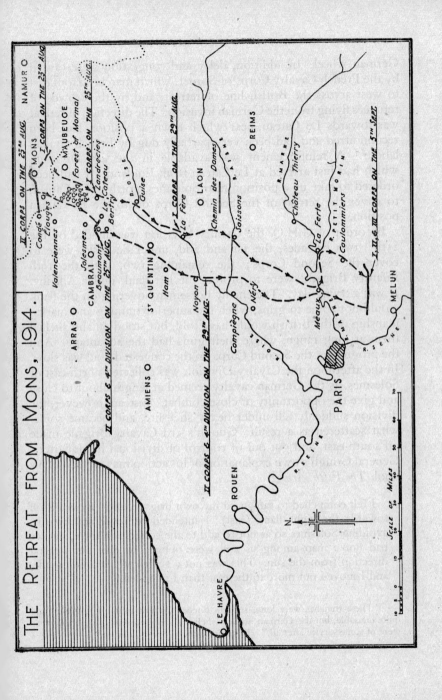

THE RETREAT FROM MONS, 1914.

NAMUR

II CORPS ON THE 23RD AUG.

I CORPS ON THE 23RD AUG.

MONS

MAUBEUGE

Congé

Élouges

Forest of Mormal

Valenciennes

I CORPS ON THE 25TH AUG.

Landrecies

Le Cateau

I CORPS ON THE 25TH AUG.

Solesmes

Beaumont

Bertry

CAMBRAI

II CORPS & 4TH DIVISION ON THE 25TH AUG.

ARRAS

R. OISE

Guise

La Fère

I CORPS ON THE 29TH AUG.

LAON

Chemin des Dames

R. AISNE

Soissons

REIMS

R. MARNE

Château Thierry

ST QUENTIN

Ham

Noyon

II CORPS & 4TH DIVISION ON THE 29TH AUG.

AMIENS

Compiègne

Néry

R. OISE

La Ferté

R. PETIT MORIN

Coulommiers

I, II, & III CORPS ON THE 5TH SEPT.

Méaux

R. MARNE

MELUN

ROUEN

PARIS

R. SEINE

R. SEINE

LE HAVRE

N.

SCALE OF MILES
10 5 0 10 20 30 40 50 60 70

German wheel. In addition, delay and congestion were caused by the French Cavalry Corps of Sordet, which marched from east to west across the British line of retreat, and by the crowds of refugees flying from the German invasion. The direction of retreat was towards Le Cateau, near which town a position had been reconnoitred and had been very partially dug by French civilian labour.[1] A reinforcement was available in the 4th Division, which had just arrived at Le Cateau from England. It had been ordered to take up a position near Solesmes, north of Le Cateau, to cover the retreat of the Second Corps on to the Le Cateau position.

By order of G.H.Q. the Cavalry Division was divided on the 25th: two brigades, the 1st and 2nd, under de Lisle, were to cover the Second Corps; the remaining two, with the 19th Infantry Brigade, were to protect the left flank under Allenby. It was a trying day. The enemy horsemen hovering on the flank would not come to grips, when the superior training and marksmanship of the British would have told, but stood off and shelled them at long range, where their guns had the advantage. And the progress of the Second Corps on the congested road was slow. In the afternoon the Cavalry Division was collected north-east of Solesmes, as the German cavalry seemed at length about to close and give the opportunity of close combat. Instead, however, the division suddenly fell under heavy shell-fire, and became somewhat scattered as a result. Gough's 3rd Cavalry Brigade made off south-east, and got out of control of divisional headquarters. General Gough's own explanation of his action may be read in his book *The Fifth Army*:

> I felt compelled to safeguard my own brigade, and I moved it off towards the right flank (east). I intended to retire southwards, avoiding Solesmes so as not to add to the congestion there, but we had not a map among us and were obliged to take our general direction from the sun. This was not a sufficiently accurate guide, and I moved out more to the east than I intended.

[1] " These trenches were long, straight ditches without turns or traverses, and quite unusable, but the German artillery shelled them mercilessly, so perhaps they were of some service after all." (Brigadier-General Spears, *Liaison*.)

The 3rd Brigade eventually reached Catillon, east of Le Cateau, and spent the night of the 25th there, without informing the Cavalry Division of its whereabouts. Next day it did good work in helping to cover the retreat of the right of the Second Corps. It never again came under control of the Cavalry Division, being eventually attached, with Chetwode's 5th Cavalry Brigade, to Haig's First Corps, of which General Gough's brother was the principal staff officer. De Lisle, with part of his 2nd Cavalry Brigade and most of the 1st Cavalry Brigade, also became separated, and spent the night east or south of Le Cateau.

Meanwhile Solesmes, a long, straggling village which formed a defile on the main route of the Second Corps' retreat, had become congested with men and transport, and there was considerable danger that the advanced German troops would arrive before the village could be cleared. Allenby enlisted the assistance of the rearmost brigade of the 3rd Division, McCracken's 7th Infantry Brigade, to aid the cavalry in keeping the enemy at arm's length till Solesmes was clear. This was successfully done, and between sunset and midnight the Second Corps settled down on the high ground west of Le Cateau, with the men considerably exhausted and drenched by a heavy storm of rain which broke about dusk. The 4th Division, which had been in position on the high ground west of Solesmes, did not reach their bivouacs to the west of the Second Corps till long after midnight.

The original intention had been for the First and Second Corps to reunite south of the Mormal Forest about Le Cateau, and to make a stand on the line of high ground to the east and west of that town; and the troops of the Second Corps had reached their bivouacs with that intention still in the minds of their leaders. But late in the evening of the 25th Sir John French issued orders for a continuance of the retreat, directing Allenby to cover the Second Corps. The 19th Infantry Brigade, which was by this time in Le Cateau, was transferred from Allenby's command to the Second Corps. The orders reached Allenby at Beaumont, five miles west of Le Cateau, a little after 11 P.M., just when he had received reports of the withdrawal of the cavalry rearguard from the heights to the north. He quickly realized the seriousness of the situation. To cover the first stages of the Second Corps' retirement from its present positions it would be necessary for the cavalry to hold the high ground to the north, about Solesmes and Viesly, which they and the 4th Division had held on the previous afternoon and evening. But they had withdrawn at nightfall, when the last of the Second Corps had passed through, and the ridge was now in German hands. Even had Allenby had the whole of the Cavalry Division closely under his control he could hardly have won back the ridge from the German advanced guards. Actually, as we have seen, a large part of the cavalry had escaped from his control, and was a considerable distance away.

As soon as the facts were clear to him Allenby motored to the headquarters of General Smith-Dorrien, commanding the Second Corps, at Bertry. He arrived at 2 A.M. on the 26th. The meeting, on which the fate of the greater part of the British Expeditionary Force hung, might have been dramatic. But both Smith-Dorrien and Allenby were direct, courageous, and quick of decision in a crisis. Allenby stated at once that his cavalry was scattered, and that it was impossible for him to interpose a screen between the Second Corps and the enemy next morning; unless the Corps could move before daylight the enemy would be in a position to attack it before it could get clear. After ascertaining from the commander of the 3rd Division, whose headquarters lay near by, that it was quite impossible for the exhausted infantry, some of whom had only just arrived, to move earlier than 9 A.M., Smith-Dorrien made his famous decision to stand and fight, asking Allenby and Snow (4th Division) to act under his orders, to which Allenby gave instant acceptance and Snow so soon as he could be communicated with.

Early next morning the battle of Le Cateau began. Smith-Dorrien hoped that his right would be covered by the First Corps, which should by G.H.Q. orders have marched towards Le Cateau. But the action, unimportant in itself, at Landrecies, on the evening of the 25th, in which some German troops stumbled in the dark on to the billets of the 1st Guards Brigade, had a most unfortunate effect on the mind of Sir Douglas Haig, the commander of the First Corps. He was persuaded that large German forces were already between him and the Second Corps, and marched south-east on the 26th, instead of south. Thus the right flank of Smith-Dorrien's force was exposed and suffered heavily.

The obvious task of the cavalry at Le Cateau was to cover the flanks of the infantry battle. The battle was, however, no ordered affair; as has been seen, the decision to fight was taken only a few hours before the action began, and orders to stand had barely reached the troops in the front line before they became engaged. On the right wing, where the main brunt of the German attack fell and losses were heaviest, the truant 3rd Cavalry Brigade and the greater part of the 1st and 2nd Brigades assisted in somewhat haphazard fashion to protect the flank and to cover the withdrawal, but they acted independently and were for the time being outside Allenby's control. On the other flank, where he had one complete Brigade (the 4th) and some portions of the 1st and 2nd at his disposal, he was in a better position to influence the course of the action. But this flank was already covered by the French Cavalry Corps of Sordet, and was in consequence never seriously threatened. Sordet, in response to the British request to protect the flank, advanced towards Cambrai and engaged enemy columns with his artillery and some cyclists, delaying their advance with little loss to himself. Allenby meanwhile held a watching brief with the 4th Brigade. His chief personal action in the battle was when Snow, commanding the 4th Division, asked for the support of some cavalry. Allenby refused. He had only one complete brigade available, and he judged that the crisis was not yet come. His manner of refusal was typical of the man. A staff officer had written a reply to Snow's request, and showed it to Allenby for approval. Allenby insisted on writing the reply in his own hand and signing it himself. " When I take such a step," he said, " as to refuse assistance to another commander it must be made quite clear to him that the decision is mine and the responsibility mine."

The retreat continued for another ten days after Le Cateau. The Cavalry Division, except the 3rd Brigade, which continued to act under the First Corps, was reunited under Allenby's hand by August 30, and continued to cover the western flank and rear. But the German pursuit had slackened, and von Kluck's First Army was in the course of those erratic movements which were

soon to expose it to the French counterstroke. The cavalry were
continually in action, occupying rearguard positions and exposed
to shell-fire, but had little further close contact with the enemy
during the retreat, except for the brilliant episode of Néry in the
early morning of September 1, when Briggs' 1st Cavalry Brigade,
surprised in its bivouacs by a German cavalry division, which
had passed through a gap between the Second and Third Corps,
held its own until the arrival of reinforcements, drove off the
Germans, and captured their artillery.

The record of the Cavalry Division during the great retreat
from Mons may not sound brilliant. The fact remains that the
British flank and rear were protected from a greatly superior
force of hostile horsemen, who were roughly handled whenever
they came within reach. That Allenby partially lost control of his
command during the crisis of the retreat, from the afternoon of
the 25th till the morning of the 30th, cannot be denied. The
reasons, technical and human—a clumsy organization, insufficient
means of intercommunication, his failure to command the
confidence of all his brigadiers—have been indicated. Allenby
himself never for a moment lost his head or his sureness of judgment; he realized from the first that the danger lay on the left
flank, and did all he could to safeguard it. He resisted all urgings
from above that the cavalry should undertake some spectacular
intervention to ease the pressure. His clearness of vision and
quickness of decision on the night before Le Cateau probably
saved the Second Corps and 4th Division from disaster. His
personal courage was evident to all. Here is testimony from one
of his squadron commanders:

> He was an extraordinarily brave man personally. I remember on
> the Mons retreat when Divisional H.Q. had taken refuge with the
> 4th Cavalry Brigade and we nearly had an unfortunate experience,
> being almost surrounded. He took charge, and I remember his
> words of command being spoken with, if anything, less concern
> than most fellows would show at a field day at home.

Another staff officer has a vivid recollection of seeing Allenby
gallop along a line of dismounted men when there was a certain
amount of unsteadiness under heavy shelling. His voice and

example immediately checked the drift towards the rear and restored confidence. He never tired, in spite of long days in the saddle, a heavy load of responsibility, and short rations. He still insisted on the same details of peace discipline—chin-straps down, rifles home in the bucket, limbers properly drawn into the side of the road. This had a curious moral effect; a subaltern who had been sharply checked because some of the chin-straps in his troop were not down consoled himself with the reflection, " If the General still has time to worry us about his old fads things can't be as bad as they look." [1]

A letter written by Allenby to his wife on August 30, the first he had had time to write since the 20th, is worth quoting to show the equanimity he preserved during the strain of the retreat:

We have had a strenuous time, and have been fighting every day for a week, very short of food and sleep. I, personally, have done well in the way of food, and have had two good nights' sleep; but the men had a very bad time. Their spirit is splendid, and they have fought like tigers. We are in close touch with the French, and hope to go forward soon with them again. We are in a lovely country now, and I have been billeted in one or two magnificent *châteaux*. Even the poorer houses are very clean and comfortable, and the French women are kindness itself, and often refuse any payment for food, etc. . . . I've had a good many casualties in the division, but not as many as you would expect. These Germans fight chiefly, so far, at long range, with artillery; and the shells are not very effective, though they are alarming at the time.

An illustration of Allenby's sense of humour may be quoted here. Some years after the War he was present at a lecture by a distinguished military writer, who spoke of him as one " who had taken a leading part in the retreat from Mons." When asked to speak at the end of the lecture Allenby said, " I must contradict the somewhat equivocal statement of the lecturer that I took a *leading* part in the retreat from Mons. I was on a very slow horse."

[1] The retreat showed the justification of Allenby's insistence on the chin-strap rule. A number of men had lost their caps through disobedience of his order, and either suffered from the hot sun or wore any form of headdress, such as old French straw hats, or had handkerchiefs on their heads.

III
The Advance to the Aisne
(September 6–30, 1914)

On September 5 the long retreat ended, and on September 6 the French and British turned about and began to advance. There is no need here to retell the story of the counterstroke of the Marne. It was a manœuvre rather than a battle, and the decisive thrust was the advance of the British Army, which the Germans had discounted as beaten, into the gap between the armies of von Kluck and von Bülow.

During the advance the cavalry operated in two portions. The 1st, 2nd, and 4th Brigades, on the right flank, formed the Cavalry Division under Allenby; the 3rd and 5th Brigades worked together under Gough on the left flank. The instructions to the Cavalry Division were " to guard the front and flanks of the First Corps, connecting with the Fifth French Army." Similar instructions were given to Gough on the left flank. Thus the mission of the cavalry was entirely protective, and their principal task to keep touch with the French forces on the flanks, which were throughout the advance half a day's march behind the British. The truth is that Sir John French, having been so badly let down by the commander of the Fifth French Army at the opening of the campaign, had no mind to be exposed again to a similar experience. It was not till September 11 that any hint of aggressive purpose came into G.H.Q. orders in the words, " Every endeavour will be made by the cavalry in co-operation with the French cavalry on right and left to harass the retreating enemy."

There is no doubt that the cavalry missed opportunities during this advance, especially on September 9, the day that the B.E.F. crossed the Marne, when there was a gap in the German front and a confused mass of transport was retreating with little protection, at the mercy of boldly handled mounted men. The opportunity is easy enough to see now, with all information at our disposal, but at the time there was little to indicate it. The " G in ' gap ' " was as elusive then as it was found to be later in the War. Critics of these lost opportunities are apt to assume fresh horses, fresh men, fresh minds. In truth, all were weary. After a fortnight's constant retreat in the face of an active and greatly superior enemy it was difficult to realize that the same enemy was in confusion and on the run. A trap was suspected, so that a mistaken air report was sufficient to halt the First Corps half-way across the Marne and to place it on the defensive. The fighting on the Petit Morin and elsewhere had shown the vulnerability of horsemen to modern fire power, and the German use of Jäger battalions, well equipped with machine-guns, to support their cavalry put an effective brake on mounted action. Great difficulty was being experienced in keeping the horses shod, since the *pavé* roads of France and Belgium wore out shoes so quickly. But it was the instructions to the cavalry from G.H.Q. that formed the greatest bar to bold offensive action.

During the advance to the Aisne the separation of the cavalry into two bodies was confirmed by the creation of a 2nd Cavalry Division under Gough, Allenby becoming commander of the 1st Cavalry Division. When the obstacle of the Aisne river was reached the cavalry were soon checked, and close infantry fighting began again. During the Aisne battle the cavalry did much useful work as a mobile reserve. Presently the stalemate which had been reached in the operations was recognized by the phrase which began to appear regularly in the G.H.Q. reports, " There is no change in the situation," and was more tersely telegraphed to lower formations as " Situation unchanged." It was to remain practically unchanged on the Aisne for the next two and a half years. Allenby, with his usual foresight and common sense, ordered his cavalry to collect bayonets and entrenching tools. The brief period of open fighting was over, and trench warfare had begun.

Here are two vignettes of Allenby under fire on the Aisne. The first is from a regimental officer:

On the Aisne one day I was sent from Brigade H.Q. to Divisional H.Q. with some message or other: they were well up somewhere near Paissy and in the open lying down, except Allenby and one or two others who were standing up, being shelled to hell by a 5·9 gun or howitzer. A shell fell close to where he was standing, and my horse sat down backwards with terror. I was watching Allenby; he stood looking towards the Chemin des Dames and merely turned his head slowly and looked back for a second. I've never forgotten it.

The other is from an officer attached to divisional headquarters:

One morning advanced headquarters was established in a barn on the heights above the Aisne. All seemed quiet, and the General was reading a newspaper. Presently heavy shells began to fall near the barn, and it became obvious that the German observers had noted the occupation of the barn and were determined on its destruction. Obvious, that is, to all except the General, who had never even looked up from his paper as the shells came gradually closer, and who seemed quite unconscious that anything unusual was happening. When, to the great relief of the junior members, a senior staff officer explained the situation to him and recommended instant evacuation, he rose, took off his spectacles, placed them in the case, deliberately folded his newspaper, and made a slow and dignified retreat, without once looking back. We junior members, as soon as the General was gone, stood on no ceremony, and our retreat was neither dignified nor slow. The next salvo of shells, a few seconds later, burst fairly in the barn.

IV

THE CAVALRY CORPS
(*October* 1914–*May* 1915)

Towards the end of September 1914, when the battle on the Aisne had trenched itself into immobility, both French and Germans naturally sought a new decision by outflanking movements to the north, with troops freshly raised or withdrawn from parts of the line where trench warfare had already set in. This " Race to the Sea," as it was termed, continued throughout the first half of October. Neither side could gain any decided advantage, but the initiative generally remained with the Germans, who had more fresh formations available, so that the French were hard-pressed to hold them. By the middle of October the transfer of the British Expeditionary Force from the Aisne to Flanders filled the gap between the French armies of the north and the

Belgian army retreating from fallen Antwerp, and a practically continuous front from the sea to Switzerland was thus formed. Then began the long, desperate struggle of the Germans to break the British line at Ypres and to gain the Channel ports. The first great crisis of the War, the Marne counterstroke, had been decided by a manœuvre, in which the advance of the B.E.F. had turned the scale; the second great crisis, the defence of the Channel ports, so vital for Great Britain and thus for her allies, was determined by sheer hard fighting, of which the brunt fell on the British, and not least on the British cavalry. It is not too much to say that the fate of the War depended on the fact that this cavalry had been trained to use the rifle with an effect that no horsemen or infantry in the other European armies could match.

Towards the end of September, soon after the extension northward from the Aisne began, Sir John French urged that the British force should be transferred to the left of the line near the coast. There were good reasons for the request. Fresh British troops, a Marine Brigade, the 7th Division, and 3rd Cavalry Division, were being landed in the north in the hope of preventing the fall of Antwerp; it was obviously desirable that all the British forces should be united, if possible; the move would shorten their lines of communication, and the defence of the Channel ports was a specially British interest. Accordingly, early in October the British began to leave the Aisne. The Second Corps and the cavalry divisions moved first, the former by train, the latter by road. It was a week's march for the cavalry. They gladly left the Aisne, where the trenches were close-locked and the only employment for cavalry was as a mobile reserve of riflemen, and welcomed the prospect of a renewal of open warfare. The weather, which had been wet and cold on the Aisne, improved; Picardy was pleasant, and the plains of Flanders were pictured as a fair field for mounted action. None realized the grim work ahead of them and the approaching fate of cavalry on the Western Front. They were halted for one day as a reserve to a hard-pressed French force, but did not come into action. On October 9, while covering the concentration of the Second Corps, which had detrained at Abbeville, the two cavalry divisions were formed into a Cavalry Corps, of which Allenby received command.

After covering the concentration of the Second and Third Corps the cavalry advanced into Flanders on their left. On October 12 they drove a German cavalry corps from the high ground about Mont des Cats and Kemmel, south-west of Ypres. In the following days they advanced to the line of the Lys between Armentières and Menin, but found the river too strongly guarded to cross. On October 20 they were compelled to fall back from the line of the river and dig in on the high ground to the west. The great German thrust for Ypres and the coast was now about to be made. The First Corps, the last British troops to leave the Aisne, had just time to detrain and advance to the east of Ypres before the fateful conflict began. The Cavalry Corps found itself lying in the line of battle between the Third and Fourth Corps,[1] like a frigate between two ships of the line. Opposite it was the great mass of the German cavalry, similarly wedged between two bodies of infantry. Thus in the first stages of the Battle of Ypres the German and British cavalry strove for mastery on foot, instead of on horse. In numbers, and especially in artillery, the odds were heavily against the British. Allenby's two divisions, some 9000 strong, held a front of six miles, and were opposed by six German divisions with four Jäger battalions, a total of over 24,000 men. The 13-pounder guns of the R.H.A. were not only heavily outnumbered and outranged, but were also very short of ammunition. Yet the Germans completely failed to make any impression; in truth, except for the Jäger battalions, they were poorly equipped and trained for fighting on foot.

The 3rd Cavalry Division, fighting on Allenby's left, was now placed under his orders and included in the Cavalry Corps; and the Ferozepore Brigade of the Indian Lahore Division was sent to him as a reserve. After taking part on October 26 in an abortive attempt of the corps on their left to advance, the cavalry had a few days' comparative quiet, since the German cavalry opposite them had acquired too shrewd a respect for British

---

[1] The Fourth Corps consisted of the 7th Division and 3rd Cavalry Division, under Sir Henry Rawlinson (afterwards General Lord Rawlinson), which had landed in Belgium and advanced south.

musketry to make any further attempt to push to close quarters. But on the night of the 29th/30th German infantry relieved the cavalry; and on the 30th Allenby's widely extended force had to withstand the buffet of the Fourth Bavarian Corps and the 26th Division of the Thirteenth Corps.[1] The Cavalry Corps lost some ground, but prevented any breach of the line. From now on the principal fighting in this part was for possession of the villages of Messines and Wytschaete, standing on the high ground overlooking Ypres.

The 31st was the most critical day of the whole battle. The Germans brought yet another infantry division into line against the cavalry, and attacked vigorously. But the weak and scattered squadrons still held on. Some infantry arrived from the Second Corps as reinforcement, and only part of the village of Messines was lost, though the odds against the British were five and six to one. On this same day on the First Corps front Gheluvelt was lost, and the line breached till the last reserve, the Worcesters, re-established it by counter-attack. Repulsed by day, the Germans on the cavalry front tried again at night, hoping under the cloak of darkness to avoid the deadly British rifle-fire; and by sheer weight of numbers they drove the cavalry from the village of Wytschaete in the early hours of November 1. With the help of a French division the village was eventually retaken, but Messines, to the south, had to be evacuated at last. Wytschaete was finally lost by the French next day. The battle continued for almost another fortnight, but the crisis had passed. The Regular forces of Great Britain had been almost annihilated, but they had saved Europe from German domination. The Cavalry Corps, which had fought as infantry and had suffered as heavily as the infantry, was gradually relieved from the trenches and became a mobile reserve.

In such a battle, where the resources were barely adequate even for defence, the commanders had no opportunity to show their skill in manœuvre. They could influence the fight only by using

---

[1] To continue the naval metaphor, the frigate which had up till now been engaged with an enemy frigate, though a much heavier one, had now to fight a three-decker ship of the line. By all the rules of war the frigate should have been blown out of the water.

such scanty reserves as they could collect or borrow to patch the rents in their line and to prevent it from breaking altogether; and by maintaining their belief in victory and inspiring their subordinates with that belief.

Allenby, needless to say, remained cool and confident. The men in front of him required little urging or encouragement to do their best, but the knowledge of their leader's strength of purpose and courage was invaluable to them. They need fear no weakening or panic orders from above, need expect no mildness if their own nerve failed. The sight of him—and he visited his forward units frequently—was enough to show that here was a man who would never lose heart and did not give ground easily. He managed usually to have some reserves, however small, at the critical moment, and parcelled them out shrewdly with an instinct for the ' sore spots ' in his line. He was generous in lending aid when other corps were in greater danger than his own. At one of the crises of the battle he was wakened at night by his staff to hear that one of the most important points in his line had been lost; it was typical of his calmness and strength of spirit that, after ascertaining that everything possible was being done to restore the situation, he returned to bed and slept till dawn.

Allenby's letters to his wife at this period, written in the stress of the fighting, say little of war or of himself. As in South Africa, a garden or a flower is more likely to move his pen than any incidents of battle. He is generous in praise of his men and of his staff:

> I have now the biggest command of cavalry that anyone has had in the history of our army, and am sure that I have the best-trained and most efficient officers and men that have ever taken the field in European war. I have also a first-class staff. So I have no excuse if I do badly.

Of his A.D.C. Marshall, of the 11th Hussars, who was killed during the battle by a shell while visiting Ypres, he writes, " My poor little A.D.C., Marshall, was killed to-day. He was a good little lad; and was very kind to me, though I was always pitching into him." As in the South African War he had expressed his admiration for his enemy, the Boers, so now he writes of the

Germans, " It is not true that the German officers have to drive their men into battle. The men come on like lions."

After the battle the Cavalry Corps went into reserve round Hazebrouck, south-west of Ypres.[1] On his way up to the battle Allenby had had his headquarters for a night at the Château de la Motte au Bois, on the edge of the Forest of Nieppe. To this billet he now returned. Its *châtelaine* was a remarkable Frenchwoman, the Baroness Ernest de la Grange, aristocratic, witty, capable, and charming, a widow whose son was serving with the French cavalry. Her book *Open House in Flanders* tells much of Allenby, whose character she greatly admired, and whose firm friend she became. Of his love of observing birds and fishes she writes:

> Very susceptible to the beauties of nature, he seems to know all the birds, their songs, plumage, and habits. He watches the ways of the fishes in our little Flemish canals and irrigation creeks, and he has shown me a nest of perch. The eggs were hanging to the water weeds, for the mother seemed to be resting, while the father rushed to catch a big grasshopper and then to fight a fish twice his own size.

Of another great characteristic, his love of children, she tells the following tale:

> He never goes out on foot without stuffing his pockets with sweets and oranges. All the village children run after him, search his pockets, and feast. He has adopted two little refugees called Marthe and Sidonie. He has brought them dolls from London, and one day early in the week he met them out without the cherished dollies. When asked where they were, they said tearfully that their mother was keeping them as a " Sunday toy." The General took a hand of each, and, going to their home, said they must have their dollies every day; and if they got broken he would bring them others.

Another firm friendship that Allenby established at this time was with a man much younger than himself, Lord Dalmeny,[2]

---

[1] An Indian Cavalry Corps was formed in December 1914, and placed under the command of General Rimington. Thus both Cavalry Corps were commanded by officers of the Inniskilling Dragoons.

[2] Now Lieutenant-Colonel the Earl of Rosebery, D.S.O., M.C.

who had become his Camp Commandant. He served on Allenby's personal staff for the rest of the War, first as A.D.C. and then as Military Secretary; and when, after the War, Allenby became High Commissioner for Egypt, remained for some time on his staff at the Residency in Cairo. Allenby did not make friendships easily, nor often confide in others; to Dalmeny in these years he probably spoke more freely than to any other man.

There is little to chronicle of the doings of the Cavalry Corps in the winter of 1914–15 and the spring of 1915. For the abortive attack by the Second and Third Corps in the middle of December 1914 it was placed under the Second Corps, but was not engaged. In February each division in turn spent ten days in trenches in a part of the French line in the Ypres Salient. Otherwise there is nothing to record till the first use of poison gas in warfare, by the Germans on April 22, 1915, caused a panic among the French black troops and set the whole Ypres Salient alight again. Allenby was at this time on leave in England; while there he had a severe attack of influenza, and he did not return to France till May 3. Within a few days of his return he was appointed, on May 6, to command the Fifth Corps, in succession to General Plumer, who took over the Second Army from General Smith-Dorrien, the hero of Le Cateau. The latter's relations with the Commander-in-Chief, Sir John French, had never been happy, and had now culminated in his removal from his command at the crisis of a battle.

CHAPTER VII

CORPS AND ARMY COMMANDER
(May 1915–June 1917)

I

THE FIFTH CORPS
(May–October 1915)

THE spring of 1915—and, indeed, the whole of that year—was a period of disappointment and disillusion for the British people and the British Army. Having checked the first great German onslaught in 1914, and having lived through a winter of discomfort and inaction, they looked forward to driving the Germans out of France as soon as the weather permitted large-scale operations. The French were confident; the enemy, who had counted on a speedy victory, must surely be disheartened; and the great Russian masses would be irresistible when they got on the move. The initial success of the attack at Neuve Chapelle on March 10 seemed to show that the enemy lines could be broken if the lessons learned in that attack were applied. But that day was almost the last of success; thereafter it was a year of triumph for the enemy and of defeat, almost of disaster, for the Allies. The two great French efforts to pierce the German line failed with heavy loss; the Russian hosts, far from invading Germany, were driven back many marches into their own territory; the attempt to force the Dardanelles, which might have shortened the War by two years, met the failure that irresolute strategy deserves and usually receives; the Italian decision to join the Allies brought little advantage; and at the end of a gloomy year Serbia was overrun. The British Army in France had close on 300,000 casualties, and lost on balance more ground than it gained. It was not yet ready for a great effort, and was short of the guns, ammunition, and trained men necessary for a blow heavy enough to break through the defences that German skill and industry had set up in France. Perhaps the one great fortune of the year, though it could only be appreciated in retrospect, was that the Germans chose to use their reserves in the east, where the Russians could retire almost indefinitely without suffering a vital loss, rather than on the Western Front, where French and British could not have yielded much ground without exposing the Channel ports or Paris.

In the Ypres Salient, where the Fifth Corps front was during the whole of Allenby's five months of command, conditions were especially onerous. Of the three great battles that were fought over that small parcel of Flanders and bear the name of the Battles of Ypres, the second, in April and May 1915, was the most dolorous and unsatisfactory. In the first battle, in 1914, the old army died grimly, confident in its warcraft and giving harder punishment than it received; and in 1917 at Passchendaele, the third battle, our forces had at least the impetus of the offensive, however bloody and unconvincing. But the troops that fought in the Salient in 1915 had neither confidence of skill nor hope of gaining ground. The old army was dead; the new armies and the new equipment were not yet ready. Struggling in a muddy plain, with the enemy holding the advantage of higher ground almost everywhere, they were overlooked, outgunned, outmanœuvred, and not a little bewildered by the new weapons of gas and liquid fire used against them. Only their obstinate courage kept a footing in that cramped semicircle and held the Germans from setting foot on the ramparts of Ypres.

When Allenby took over the Fifth Corps from Plumer the battle had already been raging for a fortnight. The first phase began with the German gas attack of April 22 and the abandonment by the French black troops of the northern face of the Salient, thereby exposing the Canadians at the eastern extremity and the British 27th and 28th Divisions on the southern face. It ended on May 3 with the withdrawal of the British forces from an untenable position at the apex of the Salient, when it became obvious that the French were unwilling or unable to carry out the promises repeatedly made by them to recapture the ground lost on the northern face. The second phase began on May 8, with a violent attack on the new positions of the Fifth Corps, within twenty-four hours of Allenby's assuming command, before he had had time to become acquainted with the troops or the ground. The Corps comprised the 4th, 27th, and 28th

Divisions,[1] all in the line. Several of the commanders who fought in them were to serve under Allenby in Palestine: Bulfin, who now commanded the 28th Division, became commander of his Twenty-first Corps; Longley, who commanded the 82nd Brigade, was to lead the 10th Division; and Bols, his future Chief of the Staff, was commander of the 84th Brigade.

The battle of Frezenberg, as it was called from the ridge which was the main objective of the German attacks, lasted from May 8 to 13, and cost the Fifth Corps over 9000 casualties. But they lost little ground. In the words of the Official History:

> Assisted by less than a dozen modern heavy guns, handicapped by lack of ammunition, the miserable condition of the trenches, and the unquestioned domination of the German artillery, the British had by their endurance and tenacity made even such a small success too costly to be continued.

After a pause of ten days the Second Battle of Ypres was brought to a close by a gas attack on the Fifth Corps line just north of the Menin road.[2] Two days' hard fighting with heavy casualties brought the Germans but slight gain of ground, and exhausted their battle-worn troops. By the end of May the fighting had died down, and the battered Salient had a short rest. As in the defence of the Messines–Wytschaete position by the Cavalry Corps in 1914, there had been little that Allenby could do to influence the fight except to place his scanty reserves at the disposal of his divisional commanders and to exhort them vehemently to recover by counter-attack the ground lost. This policy of counter-attack, which undoubtedly led to heavy losses, often with no corresponding gain, was laid on Allenby from above. It was, in fact, the accepted procedure of the British Army at the time. Allenby differed from other commanders only in the degree of his obstinacy. The policy had succeeded at the First Battle of Ypres in saving a desperate situation on many occasions. In 1915 the balance was changed: the Germans were better trained

---

[1] The 28th Division was relieved during the fighting by a dismounted cavalry force under General de Lisle.

[2] Allenby used to say of this period that the only meteorological service which told him whether the wind favoured a German gas attack or not was whether the smell from a pigsty near his headquarters was strong or faint.

and equipped for siege warfare; our troops and junior leaders were, except in bravery, the shadows of the men of 1914; and equipment, especially heavy artillery, was almost totally lacking. There was, however, little margin for retirement if Ypres were to be held.

Meanwhile farther south the French were making the first of their great efforts to break through the German front in what they call the Second Battle of Artois. The support by the British of their allies involved them in the bloody battles of Aubers Ridge (May 9) and Festubert (May 15–27). In mid-June the French effort was drawing to a close, but the First Army was directed to aid its final struggles by an attack at Givenchy, and the Second Army to support it by an operation in the Salient. The Fifth Corps, which now consisted of the 3rd, 50th, and 14th Divisions, accordingly made an attempt on June 16 to improve its line by a minor operation at Bellewaarde, in the very apex of the Salient. The attack, which was well planned, failed to reach its final objectives through no fault of the attackers; the German superiority in observation and in heavy artillery practically doomed such efforts in advance.

A characteristic story of Allenby relates to this offensive. He visited the division responsible for it while the preparations were being made, and asked if all their requirements were being met. He was told by the artillery commander that it was essential to triplicate all cables if artillery communications were to be maintained in the battle. Allenby asked how many miles of cable were required, and was told ninety. The staff officer with him said that such a request was unreasonable and quite impossible of fulfilment. But Allenby merely said to the gunner, " You shall have your ninety miles," and to the staff officer, " You will see that it is supplied," in a tone that admitted of no further discussion. The cable duly arrived in good time, and artillery communications held throughout the engagement.

Fighting continued in the uneasy Salient during July and August, and on July 30 the Germans, who apparently considered it a suitable area for experiments in frightfulness, won a few hundred yards of trenches near Hooge by the first use of machines for spraying liquid fire (*Flammenwerfer*).

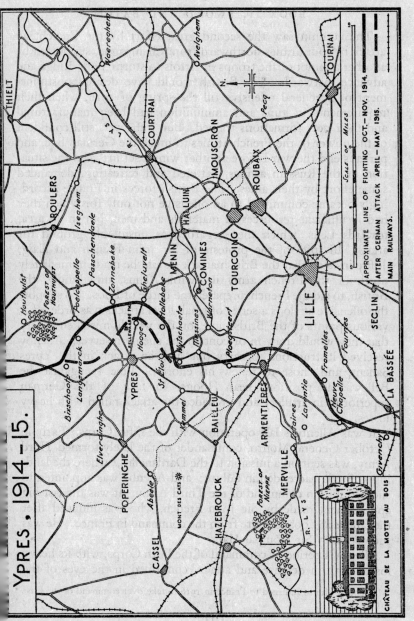

YPRES, 1914-15.

CHÂTEAU DE LA MOTTE AU BOIS

APPROXIMATE LINE OF FIGHTING OCT.—NOV. 1914.
AFTER GERMAN ATTACK APRIL—MAY 1915.
MAIN RAILWAYS.

SCALE OF MILES

N.

THIELT
Waereghem
Aveleghem
TOURNAI
Pecq
COURTRAI
R. LYS
MOUSCRON
HALLUIN
ROUBAIX
ROULERS
Iseghem
Passchendaele
Zonnebeke
Gheluvelt
MENIN
COMINES
TOURCOING
Poelcappelle
FOREST OF HOUTHULST
Houthulst
Bixschoote
Langemarck
Hollebeke
Wytschaete
Messines
Warneton
LILLE
SECLIN
Elverdinghe
BELLEWAARDE PARK
Hooge
YPRES
St. Eloi
Ploegsteert
Fromelles
LA BASSÉE
POPERINGHE
Abeele
Kemmel
BAILLEUL
ARMENTIÈRES
O Lavantie
Neuve Chapelle
Fauquissart
Fromelles
Fournes
Givenchy
CASSEL
MONT DES CATS
HAZEBROUCK
MERVILLE
Vieux Berquin
FOREST OF NIEPPE
R. LYS

E

The autumn saw the second great effort by the French, an attack by four armies northward from Champagne, supported by another attempt of the troops in Artois to storm Vimy Ridge and advance eastwards. The British would have desired postponement of a general offensive till the spring of 1916, when their requirements in guns and ammunition had been manufactured and their new formations trained. But Joffre was still confident of the power of the French armies to break the German line, and perhaps end the war before another winter set in; also the situation of the Russian armies, battered and retreating, demanded some effort by their allies. The British forces in France accordingly became committed to an offensive not only for which they had insufficient resources in materials and men, but in an area, towards Lens, which they regarded as unsuitable ground for attack. In spite of the protests of Sir John French and Haig, Joffre insisted that the British attack should be made immediately north of the French army in Artois. Thus, unwillingly, the British, to aid the French, prepared the Battle of Loos. To support the offensive at Loos a series of small local attacks was ordered at various points of the British line, on the wholly mistaken theory that they would draw in or contain the enemy reserves. Allenby received instructions to carry out such an attack in the Ypres Salient, and chose to renew his effort of June 16 against the Bellewaarde position, near Hooge. In face of the German superiority in artillery and grenades the attack failed with heavy losses.

It was Allenby's last operation with the Fifth Corps. Early in October General Monro, commander of the lately formed Third Army, was sent on a mission to the Dardanelles,[1] where the landing at Suvla had ended in failure; and Allenby was appointed to succeed him in command of the Third Army. It was the last big appointment made by Sir John French, who was induced after the failure at Loos to retire from the command in France. He was succeeded by Sir Douglas Haig.

Allenby's period of command of the Fifth Corps, with its heavy losses both in defence and attack, confirmed in the eyes of the

---

[1] General Monro returned to France in 1916 to take over command of the First Army.

majority of the Army his reputation as " the Bull." Yet the policy of continual counter-attack to recover lost ground and of local offensives on a limited front was not Allenby's; he merely carried out the orders of superior authority. Nor was that policy, nor the losses that resulted, confined to the Fifth Corps. At Neuve Chapelle, at Aubers Ridge, at Festubert, Givenchy, Loos, at all the battles fought by the British army in 1915, attacks and counter-attacks were ordered where failure was already obvious to the troops in the line; and the slaughter was as heavy as in the Salient. But Allenby's gospel of absolute loyalty to the orders of those above made him wholehearted in his persistence to push in while any possible chance of success remained. He never apologized, explained, or whittled down the orders received from above, and his strong, rough personality identified him in the eyes of the troops with the policy of ' drive at all costs.' [1]

The character of the Corps and Army commander, General Wayland-Leigh, nicknamed " the Buffalo," in C. S. Forester's well-known novel *The General*, is undoubtedly intended to represent Allenby. To those who knew him it is a grotesque caricature of the man, but it is possibly no more than a slightly exaggerated picture of him as he appeared to those who knew him by reputation only. The characteristics of the real man, his love of nature and of children, his disregard of danger, his loyalty and modesty, were recognized, as usual, by those who stood in close contact with him. His principal Staff officer of those days, General Jeudwine,[2] has written thus of him:

> During the time that I served under Allenby he was always a bulwark to his side and seemed a guarantee of the impossibility of defeat. He took care to explore personally the positions held by his troops, and on such expeditions he seemed regardless of danger from the enemy's observation. In any ramble with him about the lines

[1] A senior staff officer has said of this period, " Allenby's silent loyalty to his superiors had the effect of leading his subordinate commanders to assume that the responsibility for a mistaken policy was his own, and in certain instances some endeavoured by approach to G.H.Q. behind his back to effect his removal. Allenby was fully aware of this, but never allowed his knowledge to affect his treatment of the culprits."

[2] The late Lieutenant-General Sir Hugh Jeudwine, K.C.B., Director-General of the Territorial Army after the Great War.

we were then holding one of the pleasures of companionship with him came from his knowledge of animals, birds, trees, and flowers. He would often strike off from the safer route to follow a bird among the scrub surrounding a communication trench, or to examine a plant in a deserted cottage garden not far behind the front line. . . . When I call up memories of this great soldier, there comes before me a picture, not of a battleground, the grim and dreary waste of Flanders trenches, riven trees, and shattered houses, but of the enclosed yard of a girls' convent school at Abeele, in Belgium, the headquarters of the Fifth Corps in the latter part of 1915. In the school yard some two or three score of little Belgian girls are merrily executing complicated dance figures to the accompaniment of their own quite tuneful voices—their favourite air often haunts me still. And in a small, plain, square room, furnished with a table and a couple of chairs, his office, sits Allenby, glancing out occasionally with kindly interest from his window, commanding a view of the yard, at the noisy throng outside, and totally undisturbed by their chatter—in fact, often enjoying it. To him as he sits there come instructions from higher commanders, officers of his staff with reports or for orders, messages from his front needing immediate decision and action. Most men would have been hopelessly rattled by such incongruous surroundings at such a time. But not Allenby; he remained, as always, serene and unruffled, his brain working as clearly as ever. This serenity of disposition was an outstanding feature of his character; it never deserted him and helped to give the impression of a special dignity to his imposing figure. His mental qualities I will not discuss: they are apparent from his deeds. But for his great virtues of loyalty and modesty one cannot fail to record one's deep admiration. He was a great man and a great soldier, body and soul, and may perhaps come to be generally reckoned, as I reckon him myself, the greatest figure of the greatest war ever waged.

II

THE THIRD ARMY (TO THE BATTLE OF ARRAS)
(October 1915–November 1916)

The Third Army, when Allenby assumed command of it, consisted of two Corps, the Seventh and Tenth, to which were added a little later two more, the Thirteenth and Fourteenth.

By January 1916 the front held was twenty-two miles, from the Somme to near Arras. North of it, between it and the First Army, lay the Tenth French Army on a twenty-mile front. In March this front was taken over from the French, the First Army extending southward and the Third Army northward. At the same time the Fourth Army, under Rawlinson, took over the right of the Third Army front, from the Somme northward for some twenty miles. The British forces then held a continuous line of about ninety miles, from the east of Ypres down to the Somme, the order of the Armies from north to south being Second, First, Third, Fourth.

It was undoubtedly a disappointment to Allenby when the Fourth Army was put in on his right instead of on his left, and thus became responsible for the front immediately north of the Somme, which had been chosen some time before as the scene of the main British effort for 1916. Allenby had during the winter been studying plans for an offensive in that area, and naturally expected to have the command of the troops engaged. Now the battle was handed over to Rawlinson's Army; and the share of the Third Army was to be one of those subsidiary attacks to draw in reserves which had already proved so costly and so fruitless. This attack, made by two divisions on July 1, 1916—the opening day of the Somme battle—against the Gommecourt salient, on the right of the Third Army front, was intended to assist the main offensive of the Fourth Army, " by diverting against itself the fire of artillery and infantry which might otherwise be directed against the left flank of the main attack," as the official order put it. A thankless operation, for Gommecourt was probably the strongest point in the whole German line. Allenby, though he did not approve, was not the man to shirk such a task. As the Official Historian says:

> Neither General Snow of the Seventh Corps nor his Army commander were men of half-measures. If the enemy's attention was to be attracted to Gommecourt in order to ensure the success of the Fourth Army, they were ready to take all risks, but they did go to the length of suggesting that a threat from Arras would be more effective and less costly.[1]

[1] Official History, vol. v, p. 454.

In spite of some initial success, the attack ended in complete failure, so far as gaining any ground went, though it certainly fulfilled its mission of attracting fire. Both divisions lost heavily, and were compelled to fall back to the line from which they had started. The attack by the left Corps of the Fourth Army, which the diversion at Gommecourt was designed to assist, was equally ineffective.

During the autumn and early winter of 1916, while the Somme battle continued on its right, the Third Army front was comparatively quiet. The left of the Fourth Army front was taken over by the Fifth, under the command of Sir Hubert Gough, who had commanded the 3rd Cavalry Brigade and later the 2nd Cavalry Division under Allenby in the early part of the War. Gough had never at any time made a secret of his dislike of Allenby or of his poor opinion of him as a commander. Allenby was perfectly aware of what Gough said of him, but took no notice by word or deed.

In contrast to the continual storm of his six months with the Fifth Corps in the Ypres Salient, Allenby's command of the Third Army during 1916, the year of the 'attrition battles' of Verdun and the Somme, was uneventful. The Gommecourt operation, described above, was the only considerable fight on his front during this period, and any detailed account of the process of holding the line would be tedious. The trenches originally taken over from the French were poor, and required much improvement before they could be held on the British 'offensive' system; [1] but the chalk downs of Picardy were certainly better than the waterlogged fields of the Salient. Minor fighting above ground by artillery fire, raids, and sniping, and underground warfare by gallery and mine, continued on a smaller scale the attrition process which was taking place on so ruthless a scale at Verdun and on the Somme, but produced little decisive result. [2] During the Somme battle, by the process known as

[1] The thrifty French held a trench line on the 'Live and let live' principle as far as possible; the motto of the prodigal British was usually 'Kill and be killed.'

[2] The following figures show the relative pugnaciousness of the three Armies not engaged in the Somme battle. During the period from July 1 to November 15 the First Army made 166 raids on the Germans, and were raided 37 times; the Second Army made 104 raids and received 21; while the Third Army made 40 raids against

' roulement,' exhausted divisions from the French Army were constantly being exchanged for fresh ones from the other armies. So that the Third Army during the period consisted largely of divisions resting and recuperating from the Somme battle.

" Situation unchanged " was the normal daily report of the Third Army in 1916. But the life of an army commander, even though the front for which he was responsible might be comparatively quiet, was a busy one, especially for one like Allenby, who insisted on knowing men, places, and events at first hand so far as possible. Some account of the daily life and atmosphere of Third Army headquarters during Allenby's command will be sketched in the following pages.

The Army's original headquarters were at Beauquesne, a village about five miles south-east of Doullens. Allenby's residence was a small *château* about a mile outside the village. With him lived his two principal staff officers, Bols [1] and Sillem,[2] and his personal staff—Dalmeny, who had become his Military Secretary, and his two A.D.C.'s. Bols, the Major-General General Staff, was a gallant, sprightly little man, with a quick sense of humour, whose ready optimism and willingness suited Allenby. The principal officer on the administrative side (Deputy Adjutant and Quartermaster-General was his full official title) had broken down in health soon after Allenby took over the Army, and was succeeded by Major-General Sillem, an able and kindly staff officer, a little in awe at first of his formidable Chief, but soon on very good terms with him. Allenby's practice, by no means universal with generals, of never interfering with the work of his staff, and trusting them absolutely once he knew them, made him easy to serve in spite of his occasional gusts of temper. And Bols and Sillem were both men of sunny and attractive disposition, under whom it was pleasant to work; so that the Third Army staff, by the testimony of all its members, was a singularly happy body.

the German 7. The average of casualties per week were: First Army, 1000; Second Army, 2000; Third Army, 400.

[1] The late Lieutenant-General Sir Louis Bols, K.C.B., K.C.M.G., D.S.O., afterwards Governor of Bermuda.

[2] Major-General Sir Arnold Sillem, K.C.M.G., C.B.

The headquarters mess in the *château* was a cheerful one. Allenby, though never faddy about food, liked a good table,[1] and liked good talk; Bols was always lively, and Dalmeny had a very quick, if mordant, wit. Allenby, who kept personal contact with the whole of his staff, often had one or more members to dine, and every officer on first joining the Army staff was invariably summoned to dinner. For the junior officer who found himself on the right hand of this large general with the alarming reputation this was apt to be something of an ordeal. Allenby, with his very wide general knowledge and dislike of loose thinking, was not an easy conversationalist for a young or nervous man, who might, if he ventured on some conventionally held opinion, based on no sound knowledge, find himself flatly contradicted or sharply cross-examined on his reasons for advancing such views. But if he had anything to say or special knowledge of any subject Allenby would listen with interest and bring out his knowledge by shrewd and kindly questions. His personal contact with and interest in his staff did not end with this first dinner. He frequently visited quite junior members of it in their offices, and questioned them on their work.

One of the chief anxieties of the A.D.C.'s in this *château* was the lamps. There was no electricity, and the oil-lamps, unless very carefully tended, were apt to smell and to smoke, to Allenby's extreme annoyance. One evening, when this had happened, Bols came from Allenby's room, where he had left him in a state of great irritation, and told an A.D.C. that the Chief was complaining of a smell. The A.D.C., a newcomer who was unaware of the lamp troubles, suggested that it was probably the smell of the cider press in the cellar under the Chief's room, and that what he smelt was the cider-making. Bols, with his impish sense of humour, was delighted. " I should go and tell him that at once," he said; " he'll be very pleased to know." The unsuspecting A.D.C. went into Allenby's room and informed him that the smell was due to apples. Allenby looked up, surveyed him for a moment over his glasses, and then dismissed him in one explosive sentence. The crestfallen A.D.C. made a hurried exit, to find Bols and the rest of the staff assembled outside in great merriment,

---

[1] He had succeeded in borrowing a cook from the French Army.

anxious to hear exactly what the Chief had said to the cider suggestion.

When the Third Army went north, in March 1916, head-quarters moved to Saint-Pol, a small town about twenty miles west of Arras. Allenby and his personal staff lived in a small and not very convenient villa on the west of the town, which had been previously occupied by the French general d'Urbal. The water in the well which served the house was afterwards found to have been contaminated, and, probably from this cause, Allenby soon began to suffer badly from neuritis in the arm. In the autumn he moved to Bryas Château, a few miles north of Saint-Pol, where King George V had stayed while visiting the Front in the summer. This was a spacious and comfortable billet.

During the whole of his command of the Third Army Allenby spent the greater part of most days with his troops, visiting the front line, the headquarters of his Corps and divisions, or the administrative establishments behind the front. His frequent appearances in the trenches were a source of considerable anxiety to commanders and to the troops. In the first place, he never displayed the least concern for his own safety, and was not to be deterred from inspecting any trenches he wished to see because they, or the approaches to them, were being shelled; and, in the second place, Allenby's sudden explosions of temper, if he found anything wrong, were to be dreaded almost as much as an enemy bomb. These unfortunate outbursts, often over some compara-tively trivial breach of discipline, did much to destroy the good impression that the sight of the Army commander in the front trenches made, and to confirm the legend that " the Bull " was merely a bad-tempered, obstinate hot-head, a ' thud-and-blunder ' general.

When steel helmets were introduced Allenby was as insistent that they should be worn at all times as he had been over the matter of chin-straps when he commanded the cavalry. Again Allenby was right in principle. Steel helmets saved numerous casualties, and enemy shelling might begin at any time. Again, in the careless British way, the order, because irksome, was often ignored. Men, and officers, preferred the chance of additional risk to the certainty of additional discomfort.[1] Again Allenby met with unsparing condemnation any laxity that came to his notice, whatever the circumstances. On one of his visits to the trenches he found the body of a man, recently killed, on which was a cap instead of a helmet. He called attention to this with his usual anger at such breaches of discipline. The senior commander present pointed out, on the *De mortuis* principle, the indisputable fact that the culprit was dead. Allenby insisted, with force, on the equally unchallengeable fact that the corpse was proof that his frequently repeated orders were not being obeyed.

The story of this incident was widely told to illustrate what was supposed by many to be Allenby's rough, unfeeling nature. Actually it was part of the unsparing thoroughness to which a naturally kindly and sensitive man had schooled himself, to overlook no least disobedience of orders at any time. The same characteristic had caused him during the retreat from Mons to rate tired troopers, riding out from a hard-fought action, because their chin-straps were not down. His tours of the front line were, of course, by no means all sound and fury; but Allenby in his wrath was so notable a phenomenon that it was remembered as a thunderstorm is remembered, and the hours of fair weather forgotten. On one of these visits Allenby had found, while passing down a trench, a man sitting on the fire-step deeply engrossed in the delicate, or indelicate, task of delousing his shirt. He paused opposite him and remarked, " Picking them out, I see." " No, sir, no," said the man, without looking up; " just taking them as they come." The reply appealed to Allenby, who was himself meticulous in the use and meaning of words, and he related it with amusement.

In the back areas of his Army Allenby saw for himself every establishment that ministered to the welfare of the troops, and satisfied himself on its working. Few generals of high rank have been more scrupulous administrators. Especially was he careful with regard to the medical arrangements ; and when, as frequently happened, there were conflicting claims between the ordnance,

---

[1] A London hat-maker specialized in a light *papier mâché* helmet painted to resemble a steel helmet. It is said to have been advertised in his shop-window "As worn in the rear areas of the Third Army."

supply, and medical services for the use of a site or building, Allenby insisted always that the safety and comfort of the sick and wounded should be the first consideration. He issued strict orders that no ammunition depot or similar military store which might invite enemy shelling or bombing was ever to be within near range of a hospital or casualty clearing station. His care for the sick and wounded was shown outside rather than inside the hospitals, and was known to the medical staff rather than to the troops. For, though he frequently inspected the wards, he seldom spent much time in talking to the men in hospital. Perhaps he felt that bedside visits would accord ill with his reputation.

It was different with children. When a small girl was injured during a German bombardment of Saint-Pol and had to have her hand amputated Allenby visited her almost daily, and sent home to England for toys for her. After his visits he would drive round by her mother's house to give her the latest reports of her daughter and reassure her of her progress. This love of and gentleness with children seemed strange to those who did not know Allenby well. A staff officer who had with awe and pity listened to his furious denouncement of some comparatively trifling delinquency was surprised a few hours later to see the same man's encounter with a small child. The redoubtable Chief was striding up and down outside his headquarters when there appeared on the scene a small baby, two or three years old, cruising about on its own and crying. Allenby, thinking himself unobserved, picked it up and walked up and down with it, rocking it, talking to it, and soothing it till it stopped crying.

Till he left France Allenby continued his interest in the two small refugee children, Marthe and Sidonie, whom he had adopted as friends during his command of the Cavalry Corps. He had made another small friend—Aline, about four or five years old, at his headquarters of the Fifth Corps; and he used to correspond with her through one of the nuns. He always showed consideration and friendliness to those on whom he was billeted. The nuns at the Mont des Cats when he was commanding the Cavalry Corps, and those at Abeele when he commanded the Fifth Corps, always remembered gratefully *le bon général Allenby*, and Allenby always visited them when he passed that way. His friendship with the Baroness de la Grange has already been described.

The kindly side of Allenby's nature was often unsuspected by those who knew him only slightly, and came as a surprise when it was revealed. One of his staff has recorded a typical experience. He writes:

> When I first came to Army headquarters I saw little of him except when he came casually into the office; on these occasions he always gave one the impression of being very gruff. Later I had to drive alone with him on several occasions to the Army School, which was an hour or more away by car. The first time we did the drive I was horror-struck at the idea of spending an hour alone with " the Bull "; but I soon found that we had a common interest in birds, animals, and flowers, and that his knowledge of them was considerable; also that he enjoyed talking about them; so our other drives passed most pleasantly. I remember being impressed in the various things he said by his kindly outlook towards people, which seemed so much at variance with his brusque manner.

The year 1916 was not altogether a happy year for Allenby. To begin with, his health, almost for the first time, bothered him. The contaminated water at Saint-Pol had, as already mentioned, induced a severe attack of neuritis in the arm. To cure this he was advised to take a course of electrical treatment at Boulogne, where he went for a fortnight in July.[1] This treatment did little good to his neuritis, and the rays burned his skin and started boils, from which he suffered the greatest pain for several months. It was a marvel to his staff that he bore it so patiently, with so little increase of irritability.

Secondly, his relations with the Commander-in-Chief, Sir Douglas Haig, and with the staff at General Headquarters were increasingly difficult. The difficulties were none of Allenby's making. It did not take any member of the Third Army staff long to discover that the surest way to ' ship a green sea ' (the term current at Third Army Headquarters for incurring Allenby's displeasure) was to criticize or question in any way, in speech or on paper, any order or decision from General Hadquarters. But

---

[1] His absence caused a rumour that he had been *dégommé* as a result of the Gommecourt failure.

at the periodical conferences of Army commanders it was obvious that Allenby's opinion carried little weight, and received scant attention, especially if Gough, commander of the Fifth Army, had a different view. Often Sir Douglas Haig would turn to one of the other Army commanders and ask his opinion on some point while Allenby was still speaking. Such treatment naturally disconcerted Allenby, who was never a very quick debater—few soldiers are—and caused him to show himself at a disadvantage. He and Haig had never been congenial to each other, and there probably was some touch of jealousy in Haig's attitude. He must have known by the end of 1916 that others were being considered for his place at the head of the British forces in France, and that the new Prime Minister, Mr Lloyd George, would be glad to find a commander more tractable to his ideas. Allenby obviously was a possible rival, and his qualifications for the appointment were certainly reviewed by those who directed policy in England. Allenby, needless to say, did nothing whatever by word or deed ever to put himself forward.

To add to Allenby's anxieties, his only son, Michael, had come to France in the autumn of 1916 and was constantly engaged. Though still under nineteen he had already a year's service as an officer. He had joined the Royal Military Academy in the spring of 1915, a few months after his seventeenth birthday. Six months later, on October 26, 1915, he was commissioned in the artillery. Within six months he had the distinction of being specially selected for posting to the Royal Horse Artillery. He came to France at the beginning of 1916, and in February 1917 was awarded the Military Cross. The record in the *Gazette* runs:

> For conspicuous gallantry in action. He ran out communications to the two forward companies and sent back very useful reports on the situation. Later he rescued a wounded man under heavy fire. He displayed marked courage and determination throughout the operations.

The battery to which he belonged was in the Third Army, and whenever there was heavy fighting Allenby would come stamping down the corridor in the evening to the office to which the casualty reports came, push the door open with his stick, and would say, looking out of the window with his back to the room,

" Have you any news of my little boy to-day ? " When the officer in charge replied, " No news, sir," he would stamp out without ever showing his face. He knew only too well the rate of mortality of second-lieutenants in France.

III

THE BATTLES OF ARRAS: PREPARATION AND EXECUTION
(*Winter* 1916–*June* 1917)

> Even so my sun one early morn did shine
> With all-triumphant splendour on my brow;
> But out, alack! he was but one hour mine.
>
> SHAKESPEARE, *Sonnet* XXXIII

The idea of the Arras battles was first formed in October 1916, when the Allies began to lay their plans for the following year. The experience of the long struggles at Verdun and on the Somme seemed to show that neither side could obtain quick results, and Joffre's proposals for 1917 amounted to no more than an extension of the Somme battle and a continuance of the wearing-down process. On the British front the dent made by the Fourth and Fifth Armies opposite Albert had placed the German defences in front of Bapaume in a salient which invited attack. The Third Army was to break into the north side of this salient and move south-east in conjunction with renewed attacks by the Fourth and Fifth Armies, while the First Army covered the northern flank by an assault on the Vimy Ridge, for which the French had striven so often and so vainly. To the south the French armies were to broaden the front of attack still further by an assault between the Somme and the Oise. The opening of the offensive was to be on February 1. Joffre promised no quick, cheap, or easy results. But the battles of 1916 had obviously gone far to sap German endurance; the Allies were still capable of a great effort, though for the French, in view of their waning man-power, it was probably the last great effort. The technique of attack had greatly improved during 1916, and the front of attack would be broader than ever before. If the Russians and Italians by simultaneous offensives could hold the enemy divisions in their theatres the German defences in the West might well collapse under the strain.

It is probable that Joffre's plan, though unspectacular, was the best available, and might have had a great measure of success. But it was never to be tried. The French had grown restless, feeling themselves near the end of their resources. A large part of France had lain under the invader's heel for over two years, and to win it back piecemeal, as the shattered fragments of an endless battlefield, was a repellent prospect. Theirs was not the British method of fighting, to take punishment grimly for round after round and to wear down the opponent by heavy, if clumsy, body blows and tireless infighting. Their genius lay in the lightning attack, a quick rain of blows on a bewildered adversary, and victory by a knock-out. Their headlong attempt in 1914 had brought them to the very edge of disaster, and had led them to trust in the solidity of Joffre for over two years. Now their patience was wearing thin, and at the crucial moment a new prophet of the unlimited offensive and of quick victory was found.

Nivelle, like Brusilov on the Russian side, is known to the casual reader of war histories only as the author of the offensive which bears his name. He was an artillery officer whose courage and skill had brought him rapid advancement during the War. In the summer of 1916 he succeeded Pétain as commander of the Verdun front, and on October 24 won a great success by a brilliant stroke which recovered much of the ground lost to the German attacks of the previous spring and summer. He persuaded himself, and all those whom he met, that he could repeat the same success on an unlimited scale for the whole Western Front. He was the type of soldier who appealed to the civilian statesmen who directed the War. He was sympathetic in manner, clear and fluent in exposition, supremely confident of success. Joffre seemed to offer only the nightmare of heavy losses and slow progress; this new commander had dreams to sell, dreams of quick and crushing victory.[1] On December 12, 1916, he was appointed to succeed Joffre in command of the French armies,

---

[1] The state of mind that Nivelle had induced in some French officers is illustrated by a visit paid to Allenby's headquarters by some senior French officers shortly

and at once issued a fresh plan of campaign. On December 15 he appeared to confirm his reputation by a second and even more successful attack at Verdun.

By Nivelle's plan the main battle was moved south, to the Aisne front, and was to be purely a French effort. The British share was to consist of a holding attack on the Arras–Somme front, a little before the French attack. Further, the British Commander-in-Chief was to relieve French troops on some twenty miles of front south of the Somme, in order to enable Nivelle to form the 'mass of manœuvre' of twenty-seven divisions with which he proposed to exploit the initial break through. Haig reluctantly agreed under pressure from the Prime Minister, Mr Lloyd George, who had been so captivated by Nivelle's confidence and eloquence (he spoke English perfectly) that he made an attempt to place the British army directly under his command. This extension of the front meant that the Fourth and Fifth Armies would have little strength available for offensive operations; and thus the brunt of the British effort fell on Allenby's Third Army, though the First Army, on his left, was still to secure the Vimy Ridge.

Allenby submitted his plan to General Headquarters early in February. The project shows clearly his realization of the importance of administrative questions. The necessity for close control of traffic on the roads is one of the first essentials that he mentions, and he rightly insists on the supreme importance of the road problem. He knew that if troops were to maintain their energy over a long day's fighting they must start well fed; and the time of the original assault was to be " at an hour which will admit of the troops having a satisfactory breakfast in daylight before attacking—care is to be taken that this meal is a good one." He saw that if rapid progress was to be made rapid decisions would be necessary, and announced that " staffs will move with the troops, and staff and other officers will require horses." But the principal feature of his plan was the determination to secure

before the battle. When they saw his map with the various objectives marked in colours they threw up their hands and with much Gallic gesture exclaimed, " What is it, this green line, this black line, this brown line? The word is, ' To Berlin, to Berlin! ' "

surprise as far as possible by a short, intensely violent artillery bombardment. His artillery chief, General Holland, was a man of ideas, and, like his Chief, had the character to put his ideas into practice. By experiment he satisfied himself, and Allenby, of the feasibility of maintaining a continuous rate of rapid fire without exhausting the *personnel* or causing undue wear on the guns. A week was at this time considered the minimum period of artillery preparation necessary for a great battle. In Allenby's plan it was to last for forty-eight hours only.

G.H.Q. was profoundly shocked at these revolutionary ideas. The reply sent to Allenby objected that he had miscalculated the factor of wear on the guns, that the artillery *personnel* had not sufficient training to maintain rapid fire for so long, that it would be impossible to observe the effects of the fire, that the wire on the further objectives would be insufficiently cut, and that in any case the attempt to obtain surprise was useless, since other preparations would betray to the enemy the imminence of an attack. Allenby stood firm. He was satisfied with his experiments in sustained rapid fire; he did not believe that even a week's bombardment could guarantee fully cut wire on distant objectives; he thought that a rapid advance by surprise would be likely to find such defences so thinly manned that the cutting could be completed by hand, and that, while absolute surprise as to the front of attack was probably impossible, it was quite possible to surprise the enemy completely as to the date and time of attack, and thus to make use of this most powerful, but sadly neglected, element of war.

G.H.Q., faced by the unpleasant prospect of having to change either its laboriously acquired ideas of war on the Western Front or the commander of the Third Army, hit on a brilliant compromise. General Holland was promoted to command a Corps, and Allenby was given in his place an artillery commander of orthodox views. Thus outflanked, Allenby consented to doubling the period of preparation to four days. But he still sought by every means to obtain as great a measure of surprise as possible.

While the Allies were slowly elaborating their plans, the Germans, who were usually a move ahead of their opponents strategically and tactically, were quietly preparing to slip away from what threatened to be a deadly fall. Soon after the middle of February they evacuated the dangerous Bapaume salient, and in the middle of March began their retreat on a fifty-mile front to the famous Hindenburg Line. Joffre's plan, had he still been in power and had it been possible for his plan to be executed punctually, might have caught the Germans at a disadvantage. As it was, their withdrawal was unmolested, and the Allies could only push forward slowly through a countryside devastated with Teuton thoroughness and with a ruthlessness that had not been seen in Europe for some hundreds of years.

The effect on the Allied plans in general, and on the Third Army plan in particular, was considerable. The Fourth and Fifth Armies had to move forward opposite new and unreconnoitred positions of great strength over an area in which all communications had been systematically destroyed. Their power to assist the Third Army's attack was very materially reduced, almost negatived. The same applied in a lesser degree to the southern front of the Third Army, in which the right-hand assaulting Corps would now have fresh positions to face and an entirely new problem. As it turned out, it would have been better if this Corps had not attacked at first, and if the whole weight of Allenby's initial blow had been shifted farther north. But it was late for recasting plans on which so much preparation had already been spent.

Nivelle professed that the German retirement was entirely favourable to his project. But Nivelle's stock was already falling. Not only were the French Army commanders critical of his panacea for victory, but the Government which installed him had fallen, and some of the new Government were sceptical. There was even some talk of a fresh Commander and a fresh plan; but it was rightly decided that it was too late to change. The German move had been well timed. By the sacrifice of a pawn they had disconcerted the whole of their opponent's game. Not only had they escaped from a dangerous position, but by shortening their line they had made available more guns and reserves to meet the impending attack; and it was this fact that in the event was to limit the British advance and to swell their losses.

The Arras battles were fought on the eastern spurs of the

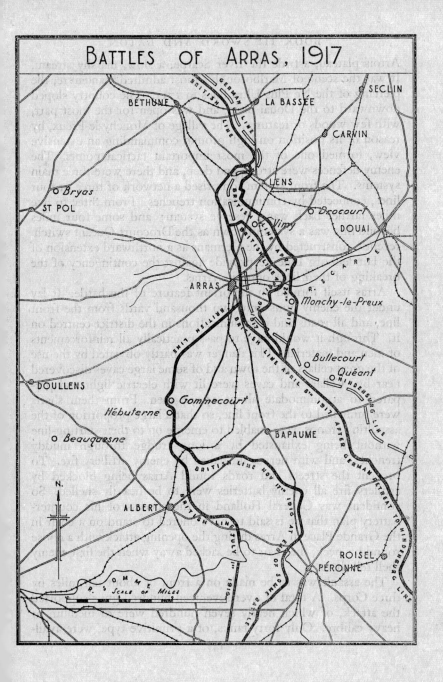

BATTLES OF ARRAS, 1917

SECLIN

BÉTHUNE

LA BASSÉE

CARVIN

Bryas

ST POL

Drocourt

DOUAI

Lens

Vimy

ARRAS

R. SCARPE

Monchy-le-Preux

Bullecourt

Quéant

HINDENBURG LINE

DOULLENS

Gommecourt

Hébuterne

Beauquesne

BAPAUME

ALBERT

ROISEL

PÉRONNE

R. SOMME

N.

Scale of Miles

BRITISH LINE

GERMAN LINE

BRITISH LINE APRIL 9th 1917

BRITISH LINE APRIL 24th 1917

BRITISH LINE APRIL 8th 1917

BRITISH LINE NOV 17th 1916

BRITISH LINE AT END OF SOMME BATTLE 1916

BRITISH LINE JULY 1st 1916

AFTER GERMAN RETREAT TO HINDENBURG LINE

Artois plateau, astride the river Scarpe, a slow, marshy stream. It was the scene of Marlborough's most admired manœuvre, the piercing of the Ne Plus Ultra lines in 1711. The country sloped downward to the Douai plain, and was open for the most part, with few woods or features. The village of Monchy-le-Preux, by reason of its position on high ground commanding an extensive view, formed one of the most important tactical points. The enemy defences were strong and deep, and there were three main systems. The front system comprised a network of three or four lines, connected by communication trenches. From three to five miles farther back was a reserve system; and some four miles beyond this was a system known as the Drocourt-Quéant switch, recently constructed by the Germans as a northward extension of the Hindenburg Line, to provide against the contingency of the breaking of their lines opposite Arras.

Arras itself formed an important feature of the battle. It lay under the enemy guns only two thousand yards from the front line, and all roads and communications in the district centred on it. Through it would have to pass practically all reinforcements of men and material. This danger was partly obviated by the use of the great cellars of the town and of some large caves discovered near by. Cellars and caves were lit with electric light and prepared to accommodate about 25,000 men. From them shafts were tunnelled to the front line, so that a large proportion of the assaulting troops were enabled to emerge on to their starting-line without being exhausted by a long trudge through muddy trenches, and with nerves unshaken by enemy artillery fire. To prevent the streets and roads round Arras being blocked by artillery fire all enemy batteries were to be heavily shelled. So confident was General Holland in the success of his counter-battery plan that he is said to have offered to stand on a chair in the Grande Place in Arras during the opening attack with a noose round his neck, the chair to be kicked away when the first enemy shell fell there.

The assault was to be made on a front of about ten miles by three Corps. A total of over seventeen hundred guns supported the attack, of which nearly seven hundred were of medium or heavy calibre. Only forty tanks, of a primitive type, were available, and they were distributed along the front and worked in small groups. Though they did some useful work in the Arras battles, they were on the whole a disappointment. The technique of a mass attack by tanks had not yet been evolved; the weapon and its tactics were still in the experimental stage.

The following is from a book written by the officer in command of the Tank Corps unit supporting the Third Army, a man of very independent and outspoken views:

It was an anxious moment when I took my seat at the first conference held by General Allenby, commanding the Third Army, in whose area the main battle was to take place.

From the outset there was only one person in the room, and that person was Allenby. He completely dominated. With the utmost clearness and a minimum expenditure of words, he outlined his plans. He put a few queries to various members of the conference and noted their replies. I was asked one or two questions concerning my proposed co-operation, which, fortunately, I was able to answer without hesitation.

After the conference was over Allenby detained me for a few moments and told me how confident he felt that the tanks would prove of great value, and assured me that he, personally, would give all the help he could and would watch the activities of the new arm with the keenest interest. It was a most thoughtful and encouraging gesture and served to spur us on to further efforts towards success, if that, indeed, were possible. It is small things such as these which distinguish the great man from the lesser and ensure a loyalty and devotion which go far to bring about the best results.

At one time or another I served under most of the senior commanders in France during the War, but I never met one under whom I would serve so gladly again as under General Allenby.

Of all the commanders in the field who occupied high positions in the British Army during the War, General Allenby must be regarded as the greatest. Not only was he a born leader of men, with a most determined and resolute character, but he possessed an extremely imaginative and far-seeing mind and was not afraid to depart from the stereotyped methods of warfare.[1]

The date of the assault was originally fixed for Easter Sunday, April 8. It was to precede the great French offensive on the Aisne

[1] *From Chauffeur to Brigadier*, by Brigadier-General Baker-Carr.

by about a week. At the last moment, after the bombardment had begun, the French asked for a postponement of twenty-four hours, and the attack actually began on the morning of Easter Monday, April 9.

Easter Sunday was fine and sunny, and facilitated the final stages of the artillery preparation. But during the following night the troops waiting in the trenches to assault were drenched with heavy rain and sleet, a presage of the unfavourable weather which was to continue throughout the Arras battles. Next day storms of sleet and snow, fortunately driven into the enemy's face by a strong wind, alternated with fine intervals. The success of the initial attack was the greatest yet achieved by British arms on the Western Front, and the action ranks with the Messines battle two months later, the Battle of Cambrai at the end of the year, and the day of August 8, 1918, as one of the most considerable victories won by the British on the Western Front in a single day's fighting. The artillery preparation had been well done (the enemy was undoubtedly surprised by its comparative shortness); and the assaulting battalions, of whom over one-third were Scottish, went forward with great dash. Over 6000 prisoners and many guns were taken, and on part of the front an advance of some three and a half miles was made. On the left the First Army stormed the famous Vimy Ridge, which had resisted so many assaults.

It seemed for a moment as if the fabric of the enemy defence had at last been irretrievably torn. Undoubtedly much ground could have been won at little cost on the 10th had the leading troops pushed on at once. Allenby's orders were clear that the advance was to be continued on that day, but were perhaps not sufficiently emphatic on the need for vigorous action, and valuable time was wasted. Next day the order was given for a ' pursuit,' but it was twenty-four hours too late. The cavalry brought forward for exploitation jammed the roads and accomplished little.

Progress on the 10th and 11th was both slow and costly. The commanding height of Monchy-le-Preux was won, where a brigade of cavalry suffered heavy loss in attack, but did valuable work in defence. The enemy had sewn the rent in his line, hastily and crudely, but strongly enough to resist anything but a full-dress attack. On the 14th Sir Douglas Haig ordered the opening

stage, known officially as the First Battle of the Scarpe, to be
brought to an end. Over 7000 prisoners and more than a hundred
guns had been collected. He announced that he himself would
make the plan for the next stage, which was to be a combined
attack by the Fifth, Third, and First Armies. But the intended
offensives of the Fifth and First Armies were reduced or postponed for various reasons. The Second Battle of the Scarpe
(April 23–24) became for all practical purposes an attack by the
Third Army alone, with troops already tired, and thinned by
hard fighting and hard weather. Two days' fierce struggle
brought comparatively small gain of ground, but inflicted heavy
loss on the enemy, who yielded over 2250 prisoners, at a cost to
the Third Army of some 8000 casualties. The battle was fought
under the shadow of the failure of the French offensive, which
had begun on April 16, and, in spite of some success, had completely failed to achieve the break-through which Nivelle had
promised and on which his whole plan depended. By April 23
it was even doubtful whether the French would persevere in their
offensive at all. Unless the French could break through, the Arras
battles had no strategical objective; and unless the French offensive was to continue they had no tactical meaning, since their main
purpose was to draw the enemy reserves from the French front.

There were some isolated actions during the remainder of
April, at the end of which the total British captures were 18,000
prisoners and 250 guns, of which the Third Army share was
11,300 prisoners and 185 guns. But the casualties had been heavy,
and the troops were desperately weary. They had been fighting
in appalling conditions of weather and ground for nearly a month
without relief. Yet they were called on for a final effort. The
First Battle of the Scarpe had been fought in sure faith of victory;
the Second in good hope of success; but this Third Battle, on
May 3, was mere charity. It was now practically certain that the
French effort was spent, though it was not yet known that it had
resulted in the mutiny of a large part of the French Army. The
main object of the new British battle was to gain a good defensive
line on which the struggle could be stayed. It was again planned
by G.H.Q. as a combined effort by the First, Third, and Fifth
Armies; and this time all three Armies attacked. But the fatal

mistake was made of fixing the hour of attack in the dark, to suit the ideas of the Fifth Army, against the advice of the commanders of the First and Third Armies, who wished to wait for the dawn. Allenby protested strongly, but Gough had the ear of the Commander-in-Chief, and his protests were overborne. The result, owing largely to the confusion of untrained reinforcements in the darkness, was a complete and costly failure.

Desultory fighting continued for a little longer on the Third Army front, and the Fifth Army still battered at Bullecourt, but by the middle of May the Battles of Arras were over. By that date Nivelle had fallen, and Pétain, a general of the sound and stubborn type, with little mind for brilliancies, had succeeded him. The policy of attrition was again the order of the day, and the British Commander-in-Chief, Sir Douglas Haig, turned with a sigh of relief to the preparation of his long-cherished Flanders offensive. The Battles of Arras and the high-flown projects of Nivelle had never been to his taste. He was confident of British ability to endure and outstay, but was mistrustful of short cuts and unorthodox schemes. The whole history of this April offensive, like many an April day in its brilliant, treacherous promise and bleak ending, had been unfortunate. In Joffre's original plan for 1917 it had a clear strategical purpose, which became less clear in Nivelle's grandiose scheme and almost vanished when the Germans withdrew to the Hindenburg Line. What was designed as a three-act drama became a mere curtain-raiser—a curtain-raiser to Nivelle's failure that was hissed from the stage.

The Third Army, on which the brunt of this spring offensive fell, bore the consequence of the change of policy and of the Commander-in-Chief's attitude to the battle. Haig, with an eye always on his Flanders offensive, would not relieve the hard-ridden Third Army divisions with fresh divisions from the Second Army in the north. He was never very sympathetic to the Third Army and its commander. Shortly before the battle began he suggested the removal of one of Allenby's Corps commanders, who was alleged to be tired. Allenby refused to change him. On the eve of the original attack Allenby was informed that his plan of battle appeared faulty to the Commander-in-Chief, and that the responsibility for failure would lie on him. After the success of the first attack the Chief of General Staff at Haig's headquarters visited Allenby with a proposal that he should hand over his right-hand corps to the Fifth Army for better co-ordination. The proposal brought an explosion in which Allenby relieved himself of much pent-up feeling, and was not renewed.

The Arras offensive left Allenby's personal reputation much as before. The brilliant opening, which vindicated him in the eyes of those who knew his true abilities, was obscured by the subsequent lack of success and heavy losses, which were ascribed by many to his violent obstinacy. A shrewd critic, writing at the time,[1] shows how he puzzled the outside observer:

> Opinions vary about Allenby almost to the very extremes as regards his capacity. His nickname " the Bull " represents one side—the idea that he can simply bang forward in a blind sort of fashion, but won't be turned; the other rates him very much more highly as a scientific soldier. I don't know which is the true estimate, perhaps neither.

Meanwhile events on the borders of Palestine were leading up to Allenby's translation from France and his vindication as a skilful soldier and great leader of men. The Egyptian Expeditionary Force, under Sir Archibald Murray, had during the latter half of 1916 driven the Turks from the Sinai Desert by a series of skilful actions, and had bridged the hundred and twenty miles of desert by a railway and pipe-line. These successes brought the force in the spring of 1917 up against Gaza, the historical gateway of Palestine on the south. The army was twice repulsed in attacks on this natural stronghold, and came to a halt. The Prime Minister, Mr Lloyd George, who was always seeking a strategical ' soft spot ' and a way of escape from the slaughter of the Western Front, demanded that this campaign should be set going again with fresh troops and a new leader. He offered the command to Smuts, the South African, lately returned from East Africa, where he had driven the Germans from most of the territory they held, but had failed to end the activities of their enterprising

[1] F. S. Oliver, in *The Anvil of War.*

leader, von Lettow-Vorbeck, and had lost a large proportion of his men and animals through sickness and overwork. Smuts refused the Palestine command. His own account of the reasons for his refusal is that an interview with Sir William Robertson, the Chief of the Imperial General Staff, convinced him that he would not have the backing of the War Office, who disliked the idea of diverting troops from the Western Front for a ' sideshow.'

On Smuts's refusal Robertson recommended Allenby. He must have known that the relations between Haig and Allenby were not happy; and if the Prime Minister wanted a man to put fresh movement into a stagnant campaign, there could be no better choice than Allenby. Early in June, while the Third Army was taking over the front of the Fifth Army, which had been ordered north for the Flanders offensive, Allenby was summoned home, preparatory to receiving the command of the Egyptian Expeditionary Force. His first reactions were those of dismay. He believed that he was being removed from France and relegated to an unimportant command because of the limited success of the Arras battles. To his successor in the Third Army, Byng, he unburdened himself bitterly; and it was not till after he reached London and had interviews with the Prime Minister and the Chief of the Imperial General Staff that he began to reconcile himself to the change.

It was characteristic of his departure that he went out of his way and made himself late for dinner at General Headquarters in order to say farewell to one of the children he had befriended. During the Battles of Arras his staff had once sought him for some time in vain, to find him at the bedside of his child friend, who had been maimed by a bomb. One last incident of this final journey to Boulogne is worth recording. On his arrival in France in 1914 he had been allotted a somewhat ancient Rolls-Royce, which he had used ever since. During the campaign a new body, much too heavy for the chassis, had been put on it in Paris, and breakdowns had been frequent. Now it broke down irretrievably on the final stage, and his driver, who had set his heart on bringing him safely in this same car to the port from which they had set out in 1914, was left disconsolate by the roadside.

CHAPTER VIII

THE TAKING OF JERUSALEM
(*June–December* 1917)

I

THE PREPARATION OF A CAMPAIGN
(*June–October* 1917)

After handing over command of the Third Army Allenby spent about a fortnight in England. At an interview with the Prime Minister, Mr Lloyd George, he was told that Jerusalem was wanted " as a Christmas present for the British nation," and that he was to ask for the reinforcements he found necessary to take it. He left Charing Cross on June 21, 1917. On this day, at Aleppo, Enver Pasha was holding a conference of the Turkish commanders on the Caucasus, Palestine, and Mesopotamia fronts to discuss the future of Turkish operations in the Eastern theatre. The plan was to recover with German assistance the city of Baghdad, which General Maude had captured in the previous March. Jemal Pasha, the Governor of Syria, struck a discordant note by insisting that the Palestine front first required reinforcement. The problem was to form the subject of acrimonious discussion in the Turkish Higher Command for some months, and was to be decided too late.

According to the Official History, Allenby assumed command of the Egyptian Expeditionary Force " at midnight on June 28, 1917." [1]

Allenby's arrival undoubtedly caused some " alarm and despondency " at headquarters in Cairo. His reputation was not a comfortable one for a staff which had become accustomed to the fleshpots of Egypt. Nor did the first actions of the new Commander-in-Chief restore their peace of mind. He went round all the rooms in General Headquarters and, as was his custom,

---

[1] In strict military parlance there could be no such time. It should be " at midnight June 28–29."

ascertained personally what each officer on his staff was doing. He at once formed the impression that the General Staff officers were too junior and inexperienced, and should be replaced. The senior officer of the Adjutant-General's branch, a Major-General, brought him on his first morning in the office a formidable pile of papers, dealing with details of dress, discipline, the administration of martial law, and such matters. Allenby studied the first two or three with rising irritation, and then asked if they were all of a similar nature. He ended by pitching the whole pile into the far corner of the room and forcibly forbidding that his time should ever again be wasted on details that a junior officer should decide. Within a week of assuming command he departed on a visit to the front, leaving behind a slightly shaken staff.

The Egyptian Expeditionary Force lay some three hundred miles from Cairo, on the southern borders of Palestine, with its main body opposite Gaza, on the coast, where it had twice suffered defeat, and with its right extended towards Beersheba, of the Seven Wells, the desert gateway of Palestine. The original mission of the Force had been to safeguard the Suez Canal; and in pursuance of this object, and to gain elbow-room for manœuvre, the Desert Column, consisting of the mounted divisions, the Camel Corps, and two infantry divisions, had advanced across the Sinai Desert during the autumn and winter of 1916, driving the Turks before it and pulling behind it a railway and pipe-line. It was a well-organized and well-conducted little campaign, which ended in an unexpected and somewhat unlucky repulse at the First Battle of Gaza in March 1917. Murray's strangely optimistic account of this battle led the Cabinet at home to believe that an easy success would attend a renewed effort, and he was ordered to advance into Palestine, with the capture of Jerusalem as his objective. The result was another and heavier reverse, at the Second Battle of Gaza, against the now strongly fortified Turkish position; the indirect consequence was the substitution of Allenby for Murray.

The Force on the Palestine front (known at this time as "Eastern Force") comprised three mounted divisions (Anzac, Australian, and Yeomanry) and four infantry divisions (52nd, 53rd, 54th, 74th). The Anzac Mounted Division consisted of two

Australian Light Horse brigades and the New Zealand Mounted Rifle Brigade, the Australian Mounted Division of two Australian Light Horse brigades and a Yeomanry brigade, and the Yeomanry Mounted Division of three Yeomanry brigades. There was also a brigade mounted on camels (the Imperial Camel Corps Brigade) and an independent Yeomanry brigade (7th Mounted Brigade). The 52nd (Lowland), 53rd (Welsh), and 54th (East Anglian) were first-line Territorial divisions which had fought in Gallipoli and in the campaign across the Sinai Desert; the 74th was formed of dismounted Yeomanry units, and had taken as its divisional badge a broken spur. A fifth division, the 60th (London), was in process of arrival from Salonika; it was composed of second-line Territorial battalions, and had fought in France before transfer to the Salonika front. A sixth division, the 75th, was being formed in Egypt from Territorial and Indian battalions from India and elsewhere. The material of the Force was magnificent. The men, for the most part, were seasoned troops, who had not suffered the crippling casualties of the Western Front, and who still retained a good proportion of the *personnel* with whom they had begun the War. Such men were veterans, with nearly three years of experience. At present they were discouraged and cynical: they had lost faith in the Higher Command and in themselves, and were, like the Israelites of old, weary of the hardships of the desert. Moreover, they were weak in numbers, having received few reinforcements from home. The Force was in the doldrums, becalmed and dispirited, held between failure and success. It needed the wind of Allenby's tremendous personality to fill the sails and give it steerage-way.

Allenby's arrival and this first short visit to the front made a remarkable change. Word went round that he had the backing of the War Cabinet and could command reinforcements in a way that Murray never could. The news that General Headquarters would move from Cairo to the front meant that the requirements and difficulties of the troops would at last be seen at close quarters and properly understood. But more than anything it was Allenby's personality that stirred their imagination and roused their hope. The Australian Official History writes thus of his coming:

He went through the hot, dusty camps of his army like a strong, fresh, reviving wind. He would dash up in his car to a Light Horse regiment, shake hands with a few officers, inspect hurriedly, but with a sure eye to good and bad points, the horses of, perhaps, a single squadron, and be gone in a few minutes, leaving a great trail of dust behind him. His tall and massive, but restlessly active figure, his keen eyes and prominent hooked nose, his terse and forcible speech, and his imperious bearing, radiated an impresion of tremendous resolution, quick decision and steely discipline. Troops who caught only one fleeting glimpse of him felt that here at last was a man with the natural qualities of a great driving commander who, given a great task and supplied, as Allenby was, with a great scheme for its accomplishment, would relentlessly force it through to its conclusion. At last they had a commander who would live among them and lead them. Within a week of his arrival Allenby had stamped his personality on the mind of every trooper of the horse and every infantryman of the line.

An officer of a Yeomanry regiment wrote, " Seldom in the course of military history has the personality of a new commander had such a marked effect on his troops."

The commander of Eastern Force, Sir Philip Chetwode, who had succeeded Dobell after the Second Battle of Gaza, was an old friend of Allenby, and had served under him twice previously —as commander of a regiment in Allenby's brigade before the War and as a brigade commander in the Cavalry Corps in France. Each man knew and appreciated the qualities of the other. Chetwode had one of the keenest and quickest brains in the Army and a remarkable eye for ground. He now presented Allenby with one of the shrewdest appreciations made during the War, the details of which had been worked out by his staff officer, Guy Dawnay.[1] The obvious line of advance into Palestine for a force with full command of the sea was along the coast. It was the most direct; it secured the advantages of naval co-operation; it covered the main line of communication to Egypt; and it presented comparatively little difficulty in the matter of water-supply. But Gaza, which barred the coast route, had become a fortress to be taken only by slow and costly process of siege. The

---

[1] Major-General G. P. Dawnay, C.B., C.M.G., D.S.O., M.C.

Turkish centre was also strong, and the approaches to it lay over a bare, open plain, dominated by the ridge on which stood the Turkish works, and almost devoid of water. There remained the Turkish left. The main position ended at Hareira, some four miles west of Beersheba. The works here were weaker and less complete and the ground more favourable to attack. Also there was here an open flank round which the great mass of mounted troops might be passed to operate against the Turkish rear. The Turkish detached garrison of Beersheba would have to be reduced by a preliminary operation and the water-supply of that place secured. The difficulties were many, but Chetwode recommended this as the most promising line of operation. He estimated the minimum force required at three mounted divisions and seven infantry divisions at full strength, with a considerable increase of artillery. Allenby, after inspection of the whole front, including a reconnaissance towards Beersheba between the British and Turkish lines, accepted Chetwode's view of the situation and adopted his plan. On July 12, on his return to Cairo, he cabled home an outline of the plan and his requirements in additional troops.

Even in this hurried visit, when almost every moment was taken up by interviews and reconnaissances, Allenby took his usual interest in the plants, animals, birds, and people of a new land. His letters to Lady Allenby, written from a train lying in a siding at the railhead, contain observations such as the following:

Of birds, there are larks, wheatears, shrikes, bee-eaters, hawks, vultures. Flamingoes frequent the mouths of the wadis. There is a merry bird, the rufous warbler, who haunts the locality. He is pert and friendly. Looks like a big nightingale, has the manners of a robin, and flirts his tail like a redstart. I saw one to-day attack a locust nearly as big as himself. There are also jackals, jerboas, lizards and scarab beetles. . . . The country is now parched and dry. In the spring it is covered with verdure, fields of barley, grass, flowers of many sorts—red-hot pokers, irises, etc. In the oases, and near the villages, are date-palms, and great quantities of fig-trees, apricots and almond-trees. There are great patches of an inferior sort of water-melon. One of the camps is in a fig and vine plantation, near the sea. Great fig-trees, 100 years old, grow right up and on to the sand dunes. The vines either sprawl on the sand or cover the fig-trees. . . . I was astounded to-day to see the camels browsing on prickly-pear cactus. I had always thought that the prickly pear was proof against any animal that had a palate and a tongue. But I see the camels eating it greedily, and paying no more heed to the awful spines than if they were bloom on a peach. . . . The people all look like Biblical characters. Face, dress, and everything like pictures from the Bible. Keen, handsome faces; picturesque Arab dress; ornaments of beads, coins and enamel, much as one sees in the Egyptian museums. The children are beggars, all. Very pretty, some of them. All attractive to me.

Otherwise these letters are a simple chronicle of his movements; there is not a word of the momentous plans he was discussing, or of military operations. This was characteristic. It was not just discretion, nor was there any affectation about it. It was simply that birds, beasts, and flowers interested him more than soldiering. Allenby was a conscientious correspondent: he answered all letters, usually in his own handwriting. But he was not a brilliant or even an interesting letter-writer. His letters kept strictly to the point at issue, and contained no gossip or commentary; they were usually mere 'situation reports,' never epistles. Whenever there is in them a flash of illumination, a telling phrase, or a clue to the writer's personality, the subject is almost invariably some new bird or flower or trick of Nature that has caught his notice.

It was while Allenby was returning from this first trip that the strange character who was in public estimation to share his fame in the Palestine campaigns, T. E. Lawrence, first saw him at Ismailia—"a very large and superior general." [1] In the same chapter of *Seven Pillars of Wisdom* Lawrence also describes his first meeting with Allenby at Cairo. His account ends:

> Allenby could not make out how much was genuine performer and how much charlatan. The problem was working behind his eyes, and I left him unhelped to solve it. [2] . . . At the end he put up his chin and said quite directly, "Well, I will do for you what I can,"

[1] *Seven Pillars of Wisdom*, Chapter LVI.
[2] Allenby never quite solved it, but always suspected a strong streak of the charlatan in Lawrence.

and that ended it. I was not sure how far I had caught him; but we learned gradually that he meant exactly what he said; and that what General Allenby could do was enough for his very greediest servant.

Allenby spent the next fortnight in Egypt, arranging for the transfer of G.H.Q. to the Palestine front, and inspecting the Base establishments, hospitals, and workshops in Cairo, Alexandria, and elsewhere. He showed his usual thoroughness in making himself personally acquainted, so far as possible, with every one and with everything that ministered to the efficiency of his army, and his usual common sense in deciding where change was required and where confidence could be reposed. One of his first orders permitted the wearing of trousers for office work and while on leave in Cairo, in place of the breeches and boots enjoined by his predecessor.

This is a suitable place to introduce an account of Allenby written by a famous ophthalmic surgeon.[1] It shows how Allenby impressed an extremely able civilian, and also illustrates well Allenby's inquisitive mind in any matter that might forward his campaign and the well-being of the soldiers under his command.

I first met General Allenby soon after he came to Egypt, when he consulted me about his eyes in Alexandria. I had heard much of his alarming personality, but, possibly because I was an independent civilian, a soldier only as regards my uniform, I was not in the least terrified by him, though he struck me at once as a great man both in mind and stature. He asked me about my job. . . . He told me that he had not had much time to acquire a knowledge of all the work which was being done by civilian specialists in the Egyptian Expeditionary Force since he arrived, but that I must go and see him when he had moved General Headquarters from Cairo and Ismailia to just behind the front. Shortly afterwards he moved General Headquarters up to the neighbourhood of Rafa, and no one who was in Egypt at that time will forget the fresh current of hope and inspiration which swept through the Egyptian Expeditionary Force after he had been in Egypt for a few weeks.

In due course I went up to General Headquarters, and within

---

[1] Sir Hubert Eason, C.B., C.M.G., M.D., M.S., President of the General Medical Council, and former Principal of the University of London and Superintendent and Senior Ophthalmic Surgeon, Guy's Hospital.

twenty minutes of reporting my arrival I was invited to dine with Allenby that evening. He put me next to him and began pumping me on my subject. Did I know anything about diseases of the eye in previous campaigns in Egypt and Palestine? Had I written anything about it or published it? I told him that I had just been translating that part of the memoirs of Larrey, Napoleon's famous chief medical officer, which dealt with ophthalmia, and had sent a paper on this subject home. I told him something about the disastrous epidemic of ophthalmia which blinded so many of Napoleon's army in Egypt during the campaign of 1798–1801. He asked me to send him a copy of my paper. . . .

His interest in everything appertaining to Egypt or Syria which might affect the troops or the progress of the campaign was insatiable. Whether it was a fly expert from the British Museum, a railway engineer, an expert on town-planning, or a naturalist who could tell him something about the flora or fauna of the country, he had them all up and sucked their brains of anything they could tell him. If they had something to tell him, he never forgot them: if they had not, heaven help them! He borrowed from me Myres' *Dawn of History*, Hogarth's *Ancient East*, volumes of Herodotus, a history of the Crusades, and other books, carried them off with him to the front, and when he returned them asked me for more.[1] He was so convinced that in the unchanging East history would repeat itself that from the beginning he said that the decisive battle of the campaign would be fought at the Pass of Megiddo. Going round one day in the neighbourhood of Ludd, he drifted (well, 'drifted' is not quite the word to describe Allenby's entry anywhere) into a bacteriological laboratory of which an old fellow-student of mine was in charge. He saw some charts on the wall, and asked their meaning, "Well, sir," said the bacteriologist, "those are charts of the seasonal incidence of malignant malaria in the Plain of Sharon, and I think that is the reason why Richard Cœur de Lion never got to Jerusalem. His army was nearly destroyed by fever, and I find that he came down the coast in September, when malignant malaria was at its height." This sort of information was manna from heaven to Allenby, and he never forgot it. . . .

[1] An incident which occurred shortly before the Third Battle of Gaza shows the range of Allenby's knowledge. A discussion arose about the site of the ancient historical route across Sinai. Allenby suggested reference to a passage in Strabo. Extracts from his works were obtained from Cairo in the original Greek, and Allenby translated the passage without difficulty.

After the Armistice, when Allenby came to live in Cairo, I occasionally had the pleasure of lunching with him and Lady Allenby. Nothing was more striking than the entire absence of formality, parade, and ceremonial when he was, so to speak, in his own home. He unbent entirely, was cheerful and merry, with an acute sense of humour, and, as during the campaign, he was keenly interested in anything connected with the country or with the welfare of the troops. When I said good-bye to him on going home in 1919 I felt that I was leaving one of the few really great men that I have met in my life. He had determination, a strong will, an imposing and imperious personality, but he was a lasting friend to anybody who knew his job and gave them credit for all that they had done. Though it is nearly twenty years ago, my memory of him is still quite vivid, and I have seen no reason after this lapse of time to vary my original impression that he was one of the few really great men I have met in the course of my life.

In the last week of July Allenby made another tour of inspection on the Palestine front. He returned to Cairo on July 31 to meet a cable from Lady Allenby telling him that their only child Michael had been killed in France. He had been hit by a splinter of shell which went through his steel helmet while he was walking from a detached gun to the remainder of the battery. He lived five hours, but never recovered consciousness. He was half-way through his twentieth year, and had won the Military Cross and been recommended for promotion to the rank of captain.

His battery commander wrote of him:

He had absolutely no notion of fear, and in every operation wished to go forward as Forward Observing Officer, but, of course, was only allowed to do it in his turn. He was the finest practical gunner of his rank that I have ever seen in France. The men all loved him and would do anything for him. In the mess he amused us greatly with his socialistic views and his defence of conscientious objectors. He was a good rider and a thorough sportsman.

This testimony is confirmed by others; there is no doubt that young Allenby's personality made a deep impression on all who knew him. Of all that generation of youth from whom the Great War took so terrible a toll in death or disillusion, to Britain's grievous loss, there were few of more promise than Michael Allenby.[1] Allenby took the shock with his unquenchable courage. He went on with his work and asked no sympathy. Only those who stood close to him knew how heavy the blow had been, how nearly it had broken him, and what courage it had taken to withstand it.

After his son's death Allenby obtained, with some difficulty, permission for Lady Allenby to go to Egypt. She arrived in October, and went to the Villa Heller, at Gezira. Her influence in the English community in Egypt was in its way as great as Allenby's at the front. She took a part in the direction of Red Cross work, in finding occupations and interests for convalescents and for officers and men on leave, and similar activities. Her imperturbable serenity was as effective in inspiring courage as was her husband's dynamic energy. She had in her gentle way as much strength of will and purpose as he had.

By the middle of August the first and most important steps in the preparation of the campaign had been taken. Allenby had received from the War Cabinet sanction for his proposals and a promise of nearly all the reinforcements he required; he had reorganized his army into three Corps; he had outlined his plan to his Corps commanders; and he had moved G.H.Q. from Cairo to the front. The camp was a little north of Rafa, at Umm el Kelab (" the mother of dogs "). It consisted partly of wooden huts and partly of tents, on a slight rise in the bare, sandy plain.[2] Summer conditions on the Palestine borders were extremely trying. There was no shade, and the temperature often rose to 110 degrees; sometimes a hot wind from the desert, the Khamsin, blew for days on end; there was constant dust; all cuts, even scratches, turned septic; and ' sand-fly fever,' which, though not dangerous, left its victims weak and exhausted for many days, was prevalent. Only a regular sea-breeze kept the heat down and

[1] Young Allenby's memory is preserved in the battery in which he served (T Battery, Royal Horse Artillery) by a fund which Allenby and his wife established after the War from the money Michael had left. The fund is used mainly to provide and keep up a sitting-room and library for the men of the battery.

[2] It was curious to learn that a large proportion of Scotch whisky was distilled from barley grown on this dusty plain, which became green with the rains of winter.

made the nights reasonably cool. The roads were sandy tracks, negotiable only by the power and majesty of Rolls-Royce or the irrepressible mobility of Ford—the old-model 'tin Lizzie' that bumped and banged its way across Egypt, Sinai, Palestine, and Syria, often where nothing else mechanical would go, and was an invaluable asset to the Egyptian Expeditionary Force.

The Commander-in-Chief, in spite of the dust and the heat and the roughness of the tracks, was constantly round all parts of the front. His first visit to the headquarters of the Corps on the coast was made in a particularly disreputable Ford truck, as his own cars had not arrived. He sat perched up on the front seat alongside the driver, an Australian, who was clad only in a sleeve-less vest and very attenuated shorts. The picture of these two, with one of the personal staff bumping painfully in the body of the truck behind, remained long in the memory of those who witnessed it.

There was much to be done and much to see. The increase of the force involved great administrative changes and develop-ments, from the advanced base at Kantara, on the Suez Canal, to the front line. The railway was being doubled; and special construction gangs were trained to enable it to be rapidly pushed forward when the advance began. Pipe-lines for water were developed and extended. Depots of ammunition and stores of all kinds had to be accumulated. Allenby was fortunate in having as his Quartermaster-General one of the most capable and ex-perienced administrative officers in the Army at the time, Major-General W. Campbell.[1]

As usual, Allenby saw everything for himself—trench line, camps, hospitals, depots, watering arrangements, and all adminis-trative establishments. His constant presence and obvious deter-mination to do everything possible for their comfort heartened the troops; but so sudden and frequent became his appearances that Corps staffs suborned a signal officer at G.H.Q. to broadcast a warning whenever the Chief set out from camp. The warning was conveyed by the letters " B.L.," the interpretation of which was " Bull loose."

[1] The late Lieutenant-General Sir Walter Campbell, K.C.B., K.C.M.G., D.S.O., afterwards Quartermaster-General at the War Office (1923–27). He died in 1936.

His temper was under better control than in France, or he found things ordered more to his liking. Still, there were occasional explosions which showed that he had lost nothing of his forcefulness. The habit of carelessly lighting fires where they might cause damage was anathema to him. Soon after his arrival he found a fire lighted in the shelter of a pile of boxes of ammunition, and after an outburst of wrath that shook the culprits almost as much as if the ammunition had exploded he directed a senior staff officer to issue an order that any similar carelessness would be followed by a court-martial of the officer responsible. Not many days later he was inspecting the largest depot of ammunition on the front, stacked in the open near the coast. All went well till in the centre of the depot the guard were found cooking their midday meal within a few yards of a large pile of ammunition. Allenby, who was riding, flung himself from his horse, and strode up to the sentry. "Repeat your orders," he commanded abruptly. The sentry gazed in consternation at the large and obviously angry General, but at a second impatient command started hurriedly with the routine orders for a sentry: "Take charge of all Government property within view of my post; pay the correct compliments to all field officers; in case of fire, alarm the guard——" He got no further. "Well, there's a fire," roared Allenby, pointing to the dinner. "Why don't you alarm the guard?" The guard was eventually turned out, and made to stamp out the fire which was cooking their meal; whereupon Allenby remounted, observing grimly to the officers accompanying him, "Well, you've read my order. The officer responsible will be tried by court-martial, whatever his rank." On his return to camp, however, he found that the staff officer concerned had forgotten to issue the order, and there was a second, and louder, explosion.

On days when he did not visit the front Allenby rode in the afternoon or evening. Whatever his route, it almost invariably included a small copse in the desert, a mile or so from the camp. The southern border of Palestine is on one of the principal lines of bird migration, and in this copse were to be found specimens of many different birds. Allenby would ride round the copse for a quarter of an hour or so, naming the new species that had arrived

since he was last there and remarking on their habits.[1] A passage
from a letter to Lady Allenby shows his usual interest in men,
birds, and flowers in new places:

> I was up yesterday looking at the enemy's lines between Gaza
> and the sea-coast. I rode some miles along the beach, past the
> mouth of the Wady Ghuzzee. Beautiful sands and brilliantly clear
> blue sea. At the mouth of the Wady Ghuzzee is a brackish lagoon,
> wherein two or three natives were fishing. They have a circular
> net, with leaden weights on its rim. This they carry loose on their
> shoulder. When a fish is seen—usually a sole—they throw it over
> the top of him and catch him under it. The water must be clear, as
> it always is, and not more than about 2 feet deep. All along the
> beach, at the foot of earthy cliffs some 20 or 30 feet high, grow
> quantities of delicate white lilies; like large white daffodils. Along
> the water's edge are queer crabs, big and little, many sandpipers and
> stints and some lovely blue kingfishers. They are the Spanish king-
> fisher; very like the English, but bluer. They pick up the little fish
> in the pools, and are quite tame and friendly.

The seven infantry divisions required by Allenby were to be
made up by the transfer of the 10th Division from Salonika and
the completion of the 75th Division in Egypt. But the former
could not arrive till the end of August, and the latter was not
likely to be fit to take its place in the line till the end of September.
Meanwhile the Force was reorganized into three Corps—the
Desert Mounted Corps, under Chauvel,[2] an Australian; the
Twentieth Corps, under Sir Philip Chetwode; and the Twenty-
first Corps, which was given to Bulfin,[3] a stout-hearted warrior,
but lacking Chetwode's brilliance. He had come to Palestine
in command of the 60th (London) Division, which was now
entrusted to Shea. There was no general 'purge' of commanders, as some have supposed. A few elderly and obese colonels
of mounted regiments were replaced by more active men; one
divisional commander, whose abilities were not quite equal to his
position, was sent home; but Allenby was always content to
make the best of the material available, and probably dismissed

---

[1] There were on Allenby's staff two well-known ornithologists, Colonel R.
Meinertzhagen and Lord William Percy.

[2] General Sir Henry Chauvel, G.C.M.G., K.C.B.

[3] The late General Sir Edward Bulfin, K.C.B. He died in 1939.

fewer senior officers than did any other of the Army commanders of the Great War.[1] There was one important change at Head-quarters. The Chief of the General Staff, Major-General Sir Arthur Lynden-Bell, was temperamentally unsuited to work with Allenby, and the relations between the two men were never happy. It was a relief to both when the doctors decreed that Lynden-Bell had been too long in the East, and that his eyesight would suffer unless he was transferred home. Allenby at once cabled for Bols, who had served him well in the Third Army and was now commanding a division in France. As assistant to Bols Brigadier-General Guy Dawnay came to G.H.Q. He had been Chetwode's staff officer in Eastern Force, and had helped him to prepare the appreciation on which the plan of the new campaign was based. He now became responsible for working out the details to give effect to the plan, a task for which he was admirably qualified.

The plan itself was simple, as are almost all good plans in war: to concentrate a superior force against the enemy's left flank, while inducing him to believe that his right would again be attacked. The Twentieth Corps and Desert Mounted Corps were to form the striking force against the Turkish left, while the Twenty-first Corps kept the enemy's attention fixed on Gaza. It was in essentials almost exactly the same plan as Roberts had exploited against Cronje in the relief of Kimberley in the Boer War some seventeen years before; and it is certain that Roberts' move had stayed in Allenby's memory, since it was the first big military operation in which he, then a squadron commander, had played a part. Roberts' difficulties then were almost exactly the same as his own now—transport, water, and secrecy. The tracks towards Beersheba and the Turkish left were not practicable for the mechanical vehicles of the day, except the Holt tractors, so that the striking force was mainly dependent on horsed transport and camels. This greatly increased the difficulties of the second main problem, the supply of water. Not only had a great deal

---

[1] Allenby found at first that there was a tendency to offer him the failures who had been *dégommé* in France. The formula usually ran, " So-and-so has been found unable to stand the strain of operations in France, but it is thought that he would do better in a warm climate."

to be done in the development of water-supply before the enterprise could begin, but during the actual operation water would have to be carried for the greater part of the striking force. There were 30,000 camels employed, mainly in carrying water. When all calculations and preparations had been made the ruling factors as regards transport and water were found to be these: by the employment of all the transport available, including that of the Twenty-first Corps opposite Gaza, the striking force could be supplied from railhead up to Beersheba and for one march beyond; but it could be watered only up to Beersheba, and its advance beyond Beersheba was dependent on the supplies of water at that place. The early capture of the Turkish detached post of Beersheba, with wells intact if possible, was thus a keystone of the plan.

The third great problem was to move the striking force some ten or twelve miles over open country, capture Beersheba, and attack the Turkish left without the enemy becoming aware of the intention. There could be no question of concealing entirely the preparations for a move against Beersheba; but it was hoped to persuade the enemy that this move was only a feint, and that the main attack would come, as before, against Gaza. The steps taken to deceive the Turk were varied and ingenious; the most spectacular and successful was the famous ' haversack ruse,' in which a staff officer contrived to be chased by the Turkish outposts, pretended to be wounded, and dropped, with other articles, a haversack stained with fresh blood containing papers, letters, money. The papers and letters had been very skilfully prepared, firstly to give the impression that they were genuine, and secondly to convey the information that the main attack was coming at Gaza, and that the preparations against Beersheba were only a feint.[1] It is now known that these papers were one of the principal influences that determined the action of the Turks before and during the battle. But this was only one of the many steps taken to conceal the real plan and to implant a fictitious reading of it in the minds of the enemy.

[1] A full account of this celebrated ruse is given in the Official History (vol. ii, pp. 30–31) and, more dramatically, in Aston's *Secret Service* and Tuohy's *The Secret Corps.*

The details of the plan were developed at a series of conferences. Allenby presided at these and made his qualities as a commander very evident. He had a complete grasp of all sides of the plan, strategical, administrative, and tactical, and gave any decision required with authority and without hesitation. Then he left his staff to work out the details without interference.

The date at which the operation should begin was a difficult point for decision. It had been Allenby's original intention to attack in September, but the lateness of arrival of certain parts of the force soon made it clear that neither the training of the troops nor the administrative arrangements would be complete till well on in October. There were risks in postponing the operation for so long. Heavy rains might be expected from the middle of November which would turn the coastal plain of Palestine into a sea of mud; and there was evidence that the enemy was bringing down reinforcements from the north and was planning some counter-measure. Allenby sensibly preferred to wait till his preparations were complete and his troops handy at their *rôle*, and to risk being forestalled by unusually early rains or an unnaturally active Turk.

A curious Arab prophecy was discovered by some one about this time; it was to the effect that the Turks would be driven from Jerusalem only " when a prophet of the Lord brought the waters of the Nile to Palestine." Now, the pipe-line laid across the desert by Murray had already brought Nile water to the very boundaries of Palestine, and was to be continued forward as soon as operations began; and Allenby's name transliterated into Arabic could be read as " Allah en nebi " (" the prophet of the Lord ").

The date for the attack on Beersheba, which was to be the opening act of the operations, was eventually fixed for October 31. The bombardment of Gaza was to begin some days earlier. The date was the latest possible, and involved some risk of forestalment by weather or by foe; but it enabled all the elaborate administrative preparations to be completed and the troops to come to their starting-places trained, fit, and confident. The training had included long marches over heavy going and practice in working on a limited water ration. The ground between the front-line posts and Beersheba, a wide No Man's Land of some ten miles or more, had been thoroughly explored by commanders and staffs under cover of a series of reconnaissances in force by the mounted troops. There were five of these between August 24 and October 3. Their purpose was twofold: they enabled the staffs to work out the somewhat intricate arrangements for moving the troops into position for the assault on the Beersheba defences, and they accustomed the Turks to such demonstrations. It was hoped that the real attack might be mistaken at first for another reconnaissance, an impression which the Intelligence skilfully endeavoured to foster by means such as cipher messages intended to be deciphered by the enemy. These reconnaissances were not altogether popular with the mounted troops, who were not, of course, aware of their significance in the general plan, and suspected a desire of the staffs to ' picnic ' at the expense of their sweat and blood. The senior commanders were irreverently termed " The Royal Party." The Turks usually reported these reconnaissances as attempts to assault Beersheba which they had repulsed with heavy loss.

While the British stroke was being prepared with solid, expensive efficiency, typical of the nation when aroused by defeat and difficulties, the counsels of the enemy were divided and troubled. As already stated, the Germans had determined in the spring of 1917 to aid their disheartened Turkish ally to recapture Baghdad, which Maude had taken in March. The best Turkish troops remaining were assembled round Aleppo; a German force was specially formed, trained, and equipped to provide a stiffening when required; and von Falkenhayn, one of the ablest and most experienced of the German commanders,[1] with a German staff, was sent to take charge of the force, to which the Turks had given the boastful name of Yilderim ("the Thunder-bolt "). It was to be transported down the Euphrates to strike at the British left flank in Mesopotamia suddenly, a bolt from the desert. Mustapha Kemal (the late Ataturk, first President of the Turkish Republic) was offered the command of the Turkish portion of the force, but declined to serve under a German staff.

---

[1] He had succeeded von Moltke as Chief of the General Staff (virtually Commander-in-Chief of the German forces) in 1914, and had held this appointment till 1916, when the failure of the attack on Verdun led to his removal.

Not only, however, was the concentration of the force at Aleppo very slow, but doubts as to the practicability of the scheme began to arise. News of the British preparations on the Palestine front and reports on the condition of the Turkish forces in Palestine caused grave doubts whether they could withstand a British offensive without reinforcement. And it was too dangerous to pursue the Baghdad adventure unless the Palestine front was secure: if it collapsed Aleppo and the communications to Mesopotamia would be exposed.

There followed long and acrimonious discussions between Enver Pasha at Constantinople, Jemal (the Turkish Commander-in-Chief in Syria), and von Falkenhayn at Aleppo. Enver stood for the Baghdad project being carried out without delay; Jemal demanded reinforcements for the Palestine front, but had no desire for von Falkenhayn and the German headquarters of Yilderim to invade his sphere of command; von Falkenhayn rightly decided, after a visit to the Palestine front early in September, that its security must be the first consideration. He proposed to transfer the whole Yilderim army to Palestine and to drive back the British by a blow at their right flank. But he had utterly failed to grasp the poorness of the Turkish lines of communication and the impossibility of transferring troops rapidly from one point to another, as he had done in his European campaigns. It was too late when he made up his mind, much too late by the time he got his views impressed on Enver and grudgingly accepted by Jemal. The Yilderim army could never reach Palestine in time to meet, much less to forestall, the British blow. A mightier thunderbolt, launched by a surer hand, was about to strike the Turkish armies on the Gaza–Beersheba line.

II

BREAKING THE LINE
(*October 27–November 7, 1917*)

The Third Battle of Gaza is the official name for the operation by which the Turks were driven from their defences on the southern frontiers of Palestine. It is a misleading title. The operation consisted in a crescendo of blows alternating at either end of the Turkish line, over twenty miles apart, and should more properly be called the Gaza-Beersheba battle. Thus the first act was a heavy bombardment of Gaza by land and sea, designed to fix the enemy's attention on his right; it was followed after four days by the assault on Beersheba, the outpost covering the enemy's left; two days later an attack on Gaza captured a large portion of its defences, and again left the enemy uncertain where to expect the next blow; it fell, after another short interval, on his left flank at Hareira, and threw his whole plan of defence into ruin. Then once more the weight was transferred to Gaza and the sea-coast and the pursuit was pressed up the coastal plain. It was an unorthodox battle, for the two wings of Allenby's army which struck these alternating blows were fifteen to twenty miles apart, linked only by a screen of one mounted division, and open to a counterstroke in the centre. But Allenby had rightly judged that the nature of the ground and of the enemy made the danger of such a counterstroke an acceptable one.

As already explained, the whole plan hinged on the capture of Beersheba with the greatest possible speed, so that its water-supply might be intact, or at least only subject to hasty damage. Hence a force quite disproportionate to the garrison was to be deployed against it. Practically the whole of the Twentieth Corps, four divisions, was to be placed within striking distance of the main defences, on the south and west of the town; while the Desert Mounted Corps (less one division guarding the centre) was to ride round to the east of the town, by a night march of twenty-five to thirty miles over stony tracks, and enter the town from that side, where the defences were comparatively slight. It was like taking a county cricket eleven to play a village team; but the pitch was a difficult one, and there was much at stake. There had, indeed, been some discussion, during the period of preparation, about the size of the force to be employed against Beersheba, some thinking that so large an army would cause the enemy to destroy the wells and withdraw without a fight. But Allenby decided to employ the full force available and to trust to ruse and secrecy to keep the Turk from divining the plan. Hence the many devices, some of which have been related, to deceive the enemy and to conceal the weight of the blow for as long as possible. The bulk of the striking force was kept near the sea-coast as late as possible and moved over to the eastern flank by night, the troops remaining concealed in wadis during the day. Their vacated tents in the coastal area were left standing and were lit up by night. How far these measures of concealment were successful is debatable. A reinforcement of new-model aircraft had enabled the E.E.F. to wrest from the German pilots the air superiority which they had long enjoyed on this front; [1] the only hostile machine that was able to make a thorough reconnaissance of the great movement from the coast was chased and destroyed before it could get back with its possibly vital news. But there were many Bedouin in Turkish pay who could not be prevented from seeing the movement, [2] and the enemy seems to have had reasonable warning of the strength of the force approaching Beersheba. It was the measures that had been taken to deceive him, and especially the ' haversack ruse,' that blinded the eyes of Kress von Kressenstein, the German commander of the Eighth Turkish Army, to the real plans of his opponent. It is not often in war that a general, on a bare, open plain, has misled his enemy as successfully as did Allenby in this operation.

On the night of October 30–31 some 40,000 troops of all arms were on the move, taking up positions for the assault on the Beersheba defences next morning, garrisoned by some 5000 Turks. Thanks to the care with which the previous reconnais-

[1] The authorities at home were apt to be short-sighted in the distribution of new aeroplanes. When a new type was produced they usually insisted on equipping all the squadrons on the Western Front before any of the new machines were sent East. It took many squadrons to produce much effect in France, while a single squadron could change the whole balance of air-power on the Palestine front in a few days.

[2] It was confidently believed in the E.E.F. at the time that the Turks had as spy a Palestinian German, Fritz Franks, who could speak fluent English and was frequently behind the British lines, disguised as an English or Australian officer. Many were the hunts for him; and a tale was told of two senior officers, unknown to each other, meeting in the desert and riding many miles together, each convinced that the other was the redoubtable Franks and seeking an opportunity to draw his revolver unobserved and challenge him. Actually, we have it on the authority of Kress himself that no German officer in disguise was ever behind the British lines at the time, and that, though there was a Fritz Franks, he was only employed on survey work and knew no word of English.

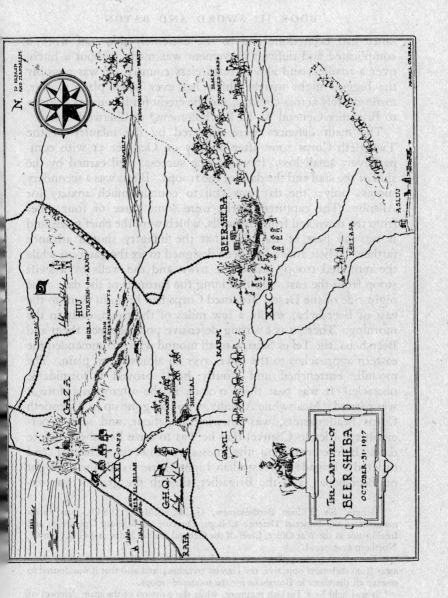

The Capture of Beersheba, October 31st 1917

sance had been done and to the extremely able staff work, a complicated and difficult movement was made without a hitch, over a roadless and almost featureless country. It was possibly the biggest night march which has ever taken place in war, made entirely across country, and the credit for its success belongs to Brigadier-General W. H. Bartholomew,[1] of Chetwode's staff.

The main defences were captured by the infantry of the Twentieth Corps soon after midday on October 31 with comparatively small loss. It was a fine success, well earned by the skill of the staff and the dash of the troops. But it was a secondary success only: the day was still to contain much anxiety for Allenby. The captured works were some three or four miles from the town and from the wells, which were the chief prize, and it was no part of the plan that the infantry should advance farther.[2] Their attack had been designed to fix the garrison while the mounted troops seized the town and the wells by a swift stoop from the east. On this hung the fortunes of the day. The night ride of the Desert Mounted Corps had brought them to the east of Beersheba, within a few miles of the town, early in the morning. There was a strong defensive post between them and Beersheba, the Tel es Saba, a small mound which commanded the eastern approaches to the town over an almost open plain. The mound, entrenched and stoutly held, proved a formidable obstacle.[3] It was past three o'clock in the afternoon before it was carried. Meanwhile Allenby, who had gone up to Twentieth Corps headquarters, was growing impatient, and sent a peremptory order to Chauvel that he was to seize Beersheba before dark. Before receiving the message, however, Chauvel had ordered a brigade of Australian Light Horse to advance straight on Beersheba; and the Brigadier, though the ground was un-

---

[1] General Sir William Bartholomew, G.C.B., C.M.G., D.S.O., later Commandant of the Imperial Defence College, Director of Military Operations and Intelligence at the War Office, Chief of the General Staff in India, and G.O.C.-in-C., Northern Command.

[2] The reason for stopping them was that any further advance was taking them away from their next objective, the Hareira trenches; and also that it was desired to reserve all the water in Beersheba for the mounted troops.

[3] It was held by a Turkish regiment, while the garrison of the main defences of Beersheba was Arab.

known and the enemy resistance unsubdued, determined to make the attack mounted. In the last hour of daylight the brigade rode over the Turks who still stood between them and Beersheba, and entered the town. The fruits of this gallant exploit were that the wells were secured almost intact, although all had been prepared for demolition, many prisoners were taken, the Turkish morale was badly shaken, and that of the mounted troops, already high, was raised to an even higher pitch. Next day Allenby visited Beersheba and saw the scene of the charge; on the field of battle he decorated Brigadier-General Grant, whose brigade had made the charge, with the ribbon of the D.S.O. It was well earned: the charge had saved the wells, without which the further operations might have suffered fatal delay.

The first day of battle had gone well. Beersheba had been captured with its water-supply almost intact, an enemy division had been destroyed, and the greater part of Allenby's force had been placed where a short march would enable it to strike the left flank of the enemy's main position. The next object was to assault and turn that flank before the enemy could reinforce or withdraw it. It will be remembered that limitations of transport prevented the Twentieth Corps being supplied for more than one march beyond Beersheba, so that even a short withdrawal of the threatened wing would place it beyond reach. All now depended on the speed with which the blow could be delivered, and how the enemy commander would meanwhile react to the loss of Beersheba. It had always been foreseen that there must be an interval of at least forty-eight hours between the capture of Beersheba and the delivery of the main blow, to develop the water-supply, to reconnoitre the Turkish position, to move the guns into action, and to complete the other measures necessary for the assault on an entrenched and wired position. The plan provided that during this period of preparation the attention of the Turkish command should be fixed on Gaza by an attack by the Twenty-first Corps.

This attack—the date of which had been left open till after the fall of Beersheba—was ordered for the night of November 1-2. It was made on a front of nearly three miles, in the sandhills along the coast. It reached practically all its objectives and fulfilled its mission of attracting enemy reserves to Gaza. But the losses of the Twenty-first Corps were just double those that the Twentieth Corps and Desert Mounted Corps had suffered in the capture of Beersheba, and showed how slow and expensive an attempt to break through on the coast would have been.

The second act of the drama had thus also gone well. But there was now an awkward and unrehearsed pause before the curtain could rise on the third act. The water in Beersheba proved unequal to the demands on it; [1] a hot Khamsin wind blew, which increased the demands; and the flank-guard of the force became involved in heavy fighting in the hills north of Beersheba, which distracted the staff from the preparations for the attack on Hareira. The enemy commander had misconceived the purpose of the force at Beersheba, and believed that a dash on Jerusalem up the Hebron road would be made by the mounted troops. This misreading of Allenby's intentions was due partly to the exploits of a small force of seventy men on camels, under Colonel Newcombe, R.E., [2] which had made a wide *détour* through the desert east of Beersheba and had cut all communications on the Hebron-Beersheba road. They caused much alarm before they were surrounded and captured, and convinced the enemy that a large force might be expected to raid Jerusalem. Hence considerable reinforcements—including the first of the Yilderim divisions, recently arrived from the north—were sent into the hills north of Beersheba, where they became engaged with the flank-guard of the British force. There was much bitter fighting in the steep, rocky hills, and two divisions (one of the Twentieth Corps, and one of the Desert Mounted Corps) became locked in this struggle, in which water again played a large part. At the time the Turkish effort was believed by the British to be an attempt to recapture Beersheba, which had, in fact, been ordered by Yilderim Headquarters. Actually it seems now that it was dictated by fear of a British raid on Jerusalem, and was a defensive

[1] All shaving and washing had to be forbidden.
[2] Colonel S. F. Newcombe, D.S.O. He had been engaged with T. E. Lawrence and L. Woolley on a survey of the Sinai Desert just before the War, and had been with Lawrence in the Hejaz in the early part of 1917. He came back to Egypt in July on account of sickness, and himself suggested and organized the raid on the Hebron road.

rather than an offensive move. Whatever the object, the fighting was hard and continuous, both sides making efforts to gain ground with little success; and it absorbed much of the attention of the Twentieth Corps staff. The attack on Hareira, in the plain, could hardly take place until the position in the hills was secure.

Allenby at G.H.Q. had a hard part. He knew well the dangers of delay, yet he could do little or nothing to hasten the stroke. For one of his temperament it must have been difficult to remain inactive while the fate of the operation hung in the balance. He must have thought of his initial success at Arras, succeeded by days of stalemate, and have wondered whether a complete success was again to elude him. Yet he remained outwardly calm and composed, and showed no sign of his anxieties till November 4. This was the day when he had hoped that the attack on the Turkish left would be made. Instead he received a message from Chetwode that it could not take place till the 6th. Allenby felt that at least he must satisfy himself that this delay was essential, and went to Beersheba in his car, determined that if will-power was required to urge the attack forward it should not be wanting. One who drove with him that day can testify to the force and energy that he radiated, and felt that it would require good arguments indeed to convince him that the attack could not be launched earlier.

The Twentieth Corps staff was a strong combination: Chetwode's brilliance was supported by an extremely able General Staff officer in Bartholomew and a solid, shrewd, and humorous chief administrative officer in Evans.[1] There was not likely to be much error in their calculations. Allenby listened attentively to Chetwode's exposition of the situation, and after a little deliberation gave his consent to the postponement of the attack till the morning of the 6th. He left with a characteristic word of encouragement (" You'll be all right; I never knew a really well-prepared attack fail yet "), and went back to wait on events with his usual cool courage.

His patience was rewarded. The attack on the 6th, made with

---

[1] Major-General Sir Edward Evans, K.B.E., C.B., C.M.G., D.S.O., afterwards Major-General in charge of Administration at Aldershot.

Phase I: DEPLOYMENT (*October* 24–30)

The Twentieth Corps moved east towards Beersheba, the Twenty-first Corps remaining opposite Gaza. The Twentieth Corps had practically the whole of the transport of the army, the Twenty-first Corps being left immobile. One mounted division covered the gap between the two corps. The remainder of the Desert Mounted Corps moved south to Khelasa and Asluj. From October 27 the Twenty-first Corps, assisted by warships, carried out a heavy bombardmentt of Gaza.

Phase II: CAPTURE OF BEERSHEBA (*October* 31)

The Twentieth Corps captured the main defences of Beersheba while the mounted troops, after a night march of thirty miles, attacked the town from the north-east. Colonel Newcombe's detachment placed itself astride the Hebron-Beersheba road. The Twenty-first Corps continued the bombardment of Gaza.

Phase III: ATTACK ON GAZA (*night of November* 1–2)

While the Twentieth Corps was preparing to attack the left of the Turkish main line the Twenty-first Corps assaulted a portion of the Gaza defences in order to attract the enemy reserves. Meanwhile the flank-guard of the Twentieth Corps became heavily engaged in the hills north of Beersheba, at Khuweilfe.

Phase IV: EXPLOITATION AS INTENDED BY G.H.Q.

While the Twentieth Corps broke the Turkish left, the Desert Mounted Corps was to pass round this flank and intercept the retreat of the whole Turkish army.

Phase IV: EXPLOITATION AS IT ACTUALLY OCCURRED

Owing to the fighting at Khuweilfe and the water difficulties, the mounted troops were scattered and tired, instead of collected and fresh, when the moment came. As the Turks still held out at Khuweilfe the mounted troops had to pass through a comparatively narrow gap, instead of round a flank. Only four brigades out of ten were immediately available.

Phase V: PURSUIT (*November* 7 *onward*)

Owing to the supply and water problem, the Twentieth Corps had to halt after November 6 and transfer all its transport to the Twenty-first Corps, who took up the pursuit along the Plain of Philistia.

THIRD BATTLE OF GAZA

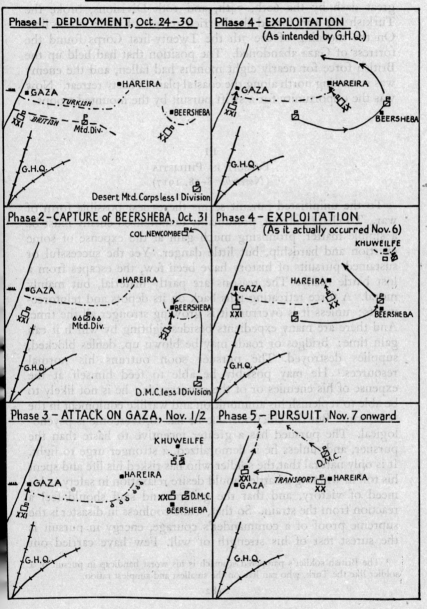

Phase 1 – DEPLOYMENT, Oct. 24–30

GAZA · HAREIRA · BEERSHEBA
TURKISH
BRITISH
XXI · Mtd. Div.
XX
G.H.Q.
Desert Mtd. Corps less 1 Division

Phase 4 – EXPLOITATION
(As intended by G.H.Q.)

GAZA · HAREIRA · BEERSHEBA
XXI
XX
G.H.Q.

Phase 2 – CAPTURE of BEERSHEBA, Oct. 31

COL. NEWCOMBE
GAZA · HAREIRA · BEERSHEBA
XXI · Mtd. Div.
XX
G.H.Q.
D.M.C. less 1 Division

Phase 4 – EXPLOITATION
(As it actually occurred Nov. 6)

KHUWEILFE
GAZA · HAREIRA · BEERSHEBA
XXI
XX
G.H.Q.

Phase 3 – ATTACK ON GAZA, Nov. 1/2

KHUWEILFE
GAZA · HAREIRA · BEERSHEBA
XXI · XX · D.M.C.
G.H.Q.

Phase 5 – PURSUIT, Nov. 7 onward

D.M.C.
XXI · TRANSPORT · HAREIRA
GAZA · XX
G.H.Q.

great dash by the 6oth, 74th, and 10th Divisions, broke the Turkish left and forced the hurried retreat of their whole line. On the morning of the 7th the Twenty-first Corps found the fortress of Gaza abandoned. The position that had held up the British force for nearly eight months had fallen, and the enemy was streaming north along the coastal plain in hasty retreat. Now was the opportunity for a swift pursuit by the mounted troops.

III

PURSUIT IN PHILISTIA
(*November 8–18, 1917*)

To the uninitiated pursuit seems the easiest possible form of war. To chase a flying, presumably demoralized enemy must be a simple matter, promising much gain at the expense of some exertion and hardship, but little danger. Yet the successful or sustained pursuits of history have been few, the escapes from a lost battle many. The reasons are partly material, but mainly moral. A force retreating falls back on its depots and reinforcements; unless it is overrun, it is growing stronger all the time. And there are many expedients besides fighting by which it can gain time: bridges or roads may be blown up, defiles blocked, supplies destroyed. The pursuer soon outruns his normal resources.[1] He may possibly be able to feed himself at the expense of his enemies or of the countryside; he is not likely to be able to replenish his ammunition and warlike equipment in the same way. But the chief obstacle he has to overcome is psychological. The pursued has a greater incentive to haste than the pursuer, and, unless he is demoralized, a stronger urge to fight. It is only natural that the soldier who has risked his life and spent his toil in winning a battle should desire relaxation in safety as his meed of victory, and that the general and staff should feel a reaction from the strain. So that, while coolness in disaster is the supreme proof of a commander's courage, energy in pursuit is the surest test of his strength of will. Few have carried out

[1] The British soldier's pampered stomach is his worst handicap in pursuit of a soldier like the Turk, who can live on the smallest and simplest ration.

pursuits with such relentless determination as did Allenby in 1917 and 1918.

An incident illustrates his attitude in pursuit. One of his staff brought to him early in a pursuit a draft order to the Twenty-first Corps to move to a certain line. Allenby at once scratched out the line indicated, and substituted two places much farther north. The staff officer, who considered the line indicated by Allenby beyond what could be expected of the troops, pointed out that he was making no allowance for any difficulties or unavoidable delays, due to the enemy's resistance or to other causes. Allenby said, " Is it impossible for the troops to reach the line I have given? " The staff officer replied, " Not necessarily impossible, but——" " There must be no buts," replied Allenby. " In pursuit you must always stretch possibilities to the limit. Troops having beaten the enemy will want to rest. They must be given as objectives, not those that you think they will reach, but the farthest that they could possibly reach." And on this principle Allenby always acted.

The proper exploitation of victory by mounted troops is an interception rather than a direct pursuit. They should aim to avoid the tail of a retreating column, where the rearguard's sting lies, and to strike in from a flank on to the line of retirement, cutting off as large a part as possible of the pursued force, and holding it at bay till the infantry can come up to complete its destruction. This was the manœuvre that Allenby had always contemplated as the climax of the battle—that his mounted troops from Beersheba should cut across the Turkish line of retreat in the plain of Philistia. And this aim he continued to urge on them with all his force while any hope remained of its accomplishment. It was not to be. He had to wait till the following year to show how mobility could be used to its right true end, the complete destruction of the enemy armies. When it was obvious that the Turkish Eighth Army on the plain, which had seemed at one time within the grasp of the Desert Mounted Corps, had eluded their pursuers, Allenby showed no disappointment and made no re-criminations. To a staff officer who remarked that the progress of the mounted troops was slow he turned with an angry challenge: " And what do you know of the difficulties of mounted troops in pursuit? Have you ever commanded such a force? I have, and can tell you what it means. The mounted troops have done all that they could, and have done it admirably."

It was the matter of water-supply more than anything else that hampered the mounted troops. When the time for pursuit came, after the Twentieth Corps had broken the Turkish line at Hareira, the Desert Mounted Corps, mainly because of water, was scattered and tired, instead of fresh and collected. One division had had to be sent back to its starting-place, after the capture of Beersheba, for water. Only four brigades out of ten were immediately available, and only two more could be added quickly. The other four could not be disengaged from the hill fighting north of Beersheba without considerable delay. During November 7 and 8, the two critical days, progress was slow. The Turkish rearguards fought stoutly, and, in spite of one of the most gallant charges in the history of cavalry, made by some Worcestershire and Warwickshire Yeomanry at Huj, the Desert Mounted Corps could never break through their screen. By the 9th the greater part of the corps was brought to a standstill by the necessity for water, few of the horses having drunk for forty-eight hours and many not having been watered for much longer periods.[1] The effort at interception had failed.

Meanwhile the Twenty-first Corps, after occupying Gaza on the 7th, had been pressing a direct pursuit up the Plain of Philistia. The Corps commander, Bulfin, had drive and energy above the ordinary, and could be trusted to second the resolution of Allenby, who himself was constantly forward, watching events and ready to give a decision. The pace and strength of the advance was dictated largely by the supply problem. Of the seven infantry divisions in the E.E.F. only two could be sent forward, and their supply strained the transport resources to the utmost. The four divisions of the Twentieth Corps were halted—three round Beersheba, to be fed from railhead; one, the 60th Division, at Huj, up to which point it had supported the mounted troops.

[1] Though there were wells in most of the villages, they were sometimes two hundred feet deep, and the only method of watering from them was to lower a canvas bucket on telephone cable. In such conditions it sometimes took a whole night to water a squadron.

One division of the Twenty-first Corps was also halted, at Gaza. All available transport of the army was gathered on the coastal plain to feed the three mounted divisions and two infantry divisions which now formed the pursuing force, the Twentieth Corps being left immobile.

The tactics of the pursuit consisted in keeping the weight on the left, near the coast. The three great watercourses on which the enemy might stand—the Wadi Hesi, the Nahr Sukhereir, the Nahr Rubin, all dry for the most part at this time of year—could be more effectively turned near their mouths. The Navy could protect and support the left flank, and supplies could be landed near it. Also, the farther the force was kept away from the hills the less it was exposed to a counterstroke from the Turkish Seventh Army, which had retreated into the hills after the Gaza-Beersheba battle. Marshal von Falkenhayn and his German staff had now reached Jerusalem, and were endeavouring to control and restore the battle. To the German eye the board seemed set for an effective counterstroke. Here was a comparatively small fraction of the British force hurrying up the plain, intent on overwhelming the Turkish Eighth Army, while the Seventh Army in the hills was within striking distance of their flank and rear. The Turks themselves, better conscious of their weakness and disorganization, counselled retreat without fighting, till the British had to halt for lack of supplies, and a solid line of defence could be re-established in front of Jaffa and Jerusalem. But the German persisted in his chessboard combination.

On November 9 G.H.Q. received warning of the impending counter-offensive through an intercepted wireless message. Allenby was unimpressed, and may be said to have done little more than give a contemptuous glance over his shoulder at his great opponent's threat, though he warned certain of his reserves to stand by to meet the thrust if required. He neither checked nor slackened the pursuit. He had gauged Turkish exhaustion and disorganization better than had von Falkenhayn, and was not the man to be turned from his purpose by a threat. His judgment was right. The Seventh Army's counter-attack, made on November 11 from the direction of Tel es Safi (probably the Gath of the Bible, and certainly Blanchegarde of the Crusaders, the fortress that held the entrance to the Vale of Elah), was held, after a critical hour or two, by the flank-guard of the Australian Mounted Division, and soon petered out from sheer weariness.

Meanwhile the Eighth Army made a last effort on the line of the Nahr Rubin to halt the pursuit and to cover Junction Station, where the branch railway to Jerusalem joined the main line to the north. This position was assaulted and taken on November 13 by the 75th and 52nd Divisions and the Desert Mounted Corps, which had been transferred to the left flank after its effort at interception had failed. This action was remarkable for a dashing charge by a Yeomanry brigade at El Mughar, and for the very gallant assaults by the 52nd (Lowland) Division on the strong villages of Katrah and El Mughar. Next day Junction Station was occupied; and a day later the same Yeomanry brigade that had charged at El Mughar overwhelmed a Turkish rearguard by another dashing mounted attack at Abu Shusheh, the site of the ancient fortress of Gezer (Mount Gisard of the Crusaders)—the strong place that from the earliest times in the history of Palestine has guarded the western passes into the Judæan hills. Allenby, with his knowledge of history, had early recognized the importance of this position.

With the occupation of Jaffa on the 16th the pursuit up the Plain of Philistia came to an end. The Eighth Turkish Army withdrew behind the river Auja, and the Seventh Army sought shelter in the Judæan range. Allenby had driven an effective wedge between the two; there was no good road to connect them farther south than Nablus-Tulkeram. In the ten days of pursuit since the breaking of the Gaza-Beersheba line the E.E.F. had advanced over fifty miles. It had taken 10,000 prisoners and a hundred guns. Thanks to the stout fighting of their rearguards and the water difficulties of the pursuing mounted troops, the Turks had avoided complete disaster. But they had suffered a crushing defeat and were in sorry plight.

Allenby had intended to halt after reaching Jaffa, and to strengthen his precarious communications before making any attempt on Jerusalem. Now he decided to advance into the hills at once. It was a bold decision, typical of the man. His line of communication could with difficulty support the force he already had at the front; in order to bring up the third infantry division of the Twenty-first Corps it was necessary to send back one of the mounted divisions. The Twentieth Corps remained immobilized fifty miles from the front. And, besides its lack of capacity, the tenuous line of communication was in no way solid; it was tied with string in many places, and might easily break, especially if the winter rains, due now at any time, should fall heavily. Lorries, horse transport, strings of camels, surfboats, the botched and patched Turkish railway, were all links in the dubious chain that brought supplies from railhead to the front. The troops too were weary, and their ranks were becoming thin. No good maps of the difficult hill country were available; and Allenby from his study of history had plain warning of the fate that had befallen many rash attempts to reach Jerusalem by these rugged western passes, where Assyrian, Roman, and Crusader had all failed. In the two books he studied almost daily, the Bible and Sir George Adam Smith's *Historical Geography of the Holy Land*,[1] he could read of the defensive strength of these hills. George Adam Smith writes of this face of the Judæan fortress:

> Everything conspires to give the inhabitants easy means of defence against large armies. It is a country of ambushes, entanglements, surprises, where large armies have no room to fight and the defenders can remain hidden, where the essentials for war are nimbleness and the sure foot, the power of scramble and of rush.

Lastly, a telegram Allenby had received from the War Office on November 11 might have given a less resolute commander an excuse for prudence. The War Cabinet, mindful, perhaps, of Townshend's disaster in Mesopotamia two years earlier, had cautioned him against involving his army in commitments too extended for its strength, and had warned him that it might become necessary to withdraw troops from him in 1918.

Allenby weighed all these factors which prompted caution and

---

[1] At least three distinguished persons, one of whom was the late Earl Lloyd George (see his *Memoirs*, vol. iv), have claimed the credit of introducing this book to Allenby's notice. Since it was Allenby's invariable practice on going to a new country to obtain and study the best books available on it, he had already discovered George Adam Smith for himself.

delay against the wisdom of allowing his disorganized enemy no respite to recover nor time to organize a defence of the passes. With no hesitation he chose the bolder, but wiser, course, and ordered an immediate advance. November 17 was a day of rest. On the 18th the advance into the hills began. Simultaneously, as if to emphasize the risks of his resolution, the winter rains began.

IV

JERUSALEM

(*November 18–December 31, 1917*)

The two Turkish armies were divided and disordered, over twenty miles apart—one in the hills, the other in the plains. But the scarcity of roads and the difficulties of the supply problem forbade anything but the simplest form of manœuvre against them. Allenby left only one mounted division and one infantry division to face the Eighth Turkish Army across the Auja and to cover the line of communication in the plain. He launched the remainder of his available force, one mounted division and two infantry divisions, into the hills, at right angles to the line of communication. Only one metalled road existed, that which ran from Jaffa to Jerusalem. There were some tracks on the forty-year-old map (the latest available), marked deceptively " Roman Road," which the local inhabitants declared fit for transport; it was realized later that by this they meant a track up which a donkey, the local means of carriage, could scramble. It was fortunate that some foresighted administrative officer had in September obtained Allenby's approval to form companies of donkey transport, in anticipation of the possibility of a winter in the Judæan hills. But these did not become available till early December; meantime the querulous camel, in conditions of cold and wet among unaccustomed hills and rocks that for once at least justified his attitude to life, was the means of transport for the great majority of the troops advancing on Jerusalem.

They were troops fit for a great enterprise. The 75th Division —the last British division to be formed in the War—consisted of West Country Territorials, many of whom had spent the early years of the War garrisoning India—men from Hampshire, Dorset, Somerset, Wiltshire, Cornwall—brigaded with some Indian battalions. They had their spurs yet to win, and were resolute to do it. The 52nd Division (Lowland Scottish) had been in practically every action of the E.E.F. since Romani, and had acquitted itself gallantly in them all. Since the fall of Gaza, ten days before, it had marched over seventy miles, and had fought nine actions; its ranks were getting thin, but its spirit was indomitable. The Yeomanry Division was drawn from the best manhood of the English countryside, and many of the troopers had three years' experience of war. Allenby knew he could trust these divisions to force the passes and to win Jerusalem, if skill and courage could do it. Nor would the leadership be found wanting. Bulfin needed no urging to get the utmost out of his infantry; Barrow, the commander of the Yeomanry Division, was one of Allenby's most trusted lieutenants, and had been on his staff in France during the retreat from Mons and the struggle at Ypres. Though a passionate believer in cavalry and in mounted action, he could fight a dismounted action as skilfully and tenaciously as anyone, and proved it now.

The general plan was to reach the main Jerusalem-Nablus road north of Jerusalem and, by thus cutting their principal line of supply, to force the Turks to evacuate the city. Allenby was determined to avoid any fighting in the vicinity of Jerusalem itself.

The skill and hardihood of the troops brought good progress at first, despite the appalling difficulties of weather and of ground. The 75th Division, on the main road, forced its way through the difficult defile of the Bab el Wad; and on the following evening, by a charge in mist and rain, stormed Kuryet el Enab, almost within sight of Jerusalem. Next day they left the main road, turned north-east, and captured Nebi Samwil (the reputed burying-place of the prophet Samuel), a commanding height which overlooks Jerusalem.[1] That marked the limit of their progress. The

---

[1] The division subsequently took as its badge a key, in token that they had captured the " Key of Jerusalem," a claim which was justified by the eight or nine attempts which the Turks made to recapture the height in the succeeding days. It was the scene of some of the most determined and bitter fighting that occurred anywhere in the War.

next obstacle in their path was the village of El Jib (Gibeon of the Bible), set on a rocky knoll which made of it a natural hill fort, flanked by fire from a spur to the south. With inadequate artillery support neither the West Country men of the 75th nor the tough Lowlanders of the 52nd, who relieved them, could win the village, gallantly as their thinned and weary ranks attacked it.

Farther north the Yeomanry Division had found only a goat-track through the Beth-horons, and had had to send back all wheeled transport and all guns, except the camel-carried Hong-Kong and Singapore battery. But they pushed on to a steep hill feature called the Beitunia spur, within a mile or so of their goal, the Nablus road. Here they met a numerous and strongly posted enemy, backed by a powerful artillery which completely out-ranged and outweighed the little guns of the camel battery, gallantly and skilfully handled as they were. The division was counter-attacked and driven down to Lower Beth-horon (Beit Ur el Tahta). That it had got as far as it did and held on so far forward may be accounted a great feat of arms.

By November 24 it was obvious that neither Bulfin's fiery determination nor Barrow's resolute skill could make any further headway; and Allenby ordered a halt till fresh troops could be brought up. He was himself well forward, having established a small headquarters in tents a few miles from Junction Station. He sent congratulations to the troops " on the unflinching deter-mination which has led to great successes under the most adverse circumstances." They had been earned. The three divisions in the hills had been fighting and marching continuously for three weeks, in extremes of heat and cold, over dusty plains and in harsh, stony hills, often on short rations of food and of water. Allenby, so careful of his men's well-being when at rest or when preparing for an operation, spent their endurance ruthlessly if it seemed possible to gain an advantage over the enemy. He applied to his soldiers the old hunting maxim, " Care for your horse in the stable as if he were worth five hundred pounds; ride him in the field as if he were not worth half a crown."

By great exertions the lines of communication had now been improved to enable the remainder of the force to be brought up; and the Twentieth Corps was ordered to relieve the Twenty-first

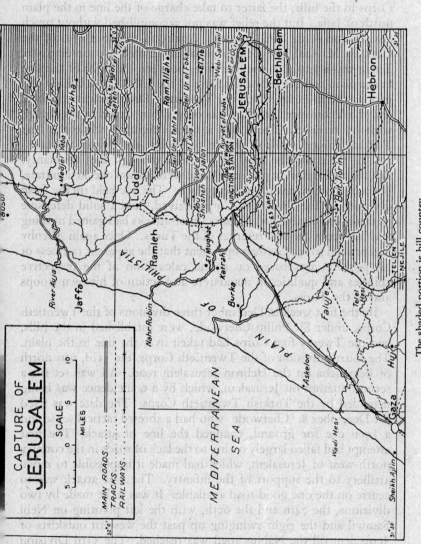

The shaded portion is hill country.

Corps in the hills, the latter to take charge of the line in the plain north of Jaffa. But the relief was not accomplished without much anxiety and some hard fighting. Again, to the keen eyes of the German Marshal, the British situation invited a counterstroke. There was a gap of some five miles between the right of the line in the plain and the left of the force in the hills. Close behind this gap lay the route by which the Yeomanry Division was supplied, and the Yeomanry Division was only a thin screen of tired men, with no reserves. There was a week's fighting while the best Turkish troops available strove to exploit the British weakness and to penetrate the gap, or to break through the Yeomanry. But their efforts were piecemeal, and were always checked in time, often by a mere handful of weary men. The line held till the fresh divisions of the Twentieth Corps arrived,[1] and a solid defensive position was established. The counter-attacks had gained nothing and had spent the best reserves of the Turks. Once again Allenby had proved to his German opponent that the apparent rashness of his position was based on sound calculation of the respective abilities and qualities in manœuvre and action of his own troops and of the Turks.

By the first week in December three divisions of the Twentieth Corps, under Sir Philip Chetwode, were established in the hills, and the Twenty-first Corps had taken over the line in the plain. The fourth division of the Twentieth Corps, the 53rd, was north of Beersheba on the Hebron-Jerusalem road. All was set for a second attempt on Jerusalem, which by a coincidence was being defended by the Turkish Twentieth Corps. The date was fixed for December 8. Chetwode, who had a shrewd tactical sense and a keen eye for ground, changed the line of attack. The first attempt had failed largely owing to the lack of roads in the country north-west of Jerusalem, which had made it impossible to move artillery to the support of the infantry. The new attack was to centre on the one good road available. It was to be made by two divisions, the 74th and the 60th, with the left pivoting on Nebi Samwil and the right swinging up past the western outskirts of Jerusalem till the Nablus road was reached. The 53rd Division

---

[1] The 60th Division had already been sent on by forced marches from Huj, and had come temporarily under the Twenty-first Corps.

was to advance up the Hebron road to Bethlehem and to protect the right of the attack, and then to pass east of the city and cut the road to Jericho.

The brunt of the attack, which was made in wretched conditions of cold and wet, fell on the Londoners of the 60th Division. After a night march down the hillside south of the main road they carried the principal Turkish defences west of Jerusalem soon after dawn. These defences were strong, and had in places been carved out of the rock; they should have been formidable works to storm. But the Londoners attacked with their usual dash, and the Turks defended with less than their usual tenacity. Little further progress was made that afternoon. Fog and rain delayed the 53rd Division, so that the 60th could advance no farther without exposing their right flank. The day closed in some disappointment and anxiety. But actually Jerusalem was won. The fall of their principal works had disheartened the Turk; and when the advance was resumed next morning it was found that the enemy had gone. The old, historic city, sacred to three of the world's chief religions, had fallen to yet another conqueror. It had often gone down in blood and ruin; this time its surrender had a touch of comedy. The mayor came out with a white flag to hand over the keys of the great city to the British; he offered them in succession to some cooks of a London regiment who had lost their way, to a sergeant on outpost duty, and to some artillery officers intent only on getting their guns into action against the Turkish rearguards. None of these felt themselves quite equal to so historic an occasion. In the end the surrender was accepted by General Shea, the commander of the 60th Division, on behalf of Allenby. Meanwhile the Turks were driven from the Mount of Olives after a sharp rearguard action.

Two days later, on December 11, Allenby made his official entry into Jerusalem. It was a simple but impressive ceremony. He entered the Jaffa Gate on foot, with the French and Italian representatives on either side of him, followed by some of his principal staff officers and by Sir Philip Chetwode, the commander of the Twentieth Corps. Among those who walked in the same procession, of twenty officers only, was Colonel (then Major) T. E. Lawrence, who had come to G.H.Q. to report on the progress of Feisal's operations shortly before the fall of Jerusalem, after his gallant, though unsuccessful, attempt to interrupt the Turkish communications by blowing up a railway bridge in the Yarmuk valley.[1] Guards, representative of the troops which had taken part in the campaign (English, Scottish, Irish, Welsh, Australian, New Zealand, French, and Italian [2]), were drawn up at the Gate, and the streets were lined by men of the 60th Division. A guard of Indian Mohammedan troops had been established over the Haram-esh-Sherif (Temple Area).[3] At the Citadel a short proclamation was read in various languages, and the notables of the city were presented to Allenby. The procession then returned to the Gate, and the ceremony ended. Israelite, Assyrian, Greek, Roman, Jew, Arab, Crusader, Turk, had entered Jerusalem as conquerors before the British. None of these nations can have been represented by one more impressive or worthier of his race than was Allenby, physically or morally.

The capture of Jerusalem stirred the imagination of the whole world. Congratulations and honours poured in to Allenby, and left him quite unaffected. He was no more moved from his usual composure by praise and success than he had been by dislike and criticism. He gave little outward sign of elation, and remained unmoved and aloof as before. As a curious instance of his obedience to orders and loyalty to the wishes of superior authority it may be noted that, though he wrote to Lady Allenby on December 9 and 10, he did not mention the fall of Jerusalem till the 11th, because he had received a telegram that the Cabinet wished the news kept strictly secret till it could be announced in the House of Commons.

The fighting of 1917 did not end with the fall of Jerusalem. More elbow-room was required in front of both Jaffa and Jerusalem before the position could be considered secure. On December 20, in the plain, the 52nd Division forced a crossing of the river Auja and drove the Turks well away from Jaffa. In the

---

[1] See *Seven Pillars of Wisdom*, Chapter LXXVI.

[2] Small French and Italian contingents with a political rather than a military purpose had taken part in the campaign.

[3] It always annoyed Allenby if anyone referred to his campaign as a 'crusade.' He pointed out that a number of his troops, and such valuable assistants as the Egyptian Camel and Labour Corps, were Moslems, not Christians.

hills an advance had been arranged for December 24, but the weather caused a postponement till the 27th. Meanwhile an intercepted Turkish wireless message showed that Falkenhayn had ordered a counter-attack on Jerusalem. This was made early on the 27th, and, though pressed with all the gallantry and self-sacrifice of which the best Turkish troops were capable, was soon checked. When the British advanced in their turn the Turks gave way and were driven back to the north of Ram Allah, over ten miles from Jerusalem. The War Cabinet, ignorant of the conditions, was now urging the immediate occupation of the remainder of Palestine, and had inquired the possibilities of an advance to Aleppo. But further operations were for the moment out of the question. Heavy rains had flooded the plain and made all movement on the lines of communication precarious; and the troops were sorely in need of rest and refit. The weather culminated in a great storm on Christmas Day, which halted all movement in plain or hills. In the Commander-in-Chief's camp near Junction Station the tents were with difficulty kept standing.

So ended 1917, a year that brought Allenby as commander of an army a taste of outstanding success in the first stage of the Arras battle, to be followed by disappointment, a change to an entirely independent command (in which his qualities had at last full scope), his greatest personal fame as captor of Jerusalem, and his deepest personal loss in the death of his son.

The Jerusalem campaign will always be a classic for the military historian; it embraced almost every form of operation in almost every variety of terrain and climate. To some extent it may be said that Allenby found a success ready made for him. Murray had laid the foundation of it by his organization of the communications across Sinai, Chetwode had devised the plan, and Dawnay had worked out the details. The War Cabinet had provided the troops he asked for, and had given him a great numerical and material superiority over the Turk. Yet all these would have been vain without the master-hand. His was the driving-power, the inspiration, and the responsibility during the eventful, often anxious, days that ended with the capture of Jerusalem. He had many big and difficult decisions to make, and he made them cleanly, without hesitation, once he had advised himself of the situation, usually by a personal visit. His energy and endurance were remarkable; long drives in heat and dust over bumpy tracks left him still fresh in mind and unfatigued in body. No one who served in the E.E.F. during the campaign had any doubt that he had served under a very great commander.

CHAPTER IX

THE FINAL CAMPAIGN

(*January–September* 1918)

I

INTERVAL

(*January–March* 1918)

EARLY in 1918 the main G.H.Q. camp was moved from Kelab to Bir Salem, near Ramleh, on the Jaffa-Jerusalem road, about ten miles from Jaffa and twenty-five from Jerusalem. Allenby had for his quarters a two-storey, stone-built house which had been a German school. It stood on a slight rise in sandy soil just above an orange-grove, and commanded an extensive view of a typical section of Palestine. To the west could be seen the stretch of sand-hills that fringed the coast-line, beyond which was the deep blue of the Mediterranean; to the north the white minarets of Ramleh marked the position of a purely Arab town; to the south were the fields and fruit groves of old-established Jewish colonies. But it was the line of the Judæan hills to the east that caught and held the eye. They stood up straight and solid out of the plain, a challenge and a warning. Their colour varied ever with the changing lights, from a hard, barren brown to a soft twilight blue: changes that seemed to illustrate their history—the hopes and promises they had inspired, the disappointments and cruelties they had seen, the attraction they always exercised. It was a setting that appealed to Allenby; he was little given to recollection and had a mind that seldom looked back, but he always remembered with enjoyment his headquarters at Bir Salem.

The house was a comfortable one, sufficient to hold himself and his personal staff and to lodge occasional distinguished visitors. The remainder of the staff and the offices were in huts or tents a short distance away. G.H.Q. remained here till the final battle of September 1918. It was within a short distance of the railway, of the Jaffa-Jerusalem road (the principal artery of communication from east to west), and of the main aerodrome at Ramleh. Not far off was Lydda, or Ludd, the traditional home of St George, who may be regarded as patron saint to Allenby, born on St George's Day.

Allenby, as ever, took the keenest interest in his new surroundings—in the birds, the flowers, the buildings, and the people. A happening of this period is worth relating to illustrate his interest in architectural remains. Somewhere near the camp he found a small, half-ruined house with a stone arch, which he identified from its form as a relic of Crusader building. He was fond of taking guests to admire this arch and of speculating on its antiquity. At last one day, when a distinguished visitor was taken to view the remains, the arch—and, indeed, the whole ruin—had completely disappeared. Investigation showed that a zealous young subaltern of Engineers, who had been told to construct a store of some kind in the vicinity, finding that the stones of the ruined house suited his purpose well, had used them in the construction of his work. Allenby's rage at this act of vandalism was great. An interesting architectural relic had been destroyed, and his strict orders for the preservation of ancient monuments had been disobeyed. The unfortunate subaltern was ordered back to the base in disgrace. Efforts made on his behalf with Allenby only raised a fresh storm of anger. Finally Bertie Clayton, Allenby's political adviser,[1] agreed to approach him, after making careful local inquiries about the arch. At first Allenby would hear no further word on the subject; but Bertie Clayton was never afraid of him, and Allenby had learned that Clayton never spoke without reason. When he agreed to listen Clayton told him that the ' Crusader ' arch had been constructed less than fifty years before as part of a local wineshop. When Allenby had recovered from the shock to the antiquarian knowledge on which he prided himself he took it very well and remitted all penalties on the zealous subaltern.

An incident which occurred about this period may serve to illustrate his interest in and knowledge of Biblical history. Sir Philip Chetwode was conducting him round the line of the

---

[1] A very fine character; see *Seven Pillars of Wisdom*, Chapter VI, for a good estimate of him.

Twentieth Corps north of Jerusalem, when he realize͟
explanation of his dispositions was receiving scant
although Allenby was gazing intently at the surroundi͟
Suddenly the Commander broke out, " Look at that big ro͟
front of us! That must be just about the place where Jonathan
and his armour-bearer climbed up and attacked the Philistine
garrison." A graphic description of Jonathan's feat followed,[1]
and Chetwode realized that the defensive arrangements of the
Twentieth Corps in that quarter stood little chance of receiving
consideration for the moment. So he removed the Chief to
another part of the line, where he got a detailed description of one
of Joshua's battles that had taken place there!

With the entry into Palestine and capture of Jerusalem political
as well as military problems began to occupy Allenby.

A lesser man might easily have become so harassed by the
many and complicated problems of administration and by the disputes and jealousies of the various creeds and sects in the Holy
Land that his conduct of the campaign would have suffered.
But Allenby refused to be in any way distracted from his primary
business of beating the enemy. He held to certain simple rules.
He insisted on the conquered portion of Palestine being administered as occupied enemy territory, strictly on the principles laid
down by international law, which enacted that as little change as
possible be made from the existing methods of government. He
chose as Administrator a man whom he knew and trusted; he
allowed him a free hand, and he never interfered in detail. As an
example of his common sense may be quoted his decision on the
vexed question of what flags might or might not be flown in
Jerusalem and elsewhere—a matter explosively charged with
religious and national jealousies. Allenby at once decreed that
the only flag permitted in Palestine during the period of military
occupation was the Union Jack flown by the Commander-
in-Chief. He refused to allow the Balfour Declaration to be
published in Palestine.[2]

The verbatim report of an interview with Allenby illustrates

---

[1] See 1 Samuel xiv.

[2] It had been made on November 2, when the Third Battle of Gaza was in full
swing. Few realized its significance or danger at the time.

his habit of wasting no time in coming to the point and of leaving all details to the subordinate concerned. It had been decided early in 1918 to start an Army newspaper (*The Palestine News*), and a certain officer had been recommended to Allenby as suitable to conduct the enterprise. His record of his meeting with Allenby runs as follows:

Commander-in-Chief's study at Bir Salem ; Wednesday, February 6, 1918

Enter General Bols with visitor

BOLS. This is the officer, sir. [*Exit.*

CHIEF. Good morning.

VISITOR. Good morning, sir.

CHIEF. I understand that in private life you were on the staff of *The Times*.

VISITOR. Yes, sir.

CHIEF. Good! Then you will produce an Army newspaper weekly [*takes up list and reads*] in English, Arabic, Hebrew, Hindi, Urdu, and Gurmukhi. All necessary arrangements will be made by you. Thank you. Good morning.

VISITOR. Good morning, sir.

[*Exit, slightly surprised at the number of languages in which the Army requires its news.*

In the early months of 1918, while the Egyptian Expeditionary Force was waiting for weather conditions to improve and for the communications by road and rail to be strengthened, the future of the campaign in Palestine was the subject of high debate in the councils of the Allies. The dominant factor in the military situation was the complete collapse of Russia, which had freed sufficient German forces to give the Germans a superiority in numbers in the western theatre and thus a last gambler's chance of defeating the French and British armies before American troops could arrive in sufficient strength to restore the balance. In the meantime, therefore, it was essential for the Allies to stand on the defensive in the west. But Mr Lloyd George had always believed that the shortest road to victory lay not in the main western theatre, but by eliminating Germany's lesser allies in the subsidiary theatres—the policy of ' knocking out the props,' as it was sometimes called. He overlooked the fact that her allies were in no sense the ' props ' of Germany (in fact, the converse was the truth), and was also inclined to disregard geographical difficulties of communications, distances, and climate. He demanded for 1918 an offensive policy in Palestine, directed to driving Turkey out of the War altogether, and wished to supply Allenby with sufficient men and material to enable him to reach Damascus and if possible Aleppo.

The Prime Minister was supported on the military side by Sir Henry Wilson, British Military Representative at the Supreme War Council at Versailles; he was opposed by the C.I.G.S., Sir William Robertson, and by the Commander-in-Chief in France, Sir Douglas Haig. The arguments of these latter ran somewhat as follows: The security of the Western Front was absolutely vital; defeat in France meant inevitably the loss of the War. Whereas an advance in Palestine, even to Damascus and Aleppo, could have little real effect; Aleppo was still many hundreds of miles from the heart of Turkey. It was doubtful, too, whether the Turks could shake off the German yoke if they wished, so strong was the German hold on the Government and Army; and Constantinople itself lay under the guns of the German warships *Goeben* and *Breslau*. Even if Turkey did sue for peace, and opened a passage through the Dardanelles, it was too late now to bring aid to Russia. To reinforce the army in Palestine would throw an additional strain on shipping, since the narrow waters of the Mediterranean formed some of the worst zones of submarine activity, and shipping was our most anxious need at the time, to maintain our food-supply and to transport the American troops to France. Turkey, already mortally wounded, could safely be left to bleed to death; and all effort should be concentrated on resisting the German blow in the west. If Turkey saw the last German effort held up she would speedily make terms; if, on the other hand, she saw her ally at or near the gates of Paris not even the loss of Aleppo would force her from the War. The Egyptian Expeditionary Force, if it remained on the defensive, could safely spare two British divisions to strengthen the Western Front, and much shipping and treasure could be economized by reducing our commitments here.

So advised the 'Westerners.' Mr Lloyd George and his supporters thought otherwise. They held that it would be a counsel of despair to stand on the defensive everywhere, and madness to take seasoned troops from a theatre where great advances could still be made and great advantages won, to fling them into the profitless slaughter of the Western Front. One more defeat and Turkey would be only too ready to make terms; an advance to Aleppo would cut the main Turkish communications to the Mesopotamian front, and enable that campaign also to be liquidated. Further, the collapse of Turkey would induce Bulgaria, also tired of the War and of the German domination, to make peace. Thus two of Germany's allies would be removed, a great step towards victory taken, and a road opened through Bulgaria to the flank and rear of Austria and Germany. The danger on the Western Front was being deliberately exaggerated, the Prime Minister declared. All the fighting of the last three years, in Champagne, in Artois, on the Somme, at Arras, in the Ypres Salient, showed that even with considerable superiority in numbers and gun power only limited advances were possible, and those at terrible cost. Why should the Germans, with a smaller advantage in numbers, and that only for a short time, be able to break through the fortified zone, when all the French and British efforts had failed? Let them beat out their strength, if they would, against the iron wall; and let the Allies meanwhile dispose of two of Germany's supporters, Turkey and Bulgaria. Such was the policy of the 'Easterners.'

The Prime Minister had his way. A meeting of the Supreme War Council at Versailles, held at the end of January, endorsed the plan for a decisive offensive against Turkey in the spring of 1918. Smuts was dispatched to Egypt by the War Cabinet with instructions to consult with Allenby and with a representative of the Mesopotamian Force and to formulate a plan for a united effort to drive Turkey out of the war. Allenby, needless to say, had taken no part in the controversy. His attitude was his customary one of complete loyalty and readiness to play his part in the War Cabinet's general plan of battle. If required to inflict another decisive defeat on the Turk he would make every effort to do so; if asked to reduce his force to a defensive basis for the benefit of the Western Front he would let no personal ambition for further distinction affect his judgment. When pressed by the War Cabinet, immediately after the fall of Jerusalem, for plans for a further advance he had replied that extensive operations were impossible in the wet season, that his immediate objectives would be to secure control of the Jordan valley and then to cut the Hejaz Railway at Amman and isolate the 20,000 Turkish troops between there and Medina, and that a movement towards Aleppo would necessitate considerable reinforcements and be dependent on the rate of advance of railway construction.

The mission visited Palestine and viewed the front, and Smuts drafted a plan which was cabled home by the middle of February. He began by stating that with the resources available it was impossible to take the offensive in Syria and Mesopotamia simultaneously; he recommended that the Mesopotamian force should remain on the defensive and transfer to Allenby all the troops that could be spared. The 7th Indian Division had already reached Egypt; it was proposed that Mesopotamia should send a further two divisions and a cavalry brigade, which would give Allenby a total of ten infantry divisions, his own three mounted divisions, an Indian cavalry division which was being sent from France, and the cavalry brigade from Mesopotamia. Smuts had accepted Allenby's views on the course of future operations, and commended them to the War Cabinet. They consisted of an immediate extension of his right flank to the Jordan and then across it into the hills of Moab, to destroy the Hejaz Railway; this was to be followed by an advance to the line Tiberias-Haifa which would give Allenby control of practically the whole of Palestine, with the harbour of Haifa and the Turkish railway that ran from east to west across the Plain of Esdraelon. Thereafter the main advance would be, not directly on Damascus, but along the coast by the ancient ports of Tyre and Sidon to Beirut, and possibly beyond it to the Tripoli-Homs gap, by which Damascus could be turned and isolated. The sea would facilitate supply, and the mountains would protect the right flank. Meanwhile a smaller column would advance into the Hauran south of Damascus to co-operate with the Arabs and Druses. Allenby held out no prospects of a rapid movement; the rate of advance would be dependent on railway construction, which would demand large quantities of additional material and rolling-stock and large numbers of labourers. Stewart considered that the railway could be advanced at the rate of a mile a day, a somewhat optimistic estimate.

The plan was, as the Official History remarks, sound enough, but stiff and mechanical. Allenby was always better at performance than at promise. His estimates on paper of future possibilities were on the cautious side, while his action in the field was daring almost to rashness. He had seen the results of Nivelle's easy optimism and extravagant promises in France a year before, and was aware of the unfortunate consequences for the Egyptian Expeditionary Force of his predecessor, Murray, having consented, against his better judgment, to attempt the invasion of Palestine with forces that he considered insufficient.

Almost before the Smuts mission had left Egypt the first stage of the operations was being executed. Between February 19 and 21 the tough, active Londoners of the 60th Division advanced directly from Jerusalem on Jericho, while farther south the Anzac Mounted Division scrambled down rocky tracks that led from near Bethlehem towards the Dead Sea, with the object of trying to reach the valley in time to cut the retreat of the Turks. The fighting needs no long description. It was a struggle against the ground as much as against the enemy. The eastern scarp of the Judæan range falls steeply, in places precipitously, to the Jordan valley, and is seamed with deep ravines, of which the most striking is the Wadi Kelt (the Brook Kerith); it is one of the most desolate and yet impressive parts of the earth. The men and horses of the Anzacs had had some strange experiences since leaving the Canal, and had been in some strange places for mounted men—marches and battle across the scorching sands of the Sinai Desert, combat in the rocky hills north of Beersheba, the waterless pursuit after the fall of Gaza, close-range fighting among the orange-groves south of Jaffa. They were to march and fight in some strange places yet. But that scramble down the eastern face of Judæa, from the chill summits of the range to the warmth of the valley, more than a thousand feet below sea-level, must have been the strangest of all their experiences. Their effort was in vain: the Turks withdrew across the Jordan in time to escape their blow.

Before the next stage, the advance on Amman, could be carried out it was necessary to gain more room to the north, both in the Jordan valley itself and in the Judæan range above it. Consequently the next operation was a general advance on the whole front of the Twentieth Corps, up the Jordan valley on the right and astride the Nablus road in the hills. The objective in the valley was the Auja stream (a namesake of the river north of Jaffa), and in the mountains the general line of the Wadi Jib—the ancient frontier between the kingdoms of Judah and Israel, between Judæa and Samaria. On the left the Twenty-first Corps was to swing forward its right in the foothills north-east of Jaffa, to conform to the advance of the Twentieth Corps.

The operation lasted from March 8 to 12, and was completely successful. But the slowness and comparative costliness in casualties of the advance of the Twentieth Corps along the spine of the Judæan range convinced Allenby that his next great attack, if he wished for speedy or decisive results, must be made in the plain, and not in the hills.

Just before this operation began Allenby became aware that he had a new enemy Commander-in-Chief to oppose him. Liman von Sanders, the defender of Gallipoli, had replaced von Falkenhayn. Allenby's other principal adversary in the Jerusalem campaign, Kress von Kressenstein, had already been removed from his command, and Jemal, the autocrat of Syria, had been recalled to Turkey. The disappearance of all these three was a measure of Allenby's success in discomfiting his opponents. Liman von Sanders had less brilliance in manœuvre than Falkenhayn, but was a staunch fighter on the defensive, and had better knowledge of the Turks and their methods. He worked through a Turkish rather than a German staff. He took to himself great credit at this time for stopping a British advance on Nablus, though no such advance was, of course, intended. It is interesting to note that the line now reached, the ' line of the two Aujas,' had been chosen by Allenby, from his reading of history, in the previous autumn, while the army was still on the southern border of Palestine, as the best line on which to cover Jerusalem and Jaffa, should he get as far.

On the British side there was also an important change. Guy Dawnay, whose clear and logical brain had been invaluable in the planning of the Jerusalem campaign, had been taken for an appointment at General Headquarters in France. He was succeeded, after a short interval, by another extremely able staff officer in Bartholomew, who had been with Chetwode during the Jerusalem operations. Allenby had the knack of choosing his assistants well.

II
TRANS-JORDAN
(*March–May* 1918)

The stage was now set for the crossing of the Jordan and an advance into the hills of Moab. To understand the strategical significance of this operation it is necessary to look at the map and to consider the lie of the railways that served the Turkish armies. For this purpose only the lines south of Damascus need be regarded. North of Damascus it is enough to know that a single, inefficient, incomplete line of railway connected Syria with Turkey.

The Hejaz Railway, the destruction of a section of which was one of the objectives of the operation, ran from Damascus through the Hauran to Deraa junction and on to Amman, the capital of Transjordania to-day (Rabbath Ammon and Philadelphia of old times); thence along the edge of the desert by Maan into the Hejaz, to the holy city of Medina—still held by a Turkish garrison. At Deraa a branch ran westward down the Yarmuk valley; this branch, which went by way of Nablus and Tulkeram, with a spur to Haifa, was the principal line of communication of the Turkish armies west of the Jordan. It will be seen that an extension of the British right flank to Amman would place it in a position to strike north along the railway to Deraa junction, and thus to cut the Turks' main line of communication. This line of advance had, in fact, been advocated by some members of the Smuts mission as the most rapid and effective means of

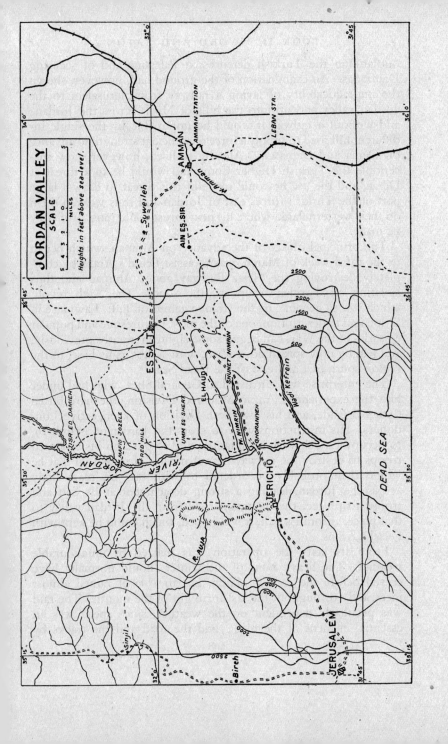

JORDAN VALLEY

SCALE

5 4 3 2 1 0 5
MILES

Heights in feet above sea-level.

32°0

36°0

35°45

35°30

35°15

36°0

35°45

AMMAN STATION

AMMAN

LEBAN STA.

W. Ammān

AIN ES-SIR

Suweileh

2500

2000

1500

1000

500

ES SALT

QISR ED DAMIEH

MAFID JOZELE

RED MILL

UMM ES SHERT

EL HAUD

SRUNET NIMRIN

W. NIMRIN

GHORANIYEH

Wadi Kefrein

JORDAN

RIVER

JERICHO

DEAD SEA

R. AUJA

500

1000

1400

2000

2500

JERUSALEM

Bireh

Sinjil

31°45

32°0

outflanking the Turkish defences in Palestine and of securing
Damascus. An examination of the ground had, however, shown
the impracticability of laying a railway from Jerusalem to the
Jordan valley and up into the hills of Moab across the Jordan;
and without a railway it would be impossible by the single indifferent hill road to supply a force of sufficient strength to advance
on Deraa and Damascus. Allenby realized, however, how susceptible the Turkish Higher Command would be to a threat at
Deraa, and the use he could make of this threat to draw a large
part of the Turkish forces east of Jordan and thus weaken them
on their western flank, where his next thrust could most profitably
be made.

The principal object of the advance on Amman, which began
in the third week of March, was to assist Feisal's Arabs by completely destroying the Hejaz Railway about Amman and thus
isolating all Turkish troops to the south. The Arab revolt,
which was to become, by the strange genius of T. E. Lawrence in
action and in description, one of the most picturesque and popular
episodes of the War, had begun some eighteen months previously,
and had by now spread northward, with Akaba as its base, to the
region south-east and east of the Dead Sea.

The enterprise was entrusted to General Shea, who had under
him the experienced Anzac Mounted Division, the hard-bitten
Camel Brigade, and his own 60th Division of keen, active Londoners. His instructions were to cross the Jordan on March 19,
to occupy Es Salt with his infantry, and to push on his mounted
troops to destroy the railway near Amman. He was told that he
would then probably be ordered to withdraw his main body
across the Jordan, leaving a strong detachment at Es Salt and
troops to protect the mountain road from the Jordan valley to
that place. From Es Salt, it was hoped, touch could be kept with
Feisal's Arabs.

From its start the operation was marred by unfavourable
weather. The heavy rains of the winter should normally have
ceased before the end of March, but in 1918 it rained almost
incessantly throughout the last fortnight of the month. The raid
was peculiarly dependent on the weather, since speed was an
essential element of the plan; and the road and the tracks by

which the advance was to be made, rough and difficult enough when dry, were almost impassable in the wet. The first stage, the bridging of the Jordan, had to be postponed for two days, from the 19th to the 21st, owing to the flooded state of that tortuous, narrow river, which rose nine feet during the night of the 20th–21st. It was the 23rd before the main body was across. The enemy holding the river were not numerous, but the river was running bank-high in swift flood. The crossing was watched by H.R.H. the Duke of Connaught, who was on a visit to Palestine.

The force reached and occupied Es Salt on the evening of March 25; the opposition had been slight, but the weather atrocious. A large proportion of the inhabitants of Es Salt, a picturesque old town perched on the hillside, were Christians, who welcomed the invaders with open but unwise delight. The mounted troops, reinforced later by a brigade of the 60th Division, then strove for four days, from March 27 to 30, to capture Amman. But the delay on the Jordan had been fatal: it had given the enemy time to reinforce the garrison, for whom the group of hills round the town formed a strong natural position, too strong to be forced by troops with little artillery or ammunition. On March 30 the withdrawal began. It was decided not to attempt to maintain a detachment at Es Salt, which had been attacked by Turkish forces from west of the Jordan; and the whole force, except a bridgehead detachment at Ghoraniyeh, had recrossed the Jordan by April 2. The withdrawal was never in any difficulties except from the weather and from the state of the tracks. A large number of refugees from Es Salt, who had too vociferously and prematurely acclaimed the entry of the British, accompanied the troops in their withdrawal, from well-founded fear of Turkish reprisals. Mathematically the operation might be claimed a success for the British, who brought back a thousand prisoners and inflicted heavy loss on the Turks at a cost to themselves of only 1350 casualties. Morally and tactically it was a reverse; the troops of the E.E.F. had failed in their object, and had turned their backs on their enemy for the first time for nearly a year. The ultimate strategical gain, in drawing a large body of Turks to the eastern flank, could not yet be recognized. Neither the handling of the force nor the qualities of the troops were in any way to blame for the failure; the conditions of weather and ground had made their task impossible.

While the force was crossing the Jordan and struggling up the hills of Moab news came of the German successes in France and of the great British retreat. The effect on the plans of the E.E.F. was immediate. Allenby was at once warned that all the troops he could spare would be required for France. Two divisions, the 52nd and 74th, were put under orders for embarkation. As Sir Archibald Murray had done two years before, Allenby responded generously, both in numbers and in quality, to the call from France. The 52nd and 74th were two of his best fighting divisions; and he sent, besides nine Yeomanry regiments, twenty-four British battalions, five and a half heavy batteries, and five machine-gun companies. For the time being the E.E.F. ceased to be an effective offensive force.

Nevertheless Allenby did not at once adopt the defensive. While the troops for France were being withdrawn for embarkation he undertook two offensive operations, one on either flank of his line. The first of these was carried out by the Twenty-first Corps on the left, from April 9 to 11, and is officially known as the Action of Berukin. It had been planned as a stage in the general advance of the army when the E.E.F. expected to receive reinforcements instead of sending them away. The idea of the operation was to force a gap in the Turkish line just where the plain and the foothills joined, and to pass through a mounted division to cut off the Turkish forces between the foothills and the sea. The plan, which had been drawn up by the Twenty-first Corps, was not regarded with any great favour by some of Allenby's advisers, who were doubtful of its practicability or of its value in the changed circumstances. The operation was finally approved somewhat in the spirit in which Bunyan claims to have published *The Pilgrim's Progress*.[1] It was a failure. The attack of the 75th Division in the foothills, which was the preliminary stage, made little headway. It was opposed by the German units

[1] " Some said, John, print it; others said, Not so;
Some said, It might do good; others said, No."
(Author's apology for *The Pilgrim's Progress*)

with the Turkish Army, who, as usual, fought stoutly and skilfully. The preparations had been too obvious, and the original attack did not achieve surprise, while the whole plan was disclosed to the enemy by the capture of a marked map from the body of an officer on the first day. The action was broken off after three days' hard fighting in the foothills. It confirmed Allenby's impression, from the March advance in Judæa, that a rapid breach in the enemy line could only be made in the plains.

The second expedition across the Jordan, which was the next move, was no more successful tactically than the first, but was shorter and more dramatic. Allenby had always had in mind another attempt to establish his right flank in the hills of Moab when the weather became more settled. The Turks, suspecting this, had delivered a strong attack against the bridgehead at Ghoraniyeh on April 11, but had been repulsed with heavy loss. Their main force on this flank then entrenched itself in the foot-hills by Shunet Nimrin, where the road to Es Salt entered the hills.

The advantages Allenby hoped to gain by an extension of his right into the hills were several. The harvest was now ripening in Moab, and was of considerable importance to the ill-provided Turk; if the British could seize and hold Es Salt they could stretch out a hand to Feisal's Arabs, encourage their activities, and deprive the enemy of the grain he was counting on to supply his forces. A force posted at Es Salt could protect the flank and threaten the railway from Amman to Deraa, without being ex-posed to the summer heat of the Jordan valley. Also, the Turkish force at Shunet Nimrin, isolated from immediate support, seemed to have placed itself at the mercy of a swift stroke at its communications by mounted men; the Turks had probably not realized that bold horsemen could operate in the hills as well as on the plains.

Allenby had designed the operation for the middle of May, when the reorganization of the Yeomanry Mounted Division [1] would be complete. But in the last week in April an exceptional opportunity seemed to offer itself. Envoys from the powerful Beni Sakhr tribe presented themselves, announced that they were

[1] See p. 218.

encamped at Medaba, nineteen miles south-east of Ghoraniyeh, and were prepared to co-operate with the British in an operation against the Turks at Shunet Nimrin, provided it was carried out before May 4, after which date lack of supplies would compel them to disperse. This seemed to fit in so well with Allenby's projects that the expedition was staged forthwith, without waiting for the Yeomanry.

Chauvel had the command of it, with the Anzac and Australian Mounted Divisions and the ever-ready London Division. Besides the main road through Shunet Nimrin, where the Turks were posted, there are three bridle tracks from the Jordan valley to Es Salt. The first of these left the valley too close to the Turkish position to be usable; the second ran from the Umm es Shert ford over the Jordan, and the third from the Jisr ed Damieh bridge, in Turkish hands. The plan was for the infantry to make a direct attack on the Nimrin position, while the mounted men, riding swiftly up the valley, reached Es Salt by the Umm es Shert and Jisr ed Damieh tracks. The main communications of the Turkish force at Nimrin would thus be cut, and their only other connexion with Amman was by the Ain es Sir track, which had been found on the previous raid to be barely passable for pack animals. This track the Beni Sakhr promised to bar, so it was hoped that the enemy at Nimrin, surrounded and cut off, would be compelled to surrender or be destroyed. The danger of a Turkish attack on Es Salt from west of the Jordan was to be guarded against by leaving a brigade in the valley to seize and hold the Jisr ed Damieh bridge, or, if this were not possible, to hold a position astride the track. It was a bold plan that promised well had it not been based on faulty intelligence of the enemy and misplaced trust in the unstable Arabs. The Beni Sakhr made no effort to fill the *rôle* they had undertaken,[1] while the Turks reacted with unsuspected swiftness and strength.

[1] Actually the sheikhs who had come in represented only a small section of the Beni Sakhr, and never seem to have expected their offer to be taken seriously. Sir Hubert Young in his book *The Independent Arab* writes of the incident from the Arab side:

" Marzuq told me that he had sent over a small party of Beni Sakhr sheikhs from Madeba to General Allenby's G.H.Q. with a letter saying that he only needed a little assistance from the British to destroy the entire Turkish army east of the Jordan.

Operations began at dawn on April 30, and at first went well. The Australian Division moved swiftly north up the valley, and the leading brigade arrived near Jisr ed Damieh by 5.30 A.M. It could not capture the bridge itself, so took up an extended position to cover the track to Es Salt, up which a second brigade rode to the capture of that town, which was occupied by the evening and its garrison captured, a fine exploit. Three other mounted brigades rode up to Es Salt by the Umm es Shert track. Meanwhile two brigades of the London Division, with the New Zealand Mounted Brigade on its right, captured the outpost line of the Shunet Nimrin position, but could make little impression on the main line, which was strongly posted and entrenched. General Shea hoped, however, that some of the mounted troops descending from Es Salt on the Turkish flank and rear, coupled with the Arab closing of the Ain es Sir route, would compel the Turks to retreat next day.

These hopes were not fulfilled. The mounted troops could make little progress down the road from Es Salt against a strongly posted Turkish flank-guard in difficult hills, and the enemy throughout the operation used the Ain es Sir track, which he had made fit for wheels, without let or hindrance from the Beni Sakhr. So that the gallant efforts of the 60th Division were made in vain.

Meanwhile disaster overtook the flank-guard in the valley. Unsuspected by the Intelligence and unseen by the airmen, a strong Turkish force was close to Jisr ed Damieh. A division of Turkish cavalry had lain skilfully concealed in broken ground just west of the river for some time past, in anticipation of a

. . . On the 29th April one of the Beni Sakhr sheikhs came back from G.H.Q. He brought a letter purporting to come from General Allenby, in which he said that he hoped to co-operate with Marzuq, and that the bearer would give necessary details. According to the bearer, General Allenby proposed to advance on Shunet Nimrin on the very next day. Mounted troops were at the same time to attack and capture Es Salt, and the Beni Sakhr were to rise immediately and join in. Marzuq was much perplexed by this letter. He had acted without any authority in sending across to General Allenby, and was rather frightened at the result of his move. He knew perfectly well that the Beni Sakhr would do nothing without guns, and no guns had arrived."

Lawrence in *Seven Pillars* (Chapter XCVI) makes some pungent comments on the folly of initiating an operation on the unverified promises of unknown sheikhs; but it was difficult for G.H.Q. at the time to realize the complete irresponsibility of Arab warfare.

fresh British advance on Es Salt; and a Turkish division had been moved up close, the day before that advance began, with the intention of attacking the British outpost at Mussallabeh, west of the Jordan. Further, a bridge had been made at Mafid Jozele, which had escaped the notice of the Air Force, and had not been discovered by the mounted troops till late on the 30th. The result was that on the morning of May 1 the Light Horse brigade in the valley, spread on an extended front from near the Nahr es Zerka (Jabbok) stream to Red Hill, was suddenly attacked from three sides by a greatly superior Turkish force. It was soon driven off the Jisr ed Damieh–Es Salt track and up against the trackless hills behind. It was only with great difficulty and the loss of nine guns and a quantity of transport that it succeeded in extricating itself. With the help of reinforcements a line was established a mile north of the Umm es Shert track, the only communication open to the mounted troops in Es Salt. It has since become known that the situation might have been more critical still but for a Turkish mistake which caused the counter-marching of a regiment which would otherwise have added its weight to the attack.

During May 2 and 3 the attacks on the Shunet Nimrin position were continued without success, and meanwhile the mounted troops in Es Salt were being pressed from west, from north, and from east. There seemed at one time a danger of their being completely cut off from the valley, and a scheme was even contemplated by which Lawrence, who was at G.H.Q. at the time, should be flown to Es Salt to lead the mounted troops east towards the area controlled by Feisal's Arabs.

Allenby went down to Chauvel's headquarters in the valley on the afternoon of the 3rd, and after hearing a somewhat alarming report of the situation at Es Salt gave orders for withdrawal.

On the night of May 3–4 the four mounted brigades from Es Salt scrambled down the narrow Umm es Shert track with surprisingly little difficulty, and by the evening of the 4th the whole force had recrossed the Jordan. Again a thousand prisoners were brought back, and the balance of losses was much in favour of the E.E.F.; again the tactical victory was with the enemy; again Allenby's strategical objective was accomplished, since from now onwards about one-third of the whole Turkish forces were maintained east of the Jordan.

Allenby had taken the loss of the guns with great calm. There were plenty more guns in the ordnance depot, he remarked; it was the trained gunners who had fallen who were the greater loss. On the afternoon of the 3rd, however, when the position of the troops in Es Salt was reported as critical, he had for the first time in the campaign betrayed signs of anxiety. His final reaction was typical. When Chauvel expressed to him his regret for the failure he replied, with his usual emphasis, " Failure be damned! It's been a great success." It had, from the strategical point of view, but it required a far-seeing man to realize it and to discount so lightly the tactical failure. A great nation is said to forget its defeats easily: the same is true of a great general.

III
REORGANIZATION AND PLANNING
(*May–August* 1918)

" Nothing is known of the climate in summer-time, since no civilized human being has yet been found to spend summer there." So said the official Intelligence handbook about the Jordan valley. Yet Allenby, after the two failures to establish a position in the hills east of Jordan, was practically compelled to maintain a considerable force in the valley, both for the protection of his right flank and to keep alive the enemy's apprehensions of another thrust at Amman and Deraa. He did so with his eyes open to the risks he ran. It was mainly a medical problem, and Allenby's dealings with his doctors were typical of his methods. Few commanders of large armies have consulted the heads of their medical services more regularly and earnestly than did Allenby; few have more boldly overruled their advice than did Allenby when his plans demanded a course of action that they regarded as dangerous. No general, probably, has ever given fuller assistance and support to his doctors in their measures for combating the risks of disease. Here are two opinions of Allenby from senior Medical Officers of his Army. The first is from

Major-General Sir Richard Luce, a Territorial officer who became Chief Medical Officer of the Twentieth Corps and afterwards Chief Medical Officer of the whole Army:

We were all greatly impressed both with his appearance and his grasp of things. From a medical point of view the most interesting point in his conduct of the Palestine campaign was his policy with regard to the question of malaria. The Jordan valley had always been regarded as an impossible habitat for Europeans in the late summer months, and the Maritime Plain almost as bad. With full realization he boldly faced the dangers of occupation, which he considered essential to his strategy; but—and here he showed his greatness—he gave unstinted help in carrying out every method of mitigating the danger that was put forward. Work on anti-malarial schemes was given priority over all other work behind the lines. Thousands of Egyptian workers were put at the disposal of the anti-malarial authorities for draining marshes and training the course of streams, such engineering projects as had never before been undertaken in the face of an enemy. The result was that the mosquito population was marvellously diminished, and malaria, troublesome as it was, never became a menace to the general health or morale of the troops.

Sir James Barrett, the distinguished Australian, has written:

In all these matters the Commander-in-Chief was quick to understand the essentials of the difficulties and prompt to act. I found that I was dealing with a man of scientific instincts; courteous, considerate, and appreciative of the service the Medical Staff could render. He never interfered in detail, but supported the Army Medical Service thoroughly, finding out where he could repose confidence. He was, as far as I know, the first Commander in that malarial region in which many armies have perished to understand the risk and to take measures accordingly.

Apart from malaria, the Jordan valley in summer was a horrible place. The historian says that Cleopatra once had a palace there, where she entertained Antony. It seemed an incredible tale to those who knew the valley in summer. The daily temperature was over 100 degrees, the atmosphere, at more than a thousand feet below sea-level, humid and oppressive; and hot winds, or the least movement of troops or transport, sent choking clouds of fine dust along the valley; scorpions, huge spiders, centipedes, and flies were the principal representatives of animal life. The positions were held almost entirely by the mounted troops—at first by the Australian or Anzac divisions, and later, after the reorganization, by the newly formed 4th and 5th Cavalry Divisions.

Allenby visited the valley frequently. If all the stories that are told of his appearances there were true, they would seem to indicate that he was like a naval depth-charge, set to explode at a certain distance below sea-level, since so many of them record his outbursts of anger at some breach of discipline. The best known is of the Australians and their ' cut-shorts.' Allenby had issued a stringent order against anyone riding in shorts. The reason was a good one; it was probable that the bare knees of the rider would be rubbed, and almost every sore in Palestine became septic and had to be treated in hospital. The Australians, in the heat of the valley, wore a minimum of clothing, and Allenby was almost bound to encounter one riding in cut-shorts whenever he appeared. His explosions at the sight became notorious.[1]

It was typical of him, of his strength and of his weaknesses, that he would make no allowances for the conditions in the valley, nor for the characteristics of the Australian. His temper had mellowed with success; and though he still lived up to his reputation as " the Bull," and always remained a very formidable personality, the explosions were perhaps less frequent and his natural kindliness reasserted itself sooner than in France. He was motoring in the valley one day when he passed a small depot of ammunition which did not conform to his ideas of arrangement or concealment. He stopped and sent for the officer in charge, who happened to be shaving and arrived with one side of his face covered with lather. Allenby at once burst out with a very forcible exposition of the shortcomings of the ammunition depot. The unfortunate officer was almost paralysed by this onslaught; but just as he was expecting to be placed under arrest he was amazed to find the Commander-in-Chief's large hand thrust out

---

[1] After the War Allenby was presiding at a meeting to decide on a suitable monument to the E.E.F. " I think we want something simple," he said, " something rather rude and rough." A distinguished General present whispered to his neighbour, " Then what about a statue of the Chief when he has seen an Australian riding in shorts? "

to him, as he concluded, "Well, those are my orders. See that they are carried out. Good-bye! I am very pleased to have made your acquaintance."

On another occasion his car, descending the steep and dusty Jerusalem-Jericho road, nearly ran into the mess-cart belonging to a certain General's headquarters. Then, said the men in charge of the cart, "out of the dust appeared a large and angry man with a lot to say." As he got back into his car Allenby said to his A.D.C., "I fairly let myself go that time, didn't I? What a joke it would have been if we had knocked old So-and-so's mess-cart over the side!"

Of this quickness with which he recovered equanimity after one of his outbursts many stories could be told. On one occasion in Palestine, furious at a breach of orders which he discovered during an inspection, he informed an officer that he would be tried by court-martial; half an hour later, at the conclusion of the inspection, he shook him by the hand and complimented him on what he had seen. Nothing more was said of the court-martial. It is unlikely that Allenby forgot about it; more probably he realized that he had been hasty, and the handshake was his method of withdrawal. At another time, on a visit to a training establishment in Egypt, he disapproved strongly of the methods of a sergeant-instructor in bayonet-fighting. Taking the rifle from him, he gave an impressive exhibition of thrusting and parrying. With his great strength, he handled the rifle like a toy. As he finished he said to the commandant, "Send that sergeant back to his regiment—he's useless." But the rest of his inspection was satisfactory, and as he left he told the commandant he could keep the sergeant if he wanted him.

The chief business of the summer was reorganization. Some 60,000 British troops had left the E.E.F. for France, and were being gradually replaced by Indian units. It was a complicated process.

To take the mounted troops first. The Yeomanry Mounted Division, together with the 5th and 7th Mounted Brigades, were broken up on the departure of nine Yeomanry regiments to France. So was the Imperial Camel Corps Brigade, which was outpaced and had lost much of its usefulness now that the Sinai Desert had been passed. From its Australian *personnel*, supplemented by a French Colonial cavalry regiment, was formed the 5th Australian Light Horse Brigade, to replace the 5th Mounted Brigade in the Australian Mounted Division. The Indian cavalry regiments which had been in France since 1915 had been sent to Palestine in March 1918; both climate and conditions of warfare there would suit them better than the bleak, close-locked warfare in the west. From them and from the remaining Yeomanry regiments were formed the 4th and 5th Cavalry Divisions. General Barrow, the former commander of the Yeomanry Mounted Division, took over the 4th Cavalry Division; and Major-General Macandrew, another Indian cavalry soldier, received command of the 5th.

The brigades in these formations consisted each of a Yeomanry regiment and two Indian cavalry regiments (except the Imperial Service Brigade of the 5th Division, which consisted of three Indian regiments). All regiments were armed with sword or lance, and were thus cavalry in the true sense. The Australians of the Australian Mounted Division also added the sword to their equipment during the summer. Their training in the use of the sword and in shock tactics was slight, but the dash and spirit of cavalry was in their blood and upbringing. The Anzac Mounted Division, though lacking nothing of the spirit and enterprise of the Australian Division, elected to remain Mounted Rifles.

Thus Allenby had four divisions of mounted troops, all of high quality and experience, of which three were armed and trained as cavalry. He was, in fact, stronger in mounted troops than at the beginning of his Jerusalem campaign. His new commander, Macandrew, was a skilful leader, of forcible personality and sanguine temperament.

It was otherwise with the infantry. Though there were still seven divisions, and five of them bore the same numbers and names as before, their composition and quality had greatly changed. Only the 54th remained unaltered, and retained all its British battalions. The 52nd and 74th, two proved and trusted divisions, had gone to France, and had been replaced by the 3rd and 7th Indian Divisions from Mesopotamia. These two had formed the original Indian contingent to France, had fought there in 1914–15, and had then gone East again, to share the failures and the hardships of the attempts to relieve Kut and the triumphs of the avenging campaign that won Baghdad. They were seasoned formations, but they had now, as will be seen, to give up a large proportion of their trained and experienced *personnel* to leaven the new units which had to be formed to complete the remaining divisions. These were the 10th, 53rd, 60th, and 75th; each of these was to keep only three British battalions, one per brigade. Of the others, twenty-three had gone to France, and ten were to be broken up in Palestine as reinforcements. In their place the divisions were gradually completed by Indian battalions; some of these came from India, and the remainder were formed in Palestine by the process of withdrawing a company from each of the existing seasoned battalions, leaving these to expand to four companies again by absorbing recruits. The process of reorganization was completed by the battalions and drafts from India arriving at intervals; the last ones did not land till August. The Official History writes of the Indian battalions that completed the ' New Model ' E.E.F. as follows:

> Twenty-one of them (belonging to the 3rd, 7th, and 75th Divisions) had proved their value in war, but each of them had given up at least one company. Ten, though composed to a great extent of men who had seen active service, had seen none as battalions. The other twenty-two had seen no service; some of their commanding officers, even, were in the same case. These battalions were largely—in some instances as to one-third of their strength—made up of recruits who had done no musketry. One had never seen the service rifle, having been armed with the Ross rifle in India. They landed in Egypt with hardly any signallers, few Lewis gunners, no bombers, often no transport drivers with experience in handling animals. Their junior British officers were almost all in need of further instruction, and few of them spoke Hindustani, while the Indian officers had for the most part been recently promoted. It is on record that in one battalion there were only two British officers who could understand their men and only one Indian officer who spoke English. Intensive training was required, not only of the units as a whole, but still more of all the specialists without whom a battalion is almost useless in modern warfare. There was indeed much to be done, and for the late arrivals little time in which to do it.

The details of this reorganization have been set out at some length, since the part played in a great victory by organization and preparation behind the lines seldom receives proper recognition in military history, which is apt to concern itself solely with the more spectacular movements and clashes of the campaign itself.[1] Yet this preparation is as important to the result of the campaign as work in the stable and on the training gallops is to the production of a Derby winner. Without it the skill of the general, as of the jockey, would be of little avail. The youthful Napoleon won his first campaign in 1796 as much by the energy and organizing power that turned a ragged, half-starved rabble of men into an army fit to march and fight as by his skill in battle; and Wellington's successes in the Peninsula would have been impossible without the tireless, careful work behind the lines of that master of detail.

Allenby was no great organizer himself, in the way that Napoleon and Wellington were; but he knew how to set his staff to work, and was always watchful to see what fruits their labours were producing—not by studying returns in an office, but by constant visits to the camps, training grounds, and administrative establishments. So much could not have been done in so short a time but for the keenness of the troops themselves, who were mostly young men of the good physique and fine traditions that fighting races of India provide. They were eager to learn the trade of the soldier, and learned quickly.

Allenby had other accessions to his army during the summer. The French contingent was increased by some battalions formed from Armenian refugees, whose discipline was perhaps more doubtful than the vehemence with which they would be likely to attack their hereditary oppressors, the Turks, if given the opportunity. There came also to Palestine, as the first-fruits of the Balfour Declaration, three battalions of Jews—the 38th, 39th, and 40th Royal Fusiliers—recruited mainly from the Jewish population of the big English cities.

Thus the army as finally organized for Allenby's last great

[1] Thus Allenby's predecessor in command, Sir Archibald Murray, has never received full credit for his great work in reorganization, in the spring of 1916, of the troops evacuated from Gallipoli.

campaign contained representatives of many countries. Of the great Dominions, Australia, New Zealand, and India provided a large proportion of the force; South Africa was represented by a brigade of artillery in the 54th Division and a battalion of Cape Boys (1st Cape Corps) in the 53rd Division; Canada was to have sent two battalions of railwaymen, had the advance planned by the Smuts mission been carried out, but their departure had been cancelled after the German successes in France. Two battalions of sturdy West Indian negroes represented the Colonies, and some Rarotongan islanders from the far Pacific used their skill as boat-men in the landing of supplies through the surf of the harbourless coast. The French and Italian contingents emphasized that the War was an Allied effort; there had even been suggestions of Japanese and Chinese troops being sent to join the E.E.F. The tale was completed by two corps of auxiliaries without whom Allenby's campaigns could never have prospered as they did— the Egyptian Labour Corps and the Camel Transport Corps. Their patience and skill were of inestimable value to the E.E.F. from the defence of the Canal to the final triumph in Syria.

There was little fighting during the summer. The British were too busy with reorganization to undertake more than active patrolling and occasional raids to test the Turkish defences and the new Indian units. Early in June a small advance was made on the coast by troops of the 7th Division in order to capture two low hills which gave some advantage in observation. On August 12 a night raid on a large scale was carried out by the 10th Division against the Turkish defences just west of the Nablus road. It was well planned and executed, and resulted in the capture of nearly 250 prisoners and fourteen machine-guns, as well as inflicting heavy loss on the enemy. The losses of the raiding brigade were only just over a hundred.

The one serious offensive operation was undertaken by the enemy. In the middle of July Liman von Sanders ordered a determined attack in the Jordan valley, with the object of cramping the British hold on the valley and thus making a fresh advance east of Jordan impossible. The main attack was directed against the salient west of the Jordan, north of the Auja stream; this had been the scene of a previous attack in April, and would have been attacked again in May had not Allenby's second Trans-Jordan raid upset the Turkish plans. It was, in fact, an obvious target, and had been strengthened by the Desert Mounted Corps accordingly. The assault was made by the best troops the enemy had available, the German battalions. Owing to the stubbornness and skill of the defending Australians and the failure of the Turkish divisions to support the German attack it ended in complete and costly failure. The Germans, passing between the scattered Australian posts in the dark, gained a momentary footing on the high ground in the rear, but were promptly counter-attacked and driven out, losing nearly 400 prisoners. The engagement was a valuable indication to Allenby both of the continued sensitiveness of the enemy Higher Command to the threat of a move east of Jordan and of the decline in the morale of the Turks, who had made little effort to second the attack of their German allies.

The plan of his final great battle had gradually been taking shape in Allenby's mind during the summer. It was based partly on thought and study—of the history of previous campaigns, of the topography of the land, of Intelligence reports on the state of the Turks—and partly on personal observation and experience during the fighting in the first half of the year. The elements of the plan must have unfolded themselves in something like the following sequence. All the fighting in the hills, from the advance to Jerusalem onward, had warned him that a quick decision and rapid progress were impossible in them, even with the aid of surprise and superior numbers; he must attack on the coastal plain, where he could employ his mounted troops to the full, if he wanted to make a speedy end of his enemy. The two Trans-Jordan raids had shown him how his adversary could be made by the threat to Amman and Deraa to stretch out his weak and wasting resources over an extended front. Liman von Sanders' willingness in his July attack to risk his best troops in an attempt to weaken the British position in the Jordan valley was proof that the Desert Mounted Corps had not endured the heat and dust of the summer in vain. The conduct of the Turkish troops in that action, together with the steady stream of deserters, was evidence of the sorry state of their forces, and an encouragement to take risks beyond the ordinary against them.

Allenby at first set his aims no higher than the occupation of the remainder of Palestine. When the new C.I.G.S., Sir Henry Wilson, telegraphed to him early in July renewing his proposal— a favourite strategical idea of Mr Lloyd George's—to send divisions from France in the autumn to carry out a winter campaign in Palestine and return to France in the spring, Allenby would promise no farther advance than the line Tiberias-Acre— *i.e.*, approximately the present northern frontier of Palestine. And when, at the beginning of August, after the War Cabinet's proposal had been dropped, Allenby outlined his plans to his Corps commanders, they were for a limited operation only. After a break-through on the coast by the Twenty-first Corps the cavalry were to make for Messudieh Junction, about half-way between Nablus and Tulkeram, while the Twentieth and Twenty-first Corps advanced to the line of these two places.

The scheme promised victory, probably a considerable victory, but would permit the retreat and escape of the greater part of the Turkish force. A much bigger conception was already in Allenby's mind, and soon came to birth. One morning, not long after his announcement of the original plan, he returned from a morning ride, strode into his office, and informed his Operations Staff that he had decided on an extension of his plan which aimed at nothing less than the complete destruction of the Turkish armies. The cavalry, instead of turning inland at the level of Tulkeram, were to continue their ride up the Plain of Sharon, cross the spur of hills that ran from the main Judæan range to the sea at Mount Carmel near Haifa, and break into the great Plain of Esdraelon some thirty to forty miles in rear of the Turkish armies, of the railway that served all Turkish forces west of Jordan, and of their main lines of retreat.

It was a daring plan, even against an enemy so inferior in numbers and morale. It would involve a continuous ride of over fifty miles for the majority of the horsemen, and over sixty for some, in the course of which they would have to cross a range of hills in the enemy's possession, passable only by two difficult tracks. There is no parallel in military history to so deep an adventure by such a mass of cavalry against a yet unbroken enemy. But Allenby had not made up his mind lightly, and there was no shaking it by the suggestion of difficulties. He left it to his staff and to his Corps commanders to work out the details of the design, but of the main framework there was to be no alteration. The long Turkish domination of Syria and Palestine, and the military power on which it was founded, were to be given their death-blow in the grand manner.

IV

THE EVE OF MEGIDDO
(*August–September* 1918)

An incalculable element in all war planning is the intentions of the enemy. But there was little uncertainty about the powers and intentions of the Turkish forces in Palestine. With an effective fighting strength of only about 33,000,[1] they were spread-eagled, thanks to Allenby's strategy, over a front of seventy-five miles, from the Mediterranean coast to Amman. The Seventh and Eighth Armies were west of Jordan, with headquarters at Nablus and Tulkeram respectively, and the Fourth Army in the Jordan valley and on the hills of Moab, with headquarters at Amman. These so-called 'armies' contained little more than 10,000 effective rifles each. Their strength and morale had steadily deteriorated during the summer.

The collapse of the Russians in the spring of 1918 had released the Turkish armies in Asia Minor, and had provided an opportunity to strengthen the Palestine front. But Enver Pasha, the irresponsible gambler who dictated the policy of Turkey at this time, trusting to his German allies to win the War, and anxious, as is the way of dictators, to display some cheaply won successes,

---

[1] The figures, as usual, are in dispute, Liman von Sanders claiming that his effective strength was much lower. It is largely a matter of difference in methods of calculation of 'fighting men.' The 'ration strength' of the Fourth, Seventh, and Eighth Armies was shown in a captured return at over 100,000; this can hardly have included less than 33,000 combatants. The ration strength of the three British Corps was under 150,000, and their fighting strength was reckoned at 66,000. The British captured 75,000 prisoners during the operations.

embarked on grandiose schemes of conquest in the Caucasus. He squandered Turkey's last reserves in seizing Batum, Kars, and Tiflis, places which had once, long since, owned Ottoman rule. Far from reinforcing Palestine, he had even attempted to withdraw from Liman von Sanders all his German troops. And so poorly organized were the lines of communication to Syria and Palestine that the Turkish soldiers at the front lacked even the means of proper subsistence.[1] They were ragged and halfstarved; and the transport animals were incapable of hard work owing to insufficient forage.

Obviously the troops of Liman von Sanders could undertake no serious offensive action; the only question was whether they would 'stay put' till the day chosen for the battle. Did Allenby, perhaps, recall the fisherman he had watched a year before on the shore near El Arish[2] flinging his net over a flat-fish, his one anxiety that the fish should remain supine till the net fell round it? He was like that fisherman now, sure of his prey if it did not withdraw before he was ready to make his cast.

The vital points in the Turkish rear over which Allenby aimed to fling his net were Deraa, the junction where the railway to Palestine, which fed the Seventh and Eighth Armies, branched off from the Hejaz Railway, which served the Fourth Army; the crossings of the Jordan at Beisan and Jisr el Mejamie; and Afule, in the Plain of Esdraelon, where the railway to Nablus and Tulkeram turned south. Deraa was beyond the sweep of Allenby's horsemen, but was within the range of his Arab allies, whose mobility was little trammelled by questions of supply or lines of communication. Allenby had no expectation of their ability to seize or hold Deraa, but had entrusted to them the mission of breaking the railway near Deraa just before his own attack, and had backed his belief in their assistance by the gift of 2000 riding camels. Beisan and Afule he intended to seize with his cavalry within twenty-four hours of the opening of the battle. Thus he aimed, not merely at the defeat, but at the complete annihilation of the Seventh and Eighth Armies. The Fourth Army, east of

---

[1] The railways had little or no coal, and many olive- and fig-trees and even vines in the Nablus valley were cut down at this time to provide fuel for the railways.

[2] See p. 167.

Jordan, would escape the first casting of the net, but might be caught by a second cast.

The details of the plan were worked out at a series of conferences, over which Allenby presided. Those who attended them will not easily forget his almost presumptuous confidence about the issue of the operations, the clearness and incisiveness of his instructions, and his occasional abrupt impatience at some objection or difficulty. It was not his way to be content with half-measures, and this was shown clearly in two aspects of the plan—the arrangements for the break-through on the coast and the measures for the deception of the enemy. No better example of the old maxim " Concentrate all available force at the decisive point " could be found than Allenby's distribution of force for his last great battle. In total fighting men he had a superiority of approximately two to one over the Turk; but when his concentration was complete he had massed on the left of his line, on a front of some fifteen miles, 35,000 infantry, 9000 cavalry, and nearly 400 guns,[1] while on the same front his unsuspecting adversary had only some 8000 infantry and about 120 guns. On the remainder of the front, nearly fifty miles, the British, with 22,000 infantry, 3000 mounted men, and 170 guns, faced about 20,000 to 25,000 Turks with 270 guns.

That such a distribution was achieved without the enemy becoming aware of it was due to the elaborate measures taken for secrecy and for deception. Allenby's plan was the exact reverse of the Gaza-Beersheba battle of nearly a year before. Then he struck the Turk's left flank, while persuading them that he meant to break through on the coast. Now that he meant to break through on the coast he took every possible step to make them apprehend a blow at their left flank. Elaborate precautions were made as if to transfer G.H.Q. from the camp in the plains to an hotel in Jerusalem, which was cleared and prepared for it, with telephone lines laid, offices marked, and so forth. This was backed by rumours of a great concentration in the Jerusalem area and the marking of billets. New camps were pitched in the Jordan valley and additional bridges thrown across the Jordan.

[1] Three-quarters of these guns were concentrated on a front of seven miles near the coast.

Fifteen thousand dummy horses, made of canvas, filled the horse lines; and sleighs drawn by mules raised clouds of dust at the times when the canvas horses should have been going to water. Battalions marched ostentatiously down to the valley by day and returned by lorries at night. Wireless traffic was continued from Desert Mounted Corps headquarters near Jericho long after the headquarters and nearly all the troops had been transferred to the other flank. Only the Anzac Division, with a brigade of Indian infantry and some other battalions, was left in the valley. It was known as " Chaytor's Force," from the commander of the Anzac Division. Farther east Lawrence's agents spread news of the large quantities of forage which would shortly be required by the British in the Amman district. Such were some of the measures taken to give enemy observers and enemy agents the impression that another advance east of Jordan was being prepared.

Meanwhile the concentration on the other flank was made with the greatest possible secrecy. Only a few senior officers knew the full details. Troops from the Jordan valley and Judæan hills were moved by night to the coastal area, where they were carefully hidden in the orange-groves and olive woods north of Jaffa. No new tents were pitched. With great foresight the units normally in reserve had during the summer been widely dispersed, so that reinforcements could be introduced without any increase in tentage. Thus a battalion had been quartered in two half-battalion camps: when reinforcements arrived a whole battalion occupied each of these camps, and the force was doubled without any change being visible from the air. No movement of any kind was allowed to the troops hidden in the woods and groves during the hours of daylight. The irrigation channels in the orange-groves provided means for watering most of the horses without their having to leave their place of concealment. Fires were forbidden by day or night. Even the local inhabitants were unaware of the great concentration. And our Air Force had gained so complete a mastery over the enemy that few hostile aeroplanes crossed our lines in September. That the enemy was unaware of Allenby's schemes was proved by an Intelligence map captured in the course of the operations. This was dated September 17, two days before the assault, and showed no suspicion of any great concentration on the coast; on the contrary, it indicated an increase of force in the Jordan valley.

A few days before the date fixed for the great assault Allenby visited all divisions and explained to the assembled commanders of units his plan of attack and his confidence of success. He radiated victory, and undoubtedly inspired those who heard him. He even alarmed his staff with what appeared as over-weening presumption, when they heard him promise the cavalry 30,000 prisoners. To a defence-minded battalion commander who inquired what line he should consolidate the Chief replied abruptly, " Aleppo." Besides animating all leaders with hopes of victory, Allenby during these visits discussed with the senior commanders, especially those of the cavalry, the probable course of operations and the difficulties that might arise. Thus they started on their great ride with full knowledge of his intentions and with the certainty that the boldest action would have his backing. His outlook had passed beyond Palestine now, and to his Corps commanders at least he spoke of an immediate advance to Damascus and even farther.

The campaign had, in fact, been practically won before a shot was fired, and Allenby realized it better than anyone. The patient work of reorganization and training in the summer, the brilliant conception of the Commander, the handicraft of an experienced staff, had combined to prepare one of the most crushing strokes ever delivered in war. The Turkish armies may have stirred a little uneasily on the evening of September 18, 1918, with some sense of an impending offensive, but of its imminence and its weight they had no conception.[1] Their traditional Ottoman stubbornness and skill in defence were of no avail to them here.[2] This was to be no soldiers' battle, but the manœuvre of a great master of war.

[1] A havildar (sergeant) in an Indian battalion had deserted to the Turks on the 17th, and presumably told what he knew of the attack. But his story apparently won little credence. Perhaps another ' haversack ruse ' was suspected.

[2] The Turkish commanders and staff wished, it is believed, to withdraw to a line farther north before the battle. But Liman von Sanders would not agree. The tactical instinct of the Turks was here better than that of the Germans, as it had been the year before, when they wished to consolidate the defences of Jerusalem, and von Falkenhayn insisted on manœuvre and counter-attack.

CHAPTER X

CAVALCADE

(September 17–October 31, 1918)

I

MEGIDDO

(September 17–22, 1918)

> If thou hast run with the footmen, and they have wearied thee,
> then how canst thou contend with horses?
>
> Jeremiah xii, 5

THERE were two curtain-raisers to the great drama on the coastal plain. The first was played by the Arabs under Lawrence, who had concentrated at Azrak, an old outpost of civilization on the edge of the desert. On September 16 and 17 they cut the line between Deraa and Amman, between Deraa and Damascus, and between Deraa and Afule. At the same time the Air Force raided Deraa. The enemy Commander-in-Chief reacted, as was hoped, by sending there a part of his scanty reserves. The other preliminary operation was carried out in the Judæan hills by Chetwode's Twentieth Corps, now reduced to two divisions only. The mission of the Corps was to advance on Nablus in step with the Twenty-first Corps and to prevent the enemy escaping eastward. Chetwode, who had a practised eye for ground, refused to take the obvious line of advance astride the Nablus road, where the enemy expected attack and had a series of strong positions. He assembled his divisions one at either end of his twenty-five-miles front, leaving in the centre only a thin screen of a cavalry regiment and two pioneer battalions. He intended, when the time came, to make a converging advance from both flanks, thus keeping to the high ground and turning the enemy's defences of the main road. The preliminary operation, carried out on the night of September 17–18, was designed to bring his right division across a deep ravine in readiness for the advance on Nablus; it would also secure an important water-supply, and would serve to distract the enemy's attention from the main attack in the plain. It was successful, after some hard fighting at some points.

Not long after the noise of battle had died down in the hills the assault of the Twenty-first Corps opened with a great roar of artillery at 4.30 A.M. on the morning of September 19. The infantry began their advance at the same moment. Allenby did not believe in long preliminary bombardments—he put more trust in surprise; the Turkish wire, which was not strong, could be cut by hand, and it was important to give the enemy no time to think. Simultaneously with the opening of the battle the Air Force set forth to bomb the principal Turkish headquarters. It was successful in completely interrupting all communication between the Eighth Army headquarters at Tulkeram and Liman von Sanders at Nazareth, besides greatly delaying communications with the Seventh Army. Fighting aeroplanes also patrolled over the principal enemy aerodromes and prevented their reconnaissance machines from leaving the ground. Thus the enemy Commander-in-Chief remained in almost complete ignorance of the grave events taking place on his front. The arrival next morning of a British cavalry brigade at his headquarters at Nazareth was his earliest intimation that something really serious must have happened to his army.

The action of the Twenty-first Corps was exactly that of men pushing open a wide and heavy door of which the hinges were in the foothills and the handle by the coast. Rightly, the greatest leverage was exerted at the handle end; here was the thickest concentration of troops and guns, and here were the leading cavalry divisions, ready to pass through the moment the door was even ajar. By a fortunate conjuncture the two infantry divisions on the left, through which the cavalry would pass, were both commanded by generals who had served with Barrow and Macandrew in the Indian cavalry. This fact did much to resolve the first critical problem, the determination of the earliest moment when the cavalry could pass through the infantry lines. On other occasions during the War, in France or elsewhere, the horsemen in search of the " G in ' gap,' " as the term was, had always come too soon or too late—to find either that the infantry had failed to break a passage, or that the enemy had recovered and re-formed, and that the fleeting opportunity had already gone. Now at last, thanks to good staff work and bold handling, the cavalry went cleanly through almost on the heels of the assaulting infantry. By 7 A.M. the 5th Cavalry Division began to move forward along the beach under shelter of the cliffs; the 4th Cavalry Division, farther inland, passed through the old front line a little later, just before 9 A.M. By 10 A.M. both divisions were well clear of all obstacles and fairly started on their great ride north. The skill with which the staff of the Twenty-first Corps had planned and the determination with which the infantry had assaulted had given the cavalry their great opportunity.

During their break-through they passed over a battlefield where an English commander had won a notable victory more than seven hundred years previously. At the battle of Arsuf (September 7, 1191) Richard Cœur de Lion, who was a skilful and prudent general, though a rash and unprofitable king, had outmanœuvred and outfought a worthy opponent in Saladin. Saladin's host had included a considerable force of Turkish bowmen, while Richard's international force of Crusaders contained an English contingent of horse and foot. So that it was not the first time that the ground over which the cavalry now rode had felt the victorious rush of English chivalry in pursuit of Turks. The marsh they crossed soon after the start, the Birket el Ramadan, had been used by Richard to protect his camp the night before the battle (malaria probably took a deadly toll of his army in consequence); but the forest in which the flying Moslems had taken shelter from Richard's charge had disappeared long since.

Once fairly through the trench line the cavalry easily brushed away the little opposition they met. Their next obstacle, the real crisis of the whole operation, was the passage of the seven-mile belt of hills, the great spur that separates the Plains of Sharon and Esdraelon and ends in Mount Carmel above Haifa. The tracks through it are few, narrow, and easily defensible; if the enemy realized his danger in time and sent his reserves to hold the passes they might easily impose such delay as would mar Allenby's great design and give the Turkish armies an opportunity of escape. The risk was comparable to the risk Allenby took in his plan for the Gaza-Beersheba battle, that the enemy might have the time and foresight to wreck beyond speedy repair all the wells at Beersheba. All plans in the dubious hazard of war must have such risks; the great commander is he who has both the courage to accept them and the skill to minimize them.

The 4th Cavalry Division was to attempt the Musmus Pass, which debouches at the ancient fortress of Megiddo. Near here, 2500 years before, Josiah, the best of the kings of Judah, was slain by an Egyptian arrow while fighting for his Assyrian overlord. A thousand years earlier still Megiddo had been the scene of a great conflict between Egyptian and Syrian, when Thotmes III took the same road through the Musmus Pass, to the consternation of his subordinate commanders, who feared to be caught in so narrow a defile. The King's daring was justified, for he led his force safely through and won a great victory over his astonished enemy.

Barrow also brought the 4th Cavalry Division through without a fight, but he had some anxious and dramatic moments. His leading brigade missed the entrance to the pass in the darkness, and was leading the rest of the division astray. Fortunately Barrow himself, who had gone ahead, discovered the mistake in time to divert the last brigade on to the right road and to turn the remainder. His action saved his command from a dangerous situation. As the leading regiment, the 2nd Lancers of the Indian cavalry, shook itself clear of the hills early next morning and deployed into the Plain of Esdraelon it met a Turkish battalion which had been sent to hold the pass, and promptly charged it with the lance. The shock of surprise at meeting cavalry at such an unexpected time and place was probably too much for the enemy's nerves and musketry; the fire was so wild that there was only one Indian casualty, while some fifty of the Turks were speared and the remainder surrendered. The fate of this battalion shows the danger of delays in war. It had received the order to hold the Musmus defile in plenty of time to reach it before the 4th Cavalry Division, had it acted promptly. The sluggishness of its commander and the energy of General Barrow had a considerable effect on the course of the operations.

During September 20 the 4th Cavalry Division continued its ride along the historic Plain of Esdraelon and down the Valley of

Jezreel to Beisan and the Jordan. It reached the railway junction and depot at Afule about 8 A.M., almost simultaneously with a brigade of the 5th Cavalry Division, which had crossed the hills farther north. A number of prisoners and many stores were taken. So complete was the enemy's surprise that a German aeroplane landed unsuspectingly among the British troops.

Meanwhile another brigade of the 5th Cavalry Division had ridden across the plain straight for Nazareth, with the object of capturing Liman von Sanders' headquarters and, if possible, the enemy Commander-in-Chief himself. It reached Nazareth at 4.30 A.M., before the enemy had received the slightest warning of its approach, and while the Commander-in-Chief was still in bed. But the brigade had been weakened by the pace of the advance, which it had led throughout, and by various detachments which it had dropped for escorts to prisoners and other purposes. Nazareth, built on a steep hillside, is a difficult town to search or occupy, and the brigade had no guide or knowledge of the exact position of Liman von Sanders' house or headquarters. Street fighting broke out in which the German *personnel* of the head-quarters put up a stout resistance; and the few squadrons which had reached the town were eventually withdrawn, as it was believed that Liman von Sanders had escaped. It was disappointing that so dramatic a stroke as the capture of the opposing Commander-in-Chief within twenty-four hours of the opening of the battle should have just failed.

After a few hours' rest at Afule Barrow's division resumed its march down the famous Valley of Jezreel, so full of history. To the north could be clearly seen Mount Tabor, whence the Israelites had swept down on Sisera's labouring host, bogged in the valley below; where also the giant Kléber, one of Napoleon's best generals, had been hard beset by a Syrian horde, so that Napoleon himself had to hasten up from the siege of Acre to discomfit his assailants. Near Mount Tabor are the caves of Endor, where Saul visited the woman with a familiar spirit and learned his doom; on the other side of the valley stands out Mount Gilboa, where that doom met him and his son Jonathan, and inspired one of the world's great poems. Below Mount Gilboa Gideon's three hundred picked men made the first night attack of which we have a detailed account;[1] the lessons it teaches—the value of discipline, the need for personal reconnaissance, the moral effect of surprise—are applicable to any night attack to-day. At the mouth of the valley stands Jezreel itself (the modern Zirin), a natural fortress on a low hill rising out of the plain, the scene of one of the most famous dramas of the Bible. Here was Naboth's vineyard; here the watchman saw the avenging Jehu driving furiously up from the valley of the Jordan; here Ahab's proud, wicked queen, Jezebel, decked herself to meet her fate, and met it royally with a shrewd taunt—" Had Zimri peace, who slew his master? "—at the upstart military dictator.

The advanced guard of the 4th Division, riding past all these memories, occupied Beisan (where Saul's dead body had hung) by 4.30 P.M.: the whole division was concentrated there by 6 P.M. It had covered, according to the official calculation, seventy miles in thirty-four hours, but the greater part must have ridden at least seventy-five to eighty miles. Only twenty-six horses had foundered, a remarkable tribute to the horse-mastership and staff work of the division. One regiment went on during the night another twelve miles to Jisr el Mejamie, and occupied the railway bridge over the Jordan.

The Australian Mounted Division, less one brigade which had been detached to work on the left of the infantry advance, followed the 4th Cavalry Division through the Musmus Pass and reached the Plain of Esdraelon about 11 A.M. on the 20th. Thence it sent a brigade to Jenin, where it made large captures of men and stores. It then disposed itself to await the retiring Turks.

Thus by the evening of September 20, thirty-six hours after the opening of the battle, the natural avenues of retreat of the Turkish Seventh and Eighth Armies were in the hands of the British cavalry. Their only way of escape was eastward across the Jordan by narrow tracks through difficult country; and even this passage was being hourly contracted by the action of the infantry in the hills advancing on Nablus, of Chaytor's Force in the Jordan valley, and of the 4th Cavalry Division from Beisan. Only the boldest and most fortunate escaped the fall of Allenby's net.

While the cavalry were occupying the line of butts the infantry

[1] See Judges vii.

were steadily driving their prey towards them. The Twenty-first Corps, after breaking a way for the horsemen on the morning of the 19th, had swung right-handed on a great wheel towards the hills; and by evening Shea's 60th Division, on the outside of the wheel—except for a brigade of Australian Light Horse—had reached Tulkeram. During the next three days the destruction of the Seventh and Eighth Armies was completed. The infantry of the Twentieth and Twenty-first Corps converged on Nablus, which was occupied on the evening of the 21st. A great part of the Eighth Army had already been captured or killed by the Twenty-first Corps. Most of the remainder retired on Jenin by the Plain of Dothan, and were rounded up by the Australian Mounted Division. Some small remnants of this Army and the greater part of the Seventh endeavoured to escape towards the Jordan.

In the narrow gorge of the Wadi Fara, which leads from Nablus to Jisr ed Damieh, a long column of guns, troops, and transport was caught and bombed by the Air Force on the 21st. The head of the transport was soon blocked, and all movement ceased; nearly a hundred guns and over a thousand vehicles were captured here when the infantry came up. The survivors of the demoralized column scattered in the hills, where the greater part were rounded up by the cavalry in the next few days. The Air Force had already wrought even deadlier, if less spectacular, destruction on the road between Tulkeram and Nablus.

Those of the enemy who broke eastward to the Jordan from Nablus had only a narrow and difficult passage to safety, for the 4th Cavalry Division advanced south from Beisan, and Chaytor's Force in the valley advanced north on Jisr el Mejamie. Among the few who had the determination and skill to escape were the commander of the Seventh Army, Mustapha Kemal Pasha, the future Ataturk, who was to regenerate the Turkish nation,[1] and Colonel von Oppen,[2] with the remnants of his German contingent, which maintained its formation and discipline in spite of the rout of its Turkish allies.

---

[1] He had taken over command of the Seventh Army in August from Fevzi Pasha, now Marshal Cakmak, head of the Turkish Army, who had become ill.
[2] He died at the end of the retreat at Tarsus.

CHAPTER X: CAVALCADE

Allenby himself—he was not a commander who was content to await news at his headquarters—had been well forward during the operations. Here, from a regimental history,[1] is a snapshot of him in the early morning of the 19th, while the infantry fight was still in progress:

> A halt was called, and the battalion stood about in groups, discussing the stupendous fact that they were standing on what had been Turkish ground only a brief hour previously. Shortly afterwards there was a stir among the crowds of men, which parted to allow the passage of a large open touring car, from the radiator of which flew a small Union Jack. It was the Commander-in-Chief, thus early up at the front of affairs, to see for himself how things were going. Those fortunate enough to be close to the car had a clear view of General Allenby, whose features showed no sign of the great triumph he was now so close to achieving. The Commander-in-Chief sat straight upright, looking ahead to where the puffs of smoke showed where our shells were falling among the flying Turks.

On the 21st, a few hours after the capture of Nablus, Sir Philip Chetwode, who had gone up to the advanced troops of his Twentieth Corps, met the Commander-in-Chief in the town, which he had entered from the west in an armoured car close behind some mounted troops. He at once ordered Chetwode to dispatch his Corps cavalry regiment, however tired it might be, down the Wadi Fara in pursuit of the Turks. Next day, the 22nd, Allenby was at the headquarters of the Desert Mounted Corps at Megiddo. Long distances over indifferent tracks in heat and dust had no effect on his determination to see for himself how things were going. He was out almost every day, and often close behind his advanced troops. On one day he motored more than two hundred miles, hardly a mile of which was over a properly made road, between 5.30 A.M. and 8 P.M. The impressions he thus gained at first hand of the spirit of his troops and leaders and of the disorganization of the enemy were invaluable to him in his planning of the next stage in his great design, the advance to Damascus and the destruction of the Fourth Turkish Army, east of Jordan.

[1] *The Kensingtons*, p. 367.

II

DAMASCUS

(September 23–October 5, 1918)

Even before the Megiddo battle Allenby had in his mind a plan
for an immediate advance on Damascus, and had certainly spoken
of it to some of his subordinate commanders. On the 22nd, when
he saw Chauvel at Megiddo, he warned him to be in readiness for
a further advance and, as a first step, to seize Haifa, Acre, and
Tiberias, thus completing the conquest of Palestine. Haifa and
Acre were occupied on the 23rd, the former after a dashing charge
by the 15th Cavalry Brigade.[1] Its capture enabled stores to be
landed, and thereby eased the supply situation. Tiberias was
occupied on the 25th, after the most fiercely contested action of
the whole pursuit. Liman von Sanders, after his escape from
Nazareth, still ignorant of the extent of the disaster that had
befallen his armies, ordered them to occupy a defensive line from
Deraa down the Yarmuk valley to Semakh, at the southern end
of the Sea of Galilee, and thence by Tiberias along the western
side of the lake. These orders were quite incapable of fulfilment,
and, in fact, never even reached the Seventh and Eighth Armies,
which had practically ceased to exist. But Liman von Sanders
himself, as he passed through Semakh, had done something to
organize resistance at that pivot of the defence, putting a German
officer in command and giving him a number of German machine-
gunners to stiffen the garrison. The brigade of Australian Light
Horse that approached the station and village shortly before dawn
on the 25th was, however, in no mood to be checked by any
difficulties or dangers. As soon as the German machine-guns
opened they formed line and charged unhesitatingly over unknown ground in the moonlight. Their loss in horses was heavy,
but they reached the buildings, dismounted, and cleared them in

[1] This is probably the only recorded charge of cavalry in which men of the Royal
Engineers have ridden. The 15th Field Troop, R.E., happened to be alongside the
Jodhpore Lancers just before the charge, and on the invitation of the Lancers' commanding officer armed themselves with lances and swords from casualties and rode in
the charge. Though none of them had ever handled such weapons before, they claim
to have killed at least one Turk with the *arme blanche*.

some grim fighting at close range, in which about a hundred Germans were killed and 350 prisoners taken, mostly Turks. The Australians had some seventy-five casualties to men and a hundred to horses. Tiberias was then occupied without further resistance.

Before dealing with Allenby's plan for the advance to Damascus it is necessary to describe briefly the situation east of Jordan. Chaytor's Force, which had been left in the valley to face the Fourth Army, consisted of his own Anzac Mounted Division, an Indian infantry brigade, two battalions of Jews, and two of West Indians. Its first task after the battle opened was to advance north up the valley to Jisr ed Damieh, which was captured on the 22nd. By that time it was obvious that the Fourth Army was withdrawing from its positions in the valley, and for the third and last time the Anzac Division advanced on Es Salt and Amman. Amman was taken on the evening of the 25th, by which time the Fourth Army was in full retreat for Damascus, over a hundred miles distant from Amman. It had, in fact, delayed too long for safety, and its march to Damascus, with the Arabs hanging on flanks and rear, was an ordeal that few survived. Chaytor did not join the pursuit of this doomed force: he remained at Amman to intercept the Turkish Second Corps, which was withdrawing from Maan and farther south. It surrendered without fighting.[1]

Thus by the 26th, when Allenby held a conference of Corps commanders at Jenin, all Palestine was his. He had nearly 50,000 prisoners, the Seventh and Eighth Armies were reduced to a few small scattered columns, and the Fourth Army was in hasty retreat. There were estimated to be perhaps 40,000 Turks either between the British and Damascus or at Damascus itself. At his conference Allenby announced briefly that the Desert Mounted Corps would advance forthwith on Damascus, while the Twenty-first Corps would send a division along the coast to Beirut, to be followed by another if necessary. Orders to this effect had already been issued. Those present at the conference will remember chiefly the summary fashion in which Allenby

---

[1] There was a curious interlude after the surrender, when the Turks and a small body of Australians to whom they had surrendered combined to keep off a horde of Arabs who proposed to massacre the Turks.

disposed of the supply problem. He turned to his senior administrative officer present with a question: " And what of the supply situation? " " Extremely rocky, sir," was the discouraging reply. " Well, you must do your best," said Allenby, and proceeded to impress on his commanders the need for boldness and rapid action. He was meticulous in his administrative arrangements before an operation, but in a pursuit like this was prepared to drive his troops forward on the shortest of rations. He realized better than anyone that his most dangerous enemy at the time was disease rather than the Turk, and that his best weapon was speed. He knew that malaria, which his protective measures had so hardly held at bay in the Jordan valley and elsewhere, was bound to take toll of his troops once they had passed into the lines of the Turks, who had taken no measures of protection. He told a senior Medical Officer that the knowledge that in fourteen days from the opening of the campaign malaria would begin to sap the strength of his force acted as a spur to his determination to press forward as rapidly as possible.

Chauvel ordered the 4th Cavalry Division to move on Deraa, to intercept the retreat of the Fourth Army if possible; if not, to follow it to Damascus by the ancient pilgrims' road. Meanwhile the Australian Mounted Division, followed by the 5th Cavalry Division, was to take the more direct road north of Lake Tiberias by Kuneitra. The distance to Damascus by this route was about a hundred miles, while the 4th Cavalry Division, which started its march a day earlier, had about 140 miles to cover. All three divisions arrived on the outskirts of Damascus on September 30 within a few hours of each other.

There is no need to relate the advance in any detail. The leading brigade of the 4th Cavalry Division suffered a temporary check at Irbid, where it tried to dispose in too contemptuous a fashion of a strong flank-guard from the Fourth Army; but the division reached Deraa on the morning of the 28th, to find it already in the hands of Lawrence and the Arabs. The Arab force from Azrak had cut in on the line of retreat of the Fourth Army and had captured or killed considerable numbers of them; and the villagers were also arming themselves and revenging many years of oppression. The 4th Cavalry Division now followed on the rear of the Fourth Army, while the Arabs continued to attack the flanks.[1]

The Australian Mounted Division was considerably delayed by a German-Turkish rearguard at the crossing of the Jordan at Jisr Benat Yakub (" the bridge of the daughters of Jacob "), and did not reach Kuneitra till the night of the 28th. After some further fighting against the enemy rearguards the Australians on the evening of the 30th cut the road and railway leading by the gorge of the Barada river westwards [2] to Rayak and Baalbek, causing great havoc in a Turkish column caught in the gorge. The 5th Cavalry Division had come up on the right of the Australians, and had gained touch with the 4th Cavalry Division. Thus as darkness fell on September 30 all three divisions were on the outskirts of Damascus, while within the city Turkish rule had already ceased, and some parties of Arab irregulars had already entered.

Next day, October 1, the city was occupied. A brigade of Australian Light Horse were the first troops to enter, passing quickly through it in quest of a Turkish column which had retired north. Damascus, probably the oldest city of the world, has never been a fortress or walled town, like Jerusalem. It is famous for trade rather than for war: though its swords are renowned, its silks and silver-work are better known. It has never stood a siege, and has usually fallen as a prize to the victor of some battle fought at a distance. And now its significance was political rather than military. To the horsemen of the Desert Mounted Corps it marked a stage in the pursuit of a beaten foe and towards the ending of a long war; to the Arabs and to their

---

[1] Lawrence's relation, in *Seven Pillars of Wisdom*, of his meetings and conversations with General Barrow at Deraa and elsewhere is inaccurate, and his whole account of these days is tendentious and quite unfair to the 4th Cavalry Division. Sir Hubert Young in *The Independent Arab* gives the following picture of the occupation of Deraa:

" We reached Deraa at about ten o'clock, to find General Barrow installed in the railway station, Sherif Nasir and Lawrence in the town, and a certain liveliness between the Allied forces. The General had entered Deraa to find it in an appalling state owing to the excesses of the Bedouin. Until the Sherifian detachment arrived there was no sign of any organized Arab force, and he naturally hesitated to leave at the mercy of what he regarded as a pack of ragamuffins a town which had been evacuated by the Turks as a result of his own advance."

[2] The Abana of the Bible.

leader, Feisal, it was the goal of all the national hopes, the former capital of the great Arabian empire that had once stretched from India to the Atlantic. After many years of foreign rule they dreamed again of independence and empire, but across their ambitions lay the shadow of the Sykes-Picot Agreement, which gave special rights to the French in Syria and to the British in Palestine. Its terms had been published in Russia after the Revolution, and had been communicated to Feisal by the Turks in the hope of detaching him from the Allied cause. Hence the Arab anxiety to stake a claim on Damascus and Syria by right of conquest, and to show themselves capable of setting up an administration.

Lawrence worked feverishly to aid the Arabs. He was in a difficult position for his high-minded but self-conscious nature. In loyalty to his country and to Allenby he had used all means and arguments to induce the Arabs to fight on our side, and had encouraged them to believe that the imperialistic designs of Britain and France did not exist, or would be set aside, if they showed their ability as a nation to unite and to rule. His self-consciousness exaggerated to himself his ' betrayal ' of the Arabs; and he was eager to do all he could to help them to stake a claim for independence. His forwardness in the Arab cause and his assumption of authority, though his official position was only that of Allenby's representative with Feisal, puzzled and troubled Chauvel, the military commander, who was not prepared to deal with delicate political problems.[1]

On October 3 Allenby visited Damascus, and sent at once for Feisal, who was preparing to make a triumphal entry into the city. The two men now met for the first time. They were a striking contrast—the burly, confident Englishman, accustomed to command and to dominate by sheer force of personality, and the slight, ascetic Arab with his princely bearing, to whom the arts of the politician were more natural than the vigour of a soldier.[2] Both were men of fine quality, and appreciated and

---

[1] Lawrence's story of the events in Damascus after the entry and of his dealings with Chauvel is not the whole truth, and is unjust to Chauvel.

[2] Allenby wrote to his wife, " You would like Feisal. He is a keen, slim, highly strung man. He has beautiful hands like a woman's, and his fingers are always moving nervously when he talks. But he is strong in will and straight in principle."

trusted each other. After greetings Allenby explained to Feisal that France was to be the protecting Power in Syria, but that Feisal, as representative of his father, King Hussein, could set up a military administration of the occupied enemy territory east of the Jordan, from Akaba to Damascus. The Lebanon was to be under direct French administration, and Feisal would have a French officer attached to him to represent French advice and guidance. It was, in fact, the Sykes-Picot Agreement, which the French Government was demanding should be observed. Feisal protested strongly, but Allenby insisted on his orders being obeyed, and that Feisal must accept the situation till the peace settlement.

After Feisal had left, Lawrence said that he could not consent to work with a French officer and asked for leave, which was granted. He left Damascus next day. Into the last year he had crowded the effort, mental and physical, of several years for any ordinary man; small wonder if he was overstrained in mind and body. He was later to fight for the Arabs at the council table as vigorously as he had led them in the desert. His name will always be connected with the Arab campaign, in which his achievements were as remarkable as his character. It is a tribute to the greatness of Allenby that Lawrence, who was no respecter of persons because they held high rank or place, always gave him implicit obedience. He wrote of him in *Seven Pillars*, " Allenby never questioned our fulfilling what was ordered. Power lay in his calm assumption that he would receive as perfect obedience as he gave trust." Lawrence had great courage, versatility, and quickness of mind, but Allenby was unquestionably the stronger and greater character of the two outstanding figures in this campaign. Lawrence wrote of Allenby and himself later as " lion and mouse friends."

III

ALEPPO

(*October* 5–31, 1918)

When the Desert Mounted Corps left the Plain of Esdraelon to advance on Damascus there had been some 40,000 Turks between it and its goal. Of these one-half were now prisoners, and several thousands had been killed. Less than 17,000 weary, dispirited, disorganized enemy troops had escaped from Damascus; and of them only 4000 were believed to be effective rifles. The enemy had no guns and little transport, and could obviously offer only slight resistance to a further advance. The obstacles to the occupation of the rest of Syria were now distance, supply, and disease. The last was the most serious. As Allenby had foreseen, the admissions to hospital from malaria began to rise at an alarming rate just a fortnight after the first break-through, a few days after Damascus had been won. To malaria was added the epidemic of influenza (the ' Spanish 'flu,' as it was called) that swept the whole world at this time, and was in its total casualty list almost as deadly as the War. All units were soon much reduced in strength. The 4th Cavalry Division and Australian Mounted Division, who had had the harder work and longer spells of the Jordan valley, suffered worse than the 5th Cavalry Division.

The War Cabinet had urged on Allenby an immediate cavalry raid on Aleppo after the fall of Damascus. He wisely preferred to proceed more methodically, by stages; and he ordered as the first stage an advance to the line Rayak-Beirut. The 5th Cavalry Division left Damascus on October 5, and occupied the railway junction of Rayak next day, picking up a number of Turkish stragglers and finding some abandoned stores and rolling stock. The 4th Cavalry Division followed a day behind; the Australian Division was left to guard Damascus.

Meanwhile the 7th Indian Division of Bulfin's Twenty-first Corps had left Haifa on October 3, and was marching up the coast by Tyre and Sidon to Beirut, which it reached on October 8. French warships had forestalled it by sea and Arab irregulars by land. These latter, sent by Feisal to support Arab claims to the Lebanon, were with some difficulty persuaded to withdraw in favour of a French military administration.

Homs-Tripoli was the next stage, reached in the middle of October by the 5th Cavalry Division inland and a brigade of the 7th Indian Division on the coast. There had been no fighting since Damascus. In fact, this advance northward seemed rather an anticlimax—like walking up a few rabbits after two drives in which the birds had come high and fast. But it was not really as simple or safe as it seemed: Damascus was 150 miles from the depots on which the original operation had been based, and Aleppo was 200 miles from Damascus. The Turks might well make a determined last stand there. The gallant von Oppen, who had kept his Germans together throughout the retreat, had died of cholera; but there were two of the best Turkish commanders, Mustapha Kemal, of the Seventh Army, and Jemal Pasha, of the Fourth, still with the Turkish remnant, and the Turk at his most miserable can put up a stout fight. Even Allenby, when he learned that the 4th Cavalry Division, which was to have followed the 5th, was completely immobilized by sickness, hesitated for a moment to send on the 5th Division, also considerably reduced, without support. But its commander, Macandrew,[1] was a forcible and confident soldier, and telegraphed that he had no doubts of his ability to occupy Aleppo. He was allowed to proceed, and justified his boldness by seizing Aleppo, with the effective aid of a column of Feisal's Arabs, in face of a very considerably superior Turkish force, which had been rallied and reorganized by no less a leader than Mustapha Kemal Pasha, who was later to rally and reorganize all Turkey.

The last engagement of the campaign was fought at Haritan, some eight miles north-west of Aleppo, on October 26, when a strong Turkish column was charged by two weak regiments of the 15th Cavalry Brigade. After an initial success the brigade was compelled to withdraw, greatly outnumbered; the Turks also withdrew, shaken by the boldness of the attack. A few days later, on October 31, the armistice with Turkey was announced.

In less than six weeks Allenby's army had captured 75,000 prisoners and 360 guns, and had moved its front forward 350 miles. Its own casualty list had been little over 5000. The most advanced troops, the 5th Cavalry Division, had actually covered some 550 miles in the thirty-eight days from the breaking of the line to the occupation of Aleppo. The greatest exploit in history of horsed cavalry, and possibly their last success on a large scale, had ended within a short distance of the battlefield of Issus

[1] Macandrew died at Aleppo in July 1919 as the result of an accident.

(333 B.C.), where Alexander the Great first showed how battles could be won by bold and well-handled horsemen. It had taken just four years to conclude the war with Turkey; it took nearly five more to conclude peace. Which proves the staying-power of the pen over the sword.

CHAPTER XI

ALLENBY THE GENERAL

ALTHOUGH Allenby was to give another eight strenuous years to the service of his country, and, as Field-Marshal, to remain on the active list to the end of his life, his career as a commander of troops in the field virtually ended when the armistice with Turkey was concluded. Therefore this seems the appropriate place to attempt some estimate of his generalship and of his place on the roll of great British soldiers. He would have claimed no such place for himself, not because of any conscious modesty, but simply because he would not have thought it worth while for anyone to spend time in discussing his merits or demerits. What he had been given to do he had done to the best of his ability; the results, good and bad, were there for the world to see and judge.

Allenby had been successful. Whether his successes were due to fortune, to the work of his staff, to the fighting qualities of his troops, to the weakness of the enemy, or to his own skill, let anyone decide for himself. He would do nothing, by speech or writing, to influence the verdict, except to give most generous tribute to all those who had helped him. What mattered now was the next job of work, not discussion of the last. If Allenby had been a bridge-player he would have permitted no *post-mortems*; he would simply have recorded the score with a word of praise or condolence to his partner and would have concentrated on the next deal.[1] And when all work was done it was surely better to spend one's last years in the study of living birds and beasts and flowers and in visiting new corners of the earth than in discussing old, dead events that had passed beyond recall, for good or for evil. " Once you have taken a decision, never look back on it," was one of Allenby's favourite maxims. Few have had the strength of mind to act on it as wholly as he did.

Not many generals, certainly few modern generals, can have

[1] On drafts of the Official History submitted to him, for instance, he made few comments, unless to emphasize the skill or coolness of one of his subordinates.

had Allenby's experience as a commander in the field and on the training ground. On active service he had commanded a troop in Zululand and Bechuanaland; a squadron, a regiment, a column (the equivalent of a brigade), in the South African War; a division, a Corps, an Army, and finally an independent Expeditionary Force in the Great War. In peace he had led and trained a troop, a squadron, a regiment, a brigade, a division—not for a season or so, in the intervals of staff employment, but each for several years. In addition to all this practical experience, he had studied the theory of his profession seriously; he had passed the course of the Staff College, and had held a staff appointment most efficiently. It would be difficult for any critic to find fault with his professional equipment for command.

He was, however, no narrow-minded specialist; he had an unusual range of interests and knowledge outside his profession. And what he knew, military or secular, he knew thoroughly; there was nothing superficial about Allenby's store of information, as many a shallow conversationalist or plausible commanding officer found to his cost. Also he had travelled widely, and had used eyes, ears, and tongue with understanding.

In all professions, and expecially in the military, character is of greater importance than brains or experience. Allenby's character can surely be judged adequate to the most searching calls that the testing profession of arms could make. He had absolute courage, physical and moral—a courage so complete that he seemed almost unaware that such a quality existed; he acted quickly and coolly in danger, not because danger excited him to action, but because there was work to be done at once. His loyalty to his superiors went beyond deeds; he would brook no word of criticism of their orders or decisions. He had an even rarer quality, possibly—that of trusting his own subordinates. Courage, loyalty, trust, straightforwardness—all these were Allenby's; and these are surely the prime qualities required of one in whose keeping the welfare, the honour, and the lives of many men are placed.

What, then, was wanting in Allenby that his greatness was so reluctantly admitted by some, that he was so unpopular a figure for a great part of his military career? He lacked a measure of self-control, a little humanity, the power to communicate enthusiasm and to inspire disciples. His sudden explosions of temper, his occasional almost childish petulance, did his reputation the more harm since he never troubled to correct the impression they created. Only those who stood near to him and saw him daily knew how little they represented the true nature of the man. Allenby never quite realized that men are governed through the emotions rather than through the intelligence. There was an aloofness about him, a suggestion of mental superiority, that kept him from the hearts of his officers and men—perhaps designedly, for any show of affection would have embarrassed him greatly. He lacked the spur of ambition; duty was the mainspring that drove him, and duty is a less powerful motive of action than ambition for a career or zeal for a cause.

As a general in high command he used surprise and mobility as his main weapons for the discomfiture of his adversaries; these, and relentless vigour in pursuit, are the principal lessons that students of his campaigns will note. They may mark also his willingness to take chances, though doing all in his power to minimize them. Allenby was no reckless gambler; he calculated the odds carefully, but when they were in his favour and the gain was great he accepted risks cheerfully. The soft modern doctrine of ' Safety first,' which so often marks the decline of businesses, of governments, of armies, and of nations, found no place in Allenby's creed. His skill in planning and in deceiving his enemy was not the result of sudden flashes of inspiration, but of much reading and study of past campaigns and of present conditions. His mind did not work very swiftly, except in action, but surely.

A less obvious quality, but one that was the real foundation of his successes, was the care for administration, which has been emphasized in the course of the narrative. Administration is not a showy quality, and is apt to receive scant attention in the writing of military histories. " Where do you read that Sir Tristram weighed out hay and corn, that Sir Lancelot distributed billets, or that any knight of the Round Table condescended to higgle about a truss of straw? " scornfully cries a character in one of Scott's novels. But if these knights had indeed not troubled to supervise such details of interior economy, be sure that their enterprises would have miscarried. Allenby made no such mistake; he never interfered in details, but he insisted on being satisfied at all times that every possible preparation had been made for the supply of food and munitions and stores, for the health of his troops, and for the care of the sick and wounded. The exception was in pursuit; then he was prepared to disregard the warnings of his supply officers and to call on his troops to live hard and fight hard, so that the enemy should be given no opportunity to live and fight again.

His method of command was a more personal one than that of most commanders of great armies—modern armies, that is. Once he knew and trusted his staff he spent as little time as possible in the office and as much time as possible with his army—by no means always with the forward troops, but also in visiting bases, hospitals, workshops, training camps, and all establishments by which the army lived, moved, and had its being. His physique and appearance stood him in good stead. He could endure continual long journeys over dusty, bumpy tracks, often in great heat, without the least apparent fatigue; and his bearing left an ineffaceable impression on the minds of his troops. No soldier who had seen Allenby—and practically all his soldiers did see Allenby—could have any doubt that he was being commanded, or that operations would not fail from lack of vigour and decision in high places.

His ideas on discipline were simple: an order was an order, a regulation was a regulation, to be obeyed without question, at all times and in all circumstances. His strict enforcement of certain orders, such as the keeping of chin-straps down and the wearing of steel helmets, and of certain prohibitions—for example, against riding in cut-shorts or tying horses to trees—has been the cause of many of the stories told of him, and has left in the minds of some an impression of a senseless martinet who delighted in petty details of dress and discipline. This is not the truth: the orders he insisted on had all a reason of good common sense; he relaxed or cancelled many restrictions that seemed to him unnecessary, and never troubled about small idiosyncrasies of dress or routine. What Allenby would never consent to do was to turn a blind eye to infringement of orders, or to make any allowance for circumstances. Hence his rating of half-dazed men who had been fighting for hours because their chin-straps were not down, his ban on cut-shorts even in the tropical heat of the Jordan valley, his explosion of anger because he found a corpse in the trenches wearing a cap instead of a steel helmet.

His critics overlook, or do not realize, how seldom Allenby punished, except with his tongue. When he commanded a regiment some of his officers thought him unduly lenient; as a higher commander, when he reviewed the sentences of courts-martial or other matters of discipline, he always took the greatest pains to understand any case brought before him, and was on the side of mercy whenever possible.[1] With officers, even senior officers, he was often harsh in words and manner, sometimes in the presence of their juniors; this was resented by many. But with Allenby duty came first and personal feelings (his own or anyone else's) much later. " I do not care if I am fair or unfair to anyone, if I think they do not do their work," he once said to one of his staff. At the same time he gave every one a chance; and if he was doing his best he seldom removed him from his post, even though his best was not very good. Allenby preferred to be served by an honest mediocrity whom he could trust than by one of better capacity of whose honesty and loyalty he was not sure.

Allenby was a purist, sometimes almost a pedant, in the use of the English language. His style, both official and colloquial, was simple and severe; good, plain, homespun English, purged of all superfluous adjectives or adverbs, all neologisms, colloquialisms, or idiosyncrasies. Once his standard was known it was easy enough to draft a document for him; but officers new to his ways sometimes met rude rebuffs when they first produced work for him. Such a modernism as ' dump ' would be removed with a caustic reproof from any official document submitted to him; if he met it verbally he might affect to be ignorant of its meaning. A split infinitive would be duly castigated, even though it were

---

[1] A senior staff officer said of him, " He was the most just man I have ever served. In the matter of courts-martial, courts of inquiry, reports on inefficient officers, and so forth he took the greatest pains to ensure that justice was done, and that no question of bias or prejudice was allowed to intrude."

in a telegram which had to be enciphered, deciphered, and para-
phrased before it reached its destination, in the course of which
process the infinitive might be unsplit and resplit without the
sender having any control over the matter.

After the Battle of Beersheba and the capture of Gaza the War
Office, feeling that the brief record of these successes sent by
Allenby would not satisfy the thirst of the public for news, cabled
for a fuller account of Allenby's victories. An officer of the
Intelligence Staff, realizing what was wanted, wrote a long
telegram, rather in the style of an imaginative war correspondent
presented with a ' scoop.' When it was placed before Allenby he
exploded in wrath at the idea that such florid journalese might be
sent in his name. His criticism having reduced the unfortunate
author to a state of collapse, Allenby himself dictated a stately
account of the operations, in which there was hardly an adjective,
and certainly nothing to satisfy any public demand for picturesque
detail.

If the foregoing is a fair summary of Allenby's military qualities
and manners, what of the results they produced in the Great War?
Some have gained the impression that he was a failure in France
who surprisingly became a success in Palestine, either because the
conditions were easier or because he was better suited by independent command. It was as though a forward taken out of the
scrum and put at wing three-quarter had showed an unexpected
turn of speed and scored several brilliant tries. But the player
must have had pace and cunning all the time; and a crossing of
the Mediterranean cannot have turned Allenby from a bad general
into a good one. His alleged failure in the close-locked, muddy
scrum in France needs further examination. In truth his record
there was at least as good as that of any other British commander.
In the hurly-burly of the Retreat from Mons and in the sudden
rebound to the Aisne he kept his head as well as any, and better
than some; the Cavalry Division may have done nothing very
spectacular, but it covered the flanks of the army and kept a far
more numerous force of enemy horsemen at a safe distance. In
the First Battle of Ypres the Cavalry Corps under Allenby, in
holding at bay so greatly superior a mass of enemy infantry,
performed a feat of defence unrivalled in history by any other

cavalry; and the chief credit was undoubtedly due to the composure, personal example, and iron resolution of its leader.

His handling of his next command, the Fifth Corps, has been much criticized. He is said to have been wasteful of life in making attacks or counter-attacks in conditions where there was little or no chance of success. Allenby, it should be noted, took over the Corps at the crisis of the Second Battle of Ypres, when fighting had been in progress for some time, much ground had already been lost, and it seemed doubtful whether Ypres itself could be held. He had no opportunity of getting to know the ground or the troops before his Corps had to withstand renewed heavy attacks. And he had orders to maintain his position at all costs. In this he was successful, and the Corps lost little ground in the closing stages of the battle. In the circumstances Allenby was bound to act as he did, and his firmness may have saved Ypres. But his harsh manner gave the unfortunate impression of a rough, obstinate commander who could only charge blindly forward.

His command of the Third Army showed that he was not careless of men's lives. In the ordinary day-to-day holding of the line its proportion of casualties was much lower than in the other Armies—this may have been partly due to better trenches—and Allenby ordered far fewer of the trench raids that were often the cause of needless losses and of costly retaliation. But again his roughness and outbursts of temper were the criterion by which the Army judged him. For the Arras battle, his one great opportunity in France, he has had less credit than he deserved. April 9, 1917, was the most successful day's fighting the British forces in France had yet had in two and a half years' warfare. Its success has been obscured by the subsequent slow progress and heavy losses. So far as Allenby himself is concerned, these later attacks were made on the plans of G.H.Q.; and the tired troops of the Third Army were never relieved by fresh divisions, as was done in the great battles of the Somme or Passchendaele. The last big attack of the Arras battle, an almost complete failure, was ordered to begin in the dark to suit the ideas of another Army commander and in spite of Allenby's protests.

While Allenby's reputation with the regimental officer and soldier was too much coloured by the sight and sound of a loud and angry man, the opinion of the higher staffs was influenced by his comparative silence and ineffectiveness at the periodical conferences of Army commanders. At these Allenby did not make the impression that his abilities warranted. He was not a ready debater; his mind, like a battleship, was powerful and weighty, but required space and time to turn or manœuvre.[1] Haig and he were never congenial and always inclined to be tongue-tied in each other's presence.

Thus Allenby, unlike a prophet, had little honour in France save in his own circle, the circle of those who worked closely with him. These all recognized both his abilities and his true character, but their testimony had no more weight to leaven the general opinion of the Army as a whole than an article in a staid monthly magazine is likely to change the views formed by the general public from the popular daily papers. Allenby had a ' bad Press ' when he was in France, and his reputation suffered accordingly. If his actual record of achievement is studied it will challenge comparison with that of any of his contemporaries.

There is no need to recapitulate his triumphs in Palestine. The manner in which they were accomplished surely gives reason for him to be regarded as the best British general of the Great War. He had more of the divine spark than the single-minded Haig, with equal resolution and courage; a greater driving-power, though less humanity, than Plumer; more force than Rawlinson and an equal shrewdness; a broader outlook than Maude; more experience of command than Robertson; a greater stability than the volatile Henry Wilson. He was of the same type as Welling-ton, with whom he had many points of resemblance, in his common-sense realism, in his flair for concealing his intentions and surprising his enemy, in his appreciation of the value of good administration, in his lack of the human touch.

Should Allenby be placed in the first rank of British com-manders—that small, select band headed by Marlborough, whose genius for war challenges comparison with that of Napoleon or any of the world's great captains? Certainly he has not many

---

[1] T. E. Lawrence once said of Allenby, " His mind is like the prow of the *Maure-tania*. There is so much weight behind it that it does not need to be sharp like a razor."

superiors. He may have lacked something of the passion and
creative energy of Cromwell, of the cold application of Wellington, of the fiery energy of Wolfe, of the warm humanity of Moore,
of the organizing ability of Kitchener. But the British Army has
had few leaders with better mental or physical equipment for the
rough test of war, less likely to lose heart in the darkest hour, or
more remorseless in pressing home an advantage and completing
a victory; certainly none with a greater sense of loyalty and duty
or more of the truth and straightforwardness that mark a great
and generous nature.

BOOK III

PLOUGHSHARE

PROLOGUE
AFTERMATH OF WAR

(Syria and Palestine, November 1918–June 1920)

THE armistice with Turkey, signed on October 31, 1918, left Allenby master of all Palestine and Syria. His lightning campaign, which had carried his troops from near Jaffa to north of Aleppo, a distance of some 350 miles, in less than six weeks, had destroyed the enemy forces opposed to him with a completeness which seemed to dispose of all military difficulties in the Middle East.

But war creates as many fresh problems as it solves old ones. Allenby, at the end of 1918 and beginning of 1919, found that the very thoroughness of his victory had stimulated the growth in the Near East of a whole crop of controversies that the overshadowing needs of war had hitherto kept from showing themselves above ground. They were political problems rather than military; but Allenby, as Commander-in-Chief, had to find at least a temporary settlement of them until the Peace Conference could make its decisions. There was the administration of the whole of Syria to be arranged, with French and Arabs urging their claims with passion and bitterness. In the area to the north of Aleppo, Turkish generals with large armed forces still under their control were disregarding the terms of the armistice; and the Armenian population was calling for protection. The methods and date of demobilization were causing some restlessness in the minds of the war-weary troops, and would be a source of trouble unless carefully handled. There was the disposal of great numbers of Turkish prisoners and Armenian refugees to be settled as well as of quantities of animals and masses of stores of every kind. All this was in addition to the daily administration

you get into a jinrickshaw drawn
by a wild Zulu. He trots as
fast as a horse, for any distance. These jinrickshaw boys
get themselves up in the most
fantastic kits. The fashion is
to wear 2 cows' horns on their
heads, besides
all sorts of feathers
adornments, something
in this fashion. I have met
one or two old friends here.
This afternoon I had tea with
an old friend named Fetchford
He has a grown up family who

LORD ALLENBY WITH HIS PET STORK IN THE RESIDENCY
GARDEN, CAIRO

of a large body of troops scattered over an area of poor communications, some five hundred miles long and varying between fifty and one hundred in breadth.

At first the troubles were only in front, in the newly conquered areas. Behind the forward area the Military Administration in Palestine was doing admirable work; there was little foreboding yet of the effects of the Balfour Declaration or of the conflict between Arab and Jew that was to cause such suffering and perplexity in the Holy Land. Farther back still, at the base in Egypt, all seemed well; the Egyptians had remained quiet and apparently contented throughout the war, which had brought their land much profit in money; there was no one who realized the strength of the hostility, caused by real grievances, that was smouldering in the minds of educated Egyptian and fellahin alike, and was to break out so suddenly and so fiercely.

The organization of conquered Syria and Palestine was Allenby's first care. He had laid down the outlines shortly before the armistice with Turkey. The whole of Palestine became O.E.T.A.[1] South, under Major-General Sir Arthur Money, who already administered the portion of Palestine occupied before the final offensive. The coastal portion of Syria from Alexandretta to Acre, including Beirut and the Lebanon, was placed under French administration, and was called at first O.E.T.A. North (later West). O.E.T.A. East, under Arab administration, was a large, somewhat indeterminate area stretching from Aleppo to Damascus to the east of the French zone and thence southward to include the Hauran and the country now known as Trans-Jordan. Later, when Cilicia was occupied in December 1918, a new area was formed known as O.E.T.A. North, under a French administrator, the name of the original O.E.T.A. North being changed to O.E.T.A. West. All four administrations were under the direct authority of Allenby as Commander-in-Chief; and complex problems of currency, finance, public works, police, justice, refugees, poor relief, and so forth were referred, in three languages, to his headquarters for decision. The Quartermaster-General, a wary Scot, refused to let his Staff or Financial Adviser have anything to do with the administration of

[1] Occupied Enemy Territory Administration.

Occupied Enemy Territory; so the General Staff, rushing in where Adjutant-Generals feared to tread, became involved in complicated financial, legal, and administrative problems.[1] Beyond the area of the O.E.T.A.'s there was a purely military control, under the G.O.C. Desert Mounted Corps, General Sir Harry Chauvel, using the Turkish officials, of an area to the north of the Baghdad railway including the towns of Marash, Aintab, and Urfa, which had been occupied at the end of 1918 to prevent the threatened massacre of Armenians by the withdrawing Turkish troops.

Allenby, following his usual practice, travelled the huge area he controlled, and settled problems on the spot as far as possible. His responsibilities stretched from his base in Egypt, still under martial law, across Sinai, where was his line of communication by the military railway; over all Palestine, Trans-Jordan, and Syria; to places more than one hundred miles north and east of Aleppo; and in Cilicia up to the Taurus Mountains in the north-west. His headquarters were now at Haifa, on Mount Carmel.

There soon arose anxious problems to be solved. The first came to a head from the refusal of certain Turkish Generals, of whom the most prominent was Ali Ihsan Pasha, commander of the forces withdrawn from the Mesopotamian front, to disband their armies in compliance with the armistice terms. They were beyond easy reach by direct action, and Allenby had no wish to become committed any deeper into Turkish territory; so he decided to bring pressure on the Turkish Government. At the beginning of February 1919 he went, in the battleship *Téméraire*, from Haifa to Constantinople, then in Allied occupation; and interviewed the Turkish Ministers of Foreign Affairs and of War. The meeting showed Allenby's personality at its most dominant. The Ministers came prepared to discuss and argue; Allenby merely read out his demands, which included the removal of Ali Ihsan, handed them a copy, and insisted on immediate acceptance without discussion or argument. The Turkish Ministers, taken completely aback, hastily promised to comply with the require-

---

[1] A basis of agreement on many of the problems common to all the areas of occupation was laid down at a conference of their administrators and staffs held at Mount Carmel in June 1919, under Sir Arthur Money.

ments, and were so impressed by Allenby's firmness that they did so with all haste. Ali Ihsan was soon afterwards removed from his command, and the obstruction ceased. Allenby had remained only thirty-six hours in Constantinople, and had accomplished his purpose in five minutes, merely by a display of his inflexible determination.

Syria was the next problem. During the early part of 1919 friction between French and Arabs was increasing; and the French were becoming exasperated at what they considered British encouragement of the Arab cause. The French claim to predominance in Syria was based on sentiment and tradition rather than on any rights or even special interests; but it was none the less real and had been recognized by the British Government in the unfortunate Sykes-Picot Agreement. The French now complained that British officers were openly supporting the Arab claim to control the whole of Syria, and they accused Allenby himself of partiality. As Allenby wrote to a friend at this time:

> There is plenty to do and plenty to think about. All nations and would-be nations and all shades of religions and politics are up against each other and trying to get me to commit myself on their side. I am keeping my end up, so far; but there is need to walk warily.[1]

Feisal had gone to Europe to plead the Arab cause, and presently Allenby was summoned, early in March 1919, to appear at the Peace Conference and to give his views on the Syrian question. At a meeting in Paris on March 20 he stated that if the French were imposed on an unwilling Syria " there would be trouble and even war " between French and Arabs. On the next day, when he had been in Paris barely thirty-six hours, Allenby received instructions from the Cabinet to return to Egypt as Special High Commissioner and to restore order there.

Before dealing with the causes of this sudden appointment, it will be as well to outline the subsequent course of events in Syria. Although Allenby continued to be responsible for the

[1] From a letter to Major-General J. Vaughan (March 2, 1919).

military administration in Syria for another seven or eight months, his main preoccupation was henceforth to be with Egypt. The Peace Conference, from which he had been called so abruptly, decided to postpone the difficult solution by appointing a Commission of American, British, and French representatives to visit Syria and ascertain the wishes of the population at first hand. This would have been, if carried out, in accordance with a pledge given by Allenby on behalf of the British and French Governments on November 7, 1918, a few days after the armistice with Turkey, to the effect that the aim of the Allies was to set up National Governments deriving from the free choice of the inhabitants. The British representatives on the Commission were Sir Henry McMahon and D. G. Hogarth, both men of well-known integrity, standing, and knowledge, as were also the Americans, Charles Crane and Dr H. C. King. The French, however, aware of their unpopularity in Syria, negatived the proposed inquiry simply by appointing no representatives at all. They preferred to seek their ends by diplomatic pressure in Paris. The British knew well that the French would refuse to accept the findings of a Commission on which they had not been represented; but could find no means to make them appoint representatives. Eventually the Americans proceeded to Syria alone. Their report showed that an American mandate would be welcomed, a British tolerated, and a French rejected; also that Syria and Palestine must be treated as a whole, as under the Turks, and not separated. But before they returned—indeed, almost before their departure—French diplomacy, working among the devious bargainings of the Conference, had gained its ends over Syria. To retain Iraq and Palestine the British Prime Minister had agreed that Syria should be placed under French mandate. The American report was not even made public.

Though no mandate had yet been issued and the decision of the Peace Conference was in theory still open, the French obtained from the British Government, which was becoming alarmed at the cost of their many Armies of Occupation, an undertaking that French troops should relieve British in Syria in the autumn of 1919. This withdrawal of British troops and the substitution of French units took place in November. It very nearly led to an armed conflict of Arabs and French between Damascus and Beirut; only Allenby's authority prevented it. He was at Beirut at the time with the French commander, General Gouraud, and sent a staff officer to interpose himself between the two forces and to dissuade the Arabs from their intention of attacking. It was the last act of his command in Syria, and postponed the conflict between French and Arabs till July 1920. In that month, as a result of the announcement in May of the terms of the French mandate for Syria, hostilities broke out; after a short struggle the French occupied Damascus, and Feisal left the country. As is known, the British Government later made to their Arab allies of the war such reparation as lay in their power by placing Feisal on the throne of Iraq, and his brother Abdullah on the throne of Trans-Jordan.

The story of Palestine under Allenby may also be shortly outlined here. His policy was to administer it, so far as possible, strictly under the international rules for enemy territory occupied in war, which laid down the principle that the administrator is merely a tenant who can make no avoidable change in the existing laws and arrangements until the country is disposed of by treaty of peace. This, Allenby considered, precluded any special privileges being accorded for Jewish settlement until the Peace Conference had given their decision. The Foreign Office, however, in contravention of these accepted principles, sent a Zionist Commission to Palestine in the spring of 1918. Allenby continued to adhere, so far as possible, to the orthodox interpretation of the duties of a military administration; and thereby became the target of some of the criticism of the impatient Zionists. Allenby's Political Officer, Colonel Meinertzhagen (who was an Intelligence officer in 1917 and had been responsible for the famous ' haversack ruse ' at the Third Battle of Gaza), considering that Allenby was not carrying out in Palestine the policy of the Foreign Office in furtherance of the Balfour Declaration, sent a dispatch to this effect to the Foreign Office. A friend, to whom he showed the letter, warned him that Allenby would not allow such criticism by one of his staff. Meinertzhagen agreed that this was likely, but persisted in what he held to be his duty. His dismissal was even swifter than the friend had prophesied, and followed immediately on Allenby seeing a copy of the letter. But Meinertzhagen had no fear of Allenby and always met him on equal terms. " I suppose you realize that you would have had to give your house-maid longer notice," was his only comment. Allenby laughed, and they parted friends. They had always had a common interest in the study of birds.

Major-General Sir Arthur Money was succeeded as Military Administrator by Major-General Sir Harry Watson in the middle of 1919, and the latter not long afterwards by Major-General Sir Louis Bols, Allenby's Chief of General Staff. The Military Administration itself came to an end in June 1920, when Sir Herbert Samuel became the first Civil Administrator. The further progress of the Zionist experiment, its successes and its failures, the prosperity it brought and the resentment it caused, and all the rights and wrongs of that unhappy conflict, are, fortunately, outside the scope of this biography.

In both these political controversies, in Syria and in Palestine, Allenby had maintained, so far as lay in his power, a strict impartiality. His sympathies, no doubt, lay with Feisal and the Arabs; but he used his authority and influence to keep the Arabs strictly within the bounds laid down by the Allied Governments, so long as he controlled Syria. He regarded as premature the Foreign Office encouragement of Zionism while Palestine was still subject to military administration and should therefore by international law have had no major change introduced; but he was not by any means unsympathetic to the aspirations of the Jews for increased immigration, and it cannot be claimed for him that he foresaw all the dangers that the Zionist experiment was to cause.

PART I

EGYPT: THE PROTECTORATE

(*March* 1919–*February* 1922)

Your good and my good, perhaps they are different; and either
forced good or forced evil will make a people cry out with pain.

KING FEISAL, quoted in *Seven Pillars of Wisdom*
(Chapter XIV), by T. E. Lawrence

CHAPTER XII

A NATION'S ANGER

(*March–April* 1919)

Double, double, toil and trouble;
Fire burn, and cauldron bubble.

SHAKESPEARE, *Macbeth*

IT is likely that few Englishmen, even of those who knew Egypt
well, would, at the beginning of 1919, have regarded the Egyptians
as a nation in the full sense of the word; or would have admitted
that they had reasonable cause for anger. Preoccupied with the
war, we had almost completely lost contact with Egyptian feeling
during the war years. The proclamation of a Protectorate [1] in
December 1914, made hurriedly as a war measure, and certainly
so regarded by responsible Egyptian opinion, had come to be
looked on by British eyes as a settlement of Egypt's political
future that needed no immediate revision. Actually, the Protectorate made little change in the Egyptian system of government.
The only Ministry which ceased to have an Egyptian Minister
was that of Foreign Affairs, which came directly under the High
Commissioner. The capitulatory privileges of foreigners, which
conferred wide exemptions from Egyptian judicial, legislative,
and fiscal authority, remained unaffected. One of the principal

---

[1] The literal translation of the word 'Protectorate' in Arabic is *Himaya*. But that
word unfortunately had another meaning for the Egyptians. By general usage it had
come to be associated with the protected position of foreigners under the Capitulations, and as such had an objectionable significance.

uses made of martial law, which had been declared in November 1914, was to render decrees of Egyptian Ministers applicable, despite the Capitulations, to foreigners.

The fact that Egypt, under martial law, had remained passive during the war had been interpreted as satisfaction with, or at least indifference to, the existing state of affairs. And from a material point of view Egypt was obviously prospering. The price of cotton, her staple product, had soared to heights undreamt of; the Army had bought forage, animals, and other produce of the country at good prices, and had paid well and fed well the fellahin who had enlisted into those two invaluable bodies, the Egyptian Camel Corps and the Egyptian Labour Corps; the troops themselves had spent their money lavishly in Cairo, Alexandria, and elsewhere. Egypt had apparently had all the benefits and none of the losses of the long weary war: why should she be dissatisfied or so ungrateful as to bite the hand that had fed her plentifully during these years when fear, poverty, and death had been the lot of many peoples?

Such a view was natural enough in the soldiers who formed the bulk of the British population in Egypt at the end of the war; all their thoughts and energies had been involved in military operations, and they had had little time to consider the Egyptian problem or Egyptian feelings. The instructed few—the Foreign Office and Civil Service officials, the military staff officers who had dealt with questions of martial law and internal security, the British residents who had made Egypt their home—were aware of the problems and of the dangers, but all had completely failed to gauge the growth of national spirit and the intensity with which both the educated classes and the illiterate fellahin felt their grievances. Nor did they realize that the nation had found a leader to express its spirit and its resentment.

The growth of the Egyptian national consciousness had begun long before the war as a result of the freedom of speech and of thought and the material prosperity brought by the British occupation; it had been stimulated by Lord Kitchener's creation of the Legislative Assembly in 1913; its quick flowering at the end of the war was due largely to its watering by the doctrines of self-determination and of the rights of small nations expressed by the leading politicians of the Allies during the war, especially by that class-room idealist, President Woodrow Wilson.

Even those who were most likely to be well disposed to Great Britain—the Sultan, who owed his throne to them; [1] Rushdi, the Prime Minister, who had administered Egypt during the war years; the other Ministers; the great landowners who had made large fortunes out of cotton (the Pasha class)—were disappointed at the lack of recognition of the assistance Egypt had provided to Britain's war effort. The Arabs of the desert were to be allowed to appear at the Peace Conference and state their case; so were Cypriots and Syrians; while the more civilized Egyptians were to be treated as a British Colony and refused admittance. They probably felt like a man whose house had been used as an hotel for a long period by uninvited, though paying, guests without a word of gratitude to their host.

The grievances of the Effendi class were mainly the usual result of a European system of education on the Oriental mind, which is apt to absorb learning quickly but superficially without the stability of character that learning should bring. The system produced a growing class of would-be Government officials or lawyers; and as the supply of both considerably outran demand, the disappointed ones turned to politics, journalism, and agitation. Their simple creed was that the British administration, which had caused the education to be provided, should have provided also safe and easy occupation for the educated. Consequently every post in the Government held by a British official appeared an infringement of their rights; and it has to be admitted that during the war the quality of the British officials had deteriorated (many of the best having gone to fight), while the quantity had been growing for some years before the war, to the exasperation of the Egyptians. From their point of view British help had declined, while British interference had increased.

The grievances of the fellahin were simpler and more material. The demands of the Army, during the progress of its campaigns, for labour, animals, and feeding-stuffs had grown beyond the

---

[1] Soon after the outbreak of war with Turkey Great Britain had declared the Khedive deposed, and had placed his uncle, Prince Hussein, on the throne. On his death in 1917 he was succeeded by his brother, the late King Fuad.

point at which they could be supplied by voluntary effort. The military had brought pressure to bear on the Egyptian Government to fulfil its demands, which in the end had been met by the crudest form of impressment in the villages. Men had been conscripted against their will for the Labour Corps; their animals and crops seized; and even sometimes money extracted from them under the guise of subscriptions to the Red Cross. As usual in such oppressions, the burden fell heaviest on the poorest and least protected. Neither the Army nor the British officials realized the injustices which were being practised in their name; but in the eyes of the fellahin they were naturally held guilty. The villagers had tolerated the rule of the British for the protection given them against injustice; but if the British had become oppressive also, then down with the accursed foreigners. There was plenty of inflammable material in the Delta in 1919.

The man who set light to it, Saad Zaghlul, who was to become the national hero and the chief opponent of British policy for the next eight years, was a not unworthy representative of the qualities and defects of his race. He was a man of the people (like Arabi Pasha, whose revolt was the cause of the British occupation) and had been the first pure-born Egyptian—*i.e.*, not of the old Turkish ruling class—to hold Ministerial office. He was honest, patriotic, with a gift of vivid emotional oratory and a shrewd sense of humour. In appearance he was tall and gaunt, with high cheek-bones and narrow eyes. At times he was courageous and outspoken, and at times hesitant and apprehensive. He could be charming, but was occasionally overbearing and rude. Childless himself, he found unlimited pleasure in the companionship of children. With women he was invariably chivalrous and courteous. His own married life represented an ideal companionship. His wife was a daughter of a famous Egyptian Prime Minister, Mustapha Fahmy Pasha, who had collaborated very cordially with Lord Cromer over a long number of years. He could not suffer cruelty to animals. It is related that when he was in exile at Gibraltar in 1923 he was invited to visit a town in Spain where a bullfight was in progress. He was so shocked by the sight that he left at once, and in his own inimitable manner roundly told his host what he thought of him and of

Spanish taste and culture. One of his sayings was, "Animals cannot talk, but they understand; humans can talk but often do not understand." Zaghlul was not naturally a leader, as those who originally selected him for the position soon discovered, and was often alarmed at the dangerous prominence in which he found himself. He was, however, inordinately vain, jealous of his leadership, and to that extent ambitious. Ambition, as Mark Antony pointed out, "should be made of sterner stuff." Discomfort and danger make little appeal to the average educated Egyptian; Zaghlul was apt to trade on the fact that he had suffered a little of both in his efforts for the nation and to exaggerate the amount he had suffered. Revolutionaries in tougher communities would have scorned to class Zaghlul's trials as sufferings at all. He had less courage, less political wisdom, and even less ability to compromise than another contemporary opponent of England, De Valera.

Zaghlul had been chosen as the first Minister of Education in Egypt by Lord Cromer, who said in a speech shortly before he left Egypt, "Unless I am mistaken, a career of great public usefulness lies before the present Minister of Education, Zaghlul Bey. He possesses all the qualities which are necessary to serve this country. He is honest and capable and has the courage of his convictions." His talents were, however, destructive rather that constructive, and he soon went into opposition. He had now for some years been preaching the gospel of complete independence for Egypt. He had not, however, been the originator of the Wafd (or Delegation), as his party came to be known. It was the creation of others, notably men like Mohammed Mahmoud;[1] and Zaghlul consented to join only after his nomination to a Ministerial appointment had been rejected by the Foreign Office.

The sequence of events which led up to the outbreak was briefly as follows. Shortly after the armistice Zaghlul called on the High Commissioner, Sir Reginald Wingate, at the head of a delegation; and, claiming to speak in the name of the Egyptian people, demanded independence for Egypt. The High Commissioner,

[1] Prime Minister of Egypt June 1928 to October 1929 and December 1937 to August 1939; died January 1941.

somewhat taken aback, gave a non-committal reply, and Zaghlul then required permission for himself and his delegation to go to London and lay Egypt's case before the British Government. On this request being referred to it, the Foreign Office sent an uncompromising refusal; and Zaghlul embarked on a campaign to rally the nation to his view of their cause. Meanwhile Egypt's official representatives, the Prime Minister Rushdi and his colleague Adly, also asked for permission to visit England and discuss the future of Egypt. This request was strongly backed by the High Commissioner. The Foreign Office reply, to the effect that " no useful purpose would be served " by the visit, was undoubtedly a grave blunder. It was a mistake of bad manners rather than of bad intentions; but in the East manners have a greater and intentions perhaps a lesser importance than in Europe, a difference seldom realized by the average Englishman. The Egyptian sets a higher value on politeness and a lower value on mere justice than the Englishman. At the end of the war we must have seemed to the Egyptians neither polite nor just, for in war standards of politeness and justice both deteriorate.

The Foreign Office also committed the mistakes of disregarding the advice of the responsible man on the spot, and of refusing to allow grievances to be aired, two proceedings which are always of doubtful wisdom. Their excuse was that the forthcoming Peace Conference was occupying all their attention. This excuse, however, was the very root of Egyptian discontent; Arabs and other less civilized people were to be allowed to state their case in Paris, but not the Egyptians. The British attitude gave fresh fuel to Zaghlul's fiery campaign, while Rushdi and Adly tendered the resignation of their offices as a consequence of their rebuff. Sir Reginald Wingate was now summoned home to represent the situation personally. He urged, without success, that both the Ministers and Zaghlul should be received. At the end of February 1919 the Foreign Secretary, Mr Balfour, invited Rushdi and Adly to London, but it was now too late. Zaghlul's campaign had made such headway that it was obvious to the two Ministers that any agreement reached by them in London would be repudiated in Egypt unless it met Zaghlul's ideas. They refused to go unless

Zaghlul's deputation was also received, and to this the Foreign Office would not agree.

The explosion could not now be long delayed. Zaghlul's agitation reached a pitch that threatened to cause disorders and dangers to the British and other foreigners in Egypt. He was warned by the military authorities to cease his activities forthwith; and on his disregard of the warning was arrested on March 8 with three colleagues, and deported to Malta. Within a few days all Egypt had flared up in revolt. Its principal feature was an organized attack on the communications of the country; railway-lines were torn up and stations burned; telegraph and telephone wires were cut; and Cairo was soon isolated from the rest of the country. The number of casualties to Europeans was not heavy; but eight Englishmen were murdered in circumstances of extreme brutality while travelling by train from Luxor to Cairo. The grim story of this tragedy was related at the time, but the story of Hanem Aaref, a public woman of Mellawi, received little publicity. It may not be out of place, therefore, to record it here. On the arrival of the train at Mellawi with the bodies of the murdered Englishmen piled up in the brake-van, it was met by a frenzied crowd. The body of one man still breathing was pulled out of the van and submitted to further indignities. Among the two thousand persons of all classes who composed the crowd this poor woman, Hanem Aaref, alone showed any humanity. She wept at the sight and tried to protect the body. She was beaten and driven away.

Members of the British community, deeply touched by this act of pity, opened a subscription list for her. They thought of giving her a gift of land, but in keeping with the characteristics of her class she preferred jewellery. She chose two heavy gold bracelets and a gold signet ring. A third bracelet was ordered with a suitable inscription, and what remained of the fund was handed to her in cash. The inscription on the third bracelet ran as follows:

To HANEM AAREF

A GIFT IN RECOGNITION OF HER COMPASSION
TOWARDS A DYING BRITISH SOLDIER ON
18TH MARCH 1919

God will reward the doer of good deeds.

General Bulfin was in command of the Army in Allenby's absence. He was an exceptionally stout-hearted, level-headed soldier, the right man for such a crisis. He promptly formed mobile columns to patrol the country and restore order, and in little more than a week had the situation well in hand. Meanwhile Allenby had, as already related, been appointed by the British Government as Special High Commissioner, with instructions " to exercise supreme authority in all matters military and civil, to take all measures necessary and expedient to restore law and order, and to administrate in all matters as required by the necessity of maintaining the King's Protectorate over Egypt on a secure and equitable basis."

Allenby was the fourth successive soldier to be appointed as chief British representative in Egypt. Sir Henry McMahon (who had been with Allenby at Haileybury, at a crammer's, and at the Royal Military College) had served in a regiment only for a few years before joining the Political Service; but the other three, Kitchener, Sir Reginald Wingate, and Allenby himself, had been active soldiers at the date of their appointment.

Allenby arrived in Cairo on March 25 and found matters fast improving under Bulfin's firm hand. He took stock of the situation and consulted his Advisers, British and Egyptian. On the evening of the day after his arrival he addressed an assembly of notables who had been invited to the Residency as follows:

I have been appointed High Commissioner for Egypt by His Majesty the King, and it is my desire and duty to assist in bringing to the country peace, quiet, and contentment.

My intentions are :

First, to bring the present disturbances to an end.

Secondly, to make careful inquiry into all matters which have caused discontent in the country.

Thirdly, to redress such grievances as appear justifiable.

It is you who can lead the people of Egypt. It is your duty to work with me in the interest of your country.

I cannot believe that any one of you will not assist me in every way, and I am prepared to rely on you to set to work at once with a view to calming the passions now let loose.

After quiet has been restored I feel confident that you will trust me to inquire impartially into all grievances, and to make such recommendations as may seem to be desirable for the content and well-being of the people of Egypt.

Lord Allenby never deviated from this programme. Almost at the same moment as he was thus seeking to pour oil on the troubled waters a speech delivered by Lord Curzon on March 24 was published in Cairo and caused great resentment. He described the disturbances as " predatory rather than political," and said that one gratifying feature had been the behaviour of many Egyptian officials. The immediate result was a strike of these officials to show that they were not as amenable as Curzon thought.

On March 31, a bare week after his arrival, Allenby telegraphed home recommending the release of Zaghlul and of his colleagues and permission for them to proceed to Europe. This recommendation came as a shock to the British Government; they had sent a strong man to reduce a recalcitrant people to control, and his first proposal was to make a concession they had already twice refused. The Foreign Office consulted Wingate, who, though he had originally recommended this permission, now advised very forcibly that concession in the present circumstances would be an inadmissible weakness.

But the Government could hardly disregard the advice of the man to whom they had just given full powers to deal with the situation; they agreed, somewhat reluctantly, to his proposals. On April 7 Allenby announced the release, with permission to proceed where they would, of Zaghlul and his three colleagues. Of these four men, three—Ismail Sidky, Mohammed Mahmoud, and Zaghlul himself—were destined to become Prime Ministers of Egypt; the fourth, Hamed-el-Bassel, was a makeweight—a Bedouin chief of little education.

The wisdom of Allenby's action was fiercely challenged, both at the time and later. A Foreign Office spokesman concluded a contemporary résumé of the events with the words, " Thus a fortnight of violence has achieved what four months of persuasion failed to accomplish. The object lesson will not be lost in Egypt and throughout the East." A British resident with long knowledge of Egypt [1] wrote:

> The proclamation of April 7th came as a bombshell to us. As affecting British prestige and security in Egypt, General Allenby's action is regarded as nothing short of calamitous. Men who were previously prepared to stand by us simply had to go over to the other side for protection.

Lord Lloyd, in his *Egypt since Cromer*, published nearly fourteen years later, said:

> It is difficult to justify this surrender to the forces of disorder. However unwise and unjust might have been the decision to deport the four leaders, or the decision to refuse them passports, the reversal of those two decisions at such a moment was certain to be given one interpretation and one only; that violence had succeeded where constitutional methods had failed.

Yet, surely, few who have studied the history of Egypt before and since this crisis will argue that Allenby was wrong, or that it would have been possible by stronger action at this stage to have changed Egyptian opinion and to have altered the subsequent course of events. Lord Lloyd implied that if General Bulfin had been allowed a free hand to complete his measures things would have been different. But General Bulfin himself was one of those who counselled some concession to Egyptian opinion, both before and after Allenby's arrival. So did Clayton,[2] who knew Egypt well and can be no more accused of weakness of purpose than can Bulfin. That Allenby himself acted through lack of firmness is denied by his whole career and character.

The key to his action at this stage may be found in a comment he made later on to one of his staff, who brought him a report in which a subordinate constantly referred to " the difficulties of my position." " What does he mean," said Allenby, " by the difficulties of his position? I have never been in a *difficult* position in my life. I have sometimes been in an *impossible* one, and then I have got out of it as quickly as I could." This remark throws a

---

[1] He afterwards became one of Allenby's staunchest supporters.
[2] Sir Gilbert Clayton, Adviser to the Ministry of the Interior. He died playing polo while High Commissioner of Iraq in September 1929.

revealing light on Allenby's whole character: it shows the strength of the man who is prepared to face any situation and to admit no difficulty in a course of action he considers appropriate, and yet has the common sense that recognizes when a task is impossible and the courage and honesty that admits it. He was quick to realize that though the Egyptian outbreak had been stirred to boiling-point by agitators, the seething mass that overflowed was the spontaneous expression of a nation's indignation that was not without causes. It would have been easy enough with the force at his disposal to take stern measures of repression and retaliation; but these could only make it more difficult to arrive at the friendly understanding with the Egyptian people without which our position in Egypt would have been impossible. He knew that his action would be criticized in most quarters as weakness; yet he was strong enough and wise enough to take it. As with all other decisions of his life, great or small, he never looked back to justify or defend it.

The immediate effect was auspicious; rioting turned to demonstrations of joy; and Rushdi again took office as Prime Minister. But the evil elements which the revolt had let loose had yet to be subdued; and there were still many ugly incidents and murders of British soldiers and of Greek and Armenian civilians, both in the cities and in the provinces; much disorder had still to be suppressed with a firm hand. The extremists made another effort to regain control by a campaign of intimidation against Government officials; and succeeded in bringing about the re-resignation of Rushdi on April 21. Allenby, by a stern proclamation on April 22, stopped the intimidation; and a month later Mohammed Said Pasha—a Turk of the old school, forceful but unscrupulous—formed a Ministry to carry on the government of Egypt. A comparatively calm period followed.

This account of the Egyptian troubles of the spring of 1919 may be ended on a lighter note in the report of a dialogue between Lord Allenby and one of his Generals at a conference in April, when the relaxation of certain measures of punishment and control were being discussed:

ALLENBY. I hear you are fining the villages in your area somewhat heavily, General X.

GENERAL X. Well, sir, when a village misbehaves itself I fine it ten per cent. of its ghaffir tax.

ALLENBY. That's not what I've heard, X. I'm told you fine them ten times their ghaffir tax.

GENERAL X. Yes, that's right, sir—ten per cent.

ALLENBY. But that's not ten per cent.; that's a thousand per cent.

GENERAL X. Oh, is it, sir? (*Pause.*) Well, anyway it's what I call ten per cent., and when I say ten per cent. they know what they've got to pay, and they pay it all right, sir.

CHAPTER XIII

THE SPHINX AND THE RIDDLE

(*Egypt, May 1919–December 1921*)

His personality alone did much to restore the name and word of an Englishman to the high pinnacle on which they stood in the East before the war.

The Times article on Lord Allenby
(July 1925)

Whether by wise conciliation, as his supporters thought, or by ill-advised surrender, as his critics alleged, Allenby had accomplished the immediate task of his commission, the restoration of law and order to Egypt, as quickly as might be and without further embittering a resentful people. There were to be outbreaks of disorder at intervals during the whole six years of his High Commissionership; and he was to be accused again of weakness and irresolution in dealing with them. But in May 1919 he had established a period of comparative stability and calm in which the second mandate of his commission—" to maintain the King's Protectorate on a secure and equitable basis "—could be usefully examined. It did not take Allenby himself very long to realize that the King's Protectorate was an impossible relationship between Great Britain and Egypt; but it took three years for His Majesty's Government to come to the same conclusion; and it was to take yet another fourteen years to establish by treaty what it is hoped will prove a secure and equitable basis of understanding between the two countries, even under the test of a new war. The first decisive step on this path of understanding was that taken by Allenby at the beginning of 1922.

In order to appreciate Allenby's stewardship of Egypt and to follow the complexities of the problem which baffled British diplomacy and statesmanship for so many years, it is essential to have a clear background of conditions and personalities. In the first place, few British observers, not even all of those who were charged with directing our relations with Egypt, had a proper understanding of its past history or of the constitution under which it was governed. The average Englishman knew that we had taken over a bankrupt, disorganized, and oppressed country; that by honest and skilful administration we had restored its finances, had established justice, had substituted order for chaos; and that we had guided and governed it ever since. He seldom realized that Egypt, under Turkish overlordship, had enjoyed, since the days of Mohammed Aly, almost complete autonomy (except in the matter of the Capitulations [1]); so that in demanding their independence the Egyptians were not seeking something they had never had, but the return of rights they had won when the Turks were their masters. It was, however, true that these rights had been won and exercised by a foreign despot and not by the Egyptian people who now claimed them.

Nor did most people understand how the British control was exercised; they did not always grasp that the British Advisers had no executive power of their own, only through the Egyptian Ministers whom they advised. In 1884 Lord Granville, the Secretary of State concerned, had laid down the principle that the advice tendered to a Minister or a Governor by a British Adviser must be accepted, and this had made the British *de facto* rulers of Egypt; but it is important to grasp that it was only the Ministers who could issue orders or make laws, and that without a Ministry it was therefore impossible to govern Egypt by civil process. The Protectorate had made no alteration to this state of affairs; the British Advisers were still powerless without a Ministry to advise; in its absence the country could only be governed under martial law,[2] obviously a vicious and clumsy method in time of peace, quite contrary to British traditions. Hence the first care of Allenby, as of any High Commissioner, must always be to secure a Ministry which would carry on the business of the country. He might be spoken of as an administrator; but in actual fact he was more often concerned with ' minister-ing ' Egypt than with administering it. He had sometimes to persuade, encourage, or convince the doubtful, timid, or unwilling politician

---

[1] The Capitulations were certain rights, judicial and economic, which had been granted by old treaties to the nationals of many foreign Powers.

[2] Allenby had actually to declare the 1919 Budget passed by martial law.

that it was his duty to take office, in spite of an unwelcome pronouncement from Downing Street or of popular clamour from El Azhar. It was work for which Allenby had no taste and no training; yet his natural qualities of sincerity and common sense, with a patience and forbearance that only those who knew him well realized, gave him a success that would have eluded many a practised diplomat. In the troubled politics of Egypt he stood as the one constant solid figure, always straight, always true to his word; whose yea was yea, and whose nay was nay; who would listen and advise with sympathy; who interfered as little as possible in Egypt's internal affairs, but when he did, left no doubt that he meant to be obeyed.

Besides the Ministers of the moment, there were two personalities in Egypt whose influence had always to be taken into account. The first was Zaghlul, the champion of independence, the popular idol, whose vanity, obstinacy, and jealousy were growing with the crowd's acclamation and making him less and less open to reason. The second was the Sultan (afterwards King) of Egypt, Fuad, a very different character. He was shrewd rather than forcible, politic rather than vehement; he could play the autocrat but had not the vigour to be a dictator. But his abilities and his influence were very far from negligible, though he was never popular with the majority of his subjects. His relations with Allenby were usually good, and their liking was mutual; but when it came to a difference of opinion there was never any doubt as to whose was the stronger will.

There was a third, and more baffling, personality which demanded attention—that of the Egyptian crowd. Egypt is a country where no man, be he King or Minister or demagogue can rely for long on public opinion, so sudden and so changeable are its enthusiasms or its angers. In a land with a large proportion of illiterates the Press exercises a comparatively small, but seldom moderating, influence. The preachings in the mosques, the whispers in the cafés, the rumours of the bazaars, are the means by which popular beliefs are spread and passions roused. The Egyptian mob was dangerous from the suddenness of its uprising, from the extravagance of its violence; but it usually required little force to suppress it, if quickly and firmly applied.

Egyptian popular leaders, and especially Zaghlul, used the student classes as a political weapon. They could easily be excited by a little heady oratory, and naturally found street demonstrations more amusing than the dull routine of education. School strikes became a regular game and were proclaimed on the slightest occasion; should a British Cabinet Minister in London make a speech which displeased the students they left their desks and paraded the streets in noisy demonstrations; anniversaries of certain events since 1918 also provided excuses to neglect work in favour of noise. Over a period of years both learning and discipline were almost unknown to a large proportion of Egypt's schoolboys.

There was another current of opinion in Egypt which, though it exercised little influence on Allenby, might have disturbed one less careless of criticism. It was that of a large section of the British community, official and unofficial, resident or migratory. Such opinion in general accused Allenby of lack of resolution in dealing with the Egyptians. Things had gone all right in the old days, they claimed, when there was none of this talk of independence and Egyptians had just done what they were told to do; it needed only a little firmness, and perhaps a sharp lesson, and the Egyptians would again come to heel. " This didn't happen in Cromer's time," was the watchword of such people. Allenby took no notice of these imperialistic murmurings of the idle tourist or of the discontents of the disgruntled official; though he listened attentively to those who had real knowledge and understanding of the country.

Such were the conditions with which Allenby had to deal at the Cairo end of the London-Cairo cable route. At the other were the personalities of Downing Street; and the influences which were shaping the policy of the British Empire at home and abroad.

The Foreign Secretary was Lord Curzon. If experience, knowledge, diligence, aptitude had been the only qualities required the direction of foreign affairs could not have been in better hands. Nor was his judgment often at fault; yet since he lacked the force of character and the resolution to maintain his point of view in the face of opposition, much of his work was wasted, and British policy in the years after the war was usually inconstant, irresolute, and ineffectual. Lord Curzon realized the mistakes that were being made, but, though disapproving, gave way. Affairs at home occupied so much of the Cabinet's time that foreign policy had often too little attention. The rebellion in Ireland seemed to drag on interminably and with ever greater bitterness; and industrial troubles were frequent. There were many awkward foreign engagements besides Egypt, and the temper of the British people made difficult any strong policy abroad; they were utterly weary of foreign adventures and expensive foreign commitments, and wished to get back to normal as soon as possible. For the first time in its history the nation had fought as a nation. It had not liked it and wished to return to its traditional occupation of trading as soon as possible. The Chief of the Imperial General Staff, Sir Henry Wilson, when asked his recommendation on the disposition of the numerous British forces still abroad, never tired of repeating his advice to " get out of the places that don't belong to you and hold on to those that do." In this latter category, it may be remarked, he included both Ireland and Egypt.

The above sketch of the conditions in which the Egyptian problem was treated during the years following the war is necessarily imperfect; it omits much, and some of its estimates may be disputed. The essential figures in the picture were these. In Egypt a people, largely ignorant and illiterate, led by an obstinate demagogue, clamoured for independence, with no sense of the responsibilities it would bring; more moderate Egyptians, fearing responsibility, followed the dictates of the mob rather than directed it. In England a Coalition Government of discordant members, led by a Prime Minister who had little understanding of foreign peoples or foreign affairs, was distracted by a whole series of difficult problems, internal and external, among which Egypt seemed relatively unimportant, and had certainly little interest for the nation at large. Between them stood Allenby, the soldier trained to receive definite orders and to execute them precisely. He now found that in place of definite orders he was given only a vague policy, not always easy to interpret and sometimes impossible to execute.

Instead of being able to command and to receive instant obedience, he had to persuade and conciliate. He had force at his disposal as a last resort, and temptation enough to use it; but he knew that force could never solve the problem of Anglo-Egyptian relations. Many spoke of " Allenby's policy " at this time or later. He had and could have no policy of his own; he was charged with executing the policy of the Cabinet, and so far as he could interpret it, did so with his usual loyalty. But he gradually established out of his fund of natural common sense certain principles that guided him in his day-to-day conduct of affairs in Egypt. Firstly, if our avowed policy of training the Egyptians to govern themselves was sincere and meant anything it was useless to interfere and take the direction into one's own hands as soon as any difficulty arose. If the Ministers and officials were to learn to govern, if the Police were to be efficient in keeping order, if the Egyptian Army was to be able to support their authority at need, then they must learn to face their difficulties and dangers by themselves, and must not rely on the British when anything disconcerting or alarming took place. Two extracts from Allenby's letters to his mother (to whom he wrote regularly from Egypt, once every week or ten days up to the time of her death in 1922) show his observance of this principle.

April 6, 1921:

Saad Zaghlul arrived in Cairo yesterday. I kept all officers and soldiers out of the streets and left the whole management to the Egyptians. There was a gigantic and enthusiastic but quite orderly crowd, and not a single mishap occurred.

May 20, 1921 (after some disturbances had taken place):

I bide my time, as I want the Egyptians to settle their politics for themselves, and I don't want to interfere with my troops unless the life, limb, or interests of Europeans are in danger.

The principle had obvious risks, especially with the explosiveness of Egyptian crowds; and Allenby was criticized on several occasions, especially after the Alexandria riots in May 1921, which caused considerable loss of life, for not taking charge early enough. But his principle was sound, though it took a bold man to face the risks involved.

His second principle, never to bargain in matters of policy, was also wise. Bargains are for the weaker, a generous firmness for the stronger. When it had been decided that it was necessary, or desirable, to make a concession he held that it should be made freely and at once without trying to extract advantages in return. This belief was at the root of his action in obtaining the 1922 Declaration.

Thirdly, it was his firm conviction that our position in Egypt depended ultimately on our sea-power in the Mediterranean. So long as that was maintained we could afford to make all reasonable concessions to the Egyptians, since we could control Egypt just so long and so firmly as we controlled the Mediterranean. If we lost control any rights granted by the Egyptians would be valueless.

One of the most striking tributes to Allenby's work was paid by an Englishman who had a very great knowledge of Egypt and the Egyptians. Harry Boyle, who had been one of Cromer's most trusted assistants, came out to Egypt in the spring of 1921. It was nominally a holiday visit, but there is no doubt that Boyle was commissioned by the Foreign Office to make an unofficial report, in view of the many criticisms of Allenby which were reaching England. If he was sent to curse he remained to bless, as the following extracts from his diary show:

I had the privilege of seeing a good deal of Allenby, for whom I conceived a high admiration. His position in Egypt was a most difficult one, involving as it did dozens of matters with which, as a soldier, he was wholly unfamiliar. His period of office coincided also with the most active period of the Zaghlul movement. Nevertheless he did extraordinarily well, and I have no hesitation in thinking that a great part of his success with the native element waa due to his extraordinary resemblance to Lord Cromer, both in physique and manner.

Allenby is the one and only good point I can find in the whole horizon.

I like Lord Allenby more and more. He is a fine fellow and the best possible for the present circumstances. Intrigues against him, either here or in London, make me furious.

Allenby's staff also, of the Diplomatic Service,[1] found him to their liking as a chief. They soon came, in fact, to regard him with affection and admiration. If they expected a rough, blunt soldier, with little literary or classical knowledge and no skill of the tongue or pen, they were soon undeceived. " He wrote the best short minute of any whom I have served," one of them has recorded. Another, having introduced into the draft of a dispatch a translation of a passage from one of the Greek dramatists, was surprised to hear Allenby say, on reading it, " If we are going to quote Æschylus let us do it in the original Greek," which he gave.

All, at one time or another, came under the lash of his temper and the severity of his tongue; but all learned how quickly it passed, leaving no grudge or remembrance; and all appreciated his quickness to grasp the essentials of a problem, his strength of decision, and his complete loyalty to those who served him. As an instance of this last, he caused to be placed on record in the official file the privately expressed advice of one of his subordinates which he had not taken, but which had afterwards proved to be right. Allenby, on his part, soon learned to appreciate the qualities of his staff and to cease to regard them, or to address them, as " weak-kneed blackcoats." The Residency staff never worked more loyally or more harmoniously as a team than under the direction of Allenby.

The Residency at Cairo—house and office in one—where Allenby spent more than six years, is a pleasant building on the banks of the Nile. A spacious garden runs down to the great river, the water and silt of which enable almost anything to be grown. Allenby spent much time in his garden and liked showing it to visitors; their pleasure was sometimes mixed with justified apprehension of a formidable marabou stork which followed Allenby everywhere, almost like a dog, and had a jealous dislike of any children or ladies with him. The stork himself, however, had a severe fright one day when two young lions, which had been brought to visit Allenby on their way to the Zoo, broke

[1] He also had with him for a time one of his former military staff in Palestine, Lord Dalmeny; and Sir Gilbert Clayton, who had been his Political Officer in Palestine, was Adviser to the Ministry of the Interior.

loose and chased the stork round the garden. Not far off, on the other side of the river, was the Cairo Zoo, to which Allenby was a frequent visitor, improving and indulging his already intimate knowledge of beasts and birds. His interest in and love of animals did not, however, extend to dogs; he never owned one and was not fond of them. He made no parade of his position, and walked in Cairo without ceremony and without escort other than an A.D.C. till near the end of his time, when he was officially ordered not to go abroad unguarded.

Allenby still rode, but less frequently as his official duties claimed more of his time. In the winter, when he could spare the time, he shot duck, which visit the Egyptian Delta in large numbers. In the summer, when official Egypt moves to Alexandria, he bathed regularly; and on one occasion, in July 1920, nearly lost his life in the sea. It was a rough day, and Allenby, who was a strong swimmer, went out too far; he had great difficulty in getting back to shore and broke a blood-vessel and strained his heart and lungs. He was in bed for a fortnight afterwards. A less determined man would have been drowned.

There was much entertaining at the Residency, official and private, and it was seldom that there was not a large party both at luncheon and dinner. Allenby and Lady Allenby were admirable hosts in every way; even the most official parties were friendly as well as dignified. Allenby's kindliness and humour as a host are illustrated by the following story. A senior officer from Palestine, who was going on a visit to Egypt, told one of his subordinates to telegraph to the General Commanding in Cairo, an intimate friend, that he was coming to stay the night with him. " Tell him I shall be late," he said, " and that he is not to bother about dinner for me; just to put a pint of champagne and some *foie gras* sandwiches in my room." The telegram was by some mistake delivered at the Residency instead of to the G.O.C.; and when the officer arrived at Cairo he found to his surprise the High Commissioner's A.D.C. awaiting him at the station with the announcement that his telegram had been received, that the High Commissioner regretted he was dining out, but that his room was prepared. The officer in question was not easily disconcerted; but when he found champagne and a large plate of *foie gras* sandwiches in his room he felt that some explanation was needed. On meeting his host at breakfast next morning he began at once to apologize for the "awful mistake last night." "What mistake?" said Allenby. "Weren't the sandwiches the right kind?" And would hear no word of apology or explanation, merely saying he was delighted to see his guest, and to be able to provide the supper to which he was accustomed.

Lady Allenby's influence and personality were, in their sphere, as marked as Allenby's in his. Under a gentle manner and great personal charm she hid a character as strong as his; she was less swayed by sentiment and had more realism and common sense than most women; she was always punctual, never in a hurry; quite above intrigue or gossip; serene, dignified, and unaffected. A great woman and a fitting complement to Allenby's greatness.

CHAPTER XIV

THE MILNER MISSION

(*May* 1919–*December* 1921)

> Government is such an imperfect business at the best that it is
> more important that people should have the system which they
> like than a better system which they like less.
>
> LORD MILNER

AT the beginning of April, shortly after the appointment of
Allenby as High Commissioner, the Government had proposed
to send to Egypt a Commission of inquiry headed by Lord
Milner; and had suggested to Allenby the announcement of this
as an alternative to his proposed release of Zaghlul and his
associates Allenby declined to be diverted from his purpose
even by so illustrious a red herring as Lord Milner, but agreed
that the visit would be useful later.

A Commission (or mission) of inquiry is the favourite device
of British Governments for dealing with awkward problems,
internal or external. It has many obvious advantages. It post-
pones the necessity for making a difficult decision for at least a
time—the Milner Mission and the negotiations arising out of it
provided a breathing-space of more than two years; it gives
interesting employment to a number of distinguished public
servants or ex-servants; it produces a volume, often very read-
able, full of valuable information and orderly statistics; and
finally, there is always the possibility that the Commission may
light on an acceptable and workable solution of the problem.[1]

To be most effective, the Milner Mission should have reached
Egypt in May, during the quiet period following the restoration
of order. But Milner himself, who was a member of the Cabinet,
was deeply engaged in other activities; it was not easy to find
suitable members at short notice (there is a recognized principle
of such Commissions that the more difficult the problem the

---

[1] This is unusual. Four Commissions have visited Palestine since 1921, but none
of them arrived at the right answer: the Sankey Coal Commission had no better fate
at home.

greater the number of members required); and the hot season in Egypt is not the best time for good work. The arrival of the Mission was postponed till the autumn, and eventually till the winter. By then opposition to it had been organized and consolidated.

Meanwhile Allenby went on leave to England, which he had not visited for more than two years. He had left it in June 1917, comparatively unknown, somewhat disappointed; removed to a secondary theatre as a result of his failure at Arras, many believed. Now he was famous. Honours had come thickly to him. He had received the thanks of both Houses of Parliament, had been made a Viscount, had been given a grant of £50,000. Sadly enough, he had received the official announcement of his elevation to the peerage on what would have been his son Michael's twenty-first birthday. In the summer of 1919 he had been promoted Field-Marshal. In 1920 he was made Colonel of the Life Guards, which carries with it the Court appointment of Gold Stick in Waiting. Most of the Allied countries at war with Germany had sent him decorations: the United States, France, Italy, Belgium, Rumania, Greece, Egypt, China, Japan, the Hejaz. A Cockney soldier of his Army was heard to remark, on reading of his many rewards, " They 'aven't 'arf put it across old Allenby."

A new peer has to choose a place or places from which to derive his title. Allenby took Megiddo, the scene of his greatest victory,[1] and Felixstowe, where his mother still lived. As supporters to his coat of arms he chose a horse, to symbolize the cavalry arm to which he belonged and owed so much for his victories, and a camel, to record the part that useful but unlovely animal played in the Palestine Campaigns. A British General of the future may have difficulty in finding comparable supporters to his arms, for a tank or lorry would hardly gain admission to the College of Arms as " heraldic beasts."

Many institutions, guilds, or societies, whose aim and setting were peace, offered him honours for his success in war. Several universities—Oxford, Cambridge, Edinburgh, Aberdeen, and

---

[1] Certain of the lighter-minded members of his staff were convinced that Bashan, where the bulls come from, was the most suitable place in the Holy Land to be connected with his title.

Yale—offered him degrees; the ancient City Companies of London, such as the Goldsmiths, Fishmongers, and Grocers, invited him to become a freeman; a racehorse (which ran unsuccessfully in the Derby) was named after him, and several race-clubs made him a life member. Perhaps the most curious distinction he received was honorary membership of that most exclusive cricket club, the I Zingari. Its three chief rules are " Keep your promise; keep your temper; keep your wicket up." To the first and last of these precepts Allenby could faithfully subscribe; he had observed them all his life.

The crowning civic honour of the freedom of the City of London—the equivalent of a Roman ' triumph '—was bestowed on five commanders of the war: Jellicoe, Beatty, French, Haig, and Allenby. For Allenby the ceremony took place on October 7, 1919, when he was received at the Guildhall and was presented with the freedom and with a sword of honour. He was afterwards entertained at a luncheon at the Mansion House. A week or two earlier he had had a more homely reception at Felixstowe when he had gone to visit his mother, now aged eighty-eight.

Allenby returned to Egypt in November to find that the political situation had deteriorated in his absence, and that the period of calm was over. Zaghlul, still in Paris, had, through his followers in Egypt, organized opposition to the Mission, of which they intended to order a boycott. The Prime Minister, Mohammed Said, resigned on the plea that the arrival of the Mission should be postponed till the peace treaty with Turkey had been concluded; [1] and a successor had to be found. The Mission arrived early in December. Its composition was distinguished and was intended to be sympathetic to Egypt. The other members besides Milner were Sir Rennell Rodd,[2] who had served Egypt under Cromer; General Sir John Maxwell, who had many years' service with the Egyptian Army and was a popular figure in Egypt; Mr C. Hurst,[3] Principal Legal Adviser of the Foreign Office; Mr J. A. Spender, a prominent Liberal, formerly Editor

[1] Actually it was not signed till three and a half years later, in July 1923.

[2] Raised to the peerage as Lord Rennell in 1933, Ambassador to Italy, 1908–19, M.P., 1928–32. Died 1941.

[3] Sir Cecil Hurst, G.C.M.G., K.C.B., President of International Court of Justice at The Hague, 1934–36.

of the *Westminster Gazette*; and General Sir Owen Thomas, to represent the Labour Party. But the Mission had two fatal defects in Egyptian eyes. Its terms of reference included the maintenance of the Protectorate; and although an exclusively British body, it proposed to recommend a Constitution for Egypt, a task for which Egyptians considered themselves fully as capable and more concerned. The boycott by Egyptians was successful; and the Mission left Egypt three months later without having had any open contact with Egyptian opinion other than by the vociferous and uncomplimentary clamours of the mob. It had had, however, certain important contacts behind the scenes.

Allenby, largely with the idea of leaving a free field for the Mission, spent the first six weeks of 1920 touring the Sudan with Lady Allenby. He first paid a visit at Jeddah to King Hussein of the Hejaz, who had long expressed a wish " to kiss him on his intelligent forehead." Hussein as a ruler was difficult and unreasonable; as a host, he was courteous and charming. He presented Allenby with a sword of honour and entertained him at the traditional Arab banquet called ' Sumat,' held only on special occasions and usually to celebrate the visit of a conqueror. Slaves walked along the middle of the table to feed the guests, over two hundred of whom were present, including tribal chiefs from all parts of the Hejaz.

From Jeddah Allenby went by Port Sudan, Suakin, and Atbara to Khartoum; and then on up the river as far south as Lake No in the Bahr el Ghazal Province. On the return journey he visited the Kassala and Dongola provinces. At Korosko, just north of Wadi Halfa, he found a crashed aeroplane; it was one of the earliest of those ventures by which the long-distance air routes of the world were laid out in the years following the war. The pilots were South Africans, Pierre Van Ryneveld and Quintin Brand.[1] They had reached Korosko from London in seven days, a record at that time. Allenby took the two pilots aboard his steamer. On return to Cairo they renewed in another plane their

[1] Now Lieutenant-General Sir Pierre Van Ryneveld, K.B.E., D.S.O., M.C., Chief of the General Staff, Union Defence Forces in South Africa, and Air Vice-Marshal Sir Quintin Brand, K.B.E., D.S.O., M.C., D.F.C., Director-General of Civil Aviation in Egypt 1932–36.

LORD ALLENBY AT HIS INSTALLATION AS RECTOR OF EDINBURGH UNIVERSITY IN APRIL 1936

This is probably the last portrait taken of Lord Allenby, who died on May 14, 1936.

Photo Ian Smith, Edinburgh

FISHING THE STANLEY POOL, RIVER TAY

Photo Star Photos, Perth

attempt to reach South Africa by air and eventually did so after a mishap in Rhodesia. They were the first men to complete the journey from England to the Cape by air.

Milner and his Mission returned to England in March 1920. Although moderate and responsible Egyptians had not dared to break the boycott imposed by students and agitators in Egypt, some now bethought themselves that it would be well to get into touch with the Mission before it reported. After some face-saving negotiation they induced Zaghlul to accompany them to England and to open discussion with the Mission at the end of May. Early in August, after protracted and difficult negotiation, Milner produced a scheme which went a long way towards meeting Egyptian claims. The Protectorate was to be replaced by a Treaty which granted Egypt independence, subject to certain reservations for special British interests. Allenby, who came home on leave in August,[1] strongly advised that the scheme should be put at once before the Cabinet, and, if approved by them, announced as the solution of His Majesty's Government; and that its terms should on no account be made public before Cabinet consideration.[2] His advice was not taken, or came too late. Milner, with a rashness curious in so experienced a diplomat, had given Zaghlul a note of his proposals without obtaining from him any acceptance of them or even undertaking to recommend them. Zaghlul, fearing to lose the favour of the fickle mob if he made the least concession, had declared that the proposals must be accepted by the Egyptian nation, of which he had so often

[1] There were strong rumours at the time that he would not return to Egypt; and the War Office intended to recommend him for the Aldershot Command if the Foreign Office did not require him for Egypt.

[2] The following is an extract of a letter of Allenby to a friend, dated August 27, 1920:

" Milner gave me the outline of his projected settlement. Apparently Egypt is to have control of all but Finance and Justice. She will conduct her own foreign affairs. The Sudan question had not been seriously discussed; and it seems that the present dual control is to endure on Egypt receiving a guarantee that she gets her Nile water. Here is, I fear, likely to be trouble. I told the King, Curzon, and Milner that I hoped the Milner proposals would not be published; but submitted to H.M.G., who would take what action they deemed requisite. However, it appears that the whole thing is public and a cockshy for criticism by every one— before the Cabinet has ever had a chance of considering it. Zaghlul, I hear, is not content; and will not return to Egypt."

claimed to be the sole accredited representative. He was allowed to send some of his colleagues to Egypt to sound national opinion; the terms of the proposal, of course, became public at once, and were thenceforward regarded, as Allenby had foreseen, as the minimum offer to which the British Government was committed. It was useless for Curzon to announce that the agreement was merely the recommendation of the Milner Mission and not necessarily acceptable to the Government. Milner, a member of the Cabinet, had always been regarded by the Egyptians as a plenipotentiary in the negotiations, and any assertion to the contrary was taken as evidence of British bad faith. Allenby's dislike of the bargaining process of a Treaty was justified.

The agreement might, even so, have had a good chance of acceptance if Zaghlul had shown any leadership. But by refusing to commit himself either to recommendation or condemnation, he left his supporters puzzled and gave his enemies their opportunity. After some further fruitless discussion the Mission submitted its report, and it was decided to open negotiations on its proposals with an official delegation from Egypt.

It was now 1921, nearly two years since the troubles into which the Commission was appointed to inquire, and one year since its visit to Egypt. But there was to be still more delay. The negotiations on the composition of the delegation were long and tortuous. The Sultan, Fuad; the Prime Minister, Adly; and the popular favourite, Zaghlul, all wished to have the predominant voice in its formation.

Zaghlul, getting anxious about his position, and jealous of Adly's growing influence for moderation, telegraphed from Paris on March 20 saying that he would support the Adly Ministry on condition that martial law and the censorship were abolished and that he should lead the official delegation, which should contain a majority of members from his following. He then made hurried plans for his return to Cairo, where he arrived on April 5. Adly showed every friendliness towards him; he went to the station to greet him, and no action was taken to prevent the nation from giving the warmest welcome to the nationalist leader.

The journey by rail from Alexandria to Cairo was one of

triumphal progress, and extraordinary scenes marked his arrival in the capital. The day automatically became a national holiday. Women left the seclusion of the harems, an unprecedented thing, to participate in one of the most remarkable receptions ever accorded to a citizen of any country. At least 400,000 people must have thronged the relatively short distance from the railway station to Zaghlul's house. Tram-cars bedecked with flags and palms, vehicles of all descriptions covered in flowers, dancing-girls, native musicians, camels and donkeys, all combined to make a striking picture.

It was not long before Adly and Zaghlul came into open conflict. Three weeks after his return Zaghlul in a speech made it clear that collaboration between himself and Adly depended on the entire acceptance of his conditions. Meanwhile Adly announced that Zaghlul had found himself in agreement with the Ministry, except as regards the presidency of the delegation. The Ministry maintained, said Adly, that according to precedent the Premier must preside over an official delegation. Zaghlul was beginning to lose ground, and five members of his delegation declared their confidence in Adly. As he found his influence waning, so Zaghlul became more violent in his campaign against Adly. As a direct result there were serious riots with much loss of life at Alexandria in May. The casualties were thirty Egyptians and fourteen Europeans killed and a hundred and thirty Egyptians and sixty-nine Europeans wounded.

Allenby has been much criticized both for allowing Zaghlul to return and for failing to take strong enough action to prevent the Alexandria riots or to check them in time. The return of Zaghlul was obviously a dangerous measure likely to disturb the peace, but it would have been difficult to refuse admission to Egypt to one who had been admitted to negotiation in England and with whom Adly himself was in correspondence over the formation of a joint delegation. The Alexandria riots were a direct sequel to an incident at Tanta at the end of April, when the police fired on an unruly and dangerous mob, killing a few and wounding others. Allenby strongly advised a firm attitude to the popular outcry against the police, but Adly, always weak in a difficulty, agreed to an inquiry, which passed some criticism on the police and shook their morale. As a result they would not fire in similar circumstances at Alexandria, and the mob got completely out of hand. If Allenby's advice had been followed about the Tanta incident the Alexandria riots would never have assumed such proportions. His reluctance to intervene at once with British troops was in accordance with his policy that the Egyptians, if they were to be fit for independence, must learn to check their own disorders.

At last the official delegation, led by Allenby, departed for London on July 1. As Allenby had repeatedly warned the Foreign Office during these months, the negotiations between Curzon and Adly had no greater prospect of success than those between Milner and Zaghlul. With Zaghlul still commanding the voice of the crowd, Adly dared make no withdrawal from the position the former had taken up with Milner. The discussions, with an interval of some five or six weeks, lasted from July to November, but the question of the location of British troops in Egypt proved an insuperable obstacle that no council-table formula could surmount.

During Adly's absence the political atmosphere had been reasonably calm in spite of Zaghlul's agitation and of a singularly ill-timed visit, at Zaghlul's invitation, of four Labour M.P.'s, which was permitted by the Cabinet in spite of the protests of the Residency. The Ministry, under Sarwat Pasha, acting as Prime Minister, during Adly's absence, had made considerable headway; the majority of Egyptians were genuinely anxious for a settlement and calm. Zaghlul had made many blunders and had lost much ground. But disappointment at the failure of the negotiations was accentuated by a peevish admonitory note from the British Government, which Allenby was ordered to present to the Sultan early in December.[1] Adly resigned shortly afterwards. The tone of this note caused great resentment in Egypt, and undoubtedly very much increased the difficulty of forming a new Ministry. The strong political position which Adly had gained in Egypt for himself and the moderate elements crumbled to pieces, and Zaghlul rose again like a phœnix from the ashes of his own folly. His

---

[1] It came to be known as the " Allenby Note," though Allenby had no hand in its composition and had never seen it till he was ordered to hand it to the Sultan.

relief at the breakdown of the Adly negotiations was obvious. He welcomed it not on national but on personal grounds.

There was a moment when Sarwat was prepared to take office on a programme accepted by the Foreign Office; but renewed agitation by Zaghlul destroyed the opportunity. The situation by the middle of December was that no Minister could be persuaded to form a Government to carry on the affairs of Egypt. The attempt to bargain a Treaty had brought a complete deadlock from which Allenby was left to find an exit.

In the meantime disorders had broken out in Cairo. On the advice of the officials responsible, who feared widespread and dangerous disturbances, Allenby decided to prohibit a meeting summoned for December 22 by Zaghlul, the prime mischief-maker. Zaghlul challenged the decision by an appeal to the nation.

Allenby now made up his mind that there was no way of removing the deadlock in Anglo-Egyptian relations while Zaghlul and his immediate entourage remained in the country. So he took the bold step of ordering the arrest of Zaghlul and five of his colleagues on December 23, and they were removed under military escort to Suez for deportation.[1] There was some apprehension that Allenby's drastic action would plunge Egypt once again into a state of widespread disorder. There were many portents to support this view, but Allenby did not share it, and was determined vigorously to suppress all attempts at disturbance. He had strong forces on the streets of Cairo, where the outbreaks were promptly suppressed, and sent warships to Suez, Ismailia, Port Said, and Alexandria, while naval parties went up the Nile. The natives of Alexandria, doubtless mindful of the lessons of the preceding May, showed little disposition to stir up trouble, and mischief-makers in general soon realized that they were to be given little chance of organizing outbreaks on any large scale. Thanks to Allenby's firm measures, calm had been practically restored before the end of December. Disorders had ceased; all Government officials, after a short face-saving strike, were again

---

[1] Zaghlul was entertained on Christmas Day by the officers of the British regiment at Suez. On December 30 he left for Aden, where he remained till March 1, 1922, when he was removed to the Seychelles Islands.

at work; the schoolboys were still out, but were soon to return to their studies under the threat of an indefinite lock-out; and the native Bar had decided to call off their strike, and, instead, to go into mourning for two months. The public services were again working normally.

But all this did not mean to say that Egypt had settled down to any political stability. Order had been re-established by strong military action, but for Allenby the same fundamental political problems remained to be solved. There was still no Ministry and no chance of getting one until some way could be found out of the political impasse. On December 28 Allenby had been compelled to issue a proclamation authorizing the Under-Secretaries of State—who, with one exception, were all British—to exercise the powers and functions of Ministers in administrative matters until a new Ministry was formed. But it was an impossible task for a group of British Under-Secretaries to carry on the government of the country for any length of time with a hostile Egyptian personnel. Allenby had to find some solution of the deadlock.

CHAPTER XV

THE 1922 DECLARATION

Content you, gentlemen, I'll compound this strife.
SHAKESPEARE, *The Taming of the Shrew*

THE announcement made by His Majesty's Government on February 28, 1922, by which the Protectorate was abolished and Egypt declared an independent Sovereign State, is a notable landmark in the relations between Britain and Egypt, and is Allenby's principal contribution to political history. His action has been much criticized, misunderstood, and misrepresented, so that a somewhat full account of his doings and his motives during December 1921 and the first two months of 1922 is an essential part of his biography.

Allenby had during 1921 repeatedly warned the Government to be prepared for a failure of the negotiations with Adly and to have a policy ready to announce if the plan for a treaty broke down. He had made no secret of his own view that the policy should include the abolition of the Protectorate. Now, however, he was left, after two years of bargaining, with an impracticable policy, no Ministry, and a complete stoppage of the administrative machinery of Egypt. Co-operation with the Egyptians, on which basis British rule had rested during and since the days of Lord Cromer, had come to an end. Allenby determined that the time had come to compel the Government to recognize the true facts of the position.

During the last week of December 1921 and the first week of January 1922 he ascertained, mainly through one of his staff as intermediary, the conditions in which the moderate party, the leaders of which were Adly and Sarwat, could undertake to form a Ministry. On January 12 a formula had been agreed on, Sarwat had produced a satisfactory list of Ministers who were prepared to take office under it, and Allenby was in a position to telegraph his solution to the Foreign Office for approval.

Put as briefly and simply as possible, the difference between Allenby's standpoint and that taken up hitherto by His Majesty's

Government was as follows: the Government was prepared, subject to the approval of Parliament, to abolish the Protectorate and to recognize the independence of Egypt, provided the Egyptians would first bind themselves to conditions regarding certain British interests and rights, of which the chief were the safeguarding of our Imperial communications, the protection of foreigners in Egypt, and our position in the Sudan. This the Egyptians had refused to do. Allenby proposed that the Government should abolish the Protectorate and grant independence forthwith, but should announce at the same time that Great Britain retained liberty of action, if her interests demanded it, in certain matters, afterwards known as " the reserved subjects," until such time as an amicable agreement on those matters could be reached. The Government contended that it was impossible thus to give away our position in Egypt by the abolition of the Protectorate, until we had satisfactory pledges from the Egyptians as to our special interests. Allenby retorted that our position in Egypt in fact depended not on the existence of a shadowy, undefined Protectorate, but on our sea-power in the Mediterranean and the presence of our garrison in the Delta, and that these constituted our real pledges.[1] As long as we announced that, as the stronger party, we intended to reserve our rights in the essential matters, there was no danger in granting independence to Egypt, and much profit, since it would enable Egyptian co-operation again to be secured.

In his cable to the Foreign Office Allenby demanded an immediate reply. This led to accusations of " aggression "; of presenting a pistol at the head of the Government; of delivering an ultimatum; of being, in fact, rough and soldier-like. The real explanation was that Allenby knew he had no time to lose. He was aware of the changeable mood of Egyptian politicians; and the solution he was now urging was no new thing but one that he had presented to the Government many times in the last year. He was now determined on forcing an issue without further

[1] " Whatsoever may be the final solution of the problem, our effective guarantees are our military and naval position in Egypt, and the variously penetrating influences of our forty years' moral predominance in the country."—Allenby's dispatch to the Foreign Office (February 2, 1922).

delay. He sent at the same time as his official cables a private telegram to the Foreign Secretary, Lord Curzon, urging his support. Curzon answered that he would do his best to obtain an early decision from the Cabinet, and that he hoped for a favourable reply. He did in fact recommend Allenby's proposals most strongly in the Cabinet, but, on meeting opposition, wilted before it as he had done on other occasions. On January 18 a telegram was sent to Allenby saying that the Cabinet were unable to accede to his proposals as they stood, and suggesting that he should send home two of his Advisers, Sir Gilbert Clayton and Mr Amos,[1] to explain them further. It was not a suggestion that had the least chance of appealing to Allenby. He replied at once that his Advisers were in entire agreement with the solution he had proposed, and that it would be a useless waste of time to send them home; that one of his staff, Mr Selby,[2] would very shortly be in England, and could give any detailed explanation necessary. In a personal telegram to Curzon he again repeated his main arguments; urged the dangers of delay; and ended by tendering his resignation if his advice was not accepted. Since Allenby was subsequently criticized for the manner and hastiness of this resignation, it should be made clear that this was a personal telegram to Curzon and not, therefore, a formal resignation. Allenby's intention was to strengthen the Foreign Secretary's hand in his discussions with the Cabinet. Curzon had telegraphed to Allenby that he was supporting him in the Cabinet " up to the point of resignation," [3] and Allenby hoped by placing his own resignation in Curzon's hands to give him an additional weapon to use in the Cabinet. Such personal telegrams are not usually circulated to other members of the Cabinet, as are official ones; but this one of Allenby's was, without reference to Curzon's personal telegram to Allenby; and his resignation was held by some Ministers, who were unaware of the circumstances, to be a ' footpad ' attempt to hold up the Cabinet coach.

[1] The late Sir Maurice Amos, K.B.E., Judicial Adviser to the Government of Egypt, 1919–25.

[2] Sir Walford Selby, K.C.M.G., C.B., C.V.O., Ambassador in Lisbon 1937–40. He had been First Secretary at the Residency and was now on his way home to take up an appointment at the Foreign Office.

[3] " Up to " but not " including," he explained subsequently.

On January 24 the Foreign Office cabled to Allenby an alternative formula, which Curzon afterwards described as a " bridge " which he had at great pains constructed for Allenby. In essentials it was, however, the same proposal—that the Egyptians should accept our terms first, and that the Protectorate should be abolished afterwards. Allenby replied, on the 25th, that he would endeavour to carry out the Government's suggested policy, but that he had not the least hope that any Egyptian Ministers would take office on it. He now formally and officially tendered his resignation. The four principal British Advisers to the Egyptian Government, in consultation with whom Allenby's proposals had been drawn up, also informed the Foreign Office that Allenby's resignation must involve theirs.

After another Cabinet meeting a long denunciatory telegram was sent to Allenby on January 28. It accused him of suddenly and without warning reversing a policy on which he had been consulted by the Cabinet, and which was largely the result of his own advice; of misleading them as to the prospects of obtaining a Ministry to carry out that policy; and of now presenting an ultimatum to the Government and demanding an instant reply without discussion. It concluded by ordering Allenby, together with Amos and Clayton, two of his principal Advisers, to return home for consultation. The majority in the Cabinet had in fact decided to replace Allenby and his Advisers; and the telegram was intended to provide the Government's subsequent justification. Actually it was such a complete misstatement of the position, and its accusations could so easily be disproved, that it gave Allenby a very strong position for counter-reply. He did not, however, make any immediate answer, but told an extremely able member of his staff to draw up a dispatch to refute the Foreign Office allegations; this dispatch, a masterpiece of argument and phrasing, which completely upset the Foreign Office case, he carried home with him. The last paragraph may be quoted as typical of Allenby:

The Commission which I hold from His Majesty is to maintain His Majesty's Protectorate over Egypt. I have done so, but I do not think it has the elements of durability, and I have now advised

298

its being brought to an end, as it was established, by a unilateral declaration. I have laid open to His Majesty's Government a course which, in my judgment, accords with the general traditions of British policy and British institutions, and is in the truest interest of the Empire, while it is consistent with that political development of Egypt which His Majesty's Government have always desired to encourage, and which has been the goal of the labours of my predecessors, men who in serving their own country have sought the welfare of the Egyptian people.

Allenby left Cairo on February 3. The report of the enthusiastic send-off given him by Egyptians, British, and foreigners—not only at Cairo but at other stations on the line and again at Alexandria—gave his opponents at home their first cause to doubt whether it was going to be quite as easy as it had seemed to dismiss so popular a figure. Their doubts were increased by articles in the Press, particularly in *The Times*, supporting Allenby, though without full knowledge of his proposals. The attitude of *The Times* is of some interest. Its very able foreign correspondent, Sir Valentine Chirol, had lately been in Egypt. He had been treated with scant courtesy by Allenby, who had been annoyed by some comments in a *Times* article, not on himself but on the Sultan. Chirol had therefore no reason to favour Allenby. But he understood the Egyptian problem; and when he learned in London of the gist of Allenby's proposals he supported them warmly, and cabled to Lord Northcliffe, proprietor of *The Times*, who then happened to be passing through Egypt on his way home, recommending him to stop in Egypt and to study the question on the spot. Northcliffe sent a telegram to Allenby to ask if he could stay at the Residency. Allenby was embarrassed; he was the last person to canvass for Press support, and mistrusted newspaper-men. He was, however, persuaded by his staff to receive Northcliffe, who spent several days gathering all shades of opinion in Egypt, and was a witness of Allenby's impressive send-off. The support of *The Times* in the succeeding weeks was a considerable factor in Allenby's success.

Lord Northcliffe pointed out that Egyptian hopes of a generous settlement had been allowed to grow up unchecked over a period of two years, and then with the breakdown of the Adly-

Curzon negotiations came such universal feelings of bitterness and mistrust as to paralyse government in Egypt. He found a very curious situation in Egypt. The government of the country since December had been carried on by Under-Secretaries of State, and that was a position which could not last indefinitely, but in the absence of any solution of the present deadlock there seemed no immediate prospect of remedying that very unsatisfactory situation. Meanwhile the position of British functionaries, to whom apparently the British Cabinet looked to carry on the machinery of government, was becoming more and more intolerable. It appeared to Lord Northcliffe that the men on the spot had taken the true measure of the situation, and had acted wisely and with courage. He had come to the conclusion that the High Commissioner had prepared the way for the best and most practical means of getting ahead with the Egyptian problem, and that it would be expedient to take advantage of his counsels, since they constituted at once a pledge of Britain's good faith, which was so urgently needed in Egypt; they would set the Egyptians well on the path they desired to tread, and they in no way imperilled the essential interests of Britain. Finally, Lord Northcliffe pointed out the fact that there was much solidarity of opinion in Egypt behind the efforts of the High Commissioner to arrive at a *modus vivendi*. This had been unmistakably evidenced by the large and representative gathering present at the station on the occasion of Viscount Allenby's departure for London.

Allenby arrived home early on February 10. He was met at the station by the Chief of the Imperial General Staff, Sir Henry Wilson, by Sir Philip Chetwode, and by Mr Selby. He was in high spirits, and at once announced to his friends that he was " not going to budge an inch and was not going to argue," forestalling advice which they had come to offer him. Though warned that it was too early for Foreign Office hours, he insisted on going at once to Downing Street to leave his dispatch refuting what he called the " wicked accusations " against him of the Foreign Office telegram of January 28.

The history of the subsequent fate of this dispatch is somewhat amusing. It was marked, in accordance with the usual custom for important State documents, " To be circulated to H.M. the

King and to the Cabinet." No sooner, however, had Lord Curzon had time to read the first pages of the dispatch than he telephoned urgently to the branch of the Foreign Office concerned and had all circulation suspended. When he saw Allenby that evening his opening remarks were on the subject of the dispatch.[1] " This is an extremely able document, Lord Allenby," he began; " it must have been written by a very clever man. You did not write it yourself. Who wrote it for you?" To this not very tactful beginning Allenby replied, " No, I did not write it, but I have been through every word of it, and am prepared to initial every line if your Lordship is not satisfied. It was written by a *very* clever man." Curzon then said that it was not a document which could be fittingly circulated to the King and to the Cabinet, since it was not the kind of document which he, as Secretary of State, or the Cabinet were in the habit of having addressed to them by their representatives abroad. Allenby replied that he regretted that fact, but that as Lord Curzon had seen fit to bring certain charges against him, which had doubtless been circulated to the Cabinet, and as his dispatch was the reply to those charges, he must insist on its circulation.

Curzon then spent some time trying to induce Allenby to withdraw his resignation, instancing his own experience as Viceroy of India, when his suggestions were frequently vetoed by the Government but he did not resign. The same, he added, was true of Lord Reading, the present Viceroy. Allenby replied that he did not wish to draw comparisons between Lord Curzon's and Lord Reading's action and his own, but that his course was clear. At present his word was current coin from Cairo to Khartoum. Were he to consent to return to Egypt, if his proposals were turned down, it would not be worth the paper on which it was written. He could not at any price sacrifice the confidence he commanded in Egypt. Curzon then asked plaintively how they were to find a successor; it would be most difficult and inconvenient. " If you ask my advice," said Allenby, " send as good a man as me, and a better if you can find him."

Having made no impression, Curzon now said that Allenby

---

[1] The account of this interview was given by Allenby to a friend immediately afterwards, and at once recorded by him.

must see the Prime Minister. Allenby again urged the need for an immediate decision. The interview ended with a bitter diatribe by Curzon about the conduct of the Advisers in supporting Allenby by their resignation. Allenby replied that he considered they had served him and His Majesty's Government loyally and that he could not discuss the point. As he was leaving the room Curzon inquired where Lady Allenby was. Allenby could not refrain from a parting shot: " I have left her behind in Egypt, as I feared there might be trouble if I brought her away."

The interview, which had lasted an hour and a half, left Allenby's determination unshaken. Next day was a Saturday. The only action taken by Allenby was to go personally to the Foreign Office to make certain that his dispatch had been " circulated." His Majesty the King afterwards told him that he had read and enjoyed every word of it.

The fateful interview with the Prime Minister was fixed for Monday, February 13, but was then postponed till the morning of the 15th. The Cabinet was now in an awkward position. Allenby had much support in the Press; his dispatch was a very damaging answer to the charges by which it had been proposed to justify his dismissal; and Allenby, as a peer, would have the opportunity and right to state his case in the House of Lords if his resignation was accepted. It was left to the Prime Minister, Mr Lloyd George, to try to turn Allenby out of his entrenched position, on which the arguments of the Foreign Secretary had had so little result.

Sir Gilbert Clayton and Amos accompanied Allenby to the meeting. Mr Lloyd George was supported by Lord Curzon. Allenby was subjected to a sharp cross-fire of questions and objections on his proposals; he began to show impatience, complaining of the number of occasions on which his advice had been rejected. " But," said the Prime Minister, " you are now asking me to abandon our entire position in Egypt without guarantee." Here Amos broke in: " That, sir, is not a fair description of Lord Allenby's proposals." Mr Lloyd George then turned on Amos and again went over the Cabinet's objections, to which Amos replied. The argument was proceeding, when Allenby broke in with: " Well, it is no good disputing any longer. I have told you what I think is necessary. You won't have it, and it is none of my business to force you to. I have waited five weeks for a decision, and I can't wait any longer. I shall tell Lady Allenby to come home." On this the Prime Minister rose and put his hand on Allenby's arm. " You have waited five weeks, Lord Allenby," he said; " wait five more minutes." He then announced that he would agree to Allenby's scheme if a few minor amendments could be made. Allenby said he would examine the amendments and give a final answer that afternoon. His Advisers, to whom he put the amendments after the meeting, soon assured him that they were quite unimportant changes in drafting, and that he had got the entire substance of what he wanted.

There was still one more effort to thwart the agreed solution. It came not from those members of the Cabinet who had always opposed it, of whom the most determined had been Winston Churchill, but from Curzon, who had originally supported it so warmly. He made a futile attempt to go back to the old proposal of no abolition of the Protectorate till after agreement on the reserved subjects. When the documents agreed to by the Prime Minister and Lord Allenby had finally been approved by the Cabinet he spoke petulantly of " the stupidity of these soldiers." His failure to move Allenby at their interview had undoubtedly rankled.[1]

The Government, too, covered its defeat with a cloud of misrepresentation. In the debate in the House of Commons on March 14, for approval of the abolition of the Protectorate, the spokesman for the Government, Mr Austen Chamberlain,[2] spoke as if it had been Allenby who had given way and not the Government. " I am happy to think," he said, " that the moment we got face to face with Lord Allenby our differences disappeared, because he saw at once that we could not alter the *status quo* in respect of those matters until we had definite security that we should be able to protect our interests and fulfil our obligations." He repeated the same travesty of facts twice more in his speech.

[1] In *Curzon: the Last Phase*, by Harold Nicolson, the 1922 Declaration is said to be Curzon's own policy. This claim and the whole account of the episode in this book are incorrect.   [2] The late Sir Austen Chamberlain, K.G.

In justice to an honourable man it should be said that he had taken no part in the discussions and was probably unaware that the brief he had been given was incorrect. Allenby made no protest. He had got his way, and cared not what was said of him. But when Austen Chamberlain later became Foreign Secretary the remembrance of that speech was present with Allenby and may have contributed to the unfortunate misunderstanding between them.

Such is the inner story of the part played by Allenby in obtaining the 1922 Declaration of the Independence of Egypt. He is still spoken of bitterly by some unrepentant imperialists as the man who " sold the pass " and gave away our position in Egypt. If anyone could have been so accused it was Milner, but actually there was no pass to sell, since there was none that could have been held. There was a last ditch that some foolish people might have died in, from which Allenby's common sense preserved us. Can there be any doubt now that his solution was the right one? The only alternative amounted to virtual annexation and military rule, which, quite apart from questions of morality and justice, was unthinkable in view of the temper of the British nation at the time and the inconstancy of their rulers. How long would British opinion have tolerated military rule in Egypt, and how long would the Government have supported their representative in such rule? Allenby had already had experience of the vacillation of the Cabinet in 1920.

Allenby's service to his country and to Egypt at this crisis lay not so much in recognizing the correct solution—that was easy to anyone who knew the real facts and conditions—as in the courage and firmness he showed in putting it forward and in carrying it through against such a weight of opposition and misrepresentation. His Advisers, who risked their careers to support him, also deserved well of the State. A contrast may be drawn between the action of Mr Lloyd George, who had been one of the chief opponents of Allenby's proposals,[1] but who, with considerable political courage, supported him in the end when the facts were brought home to him; and that of Lord

[1] He had exclaimed at one time to the King: " I know now why he is called the Bull; he has got into our Eastern china-shop and is breaking everything up."

Curzon, who realized from the first the wisdom of Allenby's solution, but had not the strength of character to support it against opposition.[1] This gives a measure of the worth of the two men in a crisis. In the council-room as in the field of action, character and courage count for much more than mere knowledge and ability. Allenby had no further respect for Lord Curzon after this experience, but he had always a liking and admiration for Lloyd George. Years later Allenby had made a speech at a Service dinner shortly after one of Lloyd George's attacks on Lord Haig and the soldiers. A friend said to him afterwards, " You disappointed the Press. They came expecting to hear you attack Lloyd George." Allenby replied immediately, " Attack Lloyd George? I like the little man. He won the war, but for heaven's sake don't tell him so."

[1] " Here was a man possessed of great intelligence, of flaming energy, of clear ideals, of unequalled knowledge, of wide experience: to this man was granted an opportunity such as falls seldom to any modern statesman; and yet, although in almost every event his judgment was correct and his vision enlightened, British policy under his guidance declined from the very summit of authority to a level of impotence such as, since the Restoration, it has seldom reached."—HAROLD NICOLSON, *Curzon: the Last Phase.*

PART II

EGYPT: INDEPENDENCE

(March 1922–June 1925)

The first of early blessings, independence.

GIBBON, *Autobiography*

Whether the People be led by the Lord,
Or lured by the loudest throat:
If it be quicker to die by the sword
Or cheaper to die by vote—

. . . . .

Holy State or Holy King
Or Holy People's Will—
Have no truck with the senseless thing.
Order the guns and kill.

RUDYARD KIPLING

CHAPTER XVI

1922: THE BIRTH OF THE NEW ORDER IN EGYPT

Always remember it is better to make a bracelet that fits the
wrist than a necklace so long that the wearer stumbles over it.

JOAN GRANT, *Winged Pharaoh*

OF Allenby's six years as High Commissioner, he had spent the
first three in obtaining a workable policy on which to base our
post-war relations with Egypt. He passed the last three years in
superintending the beginnings of the new regime which resulted
from that policy. It was a period of vexation and disappointment; it culminated in a senseless crime, for which some held
Allenby's forbearance largely responsible; it ended with his
resignation in circumstances of misunderstanding and irritation.

The mistakes and misfortunes of the period were there for
all to see, and have obscured the successes won and the real
progress made. The foundations of modern Egypt's political
life were laid in these years; Allenby played a great part in shaping
and securing those foundations; and subsequent events have

shown that the foundations were, on the whole, well, truly, and wisely laid—given the material and labour available.

In the eyes of many of his own countrymen in Egypt Allenby appeared during this period as a half-hearted defender of their rights and privileges; while certain members of the Labour Party at home represented him as a high-handed militarist who was crushing Egyptian liberties. The Egyptians themselves were in no mood to be grateful to any Englishman, and clamoured at his sternness rather than recognized his forbearance. Only those who stood close to Allenby, Egyptians as well as British, realized how much his steadfastness of purpose accomplished in most trying circumstances, and how wise his advice and judgments usually were. Fortunately, Allenby cared nothing whether he was praised or blamed, and devoted himself to the problems of the new order in Egypt without thought of personal reputation or advantage.

The immediate problems after the Declaration of 1922 were the framing of a Constitution, the abolition of martial law, which had been in force already for nearly eight years, and the compensation of the foreign officials, mainly British, who would lose their employment and prospects under the new regime. All these problems were successfully solved within the next eighteen months. The ultimate objective was the conclusion of an agreement with Egypt on the question of the ' reserved subjects '— the security of British Imperial communications, the defence of Egypt, the protection of foreign communities, and the Sudan. Had Allenby stayed in Egypt a little longer a solution of these difficult problems might have been reached earlier, for the Egyptians trusted and respected him and had confidence in his fairness. As it was, it was more than ten years after his departure before a treaty was concluded between Great Britain and Egypt.

" He gives twice who gives quickly "; and he withdraws half the value of his gift who hesitates and gives grudgingly. The six weeks that had elapsed at the beginning of 1922 between Allenby's recommendations to the Cabinet and their acceptance had allowed some of the effects of Zaghlul's deportation to wear off and had given the extremists time to poison the Egyptian mind against any gifts from the English. Certain events had helped them;

the treaty concluded by the British Government with Ireland at the end of 1921 was interpreted to show that violence and murder were the most effective means of gaining concessions from Great Britain; and the evident weakness in Britain itself of Mr Lloyd George's Government seemed to foreshadow its early fall. What might be hoped from a Labour Government was indicated to the Egyptian extremists when Mr Ramsay MacDonald, the prospective Prime Minister of such a Government, passed through Egypt shortly before Allenby's return with the Declaration. To some local Zaghlulists who entertained him at Port Said Mr Mac-Donald declared that "the people of England would soon realize it was badly governed," and that "Egypt would then come into its own"; he also expressed a hope for Zaghlul's speedy return.

Thus the generous policy which Allenby had obtained in the Declaration was accepted somewhat grudgingly by the Egyptians as an 'instalment' of complete independence. There was plenty of material for the malcontents to use. What sort of 'independence' could Egypt enjoy, they asked, while she still lay under martial law administered by foreign troops; while the chosen leader of the people was in exile; while highly paid foreign officials still held most of the key posts and could only be dismissed with costly compensation; and while the Sudan, an integral part of Egypt, was still under British rule?

The political history of Egypt during the three years of 1922 to 1924 is that of a triangular struggle for power. The three parties to it were the King, the body which comprised most of the educated and moderate Egyptians, and which may be termed the Liberal Party, and the popular party, which hailed Zaghlul as leader. Allenby may be said to have acted as referee, interfering as little as possible but blowing the whistle firmly when the worst and most obvious fouls occurred, and ignoring, like all good referees, the howls and criticisms of the mob at an unpopular decision.

Fuad, previously Sultan, had been proclaimed King of Egypt on March 15. This enhancement of title seemed to arouse his ambition and to increase his love of power. As Sultan he had exercised little influence and attracted little attention; as King, intent on reviving, as far as modern conditions would allow, the autocratic rule of his ancestor, Mohammed Aly, or of his father, the Khedive Ismail, he became a serious and disturbing factor in Egyptian politics. He sought his ends by shrewd intrigue rather than by force of character, and would always give way before a stronger personality, such as Allenby; but he had considerable adroitness as a politician of the "Tammany boss" order. He was skilful to see the value of propaganda and made much use of a subsidized Press. He always contrived to work into a Ministry one or two of his own creatures, who had access to the Palace behind the Premier's back. Thus if Fuad could not get his own way he usually contrived to make the position of the Prime Minister impossible.

The moderate party, whom we may call the Liberals, comprised the majority of the ablest and most intelligent Egyptians, including many of the old Turkish ruling class. Their principal representative was Adly Pasha; he was the 'grand seigneur' type, of good family, impressive appearance, and stately manners. He was patriotic, strictly honest, and enjoyed great prestige. But he was lacking in political courage, and would not face a difficult or unpleasant situation if he could avoid it. Allenby, after one or two experiences of his indecision, termed him "the broken reed," and put little trust in him. Adly's colleague, Sarwat Pasha, the first Prime Minister after the Declaration, had more courage than Adly and very considerable abilities and experience; if he could have commanded the prestige or following that Adly had he would have been the leader Egypt required at this juncture. Even as it was he did much towards laying the foundations of Egypt's future, in spite of the King's dislike of and intrigues against him.

Zaghlul, with his subservient party, the Wafd, undoubtedly represented the popular voice of Egypt; but he and his followers were a destructive not a constructive element. Zaghlul's character has already been sketched; himself a man of intelligence and moderation, he had been forced by circumstances to become leader of the ignorant, unruly mob, which he was not strong enough, nor wise enough, to control.

In the background hovered the shadowy, enigmatical figure of the ex-Khedive, Abbas Hilmi, nephew of King Fuad, who had been dethroned in 1914 at the beginning of the Great War and lived in exile in Europe. He had little influence on the politics of Egypt, but his intrigues, real or imaginary, had a considerable effect on the mind of King Fuad. The King, aware of his unpopularity with his people and of his unsatisfactory relations with the British Government, became obsessed with the idea that either popular outcry or the exasperation of Great Britain might demand his removal and the restoration of Abbas. Actually, the ex-Khedive was the last person Great Britain was ever likely to restore or even to allow to return to Egypt, nor did he command any popular support in Egypt itself. But it suited certain Egyptians to keep alive King Fuad's nervousness of him, while others found some advantage, political or financial, in intriguing mildly with the exile. The ex-Khedive himself both enjoyed intrigue for its own sake, and also exploited his nuisance value in the hope of a better financial settlement of his claims on the Egyptian State.

The immediate sequence of events on Allenby's return to Egypt with the Declaration were its presentation to the Sultan; the formation of a Ministry by Sarwat Pasha; the approval of the Declaration by the British House of Commons on March 14 after a seven hours' debate which showed for the most part remarkable ignorance of the real position in Egypt; the proclamation next day of Fuad as King of Egypt; and an announcement by the British Government to all Powers of the termination of the Protectorate over Egypt. The announcement contained the following passage:

The termination of the British Protectorate over Egypt involves, however, no change in the *status quo* as regards the position of other Powers in Egypt itself. The welfare and integrity of Egypt are necessary to the peace and safety of the British Empire, which will therefore always maintain as an essential British interest the special relations between itself and Egypt, long recognized by other Governments. These special relations are defined in the Declaration recognizing Egypt as an independent sovereign state. His Majesty's Government have laid them down as matters in which the rights and interests of the British Empire are vitally involved and will not admit them to be questioned or discussed by any other Power. In pursuance of this principle they will regard as an unfriendly act any attempt at interference in the affairs of Egypt by another Power, and they will consider any aggression against the territory of Egypt as an act to be repelled with all the means at their command.

This was virtually a Monroe Doctrine for Egypt.

Allenby now departed for a six weeks' tour in the Sudan, leaving the new Ministry to establish itself and to prepare a Constitution and other important measures. On his return at the beginning of May the growing pains of the new order soon made themselves manifest. The three main troubles with which Allenby had to deal for the next year or so were these: the rising agitation over the Sudan; the crimes of a murder gang against Englishmen in Cairo; and the attempts of the King to arrogate autocratic powers to himself.

The question of the Sudan was the principal weapon of anti-British agitation during the period; it was exploited continuously and malevolently as an Egyptian grievance; it led to troubles within the Sudan itself; and it was the cause of the crime that at last ended British patience. Some examination of the history and status of the Sudan is necessary to understand the elements of a controversy which touched and interested all classes in Egypt. The fellahin were concerned only with the safety of the Nile waters, the life-blood of Egypt: so long as the flow of the river was not unfairly impeded, they cared little who controlled the Sudan. For the professional class—lawyers, civil servants, clerks —an extended Egyptian hold on the Sudan would mean more jobs. For the King and the upper class it was a matter of prestige that the Egyptian title to the Sudan and power over it should be enhanced. For the professional agitator the Sudan gave unrivalled opportunities to vilify the perfidious British. The British themselves, in addition to a naturally tenacious hold on prestige and profits, were genuinely actuated by concern for the good government of the Sudanese peoples, which they felt to be safer in their hands than in Egyptian.

The peoples of the Upper Nile Valley have no racial affinity with the people of the Delta; their one binding cord is the course of the great river whose waters they share. The history of the Sudan's connexion with Egypt for the hundred years previous to 1922 had been as follows. Mohammed Aly, Egypt's national hero, who was an Albanian, sent an expedition to the Sudan in 1820 and brought it under his rule. Egypt held it for the next sixty years. She made little pretence of governing in the interests of the inhabitants, allowed the slave trade to flourish unchecked, and exploited the land unscrupulously. Sixty years of misrule led to the revolt of the Mahdi, the slaughter of an Egyptian army, Gordon's mission to evacuate the Sudan and his death at Khartoum. Sixteen years later an Anglo-Egyptian force under Kitchener reconquered the Sudan, which had suffered even more under the Mahdi's despotism than under Egyptian misrule. Great Britain supplied the military leadership and the greater part of the troops; Egypt paid by far the larger share of the bill (approximately a million and a half pounds out of a total cost of two millions).

The disposal of the Sudan, after French claims to a portion had been sternly refused at Fashoda,[1] raised an awkward constitutional problem. Was the Sudan simply a rebellious Egyptian province which had been reoccupied, and accordingly the property of the Khedive of Egypt, as heir to Mohammed Aly, the original conqueror, or had the Egyptian title lapsed during the sixteen years of the Mahdi's rule, and was the huge country now a prize of war to be shared between the successful invaders of it? What rights to it had the Turkish Sultan, the nominal overlord of Egypt?

It is not the British way to deal with a problem of this sort logically or directly. Their position in Egypt was anomalous and had never been defined; their legal status in the Sudan would be even more difficult to regularize. Lord Cromer, the British representative in Egypt and virtual ruler of the country, was called on to solve the problem. The one firm intention of the British Government (and of the British people, in so far as it was

---

[1] Major Marchand, after a remarkable march across half a continent, arrived at Fashoda on the Nile, south of Khartoum, shortly after Kitchener's defeat of the Mahdi, and claimed the southern Sudan for France. Kitchener, backed by the British Government, insisted on his withdrawal. The incident almost led to war between Great Britain and France.

interested in the Sudan) was that the troubled country after three-quarters of a century's misrule should be given peace and good administration. The logical alternatives were open annexation by Great Britain or recognition of the country as a part of Egypt and administration by British officials behind an Egyptian façade, as in Egypt. Cromer deliberately chose an illogical compromise and called it a Condominium. In the preamble Great Britain claimed her share " by right of conquest," while in Article I the Sudan was defined as having been " temporarily lost to Egypt." The two phrases were hardly consistent with each other. The practical result of the Condominium was barely distinguishable from British annexation except that Egypt paid handsomely for her title to a share. The Sudan was ruled by a Governor-General, nominated by Great Britain but appointed by the Khedive of Egypt. Egypt supplied a part of the garrison and balanced the Budget deficit, which averaged £2,000,000 a year.

This arrangement, so advantageous to Great Britain, could only be justified by the unselfish devoted work by which the British officials brought peace and prosperity to the land. So long as Egypt itself was in leading-strings British rule in the Sudan was accepted and provoked little criticism. But with the growth of Egyptian nationalism it was only natural that so one-sided an arrangement as the Condominium should be called in question. But it was especially when the 1922 Declaration had removed much of the previous ground for agitation that the Sudan question was used by the malcontents in Egypt to inflame feeling against Great Britain. No opportunity was lost to impute ill intention and arouse suspicion. For instance, Allenby's visit to the Sudan was interpreted by the Egyptian Press as a prelude to British annexation. In the end the weapon was used too often and brought a great crime and disaster.

Allenby's second great embarrassment was the murder campaign against Englishmen. During 1922 there were twelve attacks on Englishmen in Cairo, which resulted in four being killed and nine wounded. In addition two prominent Egyptian Liberals were murdered. As was afterwards shown, these murders were the work of a small gang inspired by a few well-educated fanatics. The actual murders were carried out by some weak-minded students of the Effendi class and a number of hired assassins from the criminal profession. The objects of the gang were presumably either to intimidate the British or to provoke them to reprisals. The victims were not usually chosen for their prominence or because of any supposed enmity to Egypt, but simply for the security with which they could be assassinated. It was easy to study the daily movements of some British official or officer, to discover some quiet spot that he passed daily at a fixed hour, to walk up behind him in the dusk, or even in daylight, and shoot him in the back. The murderers were aided by the average Englishman's dislike of carrying arms or taking precautions. They ran no risk from the victim, who was unarmed and was shot in the back; none from the police, provided they moved off before the police arrived; and none from the public, provided they chose a moment when no Englishman or respectable foreigner was passing. One of the British victims was shot dead in a public place outside some shops, whose owners professed to have seen or heard nothing; actual witnesses of this murder were afterwards found entirely by chance. This attitude of the Egyptian public was the principal factor which prevented the gang being brought to justice sooner; they would give no assistance to the police either by attempting arrest at the time or giving information afterwards. It was not that they approved of the murders, but they feared terrorization and reprisal, not without reason, since murderous assaults were sometimes made on those who had given evidence or helped the police.

Though the number of murders was small, they created a feeling of anger and insecurity in the British community, who chafed at the powerlessness of the authorities to stop the crimes or arrest the murderers. Some hotheads advocated reprisals and other severe measures; almost all agreed that Allenby's methods were not strong enough. Allenby kept his head and refused to be stampeded into useless violence. He may have remembered the disastrous Denshawai incident sixteen years earlier, when undue severity had left a serious stain on the British reputation in Egypt. He ordered what measures of protection he could.

British soldiers patrolled the streets, the numbers of police were increased, Englishmen carried arms. All his information, however, showed that the Egyptian people at large did not approve of the murders, and that no measures of general reprisal were likely to be effective. Only the apprehension of the gang could remove the bane. Offers of rewards up to £5000 for convicting information brought no result. The Foreign Office suggested seizing some revenue-producing branch of the Egyptian Administration from which to pay compensation to victims of attacks. Allenby replied that it would make Englishmen no safer and would ruin any chance of good understanding with the Egyptians, while liberal compensation was already being paid to the victims. A special body which Allenby set to work under a selected British official [1] tracked down the gang in the end, as will be told later. Meanwhile the attacks were a source of constant anxiety and exasperation.

Thirdly, King Fuad. Allenby's duels with that astute and ambitious monarch over the Constitution and other matters will be recorded in the course of the narrative. The two contestants had a respect and liking for each other, and between rounds had much friendly discussion on subjects of mutual interest, one of which was the various religions of mankind. Allenby appreciated the King's intelligence; the King learned to respect Allenby's sincerity and to realize his strength. In their passages of arms the monarch showed much fencing-school skill but had usually to yield in the end to the threat of Allenby's broadsword. [2] In the matter of securing a liberal Constitution Allenby fought Egypt's battle as much as Great Britain's. Though the manœuvres of the King were less dangerous than the Sudan agitation or the crimes of the murder gang, they required a constant watchfulness and gave Allenby much occupation.

The Commission which assembled to draft the Constitution, under the presidency of Rushdi Pasha (the Prime Minister of the War period), began their labours in April and continued them

[1] Sir Alexander Keown-Boyd, K.B.E., C.M.G., who had spent many years in the Ministry of the Interior and had been Oriental Secretary at the Residency.

[2] " The ingenuity of his arguments compelled my reluctant admiration," wrote Allenby after one interview.

until the late autumn. At an early stage the question of the Sudan raised an acute controversy with the British Government. The Sudan was defined in the opening clauses as an integral part of Egypt, and the King of Egypt was stated to be King of the Sudan. The British Government could hardly be expected to tolerate this attempt to alter the Condominium of 1899 and to prejudge the discussion of this ' reserved subject.' Allenby at once insisted that the clauses should be redrafted. A flood of indignation was poured out in speech and article by the Egyptian Nationalists, but Allenby and the British Government remained firm. King Fuad seized the opportunity to court popular favour by supporting the Nationalist view. He hoped thus to discredit the Prime Minister, whom he disliked, and to distract attention from his own manœuvres to alter the Constitution so as to increase the royal privileges and power.

The Committee had taken the Belgian system as a model and had prepared a Constitution on liberal lines. There was to be a Parliament elected, in theory at least, on a wide popular basis, and a Senate partly elected and partly nominated. The King was to be in the position of a strictly constitutional monarch. Fuad, who had been brought up in the despotic traditions of his family and who admitted to keeping Machiavelli's *Prince* by his bedside, was not the man to accept such a position without a struggle. His idea of a Constitution proper to Egypt was that of a monarch directing subservient Ministers chosen by himself. The functions of a Parliament should be to register the decisions of the King's Ministers. It should serve as a token of democracy rather than as the voice of a people who were, he genuinely believed, too backward to be given a voice in their rule. His attitude may be illustrated by some remarks he made to a leading Egyptian when he became aware of the main provisions of the Constitution. " If you want this Bolshevik Constitution," he said, " then I claim all the powers and privileges of a Lenin." To the reply that it was not a Bolshevistic but a democratic Constitution he retorted, " Then I claim all the powers and privileges of the President of the United States of America." The reminder that the President was elected by popular suffrage and only for a limited term was not acceptable.

At the end of November Sarwat resigned, ostensibly on the question of the Sudan clauses, actually because the King had made his position impossible by treating him with studied dislike and obstruction. This culminated in a Palace plot designed to expose Sarwat to public indignity while accompanying His Majesty to Friday prayers at the famous El Azhar mosque. Sarwat learned of the intention and realized that his position had become impossible. At the critical moment, too, the faint-hearted Adly, unwilling to share the odium of agreeing to the Sudan definition on which the British insisted and alarmed perhaps by the murder of two leading Liberals, withdrew the support of his party from Sarwat, in whose place the King nominated Tewfik Nessim.

The new Prime Minister had no great ability, but was honest and industrious. He was under the influence of the Palace and likely to prove pliable to royal wishes. First round to the King, whose confidence in his triumph was, however, disturbed by a stern warning which Allenby delivered to him on December 3, informing him of the displeasure of the British Government at his treatment of a Minister who had been appointed to implement the policy of the Declaration.

Sarwat's work has had less credit than it deserves. He had faced the difficult task of inaugurating a new regime with courage and determination. He had not only to settle some awkward problems with the British—the Sudan clauses, the compensation of foreign officials, an Indemnity Act to enable martial law to be abolished—in all of which he was likely to incur odium with his fellow-countrymen; but he had also to initiate a new system of government and to accustom to the duties of office a class almost entirely untried and untrained in the acceptance and exercise of independent responsibility. The extent of the change has not always been realized even by those who have followed the history of modern Egypt. Before the British occupation the governing class in Egypt was practically entirely Turkish in origin. During the forty years of British rule this class had lost much of its governing sense or had turned to other pursuits. The native Egyptians who were now aspiring to the direction of their country's affairs lacked for the most part the necessary moral courage and sense of responsibility. They had learned to lean on British advice in a difficulty and felt at a loss now that it was being withdrawn. As has been explained earlier, it was part of Allenby's policy to compel them to face their difficulties and dangers themselves, and he had taken some risk to do it.

The times were not easy for such an experiment. Four years of war, followed by three years of civil commotion, had overstrained the machine of government, from which the foreign advisers were now being removed with a haste dictated by nationalistic feeling rather than administrative prudence. An additional impetus to nationalism and to the desire to end British influence was given by the events in Turkey in the autumn of this year. In August and September the Greeks were completely routed by Mustapha Kemal and driven out of Anatolia. The event was hailed in Egypt as a victory for Islam over Christianity and as a British defeat. The firm stand of the British at Chanak in October did something to restore their prestige; and at the Lausanne Conference in November, called to arrange a peace treaty with Turkey, the skill of our diplomacy confirmed the resolution of the military stand. The question of Egyptian representation at this conference caused considerable diplomatic discussion and was still unsettled when Sarwat's Ministry fell.

The year had been so full of important events that Allenby was unable to go to England on leave. In the autumn his mother, whose character had done so much towards shaping his own and to whom he was so devoted, died at the age of ninety-two. To a friend Allenby wrote characteristically:

Very many thanks for your kind letter of sympathy on my mother's death. She died full of years and honour: and she kept her full mental powers and her keen interest in everything almost to the very last. Egypt kept me here this autumn; but I saw her last spring and have nothing to regret. Mabel saw her last month, and brought me her last message.

In November occurred the historic discovery by Howard Carter, financed by Lord Carnarvon, of the Tomb of Tutankhamen. Allenby was one of the privileged few who were present at the opening of the tomb and thus one of the first to see the wonderful store of treasure in it.

This eventful year of 1922 ended on a menacing note with a cruel and senseless crime. On December 27, Dr Robson, a lecturer at the Law School and especially friendly to Egyptians, was shot and killed in broad daylight while bicycling home from his work. This murder provoked the deepest feeling of indignation in the British community, much of it directed against Allenby's supposed lack of firmness.

CHAPTER XVII

1923: A YEAR OF PROGRESS

The dogs bark, but the caravan passes on.

Eastern proverb

THE year 1923, which was to be fruitful in the history of Egypt's political development, opened under unfavourable auspices. Allenby's three main difficulties were still unrelieved. The Sudan clauses had not been satisfactorily amended; the shadow of the Robson murder hung over the relations between Egyptians and British and between the British community in Cairo and the Residency; the King was unrepentant and determined to block any Constitution that did not give him a considerable measure of autocracy.

A mass meeting of the British in Cairo was held at Shepheard's Hotel on January 2 to protest against the continuance of the murder campaign and to demand strong measures of repression. Allenby had already informed the Prime Minister that martial law would not be abolished so long as such attacks continued, that an indemnity must be paid to the widow, and that police protection must be strengthened; meanwhile British cavalry would again patrol the streets.

At the beginning of February the matter of the Sudan clauses came to a head. Finding King Fuad persistent that he should be styled King of the Sudan, Allenby was compelled to seek an audience of him to insist that the point of view of the British Government must be observed. After exercising for more than twenty-four hours every effort to evade the issue, His Majesty yielded and signed the document which Allenby had presented to him. Two days later the Prime Minister, Nessim Pasha, realizing that the King's version of the Constitution was not likely to go through unchallenged, handed in his resignation, and was roundly upbraided as a coward by his royal master.

There followed a five weeks' interregnum. At first it seemed that Adly would form a Ministry. But he made the suspension of martial law a condition of taking office, and a series of bomb outrages against British soldiers made it obvious that martial law could not be removed at once. Adly, unwilling as usual to face difficulties and unpopularity, declined his task. It was left to a comparatively unregarded man, Ibrahim Yehia Pasha, to undertake what seemed the unprofitable post of Prime Minister. He lacked the ability of Sarwat and the prestige of Adly, but he was honest and patriotic and had more than a common measure of courage and determination.

He took office in the middle of March and a month later had succeeded in getting the new Constitution promulgated in its original form. That month had seen a continuous struggle between Minister and King, a struggle in which Allenby played a considerable part. During Nessim's Ministry the King had caused the draft Constitution to be altered in a number of ways so as to enhance his power and privileges. It soon became obvious that the new Prime Minister would be powerless, unaided, to restore the original text. Allenby determined to use his influence on the side of the people. In an official report he described his action as follows:

> At the time of the incident in connexion with the Sudan clauses it did not seem to me either necessary or desirable to interest myself in the other provisions of the Constitution. When, however, it became clear that, in the face of unanimous and clearly expressed public opinion, the King proposed to adhere to his version of the text, and that the Prime Minister's efforts were quite unavailing, I thought it judicious to use my influence with His Majesty. I accordingly advised him to allow himself to be guided by his Prime Minister. This advice I was obliged to give incessantly for a period of a month on successive articles of the Constitution.

Allenby explained his motives as twofold: that it was not in keeping with the policy of the Declaration that the King should arrogate undue powers to himself, and secondly, that a constitutional struggle between King and people must be avoided. He added:

> My intervention was throughout private and unofficial, and I have been at pains to explain to the many who have since come to

express their thanks that their gratitude is due not to myself but to the King and the Cabinet: still, the part I played is generally known and has, I think, gone far to promote the growing tendency amongst Egyptians to friendship towards His Majesty's Government. The King, who has little capacity for knowing when to yield, resisted Yehia Pasha until the last moment, and then consented to the modifications in question only with bad grace.

The next step was the abolition of martial law. It was not quite so simple a matter as might appear. An Act of Indemnity was required to prevent legal proceedings which might call in question any action taken under martial law.[1] Also it was found necessary to fill in gaps in Egyptian legislation to regulate certain matters which had hitherto been dealt with under martial law, such as powers to control public meetings and to take special steps for the security of the State in an emergency. On July 5 the Act of Indemnity was passed, and simultaneously a proclamation by the Commander-in-Chief put an end to the martial law that had held force in Egypt since November 2, 1914. Though its existence for so long had been denounced as harsh and tyrannical, in actual practice its interference with the life of the ordinary citizen had been negligible. It had been put to some curious uses: one of its ordinances regulated rentals between tenant and landlord and prevented profiteering; another compelled foreigners to pay certain Egyptian taxes to which they would not otherwise, by reason of the Capitulations, have been liable. Allenby had even had to declare an Egyptian Budget passed by a proclamation under martial law, since there had been no Ministry in office to do so. Of late its operation had practically been confined to enabling offences of violence against the Army to be tried by military courts. Its removal was an important step in Egypt's progress towards independence.

The next step was the Bill providing for the compensation of foreign officials, of whom half were British, who would be replaced by Egyptians. The Bill, which was naturally of great interest to the British community, provided compensation on a generous scale, at an eventual cost to the Egyptian Treasury of

[1] Since martial law is not recognized by civil law, such an Act is always required at the termination of a period of martial law.

some £6,000,000 to £7,000,000. It may sound a large price to pay for freedom from foreign leading-strings, and was so criticized by the Egyptian Press. But the terms were by no means extortionate, and Egypt had been on the whole well and faithfully served by her foreign Advisers. That she had not been plundered is shown by the fact that though taxation was light, there was a reserve of over £18,000,000 in the Treasury at the end of the financial year 1923–24.

Allenby's immediate objectives were now secured. The Constitution had been made law in an acceptable form, martial law had been abolished, the compensation of foreign officials had been satisfactorily settled, and the murder campaign seemed in abeyance. Fourteen students had been arrested and tried for conspiracy to murder in June. Thirteen were found guilty, three of whom were subsequently executed.

Egypt's future seemed to lie in her own hands: when a Parliament had been elected the ' reserved subjects ' could be discussed, and a final amicable settlement made in Anglo-Egyptian relations. Pending the elections, Allenby went home for a well-earned rest. He was in England from August till the end of October. He spent much of his time as usual in his favourite pursuit of fishing.

It is time to return to the Egyptian who had been and was to be Allenby's chief antagonist in the settlement between Great Britain and Egypt. Saad Zaghlul had, it will be remembered, been arrested towards the end of December 1921 for incitement to disturbance and had been interned at Aden. He was taken aboard H.M.S. *Clematis* on February 28, 1922, the day of the declaration of Egypt's independence, and left Aden for the Seychelles Islands the next day. This transfer had been decided some time before, and the date was fortuitous, but Zaghlul made it a grievance that this particular day was chosen for his deportation to an unhealthy island near the Equator. The climate in fact is not unhealthy, though it was too damp for Zaghlul, who suffered from bronchitis. He was accordingly transferred to Gibraltar in the early autumn of 1922, and remained there till the end of March 1923, when he was released. On the abolition of martial law in July there was no bar to his return to Egypt, and he landed at Alexandria on September 18 after nearly two years' exile. He received, as was natural, a tumultuous welcome from the populace. The King and many leading Egyptians, while expressing approval in public, were in private, however, probably somewhat apprehensive. At first Zaghlul was moderate in his professions and spoke only of the union of the nation.[1] Soon, however, his attitude changed, and he became fiercely critical of all that had been done in his absence. His one idea seemed to be to wipe out all progress for which anyone else could claim credit. His vanity and his stubbornness were again in evidence. During October he became ill and spent nearly a month in retirement. Meanwhile his party had won an overwhelming success at the primary elections.

Allenby returned to Egypt early in November to find the political situation confused. Yehia Pasha, the Prime Minister, was obviously a tired man, his Ministry was ineffective, and the administration of the country was deteriorating with the removal of the foreign Advisers. The King had seized the opportunity of the Ministry's weakness to extend his influence, and was now exercising considerable power. A future conflict between him and Zaghlul seemed probable. Altogether the position at the end of 1923 gave much ground for speculation and anxiety. The murder campaign seemed, however, to have ceased.

[1] The following, taken from his first public utterance after his return, may serve as an example of his simple and effective oratory in his more reasonable moments:
" You are accustomed to obey me, but I am not a prince. I am not descended from any royal family before whom it is the custom to bend. I do not even come from a great family. I am a fellah, the son of a fellah, the issue of a very modest family, which my adversaries qualify as even humble. Blessed be this humbleness. I am not rich that your support of me can bring you financial gain. I have no prestige. Despite all that you rally round me, showing that you court neither riches nor prestige, but rather, in certain circumstances, prison."

CHAPTER XVIII

1924: ZAGHLUL'S YEAR

(TRIUMPH, DISASTER, ECLIPSE)

THE year 1924 in Egypt was the year of Zaghlul. Its beginning saw him supreme in Egypt save for the watchful power of Great Britain in the background. That power he believed he could neutralize by negotiation with the newly formed Labour Government in England. The passing of the year showed him in his true capacity as a demagogue with power to inflame the crowd but without courage or wisdom to control it; as a jealous ruler without capacity for statesmanship or administration; as a suspicious and narrow negotiator with no talent for compromise. His downfall, inevitable sooner or later from these defects, was hastened towards the end of the year by a crime for which his failure to control his followers was largely responsible. The year ended with his virtual elimination as the central figure he had been for so long in Egyptian politics, though his name still retained its power with the people. The first native rule attempted in Egypt for some thousands of years had been tried in the balance and found wanting.

The year opened with the Yehia Ministry still in power but completely subservient to the will of King Fuad. That astute monarch, seeing a Zaghlulist victory at the polls inevitable, now openly favoured the Wafd. He had hopes, nevertheless, of a strong opposition element belonging to the landowner class, from which nucleus would spring in time a 'King's party.' January 12 was the day fixed for the first elections to Egypt's new Parliament. On January 7 Allenby, thinking it wise to be absent during the elections, departed on a tour to the Sudan. Kerr,[1] the Minister, was left in charge at the Residency.

Though the result of the elections was inevitable, the completeness of the Zaghlulist victory surprised every one—King, Residency, Egyptian moderates, even Zaghlulists themselves.

[1] Sir Archibald Clark Kerr, G.C.M.G., British Ambassador in China, 1938-42, now British Ambassador to the U.S.S.R.

In a chamber of 214 members, 190 were declared followers of Zaghlul. The Prime Minister himself was defeated, and shortly afterwards resigned. His courage and common sense had made his period of office fruitful, it had seen the Constitution and electoral law published, martial law removed, thus making the return of Zaghlul possible, and the thorny question of the compensation of foreign officials settled. His resignation upset the King's calculations. He had counted on retaining Yehia in power till the nominations for the Upper Chamber, the Senate, had been made.[1] Now he was compelled to ask Zaghlul to form a Government and consequently to accept his nominations for the Senate. On January 27, 1924, Zaghlul became the first Prime Minister of Egypt under the new Constitution. Almost at the same time the first Labour Government in Britain came into power under Mr Ramsay MacDonald, who became Foreign Secretary as well as Prime Minister. He was personally known to Zaghlul and had often professed sympathy with Egypt's aspirations to complete independence, as had many other members of the Labour Party. Truly Zaghlul seemed on the crest of success. He was supreme in Egyptian politics, the Liberals and other parties were powerless, the King dared not oppose him, while the Government in Great Britain was friendly and sympathetic. Even the Residency, with which he had had no official touch since November 13, 1918, when his visit to Sir Reginald Wingate had begun the struggle for Egyptian independence, now showed a desire to enter into friendly relations. Kerr, thinking it advisable to establish touch with Zaghlul before he became Prime Minister, made two secret and unofficial visits to him, in the course of which he succeeded in removing much of Zaghlul's suspicion and made him realize the part Allenby had played in obtaining so liberal a Constitution for Egypt. Allenby himself, on his return from the Sudan, at once called on Zaghlul, although by custom the first call should have been paid by the Prime Minister. Zaghlul was much touched by this compliment and conceived an admiration and liking for Allenby which he retained to the end, though it was never reciprocated.

[1] The Senate was two-fifths nominated, three-fifths elected. The nominations were made by the King on the advice of his Prime Minister.

Meanwhile Zaghlul's first request to the British, for an amnesty for those still undergoing imprisonment as a result of the sentences of British military courts, had been cordially met—too cordially, in the opinion of many in Egypt. The British Government agreed to an amnesty even more generous than Zaghlul had asked or expected. Such an attitude seemed to foreshadow easy negotiations on the ' reserved subjects '; and early in March, before the opening of Parliament, Zaghlul expressed a wish to go to London at an early date to discuss a settlement of the questions outstanding between Great Britain and Egypt. The proposal did not at first commend itself to Mr MacDonald, who would have preferred that the general lines of settlement should be negotiated in Egypt, and that Zaghlul should only come to London when agreement had been reached. Allenby urged that the negotiations should take place in London. He was convinced that it would be impossible to hold fruitful discussions in the turbulent atmosphere of Cairo, where Zaghlul would be subject to constant pressure from extremists. We should in fact, he said, soon find ourselves negotiating not only with Zaghlul but with the Egyptian populace and Press. Moreover, Zaghlul and his followers had set their hearts on his going to London, and it would be unwise to discourage them. Zaghlul seemed at the moment well disposed; any settlement made by him would be accepted by all Egypt, and the sooner negotiations could be begun the better. After a little further discussion Mr MacDonald sent Zaghlul an invitation to go to London in June.

It soon became obvious, however, that Zaghlul's ideas amounted to dictation of Egypt's demands rather than negotiation, and that even if he were disposed to be reasonable the clamour of the extremists, which he did nothing to check, was forcing him into a position from which he could not recede, particularly as regards the Sudan.

March 15, 1924, which marked the opening of Egypt's first Constitutional Parliament, was a day of great public rejoicing in Cairo. The crowds kept up a constant roar of cheering; their enthusiasm reached almost a state of frenzy when the royal coach appeared, in which beside King Fuad, their monarch, sat Zaghlul, their idol. He had challenged British domination; he had led and encouraged the masses in their demand for independence; twice had he been sent into exile; and now he was Prime Minister.

It is interesting to consider the feelings of the three principal figures in this day's ceremonies—King Fuad, Zaghlul, and Allenby. The King did not relish the companionship of Zaghlul; neither did he look forward to the opening of so liberal a Parliament which, according to his beliefs, ill-suited the limitations of his subjects. Zahglul himself must have had curiously mixed feelings. His seat in the royal coach was an uneasy one, for he knew only too well the working of his monarch's mind. And he certainly must have realized how paradoxical was his own position in directing a parliament derived from the British Declaration of 1922, which he had flatly rejected. There had to be some way of escape from such a dilemma, and this may explain the repeated cries from the crowd of " Indivisible Nile " and " The Sudan." Few could have realized, least of all Zaghlul himself, to what they were going to lead.

Allenby in Field-Marshal's uniform presented, as usual, a striking figure. He was satisfied as he watched the scene that the British policy embodied in the 1922 Declaration was taking its required course. British promises despite all difficulties were being honestly fulfilled; a free parliamentary institution had been established through which Egypt could produce statesmen vested with unquestionable authority to bind their country in any settlement with Britain. From the Diplomatic Gallery of the House of Deputies he looked down on the unsmiling face of the would-be autocratic King and on the craggy and uncompromising features of the demagogue Zaghlul. It was clear to him that the minds of these two men were poles apart; difficulties were undoubtedly ahead, but they would be of Egyptian making. It remained to be seen how far they would affect and retard the Anglo-Egyptian settlement for which he was so sincerely striving.

Even at this opening of Parliament, a demonstration against British rule in the Sudan was arranged, and Egyptian rights to complete control of the Sudan continued to be the principal subject of agitation in Parliament and the Press, while propaganda in the Sudan itself continued unchecked and with dangerous violence. There were other disturbing symptoms. In April a corporal of the Royal Air Force was murdered by two students, the first of such attacks for nearly a year. In Parliament the position of Sir Lee Stack as Sirdar of the Egyptian Army was violently assailed, there was a refusal to vote the annual contribution made by Egypt to the Army of Occupation, and the law for compensation of foreign officials which had been passed by the Yehia Ministry was denounced as unacceptable.

Matters reached a crisis towards the end of June, when Lord Parmoor made a statement in the House of Lords that the British Government had no intention of abandoning its position in the Sudan. This statement led to excited demonstrations and protests in Egypt. Zaghlul declared in the Chamber that in view of the British attitude nothing was to be gained by negotiations, and that he proposed to resign. Though he tendered his resignation to the King, it was not meant seriously, and he was soon persuaded to retain office. The tension was presently eased by a conciliatory statement by Ramsay MacDonald in the House of Commons, and eventually it was arranged that a meeting should take place in London at the end of September.

On July 12, when Zaghlul was leaving Cairo for Alexandria on his way to Europe, he was shot at and wounded by a student. The incident had little political result, but postponed Zaghlul's departure till the end of July, when he went to France to take the waters.

Early in August Egyptian intrigue in the Sudan bore its poison fruit. At Khartoum an armed demonstration by the cadets of the Military School was speedily quelled without casualty; but at Atbara the Egyptian Railway Battalion broke into serious rioting, and some Sudanese troops at the order of an Egyptian officer fired on the rioters and inflicted casualties. In the Sudan itself the arrival of additional British troops and the removal of the Railway Battalion prevented any further trouble. In Egypt the incident seemed at one time likely to produce a more dangerous situation. The Press and the mob at once assumed that British troops had deliberately fired on Egyptians. The acting Prime Minister, Mohammed Said Pasha, who was fully aware of the true facts, did nothing either to make the facts known or to check the violent demonstrations of the mob, in spite of repeated protests from the Residency (Allenby himself was at home on leave). In London an Egyptian Note misrepresenting the facts and delivered with studied discourtesy drew a stern rebuke from the British Government. Zaghlul, in Paris, declared that negotiations with the British Government were now impossible, though he agreed to personal conversations with Mr Ramsay MacDonald with a view to removing misunderstanding.

The conversations, which began in London on September 25, were a complete failure. Zaghlul had apparently expected private talks with the Prime Minister alone. When he found himself confronted also with a number of Foreign Office advisers, as if for formal conversations, he adopted a rigid unconciliatory attitude. The first meeting has been aptly described by Lord Lloyd as " a certain amount of ineffective recrimination upon the minor incidents of recent history," and officially by the Foreign Office as " discussions of a preliminary nature." [1] At the second meeting Zaghlul put forward a series of demands for the entire removal of British troops, British officials, and British influence from Egypt, and for the abandonment by Great Britain of any claims to defend the Suez Canal or protect minorities in Egypt. He developed this theme in greater detail at the third and last meeting. Somewhat naturally the conversations led to no result. They had shown that a Labour Government was as firm as a Conservative one on British essential interests in Egypt and the Sudan.

Zaghlul was undoubtedly disappointed and felt aggrieved with Ramsay MacDonald, who had shown a very different attitude towards Egyptian claims when he had visited Egypt as a private individual. Zaghlul had hoped for confidential talks with a sympathetic friend which would pave the way for British recognition of Egypt's complete independence. Instead he had found himself meeting a Foreign Secretary flanked by unyielding officials little disposed to abandon the British position. In the circumstances no progress was possible. Zaghlul's narrow and suspicious mind had no talent for negotiation. He could state a case with vigour and fight a campaign with courage, but he expected the fruits of victory to be handed him on a plate without discussion.

[1] *Egypt since Cromer*, by Lord Lloyd, Vol. II, p. 92.

His career was determined by two great blunders. The first was that of the British when they refused him permission to go to London in 1918; the second was his own when he failed to take advantage of the generous terms offered by Milner in 1920.

Towards the end of October both Zaghlul and Allenby returned to Egypt. About the same time Ramsay MacDonald's Labour Government fell and was replaced by a Conservative Government. Sir Austen Chamberlain became Foreign Secretary. Relations between Allenby and Ramsay MacDonald had opened on a note of mutual suspicion. The Prime Minister was inclined to regard the soldier as a heavy-handed reactionary, while Allenby had some reason to mistrust the previous utterances of Ramsay MacDonald on the Egyptian question. When the two men became acquainted, however, they worked on very good terms, and Allenby said afterwards that he found the Labour Government easier to serve than either of the other two Administrations under which he worked. With Austen Chamberlain it would have seemed natural that his relations should be cordial, for the two men had much in common. As will be shown, however, certain misunderstandings made them brief and unhappy.

The failure of the discussions in London had been received calmly in Egypt, and outwardly the situation was relatively quiet. To Allenby and his Advisers it was, however, obvious that a crisis of some sort could not be long delayed. Besides the Sudan there were several questions outstanding in which Zaghlul had challenged British interests and the policy of the 1922 Declaration. He was obviously determined to reduce the British judicial and financial Advisers to a position of impotence; he had announced his intention of cancelling the agreement for the compensation of foreign officials; and he had refused to pay certain contributions that had previously been a responsibility of the Egyptian Government.

In a dispatch to the Foreign Office Allenby shrewdly summed up Zaghlul's personal position:

It was evident that what Zaghlul Pasha could not afford to do was to lose that sort of popularity which has for years past been the breath of his life, and that now, as often before, he could hardly retain it except by extremism.

I conceive that at the end of October he was, on the one hand, rapidly losing ground through his failure to bring back from London what he had taught Egypt to want and to expect of him, and through the incompetence, injustice, and corruption of his domestic administration; and on the other, he was in danger of desertion by important adherents from the inner circle of the Wafd, and of losing with them much of the loyalty of his student army.

He was, therefore, forced to do two things; he did them, I cannot doubt, against his better judgment, and, it may be, against his will—how much or how little against his will is unlikely to be fully revealed to us. To make up for his loss in public esteem he was obliged to strengthen his tyrannical hold upon the country, and to keep the men he needed he was bound to give them office. He was in danger of losing men chiefly because he was too cautious for them: he kept them by making them more powerful; and by making them more powerful he placed the policy of caution beyond his reach.

By appointing some of his more extreme followers to important posts, with little regard to their administrative abilities, by dismissing provincial officials whom he judged insufficiently devoted to his regime, and by taking suppressive measures against his political opponents, Zaghlul fastened a tyrannical hold on the country; and then decided to provoke a struggle with King Fuad and to deprive the throne of any power to oppose his dictatorial behests. He did this on November 16 by a sudden resignation, by implying that it was owing to the King's intrigues, and by mobilizing his army of students and roughs to parade the streets and demonstrate for his return. His manœuvre culminated in a two-hour audience of the King, at which he withdrew his resignation after exacting certain undertakings from him, while outside the Palace his well-drilled student ' soldiers ' kept up a continual cry of " Saad or Revolution." On leaving the Palace Zaghlul openly thanked and dismissed them.

Zaghlul was now at the height of his power and may have dreamed of a dictatorship like that of Mustapha Kemal in Turkey. He felt himself strong enough to treat the head of Allenby's staff, who had been sent to discuss the question of the judicial adviser-ship, with such rude truculence that he had to be reminded that he was speaking to the representative of the British Government. Seldom has retribution for abuse of power been swifter; within three days of his triumph at the Palace a crime caused by his own failure to control the reckless violence of his extremists was to lead to his fall from power.

On November 19, a little after 1.30 P.M., the Sirdar, Sir Lee Stack, was shot at and wounded in three places while driving home from the Ministry of War. His A.D.C., Captain P. K. Campbell, of the Black Watch, and the chauffeur, an Australian ex-soldier named Marsh, were also hit by bullets. The shots were fired by several persons of the Effendi class, who then escaped in a waiting taxi-cab. A bomb was also thrown, but did not explode. The crime was committed as the car slowed down at the corner of a crowded street. A policeman who attempted to pursue the gunmen was struck down by a bullet.[1] The wounded chauffeur drove at once to the Residency, where the Sirdar, who was obviously seriously injured, was carried in and laid on a sofa in the drawing-room. The A.D.C. and the chauffeur, who were not so seriously wounded, remained in the hall. A luncheon-party was in progress at the time, one of the guests being Mr Asquith. Later, at about 2.30 P.M., while Lady Stack, who had been fetched by Lady Allenby, was in the drawing-room with the Sirdar, and Allenby and some of his staff and the guests were discussing the crime in the hall, Zaghlul was suddenly announced. He had learned of the crime and had come to make inquiries. Allenby pointed sternly to the wounded A.D.C. and chauffeur and said, " This is your doing." He would have led Zaghlul to the Sirdar himself had not his staff told him that this could not be acceptable to Lady Stack. Zaghlul turned with hardly a word and hurried out.

Sir Lee Stack died just before midnight the following day in the Anglo-American Hospital. He was a man of great personal charm, who had been in Egypt and the Sudan for twenty-three years. He had served both England and Egypt well, and was much liked and respected by both English and Egyptians. The

---

[1] For his courage he was given by the British Government £1000, which Lord Allenby handed to him in hospital.

crime caused the most profound sensation in Cairo and throughout Egypt. In the British community indignation ran high, part
of which was directed against Allenby, who was held by many to
have pushed forbearance with Egyptian provocation beyond its
limits. In Egyptian political circles there was consternation and a
lively apprehension of the consequences.

November 22, the day of Sir Lee Stack's funeral, was a day of
tense drama. A part of the British community had been outraged
by the announcement that Zaghlul and the Egyptian Cabinet,
whom they held largely responsible for the murder, would be
present in the British church at the funeral service. There was an
attempt, quite unsuccessful, to force Allenby to alter the arrangements. The Sirdar had been the head of the Egyptian Army and
responsible to the Egyptian Government; and it was right and
proper, Allenby held, that the members of the Government should
attend his funeral.

The scene in the British church of All Saints [1] was a memorable
one. King Fuad was represented by his Chamberlain. The
Egyptian Ministers, led by Zaghlul, showed by their faces the
strain they felt and their sense of the hostility they knew that the
British portion of the congregation bore to them. The British
Navy and Army and civil community crowded the small church;
the whole Diplomatic Corps was present in full dress, and there
were representatives of all the foreign nationalities in Egypt.
Outside a long procession had been formed, including all the
British troops in Cairo, and stretched already almost to the
cemetery. Huge crowds lined the streets. Inside the church
Allenby, in khaki uniform—a stern, impressive figure, obviously
under deep but repressed emotion—stood alone before the coffin
for some ten minutes while awaiting the arrival of Lady Stack and
her daughter. After a short but simple service the coffin was
borne to the grave by eight British warrant-officers serving with
the Egyptian Army. Egyptian princes, Senators, and Deputies
joined in the long procession which took an hour to pass a point;
all Cairo seemed to have turned out to watch it. As Allenby
stood by the grave he was obviously deeply moved and under
stress of some vital decision. The behaviour of the crowd had

[1] The present Cathedral had not then been built.

been unexceptionable in Cairo, but in Alexandria there was a demonstration and shouts of "Down with the British!" outside the church where a memorial service was being held.

The drama of the day's events was not ended by the funeral. The Egyptian Parliament was due to meet at 5 P.M., and expectation was tense as to the decisions to be taken. It was thought that the Government might resign. At the Residency Allenby was impatiently awaiting a telegram from the Foreign Office. He had determined to deliver an ultimatum that afternoon to the Egyptian Government and had cabled home its proposed terms, asking for a reply by midday on the 22nd. As the afternoon wore on and no reply was received, Allenby's impatience became acute. He was determined to hand the Note to the Prime Minister before Parliament met at 5 P.M. He feared otherwise that Zaghlul might resign and that there would be no Government to receive the terms. At 4.15 P.M. he decided that he could wait no longer for Foreign Office approval. He had directed that a cavalry regiment, the 16th/5th Lancers, should stand by at Kasr-el-Nil barracks after the funeral, and he now ordered it to parade in front of the Residency to escort him to the Prime Minister's house. Allenby seldom made use of display or ceremony, and this is perhaps the only occasion of his life when he deliberately employed dramatic methods. He had still a vital decision to make. As he was leaving the Residency to enter his car one of his staff came running from the Chancery. The long-awaited cable from the Foreign Office had at last arrived and was being deciphered; from its length it was obviously not a simple acceptance of Allenby's proposed terms. On learning that it was impossible to complete the deciphering before five o'clock, Allenby decided without hesitation to proceed with the delivery of his own ultimatum. Dressed informally in a grey lounge suit with a soft felt hat, he was driven with his escort of Lancers to the Prime Minister's office almost opposite Parliament Building, towards which the Deputies were beginning to assemble for the sitting. After receiving a salute from the cavalry and a flourish of trumpets, Allenby entered the house and walked straight to the Prime Minister's room. He read to Zaghlul in English the text of his demands, left with him a French translation, and returned to his

car. He was again received with a salute before the gathering
crowds and drove slowly back to the Residency with his escort
to learn from the now deciphered telegram how far his action
had or had not been approved by his Government.

The terms of Allenby's ultimatum were as follows:

The Governor-General of the Sudan and Sirdar of the Egyptian
Army, who was also a distinguished officer of the British Army, has
been brutally murdered in Cairo. His Majesty's Government consider that this murder, which holds up Egypt as at present governed
to the contempt of civilized peoples, is the natural outcome of a
campaign of hostility to British rights and British subjects in Egypt
and Sudan, founded upon a heedless ingratitude for benefits conferred by Great Britain, not discouraged by Your Excellency's
Government, and fomented by organizations in close contact with
that Government. Your Excellency was warned by His Majesty's
Government little more than a month ago of the consequences of
failing to stop this campaign more particularly as far as it concerned
the Sudan. It has not been stopped. The Egyptian Government
have now allowed the Governor-General of the Sudan to be
murdered, and have proved that they are incapable or unwilling to
protect foreign lives. His Majesty's Government therefore require
that the Egyptian Government shall:

(1) Present ample apology for the crime.
(2) Prosecute inquiry into the authorship of the crime with the
    utmost energy and without respect of persons, and bring
    the criminals, whoever they are and whatever their age,
    to condign punishment.
(3) Henceforth forbid and vigorously suppress all popular
    political demonstrations.
(4) Pay forthwith to His Majesty's Government a fine of
    £500,000.
(5) Order within twenty-four hours the withdrawal from the
    Sudan of all Egyptian officers, and the purely Egyptian
    units of the Sudan Army, with such resulting changes as
    shall be hereafter specified.
(6) Notify the competent Department that the Sudan Govern-
    ment will increase the area to be irrigated at Gezira
    from 300,000 feddans to an unlimited figure as need
    may arise.

336

(7) Withdraw all opposition in the respects hereafter specified to the wishes of His Majesty's Government concerning the protection of foreign interests in Egypt.

Failing immediate compliance with these demands, His Majesty's Government will at once take appropriate action to safeguard their interests in Egypt and the Sudan.

The requirements indicated in the last demand were specified in a separate document. The Sudanese units of the Egyptian Army were to be made into a Sudan Defence Force owing allegiance to the Sudan Government alone; the conditions of retirement of foreign officials were to be revised in accordance with British ideas; the British financial and judicial Advisers were to be retained.

The cable from the Foreign Office when deciphered was found to omit the demand for an indemnity and for the revision of the terms of service of foreign officials, while the demand for "unlimited" irrigation of the Gezira was changed to "such extension of Gezira irrigation as may be considered possible without detriment to Egypt by a technical commission containing a member appointed by the Egyptian Government." Also the accusatory preamble to the demands was softened. Read in a calm, unhurried atmosphere after the event the Foreign Office document may be held to be a better-balanced presentation of the British case, less open to the charges of vindictiveness or of seeking to profit by the occasion which were levelled by some against Allenby's ultimatum. These protested that a demand for 'blood-money' was undignified, and that neither the compensation of foreign officials nor the question of irrigation in the Sudan could properly be connected with the murder. Though the British Government upheld Allenby's ultimatum, they were disturbed by what they held to be his precipitate action, and asked for an explanation. Allenby replied that he considered the demand for a large sum of money necessary in order to bring home to the Egyptians the criminal results of their Government's policy; and that the Gezira irrigation demand was similarly intended to impress on Egypt the power we could wield if necessary by our control of the Sudan; he had never meant that an unlimited area should in fact be irrigated to the detriment of Egyptian interests, but that concessions should subsequently be made to a more friendly Egyptian Government.

The matter of the rights of foreign officials had been included as the best means of settling an outstanding difficulty and to avoid having to make such a demand on a friendly Government which would succeed Zaghlul's, whose resignation Allenby expected and desired as a result of his ultimatum. There was much to be said for Allenby's point of view, and his action had the practically unanimous support of the British and foreign communities in Egypt.

The Egyptian reply, while expressing horror at the crime, did not accept any of the demands except that for the indemnity. Allenby promptly informed the Egyptian Government that he was issuing orders forthwith for the withdrawal of Egyptian troops from the Sudan and was giving full liberty to the Sudan Government to increase the area of the Gezira to be irrigated. As a guarantee for the fulfilment of the other conditions Allenby ordered the military occupation of the Customs at Alexandria, again taking action without awaiting the consent of His Majesty's Government. Zaghlul's Government now resigned, having paid the indemnity of £500,000,[1] but leaving the other demands of the ultimatum unsatisfied. Ziwar Pasha became Prime Minister. He was a man of no great ability but with considerable courage and unquenchable optimism. He was of Caucasian extraction and, although a Moslem, received his early tuition at the hands of Jesuits. He was of huge stature, and had that jovial disposition which often accompanies such physique. A special chair had to be made to accommodate him in the Prime Minister's office. As a linguist he was good; in fact, he had a natural if embarrassing habit of using English, French, Italian, Arabic, and Turkish all together in his conversation. Down his left cheek ran a perpetua tear, for he was never without a cigarette drooping perilously from the corner of his mouth, with the smoke invariably ascending into his eye.

[1] The Minister of Finance had only been appointed a day or two before the murder, and it was said in Cairo that his sole administrative act was the signing of this cheque. Allenby was one of the few people who can have endorsed a cheque for £500,000. The sum was eventually used for the improvement of medical services in the Sudan.

Ziwar Pasha had held Ministerial rank several times since 1919, and in 1924, when Zaghlul came to power, he was chosen as President of Egypt's first Senate. He was a strong believer in British friendship, and by temperament and outlook he was just the man to extricate Egypt from the present difficult situation. He had the common sense to see that the only policy for Egypt was to accept the British demands without question. He knew the British well enough to realize that they would not be unreasonable once their anger had died down. He accepted the conditions of the ultimatum, and the Customs were evacuated. As Allenby had planned when he placed his demands at a maximum, it was now possible to make some concessions to a friendly Government. The amount of land to be irrigated in the Gezira was eventually settled by a commission on which Egypt was represented.

Such is the story of the Lee Stack murder and of the part played by Allenby in exacting satisfaction for it. From the point of view of the Egyptian Government it was, as was said of the execution of the Duc d'Enghien one hundred and twenty years earlier, " worse than a crime, it was a blunder." Zaghlul himself can be acquitted of any previous knowledge of the crime, and realized only too well the fatal consequences to him. " Pour moi, c'était un coup mortel," he said sadly shortly afterwards. But he never seems to have realized his responsibility for the murder by his failure to control the more extreme of his followers.

From the British point of view the murder resolved Anglo-Egyptian relations as they were approaching a crisis. It may even be said that the corpse of the Sirdar was the *deus ex machina* of an intolerable situation. Allenby's action has been praised for its courage and decision and has been blamed for its hastiness and unnecessary harshness. Those who were on the spot and knew the Egyptians were almost unanimous in upholding him; it was only distant criticism that condemned him. Egyptians themselves understood the strong hand and expected no less. The impression of events under which Allenby acted must be remembered; he had seen the wounded and suffering Sirdar carried into the Residency and had felt the wave of indignation that the crime aroused in the British and foreign residents in Cairo. And he felt that he had been betrayed by the Egyptians. He had been mainly instrumental in securing their independence, he had insisted against a great weight of opinion that they should be given every chance of ordering their own affairs, and to that end had taken risks not only with his reputation, which concerned him not at all, but with the lives and interests of his countrymen, which concerned him deeply. His championship of Egypt had been rewarded by this crime, and the reaction was strong. It was the same anger that he showed when he found an officer whom he had trusted unworthy of his trust. He never forgave Zaghlul and spoke of him afterwards as " that wicked old man."

The evacuation of the Egyptian units from the Sudan was not accomplished without serious disturbance. The Egyptian units themselves, after only a show of resistance by some of them, were withdrawn without incident, but a Sudanese battalion, corrupted by Egyptian propaganda and made of sterner stuff, broke out into a mutiny which was only repressed with considerable blood-shed. That Allenby's judgment and consideration for Egypt had not been warped by the Lee Stack murder is shown by the fact that he refused to support the strongly urged recommendation of the Sudan Government that the Egyptian flag should be removed from all Army buildings in the Sudan.

The year 1924, which had been so momentous in Egyptian affairs, ended on a comparatively peaceful note. Ziwar Pasha had met all the British demands and had received some concessions. Sidky Pasha, a forcible personality, had been appointed Minister of the Interior and was engaged in removing the damage caused by Zaghlul's administration. Parliament was dissolved, and fresh elections were to be held early in 1925. Meanwhile King Fuad with his customary astuteness had seized the opportunity of Zaghlul's eclipse and Ziwar's easy-going complaisance to re-establish much of the Palace influence.

Allenby, though it was not generally known at the time, had resigned his appointment as High Commissioner and had refused, in spite of urgings from the Foreign Secretary, to withdraw his resignation, though he had consented to serve on temporarily. Though the causes of his resignation belong to the end of 1924, they can best be dealt with in the account of 1925, when his resignation took effect.

CHAPTER XIX

1925: ALLENBY LEAVES EGYPT

Lord Allenby came to Egypt in the midst of a fierce storm. He leaves it in a calm which is striking in its contrast and full of good augury. British prestige in Egypt stands higher to-day than it has done since Lord Kitchener left the country in 1914.

The Times, June 20, 1925

BEFORE the causes of Allenby's resignation are discussed the political events of the first six months of 1925, up to the time when Allenby left Egypt, will be briefly described. The storm raised by the murder of Sir Lee Stack cleared the air and was followed by a period of comparative calm. The able if unscrupulous efforts of Sidky Pasha to lessen the power of Zaghlul's party led to a very close election contest for the new Parliament. The result of the final elections in March showed an apparent equality for Government and Opposition and was claimed as a victory by both sides. Parliament met at 10 A.M. on March 23. When it proceeded to business, after formal opening by the King, Zaghlul was elected President of the Chamber by 123 votes to 85, a shock for Ziwar's Ministry, who had counted on a majority for their candidate. The evening session began at 5 P.M., no Ministers being present, and proceeded normally till 7.45 P.M., when the doors opened, and the Prime Minister entered, followed by the rest of the Ministers. He read a Royal Decree dissolving Parliament, which thus lasted less than ten hours, surely the shortest-lived Parliament in history. Fresh elections were promised for the autumn after a new electoral law had been passed. Meanwhile the King's influence was supreme, and the easy-going Ziwar made little resistance to the royal will. The old struggle between King and people entered a new phase.

Meanwhile the internal situation remained quiet. The main event of the period was the arrest, trial, and conviction of the murderers of the Sirdar. Their conviction was the result of a very fine piece of police work, carried out mainly by British police officers. The difficulty in this, as in all the other political crimes

341

of these years in Egypt, was to obtain the necessary evidence against the criminals, who were frequently known to, or strongly suspected by, the police. The right men had sometimes been arrested but had always to be released for want of evidence. The organization responsible for the murders intimidated, if necessary, witnesses from coming forward and provided, when necessary, false evidence for the defence. Unless, therefore, the murderers could be caught red-handed the only hope was to extract a confession from one of them by guile or promise of pardon.

After much search the British heads of the police secured as their agent a former Egyptian law student who in 1915, from mistaken motives of patriotism, had been involved in an attempt on the life of Sultan Hussein. He had been sentenced to death but had received commutation to penal servitude for life, and had worked ten years in the Tura stone-quarries before being let out of prison as the result of an amnesty. When he was released and found that those who had employed him had merely used his patriotism as a tool and had no further use for him he determined on revenge; and the prospect of the ten thousand pounds' reward which had been offered for conviction of the Sirdar's murderers, together with hope of a free pardon for his original crime, brought him into the service of the police. Posing as one who thirsted for revenge on the British, he got into the confidence of the murder gang and was soon able to inform the police officer conducting the case of the names of the Sirdar's murderers. The next step was to obtain the necessary evidence. It was decided to try to frighten a confession out of the weakest member of the gang, a young Egyptian student. One of the other murderers was arrested, and a report that he had confessed was allowed to appear. The student and his brother, another of the gang, were persuaded by the police agent that the confession had actually been made, and on finding their house watched by the police were instigated into a terror-stricken attempt to escape into Libya by the Western Desert, taking with them the weapons which had been used in the murder. At the edge of the desert they were arrested, and the weaker of the brothers, panic-stricken, confessed. The arrests were made at the end of January, and by the end of May seven men were placed on trial for the murder. Six were sentenced to death, of whom five were executed, the student who had turned King's evidence having his sentence converted to penal servitude. The police agent received the reward of ten thousand pounds and a free pardon for the crime he had committed in 1915. Such was the final act of a drama which had considerable effect on the history of Egypt. Allenby, who had played one of the principal parts, left Egypt a week after the sentences had been pronounced.

The event which led to Allenby's resignation was the sudden decision of the Foreign Secretary, Mr Austen Chamberlain, at the time of the crisis which followed the Sirdar's murder, to dispatch to Egypt, without consulting Allenby, a senior diplomatic official, who automatically became the principal representative of the Foreign Office in Egypt and Allenby's chief adviser. From the military point of view it was equivalent to the supersession without warning of a general's chief staff officer during an important operation, and it was naturally regarded by Allenby as implying a lack of confidence both in his staff and himself.

Though the decision was sudden, its roots had been planted a long time previously. Ever since the 1922 Declaration there had been an influential body of opinion in London, both inside the Foreign Office and outside it, which had disliked the original decision forced on the Government by Allenby and had viewed with growing disfavour the turn of events in Egypt and the way in which the policy of the Declaration was being interpreted and handled. Criticism of Allenby grew more persistent and vocal during 1924, when Zaghlul was in power, fuel being constantly added by British, and occasionally foreign, opinion in Egypt itself. The main gravamen of the charge against Allenby was that his weakness and complacency in face of Egyptian provocation were endangering British interests and even British lives. The murder of Sir Lee Stack seemed to justify the criticism; and although Allenby's firmness after the murder was approved, the terms of his ultimatum were held to be ill-advised and his action hasty. Allenby seemed to the Foreign Secretary to have taken the bit in his teeth. It was obviously impossible at this crisis to recall him, but Mr Chamberlain decided to apply a brake. He hurriedly sent for Mr Nevile Henderson [1] and ordered him to Cairo. Had the appointment been made after previous consultation with Allenby it is most unlikely that he would have raised any objection; as it was, the terms and manner both of the public announcement and of the official communication to Allenby were unfortunate. The public announcement was to the effect that Mr Henderson had been appointed a " Minister Plenipotentiary " while employed at the Residency, Cairo. This is the normal title for the rank of Minister in the Diplomatic Service and was not meant to imply anything unusual, but coming at the time it did it was naturally interpreted in Cairo as betokening a special mission, a change of policy, and to some extent at least a supersession of Allenby's authority. In the communication of the appointment to Allenby Mr Chamberlain made what was always a fatal mistake in dealing with Allenby—he was not entirely frank with him. His explanation of the reasons for Mr Henderson's appointment was as follows:

I am impressed with the difficulty of putting you fully in possession of the mind and purpose of His Majesty's Government by a simple exchange of telegrams. I have therefore decided to send Mr Nevile Henderson to Cairo. He is an official of exceptional experience, and I have explained to him verbally with a completeness which is not possible in telegraphic communication the objects at which His Majesty's Government are arriving and the difficulties which they wish to avoid. He has my fullest confidence and will, I am sure, make your task easier by the explanations which he will be able to give you. He will join your staff with the rank of Minister, and will, I hope, lighten a burden which must be excessive with your present small staff.

Allenby's first reaction was, characteristically, loyalty to his staff. He telegraphed to the Foreign Secretary that he would be glad to have Mr Henderson's assistance during the period of stress and to learn from him the mind and purpose of His Majesty's Government, but he would be glad of an assurance that it was not intended to supersede his Counsellor, Clark Kerr, in whom, as in

[1] Afterwards famous as Sir Nevile Henderson, Ambassador in Berlin from 1937 to 1939.

all his staff, he had complete confidence. The reply was to the effect that while no reflection on the Counsellor was intended Mr Henderson would, of course, become the senior member of Allenby's staff.

Meanwhile Allenby had seen the effect in Egypt of the public announcement, and had cabled that it had been taken as amounting to his practical supersession and had seriously weakened his position. His position would, in fact, become untenable unless the Foreign Secretary could see his way to correcting that impression by making without delay a public announcement that Mr Henderson was coming solely for the purpose of discussing the situation and facilitating the exchange of views between the Foreign Secretary and himself and would leave for London within a week of his arrival.

Allenby's attitude was, in fact, that the Foreign Secretary's declared purpose of "putting him fully in possession of the mind and purpose of His Majesty's Government" could be as well, if not better, accomplished by a liaison visit than by a permanent appointment. If the appointment, however, was made because of dissatisfaction with himself or his staff it should be frankly stated.

Several further telegrams passed on similar lines, with the Foreign Secretary trying to convince Allenby that the appointment was a perfectly normal one and intended merely to assist him and to fill a vacancy on his staff, while Allenby insisted that the effect of the appointment in Egypt had been deplorable, and that unless Mr Henderson's was to be merely a temporary visit he must adhere to his determination to resign. His final telegram of this series was as follows:

Either you have confidence in me or you have not. Since you have made a striking appointment to my staff in the midst of a crisis without consulting me, and published it without giving me an opportunity of expressing my opinion, I presume you have not. It is therefore my duty to resign. You must know that in a country like this the only interpretation of such an appointment is infirmity of purpose, and this at such a moment is disastrous. I seek only the public interest, but I see no way out of the difficulty unless you can arrange to announce that Mr Henderson only comes on a specific mission and for a very brief period. As I said in my last night's telegram I shall be glad to see Mr Henderson and have his help, and maintain absolute unity with you in loyal and helpful co-operation in this important public task. I do not wish to obtrude the question of my resignation at this moment, but I adhere to my previous telegram of 27 November.

Allenby's mistrust of Mr Chamberlain's sincerity was unfortunately increased by his discovery, on the arrival of Mr Henderson, that the Minister who was to put him so fully and completely in the mind of His Majesty's Government had in fact been hurriedly recalled from a holiday and had only had one short interview with the Foreign Secretary before his departure. He had no previous experience of Egypt.

Three weeks later, when the crisis caused by the Sirdar's murder was practically over, Mr Chamberlain wrote to Allenby regretting the ' misunderstanding ' that had arisen between them and asking him to allow his resignation to be submitted

as the natural desire of a great servant of the Crown to take the opportunity offered by the end of one chapter in our relations with Egypt and the beginning of another as the proper moment to seek relief from the strain of such long and arduous service and the natural and most honourable close of your great career in the Near East, first as soldier and then as statesman.

Allenby acknowledged the spirit in which Mr Chamberlain's letter was written, but refused to admit that it had been a question merely of a momentary misunderstanding. As to the suggestion about the reasons to be given for his resignation, he wrote:

I have no personal feelings in the matter, but, though I thank you for suggesting the solution, I cannot ask to be retired with a view to relief from a strain which I do not feel. I must therefore beg that when the crisis is past you will submit my application to be allowed to resign my present appointment on the grounds given in my telegram of 26 November.

Allenby's annoyance was great when at the end of February a report that he had resigned appeared in a London newspaper and was telegraphed to Egypt. At the same time he was being subjected to particularly venomous attacks in certain sections of the London Press. No man ever paid less attention to personal criticism, but these attacks and the report of his resignation were having a most disturbing effect on the political situation just previous to the elections and were encouraging the Zaghlulists. Allenby therefore asked that the report of his resignation be denied and suggested that the papers concerned might be asked to desist temporarily from their attacks, which were harmful to our interests and might make just the difference between the success and defeat of the Zaghlulists. " If they like to return to the attack in a fortnight or so," he added, " these objections will no longer apply."

On May 2 Allenby wrote to the Foreign Secretary saying that he considered the time had come when his resignation might be submitted to the King and announced. It crossed a letter from Mr Chamberlain, written two days previously, making the same suggestion. It seems to have been the one occasion in this unfortunate business when they were entirely in agreement. Before the close of the chapter there was yet another incident that added to Allenby's resentment. He had specially asked that he should be given two days' notice of the date and hour at which the announcement of his successor would be made, so that he could inform King Fuad and the Prime Minister before the news reached Egypt. He also strongly advised that the announcement should be accompanied by an assurance that the change of persons betokened no change of policy. Less than a week later he learned from a Reuters telegram that Sir George Lloyd had accepted the High Commissionership in succession to him. The announcement, though unauthorized, was true, and Allenby was naturally angered at the disregard of his advice and the carelessness that had allowed the news of the appointment to become public property in Egypt before he himself was informed.

Allenby left Egypt a month later, on June 14. This last month in Egypt was the occasion of a remarkable series of tributes paid to his work and his personality both in the British and Egyptian Press and by all communities in Egypt. Allenby's friends at the Foreign Office used their influence with the Press at home in Allenby's favour and did its best to see that what he had done was recognized in the articles on his departure. Allenby had paid no attention to the vicious attacks made on him in some papers a little earlier and was perhaps not unduly elated by the tributes now paid him in others. He had no very high opinion of the value of the praise or blame of journalists. But the expression of opinion in Egypt of all classes and all kinds was too spontaneous and genuine to be mistaken and caused him real pleasure, the more so as its warmth may have been a little unexpected.

Perhaps the best record of Allenby's last days in Egypt can be given in extracts from the official dispatch sent to the Foreign Office by the Minister, Mr Nevile Henderson:

28th June, 1925

It is fitting that I should place on record some account of the remarkable tributes of esteem and affection paid to Lord and Lady Allenby during the period immediately preceding their departure from Egypt.

From the moment when the news of His Lordship's impending retirement became public he and Lady Allenby were the recipients of innumerable letters and telegrams—the sincerity and spontaneity of which were undeniable—not only from the British and foreign communities but from every section of Egyptian opinion other than Zaghlulist.

At the same time Their Excellencies were inundated with invitations to farewell parties and receptions in their honour.

The shortage of the time at their disposal made it impossible for them to accept more than a few of these invitations. They confined themselves, as regards Egyptians, to official dinner-parties at the Palace and with the Prime Minister, to a luncheon-party with Sarwat Pasha and to an afternoon reception at the Continental Hotel organized by Mohamed Pasha Sherei, Mabrouk Pasha Fahmy, and Saleh Pasha Lamloun.

At the last three the most cordial of speeches were exchanged; and the third of these, the afternoon reception, was pronounced by competent judges one of the most remarkable events of its kind seen in Egypt within living memory. Over fifteen hundred persons attended, all but two hundred of them Egyptians; and of the latter a considerable proportion were provincial notables, who had in many cases themselves applied for invitations. Lord Allenby spoke to or shook hands with them all, and the warmth of their feelings was patent. The fact indeed that they had come long distances, in large numbers, and without fear of possible consequences was a striking proof of the change in spirit which had been so noticeable a feature of the final phase of His Lordship's work.

On the day of Lord Allenby's departure from Cairo large and manifestly friendly crowds lined the streets. The scene at the station itself was impressive. The gathering there, which it had been found necessary to limit by the issue of tickets, was the most representative of its kind which has taken place within the memory of those present; and the many Egyptians of whom Lord and Lady Allenby have by their personal charm made close personal friends were ill able to conceal their emotion.

The special train to Port Said was stopped by request at Benha and Zagazig in order that notables might deliver speeches of farewell. Finally, the British community of Port Said organized a luncheon-party for Their Excellencies prior to their embarkation.

During their last week in Egypt Lord and Lady Allenby set themselves personally to answer all the messages which had been addressed to them, regardless of the labour involved. The impression made by this final act of sympathy on the Egyptian mind, peculiarly susceptible as it is to such forms of courtesy, was profound. More than one Egyptian has told me with obvious sincerity that Lord Allenby's parting letter to him will remain one of his most treasured possessions; and in general one may say with certainty that there are few people of any consequence in Egypt, of whatever nationality, in whom Their Excellencies' departure has not, for one reason or another, left a sense of personal loss.

The Egyptians are a kindly people and admire generous natures; they are a polite people and appreciate good manners; they are not a forceful race, but they admire and respect strength. Though Allenby's hand had lain heavily on them at times, they recognized his innate kindliness; he had been courteous, simple, and straightforward, even when stern, with the Egyptians with whom he had dealt; of his strength of character and purpose they never had any doubt, and were surprised to see them questioned by his own countrymen.

POSTSCRIPT

Such is the record of Allenby's influence on six momentous and stormy years of Egyptian history. This influence has up to now been better understood and appreciated in Egypt than in his own country, where it has been attacked or ignored. It is hoped that the story given in these chapters may cause his achievement to be better recognized. Both Great Britain and Egypt owe him a debt of gratitude. In a most difficult period in the relations between the two countries he upheld essential British interests without causing bitterness; he secured for Egypt independence from a reluctant British Government and a liberal Constitution from a reactionary monarch.

It was unfortunate that his period in Egypt should have been ended by a crime of violence and by the unhappy controversy that caused his resignation. But for this Allenby might well have crowned his work by negotiating the treaty on the reserved subjects that was not achieved until some ten years later, since there was no one in whose good faith and honesty the Egyptians had greater trust. Allenby never forgave the two persons who were primarily responsible, Zaghlul and Austen Chamberlain. This was not for any reasons of personal ambition or care for his reputation. He considered that Zaghlul had betrayed the trust he had shown in the Egyptian people, and that Austen Chamberlain had not been straightforward with him. These were the two faults which throughout his career he punished with his most severe displeasure—betrayal of a trust he placed in those with whom he dealt and lack of sincerity in speech or writing.

Of the three great British Proconsuls who served Egypt—Cromer, Kitchener, and Allenby—it is probable that Allenby appealed most to the Egyptian, to the educated Egyptian at least. Cromer, cold and correct, was respected but certainly not loved; Kitchener was liked and admired, but it is doubtful whether he commanded the same trust as Allenby, whose honesty and straightforwardness in speech and action impressed all Egyptians with whom he came in contact. Lady Allenby's personality and charm also counted for much.

Allenby was succeeded by Lord Lloyd and a policy of the strong hand. But neither the strong hand of the administrator nor the facile pen or persuasive tongue of the diplomat could alter the fact which Allenby had recognized in Egypt, the awakened spirit of a people.

EPILOGUE

(1925–35)

Sleepe after toyle, port after stormie seas,
Ease after warre, death after life, does greatly please.

SPENSER, *The Faerie Queene*

Birds are the most beautiful of all living things.

W. H. HUDSON

Poor Allenby! It is sad to see a big man in retirement and not knowing what to do. I wish we could all die in harness." So wrote T. E. Lawrence to a friend in 1932. His acute but restless mind completely misjudged Allenby and his affairs. Allenby in his last ten years neither courted the public eye nor did he, like " T. E. Shaw," conspicuously avoid it. His arrangement of his life showed his usual common sense. He did very much useful but unobtrusive public work; for his own enjoyment he spent his time on the things he had always loved—birds and travel and fishing. But for one enduring sorrow—the absence of his only son, the boy of such promise who had been killed in 1917—his last years would have been ideally happy.

His principal public work was done for the British National Cadet Association, of which he was President. A Cadet Force had been in existence, with official recognition and some slight financial aid, for many years, to give some training to working boys and boys of secondary schools. The units were military in form, but there was little militarism in them, and membership was entirely voluntary. They had undoubtedly done much to improve health and physique and to give some education in citizenship. But they had always been the object of dislike and suspicion to that class of Englishman who hates any form of discipline or elementary training, and regards citizenship of a great nation as conferring on him the privilege of criticizing everything its Government does, but as involving him in no obligation to serve or help his country in any way. In 1930 the financial crisis gave the opponents of military service the opportunity to seek to kill the Cadet movement. They secured that all financial support—only a few thousand pounds—should be withdrawn, and also all official recognition and help. The hand of the anti-militarist can be seen in the Army Order (October 31 of 1930) cancelling all recognition and support; it enacted that should a Territorial unit be willing to allow its drill hall to be used by a Cadet unit " no instruction of a military nature may be given." And this was less than three years before Hitler came into power and less than nine years before the greatest of all wars. It was, however, in accordance with the parsimonious edict that governed all military affairs at this time, that " no major war need be apprehended for the next ten years." It was not until 1935 that the Cadet Force was again recognized and assisted by the Government. But even then it still suffered from strong political opposition, and for over two years of a war vital to our national existence remained at the pitifully low figure of 20,000. Then the War Office increased the grants and, enlisting the help of the Board of Education, afforded it real encouragement. As a result, numbers jumped in a few months to 200,000. That a Cadet Force was saved at all in 1930 was largely due to Allenby, who accepted the Presidency of a Cadet Association formed to carry on the movement. He used all his personality and influence to support the Association and to secure funds; and took a lively personal interest in it to the day of his death.

In 1933 Allenby became President of an institute for old soldiers known as the Veterans' Association, and by his exertions in raising funds enabled such improvement to be made that the name of the Club was changed to the Allenby (Services) Club. It still exists to commemorate his interest in soldiers and their welfare.

His interest in birds and animals was marked by his association with the Zoological Society; his Presidency of the Central Asian Society maintained his connexion with the part of the world in which he had so distinguished himself; his appointment as Gold Stick in Waiting, which went with his Colonelcy of the Life Guards, meant attendance at Court functions when he was in London. Except when the duties of these various institutions, which he carried out with characteristic throughness, claimed him, he spent his leisure in travel in the winter and in fishing in the spring and summer. Birds he had always with him.

On his return home in 1925 Allenby was offered Deal Castle as a residence. He and Lady Allenby spent a few months there, but neither cared for the seaside, and the house was too cold. They decided to make their permanent home in London and settled in 24 Wetherby Gardens, South Kensington, a conveniently sized and comfortable house. The small back garden became an aviary, in which Allenby soon had a collection of his favourites. In the winters the Allenbys invariably set out on some distant travel. In 1925–26 they visited Australia at the invitation of the Australian Government, went on to New Zealand for three weeks, and travelled home by Canada. In the winter of 1927–28 they went to South Africa, staying first with Sir Abe Bailey at Cape Town and then at Pretoria with Princess Alice and Lord Athlone, the Governor-General. Lord Athlone had been Allenby's subaltern in the early part of the South African War. The Allenbys went on to Southern Rhodesia, where unfortunately Lady Allenby had a severe attack of malaria at Victoria Falls. They returned home by Nairobi and Cairo.

In October 1928 they went to the United States, Allenby having been invited to be present at the Convention of the American Legionaries, held that year by General Pershing in the picturesque old town of San Antonio, in Texas. They went on to Los Angeles, and spent some time in the studios of Hollywood, where they heard the first talking film—and did not appreciate it. Thence they went to San Francisco, the Grand Canyon, the Yosemite Valley, Santa Barbara, Santa Fé, Chicago, Washington, and New York.

The winter of 1929–30 was spent in India, with a week in Cairo on the return journey. Burma, Jamaica, Brazil, were among the many countries visited in other winters.

There was a curious ending to a visit to Malaya and the Dutch East Indies in the winter of 1933–34. The Allenbys arrived at Batavia, in Java, from Singapore early in January 1934. A few days later word came to the Dutch Government of a plot against Allenby's life, to be attempted by some Japanese during his stay in Java. Being warned by the Governor that he would have to be closely shadowed and protected during his stay in the Dutch East Indies, Allenby realized that his holiday would be spoilt, and he abandoned it. He flew to Sumatra by plane and went thence by Dutch ship to Colombo. Whether there was any substance in the story of the plot, which seems on the face of it improbable, is unknown; presumably it was at the time thought sufficiently circumstantial to be passed on to the authorities in Java.

The most enterprising of Allenby's journeys was his last, in the winter of 1935–36, when he was well in his seventy-fifth year. He had read some time previously an article in the *Field* about an estancia in Patagonia where salmon-fishing could be obtained. He kept the article, thinking the time and opportunity might come when he could go there. In the autumn of 1935 he decided to attempt the adventure, though no one could give any information about Lake Traful, the reputed haunt of these salmon. A cable to the landlord of the estancia, a Major Dawson, received a satisfactory reply, and the Allenbys set out for Buenos Aires. The Ambassador to the Argentine was Sir Nevile Henderson, the innocent cause of Allenby's resignation in Egypt ten years earlier. Himself a keen fisherman, he assisted Allenby to make all the necessary arrangements for the journey to Patagonia. The visit was a great success. The Allenbys spent a month in a lovely spot with a perfect climate—day after day of brilliant sunshine but with cool evenings. The fishing was unique, landlocked salmon in shape and quality equal to those of the Tay, but hard to catch except in the early morning or late evening.

At home the Tay was Allenby's favourite fishing river, and in it he caught many salmon. For trout-fishing he had a beat on the Avon, near Salisbury, rented from Colonel Bailey, of Lake. From this well-stocked stream Allenby caught many trout on the dry-fly, though his methods were once described by the water-bailiff as " a trifle military."

Shortly after his return home from Patagonia Allenby was elected Rector of Edinburgh University. He delivered his inaugural address on April 28. For some reason there is a tradition of rowdiness at this ceremony, and Allenby did not escape the usual accompaniment of hootings, cat-calls, and the like, which punctuated his address. He took it all with great good humour.

His address on this occasion is printed as an appendix to the present volume.

It was Allenby's last public function. A few days after his return to London he went out for a walk in apparently the best of health and spirits. He had arranged to go fishing on the following day. In the course of his walk he bought an addition to his aviary. When he returned to the house he talked for some time to Lady Allenby, and then went upstairs to his study. A few minutes later his butler, Pooley, entered the study and found Allenby lying dead across his desk. A blood-vessel in his brain had burst, and he had died instantly without pain or struggle. Death had given a quick and merciful end to one who had never feared him.

Allenby's death took place when conversations in Cairo between British and Egyptian delegations for the conclusion of an Anglo-Egyptian treaty of friendship and alliance were nearing a satisfactory conclusion—the fitting sequel to his work in Egypt. The leaders of all three principal parties—the Wafd, the Liberals, and the Shaab—sent heartfelt messages of condolence. There is no doubt that his death was genuinely mourned by all shades of Egyptian opinion, and that memory of his work for Egypt still lives there.

His remains were cremated and his ashes buried in Westminster Abbey on May 19, near the Tomb of the Unknown Warrior.

REQUIEM

A scholar, a statesman, and a soldier.

SHAKESPEARE, *Measure for Measure*

IN spite of some foibles and faults, he was, beyond doubt, a very great man. His greatness was the result of a few striking qualities—a perfect simplicity of character without a particle of vanity or conceit, but with a thorough and strenuous self-reliance, a severe truthfulness, never misled by fancy or exaggeration, and an ever-abiding sense of duty and obligation.

So wrote Greville of the Duke of Wellington on his death. The portrait will serve for Allenby without the change of a word. His foibles and faults were different from those of Wellington; he had less self-control, but he had less ambition and an even higher sense of obligation and duty. He had more natural tolerance and kindliness than the great Duke, but resembled him in the directness and incisiveness and sometimes in the apparent inconsiderateness of his language.

Allenby was perhaps more akin in character to another great Englishman, his contemporary, Lord Grey of Fallodon, a simple, direct, loyal servant of his country, free from all personal vanity and jealousy. His biographer wrote of Grey that " his heart was not in the streets or in the council-chamber but in the woods and beside the streams." So was Allenby's. Like Grey, he was wholly country-bred, a type becoming all too rare in these days of crowded cities, spreading suburbs, and week-end countrymen; like Grey, he loved birds and enjoyed fishing.

Allenby's qualities as a soldier have been described and summed up elsewhere. His claim to statesmanship is set out in the chapters of this volume which tell of his work in Egypt. It remains only to say something of a quality less known, his scholarship and taste for knowledge. It was a catholic taste and embraced the classics, much poetry and literature, natural history, horticulture, more than a little science, geography, and general history. When he acquired knowledge he acquired it attentively and exactly, and since he had a tenacious memory, he could always produce his knowledge accurately, thereby often confounding those with wider but less well-digested information. This memory extended to poetry, of which he could repeat much by heart. Allenby never ceased learning, just as he never ceased travelling. He had none of the vanity that leads a man to conceal or avoid what he does not know. When he came on some subject that interested him or concerned him he at once sought for knowledge, preferably by questioning some one who was informed. He had no very deep knowledge of any one subject. There were many who knew more of the ways of birds and beasts—his favourite subject; many who were wider read in his favourite authors; many who travelled more. But few can have got more pleasure out of both books and personal observation than did Allenby, or have made a wiser choice of interests.

He could on occasion talk well to a sympathetic listener, as he would listen well to some one who knew what he was talking about; but he had on the whole no great power of giving out what he knew. He was an indifferent lecturer, unless carefully prepared and rehearsed, and his impromptu speeches sometimes approached disaster. Nor did he write with freedom or ease; his letters dealt severely and baldly with the matter in hand, or were simple chronicles of events, unless some bird or beast or flower had attracted his attention; his official reports were clear and direct, but lacked any literary grace. That he had a feeling for words and the power to express himself when he took trouble may be illustrated by some extracts from his speeches and writings. Moreover, these extracts throw light on his character and attitude to life. The first is from a speech on gardens:

> There is a mystery in the beauty of a blossom. It conveys a suggestion of self-conscious life; a suggestion which stimulates the imagination of even the dullest and the dumbest among us. We seem to detect in certain flowering plants a consciousness resembling intelligence. The delight exhibited by a plant in the enjoyment of good soil and genial environment, its happiness in sunlight and fresh air, are so obvious that one can with difficulty believe the feeling to be subconscious. The ingenuity with which the orchid ensures fertilization in the interest of its race, the cunning of the

Sundew, of Venus' fly trap, and others in snaring insects for food, the shrinking from rough contact of the sensitive plants, entitle them to be considered as on a par with, at least, some of the lower forms of animal life. Flowers know slumber and waking, they know health and sickness, they riot in wilderness, yet live contentedly in confinement, they endure discipline, they profit by education. The gorgeous denizens of the wilderness and the hedgerows have, in many cases, been brought by the brain and hand of the gardener to a perfection of colour and form unattainable apart from his tutorial skill.

The second is from an address at the opening of the " Men of the Trees " exhibition:

Man's ingratitude to trees has been bad. Sinai was not always a desert; but the tamarisks which once abounded and supplied manna to wanderers in the wilderness are there no more. The forests of Palestine have disappeared; Carmel and Lebanon are bare; no longer is balm found in Gilead; and there a rider, however reckless, may urge his mount without danger of suffering the fate of Absalom.

The next is taken from a magazine article:

The peoples of the earth were broken, physically and morally, on a larger scale than hitherto experienced, yet in no different fashion than a thousand times. What we have witnessed is the customary process of evolution in man's affairs, and always, when like shocks occur, those affected believe that civilization is crashing in ruin. Human nature is, in our days, not unlike what it has ever been; that is, on the whole, well-disposed and kindly. The Great War has taught the bitter lesson that even for the victors gain is outweighed by loss; and looking back through the pages of history, we note that the winnings of one war as often as not disappear in the next. Where are now the fruits of Napoleon's dazzling triumphs, or the gains of Bismarck's victorious combinations? For Freedom no ransom is too high.

There is something prophetic in this passage from an address to the British Legion in 1932:

It is good that we should meet each other often, recalling ancient memories and renewing old acquaintance. It is good for us and good for our children and all the younger generation. Over eighteen years have passed since you answered your country's call. It is difficult to realize that babies then in arms are now of man's estate—that those men and women who are just beginning to play an active part in the service of our country knew nothing about the war of their own experience. Those girls and boys have got to learn from you, lest the lessons you learnt with such suffering be wasted. True, they can read history, and should do so. But written history is no efficient substitute for the spoken word. On you who made history lies the duty of telling these young people how the war was fought and why, show those children what sacrifices were made, that the land of their fathers—this green pleasant land—might be saved, and Great Britain and the Empire secured to them against the direst efforts of their enemies.

Unless the rising generation learn now—and learn from you who know—they may have to pay again with pain and bitter tears the debt which you have already discharged.

Let us be true to the principles which unite and guide the British Legion. Show kindness in others' trouble, courage in our own. Hold together. Trust in God; and keep your powder dry.

While as a sample of his after-dinner speaking here is one from a banquet of the Merchant Taylors Company:

Man is the only animal which eats when not hungry or drinks when not thirsty. This is a definition of man, given with intent to blame. But to-night, even if not hungry, whether thirsty or otherwise, I think no one could have resisted the temptation offered by the Worshipful Company our Hosts. Nor can blame or shame attach to any of us who have enjoyed to the full these rare meats and these generous wines. Food is the first need of mankind, to maintain internal warmth: while clothes are a useful adjunct to help in maintaining exterior warmth. Clothes are of negligible importance in hot regions, gaining in value as colder climates are reached. In Equatorial Africa food only is wanted; clothing—except for a coating of wood ash to discourage mosquitoes—is not used. In the Arctic Circle Nature has provided seals, bears, reindeer, etc., which afford both food and raiment. In temperate regions, where we live, Nature has evolved the Merchant Taylors. To their industry and ability we owe it that the materials wherewith we clothe ourselves in winter and veil ourselves in summer are of satisfactory quality. It is because of the standard established by the Guild of Merchant Taylors that we guests are able to appear to-night decently garbed in stout broadcloth, and not in sackcloth or ragged rabbit-skins. For all these benefits, for the bounteous feast of which we have joyously partaken, and for the very garb we wear, we are indebted to our Hosts. Of my own feelings it is easy to speak; but not so easy to tell those of others. Here, with us, are great legal luminaries and diplomatists. The thoughts of a Judge are never known until he speaks. The thoughts of a Diplomatist may not be known even when he has spoken. But all are human beings like the rest of us, capable of gratitude; and in the name of each and of all I express our sense of gratitude for the hospitality we have enjoyed and for the kind way in which the toast of the Guests has been honoured.

Allenby had always a great sense of humour and was capable of schoolboy fun, even in his later years. His wit was not quick but was always tolerant and kindly.

Generosity, fairmindedness, and loyalty were Allenby's most abiding qualities, and they were shown in his treatment of his friends and his foes, in his defence and support of all those who served him, in his attitude towards the Boers in the South African War, towards the Turks and even the Germans in the Great War, towards the Egyptians in the difficult years in Egypt.

Allenby was not outwardly a religious man; he seldom went to church and was broadminded in matters of belief or observance. But few men knew their Bible better or read it more regularly. That he believed in life after death is shown by the following two extracts, from speeches made at the opening of a Cenotaph at Belfast in 1929, and of the Y.M.C.A. at Jerusalem in 1933.

At Belfast:

They have passed on, from Darkness through fire, into Light. Our Memorial to them is this Cenotaph, this Empty Tomb. It holds no mortal remains. Their graves are not here; their souls are in God's keeping; but we may believe that they are in spiritual touch with us to-day. And the Empty Tomb, round which we are standing, may symbolize a Tomb which heart-broken mourners found vacant nearly two thousand years ago. In despair they went to the Tomb; they came away with a sure and certain hope. For on that morning was given to them—and through them to all the World—the Revelation that Death's dread portal is, in truth, but the gate to Eternal Life.

At Jerusalem:

Believing in life beyond the tomb, we cannot but feel that in this Land of ancient strife, myriad spirits are about and around us; souls of friends and of enemies, now united, in mutual comprehension and full wisdom; free from the toils of the flesh, willing and able to help us mortals on the upward path.

Courage and truth—these are the foundations of any greatness, a man's or a nation's. They were Allenby's outstanding qualities. He was English to the core; born and brought up in the English countryside; made vigorous and hardy by country air and wholesome food; steeped from boyhood in the countryman's lore and in observation of the ways of birds and beasts; educated in the best English traditions of duty, justice, and fair play; gifted with a clear if not brilliant mind, which was developed on the sound if easy-going methods of English schools. A character with such origins will achieve greatness if circumstances and opportunity are favourable. They favoured Allenby, and his achievement was high.

So long as England can continue to breed leaders in Allenby's mould her greatness and prosperity will remain. There were dangers ahead before the disaster of the 1939 war shook us from complacency and ignoble ease. Country life had given place to town life; courage and toughness seemed rated at lower value than of old; cleverness was being reckoned of more account than character; leadership was gained by caution rather than by daring; pleasure and personal advantage were being set before duty. The dangers and hardships of to-day are helping to bring back the old standards of courage, self-sacrifice, and hard work; they have proved that the town-bred man can show the bravery and toughness of the English race as well as his country forbears. These qualities will be very necessary in the great task before us of rebuilding a shaken world.

It may help in that task to read the story of one whose courage never failed him; who had the strength never to look back at a decision once taken, either for pride or for regret; who loved the English countryside and the English way of life and was prepared for any sacrifice to uphold it; who saw much of other lands and other peoples and was tolerant of other ways of life provided they were based on justice and fair dealing and not on self-interest; who knew much war but always spoke for peace; who was true to his own self and was never false to any man.

He was a great Englishman; may his example live and inspire us all in the testing years that lie ahead.

APPENDIX

LORD ALLENBY'S RECTORIAL ADDRESS
TO EDINBURGH UNIVERSITY

MORE than half a century ago I entered the Army, with little ambition, vague as to the future, accepting events as they came along.

I had no expectation or idea of attaining the rank of Field-Marshal; I never thought that your University might raise me to the dignity of a Doctor of Laws; that I should have the honour of receiving the Livingstone Gold Medal of the Royal Scottish Geographical Society; or—highest distinction of all—that I might be chosen by you as Rector of the University of Edinburgh.

All these things have come to pass.

Knowing that pride is a sin to be reprehended, while gratitude is commendable, I will not proclaim my pride; but I do express my gratitude to all those who have helped me on my way through life, especially to you who elected me for the exalted and honourable position in which I now stand.

As a mere soldier, I am diffident in addressing you, my fellow-members, who are superior to me in every branch of knowledge except, perhaps, the barren business of war—and, even in that, I am now no longer up-to-date.

I am fully conscious of my limitations; but the situation must be accepted, the duty has to be faced; nothing was ever won by shirking an issue or shrinking from an obligation.

Though I have not had the good fortune to enjoy a University education, I have been privileged to know men and women of intelligence and learning in all walks of life; and it has been my constant endeavour to profit by the association. In that effort I hope I have been successful. Moreover, I have always tried to keep my mind from stagnation; and in this I have been gratuitously aided by the system of continual inspection and frequent examination, by papers and word of mouth, which prevails in the Army and which no soldier—however unaspiring—is able to elude.

We soldiers are sometimes looked down on as below the average educational standard; especially so, perhaps, cavalrymen—of whom I am one. However, I assure you that your armed forces take their profession seriously; are as earnest, industrious, and competent as any equal number of civilians. We are interested in and we study each our own technical branch, while appreciating whole-heartedly and with admiration the zeal and efficiency of our brothers-in-arms belonging to the other units in the Service—here at home and throughout the Empire overseas—all bound with spontaneous loyalty to one another, under and in humble duty to the King-Emperor.

But not only in the regular forces of the Crown is that sense of loyalty found. Linked thereby, united as one, the sons and daughters of the Empire, when the supreme test of the Great War came, were equal to every trial: joined the fighting services, bore unmurmuringly the brunt, and emerged victorious.

Since victory came many years have rolled by. What has victory given us? How do we stand?

Some of our statesmen and leaders, enthusiastic and optimistic, as well they might be, acclaimed the termination of hostilities as the glorious and welcome conclusion of a war which was to end all wars. The golden age had arrived, to stay with us eternally.

We have waited long. The golden promise has not yet materialized. Still, do not let us accept the belief that all our efforts were futile, that our sacrifices were offered in vain.

Truly, the fruit for which we hungered is not yet ripe for the gathering, but we were, perhaps, hasty and premature in expectation of reward; our disappointment may thus result from impatience, natural as that might be after relaxation from the long and almost intolerable strain.

During those terrible years humanity was shocked and shaken to a degree without precedent; mentally and morally we are still unbalanced. Furthermore, the loss of our best and bravest has stripped from the world the flower and pride of its youth.

Those who to-day should have been in the prime of manhood, able and eager to join with brain, heart, and hand in the colossal task of reconstruction, are gone before their work as citizens could even begin.

But though we deplore their loss we must not let ourselves be mastered by despair. The work has to be carried on; and it is for the young generation—with broad outlook and liberal education—to undertake the rebuilding of a broken world.

Here, in this venerable centre of universal knowledge, is offered the opportunity of acquiring that breadth of outlook, and of assimilating the wisdom of ages past and present; of laying the foundation of a liberal education.

Foundation, I say, meaningly, because education is never complete. Self-education should continue while life lasts.

It is on all of you who belong to the young and rising generation that the future of our civilization depends. You have got to fit yourselves now for the enterprise awaiting you. The responsibilities to be incurred will be heavy, but you dare not attempt to escape from them; they must be courageously undertaken and carried through. The labour, though severe, is honourable in the highest degree; yet remember that you cannot expect recognition by personal honours bestowed; you will have to set about the work in a spirit of altruism, and the reward for your altruism will be the inwardly sure knowledge that so far as in you lies you have done your duty and have deserved success, even if success has not crowned your efforts.

In the protracted course of international strife many deplorable acts were committed, even by civilized nations and Christian peoples, their sanguinary and fratricidal disputes involving in the quarrel communities of other faiths and of culture less advanced.

The prestige of the elder nations has been weakened thereby, as the more backward races see their would-be mentors fallen from the exalted moral standard which the mentors themselves erected.

It will require much time to undo the harm thus brought about, to recover the ground lost; but faith and firm resolve can remedy the evil, and it is worth doing.

It must be recognized that human nature remains as it has ever been: kindly, on the whole, and well-disposed; faithful in friendship; manifesting admirable qualities of self-abnegation and of superb courage in support of high ideals of defence of kith and kin. Such qualities may—it is true—become distorted in great crises, as when existence is at stake, and may become exaggerated and changed, till marked by ferocity and even cruelty in extreme trial; but, war at an end, old hatreds weaken and gradually disappear, though persisting longer between communities than between individuals.

The pity of it is that progress towards reconciliation is hampered and retarded by the fact that after a lengthy period of general insanity, such as was experienced in the years 1914–18 and which has not even now been completely cured, each nation has difficulty in recognizing recovery of reason by other nations; hence arise mutual suspicion and distrust.

Thus fear is bred, and fear is an evil counsellor; it produces nothing better than a narrow nationalism—nationalism disguised as, and miscalled, patriotism, but which is at bottom only selfish jealousy.

Nationalism is commonly held up to admiration as a high virtue, while internationalism—which is, in other words, generous sympathy with our fellow-men—is branded as a crime, a surrender, a betrayal of our own peculiar interests and rights.

Until this view—this regrettable attitude—is altered we cannot hope for any enduring amelioration in international relations.

It is often said that war is in accordance with the law of nature, that man has always fought and always will fight, that human nature cannot be changed. As I have already suggested, human nature is not a bad nature; it need not be changed, but it can be trained and guided—by education and example—to its betterment.

From earliest days, in the evolution and rise of *homo sapiens*, competition has been bitter. From the beginning he found it cruelly hard to live; the strong arm was law, and only the fittest won through to survival. Man fought man, then family fought family; families combined for defence or aggression; tribes resulted from the association of families, and held their own for a while against tribes similarly formed, till, eventually, tribes joined forces and nations came into being.

Nations now maintain internal peace and good order by means of their own organized police forces, who restrain personal and party brawling. But as yet there are no international police, and nations continue to make war on each other freely.

To an unprejudiced and dispassionate observer there can be, however, no obvious reason why the rational procedure which has resulted in the establishment of a happy social state by the fusion in amity of once hostile tribes should not be extended to the creation of a wide comity of nations, nations independent yet interdependent—a world federation or fellowship.

And, in the end, war is not a satisfactory method of settling disputes. Ordeal by battle brings lasting benefit to neither combatant.

What have availed the victories of Napoleon Bonaparte? Where are the permanent advantages resulting from the political and military combinations, the strategical triumphs of Moltke and Bismarck?

Wars have been usually waged—in olden days—for the spoils of victory: increase of territory, acquisition of wealth, even glory to the victor. That lust for expansion is not yet quite dead, but the glory of conquest is departing; its gains are Dead Sea fruit, its legacy, bitter memories alone.

We earth-dwellers are prisoners on the planet; there is no way out. So, as we cannot escape from the proximity of our neighbours, it is surely better to live with them as friends than as enemies.

I am told on good authority that our globe can support human life for another two thousand million years or more.

If the men of science are correct in their estimate the earth is still young, barely middle-aged, and mankind is in a very early stage of babyhood. What sort of creatures our remote descendants may be in the world's old age, or under what conditions they will exist, we cannot even guess.

The old order changeth, the dragons of the prime have had their day, and a thousand million years hence evolution may have brought into being a type differing as widely from ourselves as the deinotherium from the dormouse.

But our interests lie in the problems of to-day, political, social, economic, all of immediate urgency; the near not the distant future is our instant concern, and we should concentrate on that.

There is danger in delay, for it seems likely that unless an effort in the right direction—a successful effort—is made soon the present social system will crumble in ruin, and many now alive may witness the hideous wreck. Then will loom the dreadful menace of the dark ages, returning, darker, black, universal in scope, long-lasting.

At the present moment, many years after the close of the war which was to bring enduring peace to all, we find the cleverest brains everywhere busily experimenting with new inventions for facilitating slaughter, building more horrible engines of destruction, brewing more atrocious poisons, designing more monstrous methods of murdering their fellow men and women.

If war comes on us the peaceful inhabitants of our so-called civilized communities—our women and children not excepted—will be as open to attack as the soldier in the field, for the convention that non-combatants are respected no longer obtains.

Recent progress in science has now given to the machine the mastery over man its maker. Until lately politicians and statesmen—who are the authors and the initiators of war—could feel safe in their own homes surrounded by their families. That happy security will be theirs no longer.

The knowledge of this may perhaps bring to the statesman a warning sense of his responsibility. The choice lies with him. Will the hardness of his heart prevail; must the narrowness of his outlook persist until he is schooled by poison gas and bomb; or will he call to mind the pact renouncing war as a solvent of differences, the pact signed by sixty nations, but now forgotten or disregarded? Is it too much to believe that the human intellect is equal to the problem of designing a world state wherein neighbours can live without molestation, in collective security? It does not matter what the state is called; give it any name you please—League of Nations, Federated Nations, United States of the World. Why should there not be a world police just as each nation has a national police force?

Many former obstacles have been cleared away. Science has overthrown barriers and given egress in all directions. Man is now able to navigate the atmosphere, plumb the deep seas, travel in three dimensions of space, move anywhere at a speed unimaginable to our fathers. Willingly or unwillingly, he has become a world citizen, and the duties of that citizenship cannot be evaded; duties calling for the wholehearted co-operation of every man and woman alive, joined in mind and purpose to promote the good and the advancement of all.

And machinery is ready to hand. The League of Nations is alive and active, while courts exist for determining and adjusting all international differences, judicial and financial.

No nation at heart wants war, but in the course of history it has happened and is happening that ambitious leaders, inspired by a narrow nationalism, may exercise a compelling influence on impressionable and inexperienced youth to urge them on a path of promised glory. This, especially in countries which have suffered recent territorial loss or whose overcrowded population is looking for outlet, exerts a magnetic lure on immature minds.

Dictators are, however, but ephemeral phenomena; they do not represent the democracy, the sovereignty of the people, whose common sense is in the end the sole arbiter.

Misunderstandings and petty quarrels between individuals often occur in even the happiest families, but they are composed amicably, without resort to knife or pistol. So should it be in the case of bickering between nations.

But the world is in peril because of the lack of faith. Governments, distrusting treaty-makers, no longer hold treaties in respect, regarding them as merely temporary makeshifts. Lasting agreement, permanent mutual understanding, have to be founded on truth and honesty. A pledged word ought to be as binding on the State as on the individual. In ordinary private life a partner to a contract is bound by law; the State should be bound by honour.

A distinguished scholar and profound thinker, the President of Columbia University, in words spoken not long ago, has emphasized the fact that the fundamental evil in our day is the world-wide lack of confidence.

He points out, too, that the nations of the world are now precisely where the thirteen American states were after they had gained independence and before they had organized a federal form of government.

In his opinion world organization, world consultation and co-operation, are essential to world prosperity and international peace—as essential for the nations of the world to-day as for the thirteen independent, competitive, and self-centred states of America in the eighteenth century.

I believe he is right. To my mind his are wise words. When mankind has matured in wisdom it will be generally accepted that international interests are inseparably interwoven.

When that is universally appreciated such epithets as Militarist and Pacifist will disappear, obsolete, forgotten, and none of us will be afraid to stand forth and say, with Abou Ben Adhem, " Write me as one that loves his fellow-men."

INDEX